Blackie the Talking Cat

and other favorite judicial opinions

Compiled by West Publishing

St. Paul, Minn.

WEST'S COMMITMENT TO THE ENVIRONMENT

In 1906, West Publishing Company began recycling materials left over from the production of books. This began a tradition of efficient and responsible use of resources. Today, 100% of our legal bound volumes texts are printed on acid-free, recycled paper consisting of 50% new fibers. West recycles nearly 27,700,000 pounds of scrap paper annually—the equivalent of 229,300 trees. Since the 1960s, West has devised ways to capture and recycle waste inks, solvents, oils, and vapors created in the printing process. We also recycle plastics of all kinds, wood, glass, corrugated cardboard, and batteries, and have eliminated the use of styrofoam book packaging. We at West are proud of the longevity and the scope of our commitment to the environment.

Acknowledgments: We would like to acknowledge the following people at West Publishing for their contributions to the production of *Blackie*.

Juan Abelleira
Robert Barten
Karolyn Bertelsen
Treva Bohm
Alicia DeGross
Jim Douglas

Anne Kelley
Ann Laughlin
Al Maleson
Richard Moen
John Smith

Kara L. Johnson—Editor
Steven R. Thompson—Editor

 PRINTED ON 10% POST CONSUMER RECYCLED PAPER

Preface

West Publishing has contributed to the practice of law for more than 100 years. In 1876, John B. West and his brother Horatio introduced *The Syllabi*, a weekly publication containing excerpts from the Minnesota courts. By 1887, *The Syllabi* had expanded into the National Reporter System® which to this day provides the legal profession with the full text of opinions from all federal and state appellate courts. It is this history of West and its vast compilation of case law that inspired us to compile and publish *Blackie the Talking Cat*.

To start the process, we sent a letter to judges and law professors across the United States asking them to submit their "favorite" opinion to us for this publication. The definition of favorite was left to the individual, but we explained that we were looking for cases that they enjoy reading time and again, and cases that they enjoy sharing with others.

The response was overwhelming. In fact, some people had a difficult time choosing just one opinion, so they sent several. As a result, hundreds of cases were submitted covering almost every facet of the law, and they were chosen by the contributors for practically every reason imaginable.

In our letter, we also asked the judges and law professors to include a statement as to why the opinion is a favorite. The responses ranged from the briefest of notes or just a citation, to two- and three-page letters explaining their fondness for the case.

Perhaps the largest group contained those opinions that are considered entertaining or humorous, either because of the facts, or because of the writing, or both. However, many cases were nominated because they deal eloquently or perceptively with our liberties, or because of their pedagogical value. And still others were submitted out of great admiration for the authoring judge.

Every opinion was read and appreciated by the editorial staff. Unfortunately, we could not publish all of them. The task of selecting the opinions to be included in *Blackie* was therefore extremely challenging. The final selections were made based on popularity, general interest, variety and readability. We have included majority, concurring and dissenting opinions, depending on which were suggested to us.

We wish to thank everyone who submitted a favorite opinion. (A list of contributors is located on page 445.) *Blackie* is a unique and special publication because it is a collection of judicial opinions admired and recognized by colleagues on the bench and in law schools as some of the best judicial writing in the National Reporter System.

THE PUBLISHER

P.S. If we missed *your* favorite opinion, don't hesitate to tell us about it. Maybe it will be included in a sequel to *Blackie*. Send it to:

West Publishing
Editorial Department
PO Box 64526
St. Paul, MN 55164–0526

To order additional copies of this publication, call toll free, 1–800–328–9352.

Editor's Note

For this publication, many of the opinions have been edited for readability and length. We have indicated with three asterisks (***) those portions of the opinion where material has been deleted. When necessary, editorial comments have been inserted to summarize what has been deleted. Those comments can be identified by the narrow margins and bold typeface. Case citations, parenthetical discussion of cited cases and footnotes have also been eliminated unless they are necessary either to understand the opinion or to appreciate why the opinion was submitted for this publication.

At the beginning of each opinion there will be an editorial introduction (in bold typeface) and/or a quotation from the contributing judge or law professor's letter. We have purposely chosen to identify the quotations with the contributor's title instead of his or her name, in order to respect the wishes of those who did not want to be identified with a particular case.

Table of Contents

Chapter 1

All Creatures Great and Small

Whether you are a pet owner, farmer, hunter, angler or just a plain old animal lover, you most likely appreciate the wonderful creatures in the animal kingdom and recognize the significant role they play in our lives. They provide us with companionship, livelihood, bragging rights and, more often than not, great entertainment.

Because our lives are linked so closely with the other members of the animal kingdom, we sometimes find that our furry/feathered/finned friends become the root of complex legal battles. In this chapter we find that although these court battles involve serious issues of law, the animal kingdom offers interesting scenarios and wonderful writing material for judges' opinions.

Garfield, Heathcliff and Felix the Cat are a few examples of cartoon cats who compete with one another for the affection of kids and adults around the world via their comic strips and television shows. However, they probably never met the likes of Blackie the Talking Cat. Blackie, a live cat, entertained people on the streets of Augusta, Georgia, by talking to them. Blackie's owners requested "donations" for the cat chat, which resulted in their chatting to a judge.

"The case points out conclusions some feline fanatics have long suspected—that while cats do, indeed, grin, they are not entitled to free speech under the Bill of Rights."

—Adjunct Professor, Stetson University

"Miles's third party standing argument on behalf of Blackie is truly remarkable. The court refuses Miles's jus tertii standing—pointing out that Blackie can clearly speak for himself."

—Professor, South Texas College of Law

MILES
v.
CITY COUNCIL OF AUGUSTA, GEORGIA

United States Court of Appeals
Eleventh Circuit
Aug. 4, 1983
710 F.2d 1542

PER CURIAM:

Plaintiffs Carl and Elaine Miles, owners and promoters of "Blackie the Talking Cat," brought this suit in the United States District Court for the Southern District of Georgia, challenging the constitutionality of the Augusta, Georgia, Business License Ordinance. Their complaint alleged that the ordinance is inapplicable in this case or is otherwise void for vagueness and overbroad, and that the ordinance violates rights of speech and association. The district court granted summary judgment in favor of the defendant City Council of Augusta. We affirm.

The partnership between Blackie and the Mileses began somewhat auspiciously in a South Carolina rooming house. According to the deposition of Carl Miles:

> Well, a girl come around with a box of kittens, and she asked us did we want one. I said no, that we did not want one. As I was walking away from the box of kittens, a voice spoke to me and said, "Take the black kitten." I took the black kitten, knowing nothing else unusual or nothing else strange about the black kitten. When Blackie was about five months old, I had him on my lap playing with him, talking to him, saying I love you. The voice spoke to me saying, "The cat is trying to talk to you." To me, the voice was the voice of God.

Mr. Miles set out to fulfill his divination by developing a rigorous course of speech therapy.

> I would tape the sounds the cat would make, the voice sounds he would make when he was trying to talk to me, and I would play those sounds back to him three and four hours a day, and I would let him watch my lips, and he just got to where he could do it.

Blackie's catechism soon began to pay off. According to Mr. Miles:

> He was talking when he was six months old, but I could not prove it then. It was where I could understand him, but you can't understand him. It took me altogether a year and a half before I had him talking real plain where you could understand him.

Ineluctably, Blackie's talents were taken to the marketplace, and the rest is history. Blackie catapulted into public prominence when he spoke, for a fee, on radio and on television shows such as "That's Incredible." Appellants capitalized on Blackie's linguistic skills through agreements with agents in South Carolina, North Carolina, and Georgia. The public's affection for Blackie was the catalyst for his success, and Blackie loved his fans. As the District Judge observed in his published opinion, Blackie even purred "I love you" to him when he encountered Blackie one day on the street.[1]

Sadly, Blackie's cataclysmic rise to fame crested and began to subside. The Miles family moved temporarily to Augusta, Georgia, receiving "contributions" that Augusta passersby paid to hear Blackie talk. After receiving complaints from several of Augusta's ailurophobes, the Augusta police—obviously no ailurophiles themselves—doggedly insisted that appellants would have to purchase a business license. Eventually, on threat of incarceration, Mr. and Mrs. Miles acceded to the demands of the police and paid $50 for a business license.

The gist of appellant's argument is that the Augusta business ordinance contains no category for speaking animals. The ordinance exhaustively lists trades, businesses, and occupations subject to the tax and the amount of the tax to be paid, but it nowhere lists cats with forensic prowess. However, section 2 of Augusta's Business Ordinance No. 5006 specifies that a $50 license shall be paid by any "Agent or Agency not specifically mentioned." Appellants insist that the drafters of section 2 could not have meant to include Blackie the Talking Cat and, if they did, appellants assert that section 2, as drafted, is vague and overbroad and hence unconstitutional.

Upon review of appellants' claims, we agree with the district court's detailed analysis of the Augusta ordinance. The assertion that Blackie's speaking engagements do not constitute an "occupation" or "business" within the meaning of the catchall provision of the Augusta ordinance is wholly without merit. Although the Miles family called what they received for Blackie's performances "contributions," these elocutionary endeavors were entirely intended for pecuniary enrichment and were indubitably commercial.[3] Moreover, we refuse to require that Augusta define "business" in order to avoid problems of vagueness. The word has a common sense meaning that Mr. Miles undoubtedly understood.

---

1. We note that this affectionate encounter occurred before the Judge ruled against Blackie.

3. This conclusion is supported by the undisputed evidence in the record that appellants solicited contributions. Blackie would become catatonic and refuse to speak whenever his audience neglected to make a contribution.

Appellants' attack on the vagueness of section 4 of the Augusta ordinance, which permits the mayor, in his discretion, to require a license, is not properly before this Court. As the district court indicated, defendants sought to enforce only section 2 of the ordinance in this case.

Finally, we agree with the district court that appellants have not made out a case of overbreadth with respect to section 2 of the ordinance. Appellants fail to show any illegal infringement of First Amendment rights of free speech or assembly. The overbreadth of a statute must be "judged in relation to the statute's plainly legitimate sweep." *Broadrick v. Oklahoma*, 413 U.S. 601, 615, 93 S.Ct. 2908, 2918, 37 L.Ed.2d 830 (1973). Appellants' activities plainly come within the legitimate exercise of the city's taxing power.[5]

AFFIRMED.

---

5. This Court will not hear a claim that Blackie's right to free speech has been infringed. First, although Blackie arguably possesses a very unusual ability, he cannot be considered a "person" and is therefore not protected by the Bill of Rights. Second, even if Blackie had such a right, we see no need for appellants to assert his right jus tertii. Blackie can clearly speak for himself.

The next time Uncle Joe starts to tell you the same old story about "the one that got away", hand him a copy of Judge Meekins' opinion in *Hampton v. North Carolina Pulp Company*. Talk about your fish stories. . . .

Judge Meekins' numerous allusions to the Bible are supported by copious footnote citations, but, as mentioned in the Editor's Note, they have been deleted.

"Hampton, over the years, has been a touchstone. It is always funny, well reasoned, and, today, a reminder that even during the dark years of World War II, there were individuals concerned with the environment. Moreover, it serves to remind both the bench and the bar that judges are indeed human."

—Judge, Oklahoma State Court

HAMPTON
v.
NORTH CAROLINA PULP CO.

United States District Court, E.D. North Carolina
Feb. 20, 1943
49 F.Supp. 625

MEEKINS, District Judge.

This is a civil action at law brought by the plaintiff against the defendant in which the plaintiff seeks to recover from the defendant damages in the sum of $30,000 for the alleged wrongful diversion and destruction of fish in the navigable waters of the Roanoke River near Plymouth, North Carolina. A motion to dismiss the cause for failure of the complaint 'to state a claim upon which relief can be granted' was heard by me at Raleigh in Term and thereafter briefs were filed in due course.

Well, Fish is the subject of this story. From the fifth day of the Creation down through the centuries, some of which lie behind us like a hideous dream, fish have been a substantial factor in the affairs of men. After giving man dominion over all the Earth, God gave him dominion over the fish in particular, naming them first in order, reserving unto Himself only one certain fruit tree in the midst of the Garden, and Satan smeared that—the wretch. Whatever else we may think of the Devil, as a business man he is working success. He sat in the original game, not with one fruit tree, but with the cash capital of one snake, and now he has half the world grabbed and a diamond hitch on the other half.[2]

Great hunters lived before Nimrod, who was a mighty one before the Lord, and great fishermen before Izaak Walton, whose followers are as numberless as the sands of the sea—not counting the leaves of the forest, as if anybody ever did, or could, except the quondam Literary Digest, which polled itself to death in the late Summer and middle Fall of 1936.

The most notable group of fishermen of all time was that headed by Peter, the impulsive Apostle, and his followers Thomas, Nathaniel, the sons of Zebedee, and two other Disciples, seven fishermen in all—a working majority of The Twelve.

Considered solely as a food product, fish have unlimited possibilities—quantitative and qualitative. We are told that a few little fishes and seven loaves, five loaves and two fishes, according to St. Luke, were more than sufficient to feed a hungry multitude of four thousand men, together with the women and children present, and of the fragments there were seven baskets full of fish. Quantitative.

Professor Agassiz, the eminent Harvard scientist said: 'Fish is a good brain food.' One wrote to know 'in what quantities should it be taken?' The great scientist wrote back: 'In your case, a whale a day for thirty days.' Qualitative.

Fish have their place in song and story. In song, from the nursery rime: 'Little Fishes in the Brook,' to the huge leviathans that forsake unsounded deeps to dance on sands. In story, since the dawn of civilization and the imagination of man began to build romances and tall tales, full and fruity. He was more wag than skeptic who said: 'In all the world there are only three really great fish stories—Admiral Noah, Commodore

2.   The eminent American Modernist.

Jonah and Captain John Smith.' Herbert Hoover added the fourth when, fishing in Nevada, he pulled a twenty-five pound trout from the green waters of Pyramid Lake.

Noah built an ark so many cubits high, wide and long. It had one door in the side, and one window in the top twenty-two inches square. What ventilation. We are told it rained forty days and forty nights and all the mountains were covered with water. We know that Mount Everest is 29,140 feet high. Since it was covered by the flood, the water reached an altitude of more than 29,140 feet. Divide the altitude by forty and we find that the average rainfall was more than 700 feet per day. How's that for dampness!

Apart from the Biblical account of the flood, many nations have vivid accounts of floods in which all the people, except a chosen few, were destroyed. One account, that points this story, is a fable about a flood in ancient India. A fish warned Manu that a flood was coming. Manu built a ship and the fish towed it to a mountain and thus saved everybody. We can laugh at this fable without fear of condemnation here and damnation hereafter. That was not our flood.

Jonah, like all the orthodox Jews of his time, thought Jehovah was a local Deity. Jonah did not like his assignment to Nineveh and in an effort to side-step it he took passage on a ship at Joppa for Tarshish and fled from the presence of the Lord. The Prophet thought that if he could get into another jurisdiction he would be safe. However, before he crossed the boundary line into Tarshish, Jehovah pulled down on him with a double-barrel tempest and a muzzle-loading leviathan. When he found himself a prisoner, for three days and three nights, in the belly of the great fish that the Lord had prepared, Jonah began to think things over. We all do when our 'take a chance' does not pan out as we hoped. The net result was that the Prophet, after repenting of his disobedience and praying forgiveness, was allowed to go ashore. 'The Lord spake unto the fish, and it vomited out Jonah upon the dry land.' This was before the advent of the camera enthusiast, else we might have been fortified with an authentic photograph of the minor Prophet walking ashore with the lower jaw of the whale for gang-plank. The eminent American Modernist said he was rather inclined to think that Jonah proved too tough for his whaleship's digestion and that in a fit of acute ptomaine poisoning, the cantankerous old Prophet was cast forth.

Captain John Smith, in the minds of many people, is more a joke than a myth. However, patient and interesting investigation has led me to the conclusion that he was not only a great Englishman, but a very great Englishman; that he was not only a great man, but a very great man; that he was good, useful and sane and did a very great World Service. Measured by all the standards of constructive achievement he was essentially a World Man. That Captain John Smith is less a myth than a joke is one of the glaring anomalies of history. Perhaps the raconteur had it in mind to emphasize his facetiousness by fact; to contrast his shadow with substance—his fancy with truth.

The Skeptic may scoff and the Modernist may moderate, but the story of Noah and the story of Jonah are enduring torches that lighted the way of man in his struggle upward through the immensity of the Shadow, and now as then guide the fumbling fingers of the trembling hand as with the establishment and strength of Jachin and Boas.

Divested of the insistence of the Fundamentalists on the Verbal Inspiration and Infallibility of the Bible, and accepted in the light of reason, which examines and explains, the story of Noah is the greatest statement on the importance of preparation ever penned by mortal hand. In thunder tones we are warned; in time of peace, prepare for war; in the days of ease and luxury and laissez-faire, remember that evil days are ahead; in the fat years, prepare for the lean ones just around the corner—always be ready 'to flee from the wrath to come.'

Likewise, the story of Jonah is the greatest statement on fidelity to duty, hard and inexorable, that ever fell from the lips of man. It shouts forth the consequences that follow lapses from duty through wilful disobedience or otherwise. 'Duty,' said General Lee, 'is the most sublime word in the English language.'

The fish industry is among the foremost in World Trade. Indeed, in some countries it is the chief occupation of the people and the main source of national income. Through the ages it has developed a lore and nomenclature peculiar unto itself. What is more expressive of failure than, 'A Water Haul?' What more charming password for an Ananias Club than, 'What A Whopper?' What better synonym for discomfort and disgust than, 'Fisherman's Luck,' though coarse in translation—classic in application? And where is the Lawyer who has never gone on a 'Fishing Expedition?' Who wants to 'Fish in Troubled Waters?' A whale of a bargain is a big one. Land Shark suggests Shylock, and Shylock is a type. They are synonymous and offer a perfect illustration of a distinction without a difference. 'It Sounds Fishy,' means 'Its a Lie on Its Face,' and much more diplomatic. Everybody knows that 'Fishy Smell' as well as the man 'With the Codfish Eye.' All these terms are as well understood by the Public as are the terms Bulls and Bears of the Stock Exchange. Codfish Tongues and Codfish Sounds mean one and the same thing and are interchangeable terms in the Trade.

As it is the biggest fish that always breaks the hook or bites the line in two, so, here, the huge sum of thirty thousand dollars is asked as compensation for fish that were never caught. I can remember when that sum would buy a lot of fish. I have seen six-pound roe shad retail for five cents apiece and cured herrings sell for two dollars a thousand—one hundred and twenty pounds of shad for one dollar and five herrings for one cent.

And this large sum is now asked for whose Fish? Certainly not the plaintiff's, because he never owned them. I repeat the question, whose Fish? The answer is plain: they belonged to the Public.

*   *   *

The plaintiff, in substance, alleges that he is now, and has been since 1911, the owner and in possession of those two certain tracts of land, situate on opposite sides of the Roanoke River, and known respectively as the 'Kitty Hawk' and 'Slade' Fisheries; that the properties are ideally located for the business of fishing, and have for a number of years, during the fishing season, been operated for that purpose by the plaintiff and his ancestors in title, expensive equipment having been placed and maintained thereon for the proper and profitable conduct of such business; that, from time immemorial, great quantities of fish of the kinds specified have been accustomed, during the Spring of each year, to make their way from the Ocean through Albemarle Sound, and thence into the fresh-water spawning grounds in the upper reaches of the Roanoke River; and that, by reason of this annual migration of fish, plaintiff's fishing business, and his 'Kitty Hawk' and 'Slade' Fisheries, have been 'principally and particularly valuable.'

It is alleged that the defendant is the owner of a boundary on the Roanoke River situate below the plaintiff's property which the fish, entering the river in their annual migration to the spawning grounds, are compelled to pass before reaching that portion of the river running between the plaintiff's properties; that, during the period referred to in the complaint, the defendant has maintained upon the boundary a plant for the manufacture of sulphate pulp, bleached and unbleached; that, in the course of the manufacturing operation, during the three years immediately preceding the institution of this action, the defendant has from day to day discharged into the waters of the Roanoke River, opposite its plant, a large volume of poisonous and deleterious waste and matter injurious to the fish then in passage to the spawning grounds, with the result that the annual migration of the fish upstream has been interrupted or diverted and large quantities of them have been destroyed; and that, as a natural consequence thereof, the plaintiff's business, and the usufruct of his property, during each of the three years have greatly diminished—all to the plaintiff's great and lasting damage in the sum of $30,000.00.

Measured by these allegations, it is not open to question that the acts of the defendant were palpably wrongful. They were, indeed, in violation of various criminal statutes of the State, designed to conserve the public good. If, then, upon indictment, the acts charged were admitted or established, no Court could hesitate to pronounce the defendant guilty of the creation and maintenance of a public nuisance and impose the maximum penalties of the statutes as are therein provided. But the right of the plaintiff to recover damages for this alleged wrong presents a far different question. In a case of pure tort, the wrongdoer is responsible for all the damages directly caused by his misconduct, and for all indirect and consequential damages, resulting naturally and probably from the wrongful acts, which are susceptible to ascertainment with a reasonable degree of certainty. Damages which are not the natural and probable result of the act complained of, but which are contingent or merely possible, or based upon a conjectural probability of future loss, and so beyond the scope of reasonable determination, are too remote and are not recoverable. It is well settled that in actions by private individuals, based upon the creation or maintenance of a public nuisance, there can be no recovery, even of nominal damages, upon the mere establishment of the wrongful act. In such cases it is essential to the plaintiff's cause of action that he show an appreciable injury.

*   *   *

Judge Meekins went on to explain that under North Carolina law, in order for a private citizen to sustain an action predicated upon a public nuisance, he or she must establish an injury that is not only appreciable, but special and peculiar to himself or herself, differing not only in degree, but in kind from that common to the public. Since plaintiff did not allege that defendant invaded his soil, interfered with his nets or other fishing equipment, or obstructed his right to ingress and egress, plaintiff did not show that he suffered a specific injury. Although plaintiff may have suffered loss of profits because of the destruction of fish caused by the discharge of poisonous matter by defendant, plaintiff did not own the fish or the river. The state owned both, and therefore, if plaintiff suffered an injury, so did every citizen of the state. The court concluded that the plaintiff may not recover for an injury to property in which he had no vestige of special interest.

The motion to dismiss was granted.

Could a mule have the cognizance to step in front of a train in an attempt to end its life? In the following 1920 decision, the Mississippi Supreme Court determined that it could.

HINES
v.
THOMPSON

Supreme Court of Mississippi
Nov. 29, 1920
86 So. 450, 123 Miss. 634

SAM C. COOK, P.J.

The plaintiff sued the Mobile & Ohio Railroad Company for the value of a mule killed by the running train of the appellant. The evidence offered by the plaintiff made out his case under the statute. He proved that the mule was killed by the train; he proved the value of the mule; he proved that the railroad track was straight for a mile south of the place where the animal was struck; he also proved that there was a wound on the right side of the mule. The engineer running the train testified that he first saw the mule standing near the track, and at first he thought it might be a human being, but when the animal started toward the train he discovered that it was a mule. He said it was impossible to stop the train or to avoid striking the mule. He also said that he did the only thing he could do, and that was to open his cylinder cocks, and he further testified that in seven times out of ten this would scare stock away from the track. When the mule was struck the pilot or "cowcatcher" had passed the mule, and the engineer did not know what part of the locomotive struck the mule.

As we view the evidence in this case, the physical facts did not warrant the jury in disbelieving the testimony of the engineer to the effect that he did everything he could have done to prevent the killing of the mule. It seems to have been a clear case of suicide. An unbiased study of the evidence of the engineer convinces this court that he spoke the truth when he said that he did all he could have done under the circumstances. The physical facts do not contradict or tend to contradict the testimony of the only eyewitness. This was a "touch and go" situation confronting the engineer, and he did what he believed would most probably drive the mule from the track.

"Surely a trainload of human beings need not be jeopardized to avoid killing a mule. Only reasonable care is required in such cases." *Railroad v. Wright,* 78 Miss. 127, 28 South. 806.

The defendant met and overcame the presumption of the statute, and the court should have directed a verdict for the defendant.

Reversed and dismissed.

James Wallace was accused of using his dog to hunt deer in North Carolina in violation of a state statute. Wallace alleged that the law was unconstitutional and moved to dismiss the case. The trial court granted his motion and the state appealed.

On appeal, Judge Martin took the opportunity to research and write a historical account of dogs and the courts. One can only assume that this brief dissertation will bestow upon the reader a deeper understanding of and a renewed appreciation for "man's best friend."

STATE
v.
WALLACE

Court of Appeals of North Carolina
Nov. 18, 1980
271 S.E.2d 760, 49 N.C.App. 475

HARRY C. MARTIN, Judge.

This is a case about dogs. As dogs do not often appear in the courts, it is perhaps not inappropriate to write a few words about them. The dog, a carnivorous mammal, has been kept in a domesticated state by man since prehistoric time. "The memory of man runneth not to the contrary."

Diana, the Roman counterpart to Artemis, was the goddess of hunting. She was the twin sister of Apollo and was usually pictured with her hunting dogs, given to her by the wind-god, Pan. Cerberus, the three-headed dog, served as the watchdog at the gates of Hades. In the sky we find Sirius, the brilliant dog star, the brightest star in the entire heavens. Sirius floats through time at the hand of his master, Orion.

Edmund Burke in *The Sublime and Beautiful* (1756) said: "Dogs are indeed the most social, affectionate, and amiable animals of the whole brute creation." Herodotus reports in *An Account of Egypt* (5th Century) that dogs were regarded as sacred by the ancient Egyptians. When a dog died, the people of the house shaved their whole bodies and heads and the dog was buried in sacred tombs within the city. In Sir Francis Bacon's essay *Of Atheism* (1612), we find "for take an example of a dog, and mark what a generosity and courage he will put on when he finds himself maintained by a man."

Byron wrote:

> But the poor dog, in life the foremost friend, The first to welcome, the foremost to defend.

The Talisman tells that Richard I said:

> The Almighty, who gave the dog to be companion of our pleasures and our toils, hath invested him with a nature noble and incapable of deceit. He forgets neither friend nor foe—remembers both benefits and injury. He hath a share of man's intelligence, but no share of his falsehood. You may bribe a soldier to slay a man, or a witness to take life by false accusation, but you cannot make a hound tear his benefactor. He is ever a friend of man, save when man incurs his enmity.

The shape of history was changed by a spaniel who saved William of Orange from death by the Spaniards when they made a surprise attack upon his army at night. William and his sentinels were fast asleep but a small spaniel on the prince's bed barked furiously at the approaching footsteps. It sprang forward, scratched his master's face with a paw, and enabled him to mount a horse and escape. To his dying day the prince kept a spaniel in his bedchamber.

Throughout history we find the fate of man and dog intertwined. Dogs have rescued kings and knaves, princes and paupers. Who will ever forget the heroic deeds of the great St. Bernards of the Alps? As one gazes through the window of time, the vision of a barefoot boy and his dog, walking down a dusty summer road, brings a tear to the eye. A boy without a dog! Life would be unbearable.

The dog is of a noble, free nature, yet is domesticated and dedicated to the well-being of people of all races. We find the dog's story told throughout our reports. One of the earliest cases, *Dodson v. Mock*, 20 N.C. 282 (1838), was an action for *trespass vi et armis* for killing plaintiff's dog by poison. Justice Gaston, for the Court, held that dogs belong to that class of domiciled animals which the law recognizes as objects of property. As such, the dog is entitled to protection of the law even though it may on occasion have stolen an egg, nipped at the heel of a man chasing it, or worried a sheep. Those offenses by a dog are not of a very heinous character. "If such deflections as these from strict propriety be sufficient to give a dog a bad name and kill him, the entire race of these faithful and useful animals might be rightfully extirpated." *Id.* 20 N.C. at 285.

Justice Walker speaks of the dog in *State v. Smith*, 156 N.C. 628, 629–31, 72 S.E. 321, 321–22 (1911):

> A dog is like a man in one respect, at least—that is, he will do wrong sometimes; but if the wrong is slight or trivial, he does not thereby forfeit his life.

> *   *   *

> . . . [W]e will say that the dog is not an animal of such base nature or low degree, whatever his pedigree may be, as not to be entitled to the consideration and full protection of the law, or as to subject him to outlawry if he has a bad reputation, or at least a habit of killing fowls, so that if he lurks near where they are to be found, although they are protected by a sufficient fence or other barrier against his predatory and ferocious disposition, he may be killed, even if he is not engaged in the actual attempt to slay and devour his supposed prey, or the danger of his doing so is not so imminent or immediately threatening that a prudent and reasonable man would be led to believe that his property is in jeopardy. We cannot give our assent to this principle. Admit such a right, and the peace and good order of society would be seriously endangered and could not well be preserved, for the exercise of such a right would excite the most angry passions and resentment of the dog's owner and eventually result in personal violence, thus disrupting the peace and quiet of the community. . . . He (the dog) has the goodwill of mankind because of his friendship

and loyalty, which are such marked traits of his character that they have been touchingly portrayed both in song and story.

In *Moore v. Electric Co.*, 136 N.C. 554, 557–58, 48 S.E. 822, 823, 67 L.R.A. 470, 471–72 (1904), we find:

> It is not hazarding too much to say that it is a matter of common knowledge that in the classification of animal life (not including man) the dog occupies a position in point of intelligence, fidelity and affection superior probably to all of the others. He is known to have been for ages not only an animal of prey but wonderfully acquainted with the habits and ways of both man and beast and birds, keenly sensitive as to sight, hearing and smell, and remarkably agile in all of his movements. He can, by training and association with man, become adept in many useful employments and can be taught to do almost anything except to speak. They are known ordinarily to be able to take care of themselves amidst the dangers incident to their surroundings. Where a horse or a cow or a hog or any of the lower animals would be killed or injured by dangerous agencies the dog would extricate himself with safety.

> * * *

> We think, therefore, that the dog, on account of his superior intelligence and possession of the other traits which we have mentioned in respect to the diligence and care which locomotive engineers owe to their owners and to them, must be placed on the same footing with that of a man walking upon or near a railroad track apparently in possession of all his faculties, ...

The Commonwealth of Kentucky recognized the virtues of the dog in *Shadoan v. Barnett*, 217 Ky. 205, 210–11, 289 S.W. 204, 206, 49 A.L.R. 843, 847 (1926):

> [H]istory may be searched in vain to find a living creature exhibiting as much fidelity and affection as does the dog to and for his master. Neither cold,

heat, danger, nor starvation deters him from mani-
festing those most excellent qualities in his love for
his master, and those with whom he constantly as-
sociates. History is filled with instances where all
others have fled, but the faithful dog stood guard,
either as a mourner at his master's grave or with
a determined purpose to administer to the latter if
occasion presented itself. The press dispatches constantly record his unparalleled deeds of heroism for
the protection and benefit of mankind, even at the
sacrifice of his own life. Because of those qualities,
his virtues have been touchingly described by poets
and celebrated in song, and rightfully the dog as
a companion is most affectionately regarded by all
persons who truly estimate loyalty and friendship
as factors in smoothing the path of this world's existence.

In 1897 the Supreme Court of the United States had this
to say about dogs:

They are not considered as being upon the same
plane with horses, cattle, sheep, and other domesticated animals, but rather in the category of cats,
monkeys, parrots, singing birds, and similar animals
kept for pleasure, curiosity, or caprice. They have
no intrinsic value, by which we understand a value
common to all dogs as such, and independent of
the particular breed or individual. Unlike other domestic animals, they are useful neither as beasts of
burden, for draft (except to a limited extent), nor
for food. They are peculiar in the fact that they differ among themselves more widely then any other
class of animals, and can hardly be said to have
a characteristic common to the entire race. While
the higher breeds rank among the noblest representatives of the animal kingdom, and are justly es-
teemed for their intelligence, sagacity, fidelity,
watchfulness, affection, and above all, for their
natural companionship with man, others are afflicted with such serious infirmities of temper as to
be little better than a public nuisance. All are more
or less subject to attacks of hydrophobic madness.

Sentell v. New Orleans, etc., Railroad Co., 166 U.S. 698, 701, 17 S.Ct. 693, 694, 41 L.Ed. 1169, 1170 (1897).

An opinion by then superior court judge Lumpkin (later supreme court justice) of Georgia states the history of the dog in inimitable fashion:

> "The dog has figured very extensively in the past and present. In mythology, as Cerberus, he was intrusted with watching the gates of hell; and he seems to have performed his duties so well that there were but few escapes. In the history of the past he has been used extensively for hunting purposes, as the guardian of persons and property, and as a pet and companion. He is the much valued possession of hunters the world over, and in England especially is the pack o' hounds highly prized. In literature he has appeared more often than any other animal, except perhaps the horse. Sometimes he is greatly praised, and at others greatly abused. Sometimes he is made the type of what is mean, low, and contemptible; while at others he is described in terms of eulogy. Few men will forget the song of their childhood, which runs:
>
> > 'Old dog Tray's ever faithful;
> > Grief cannot drive him away;
> > He is gentle, he is kind;
> > I'll never, never find
> > A better friend than old dog Tray.'

"Nor can any of us fail to remember the intelligent animal on whose behalf 'Old Mother Hubbard went to the cupboard.'

> "Few men have deserved and few have won higher praise in an epitaph than the following, which was written by Lord Byron in regard to his dead Newfoundland: 'Near this spot are deposited the remains of one who possessed beauty without vanity, strength without insolence, courage without ferocity, and all the virtues of man without his vices. This praise, which would be unmeaning flattery if inscribed over human ashes, is but a just tribute to

the memory of Boatswain, a dog who was born at
Newfoundland, May 3, 1803, and died at Newstead
Abbey, November 18, 1808.

*   *   *

"The dog has been very often before the courts of
the different States and of different countries, and
has been the subject of a good deal of judicial humor and of judicial learning; but it bears a tinge
of the ridiculous to contend that, however many
and however valuable dogs a man may own, he can
not be made to pay his debts if he will only invest
his money in dogs,—a contention which reminds
one of the very solemn discussions in a certain
court, at a time not very long past as to whether
the oyster was a wild animal. Before the courts, the
dog has received a treatment as varied as that given
him by authors. . . . '. . . From the time of the
pyramids to the present day; from the frozen pole
to the torrid zone, wherever man has been, there
has been his dog. Cuvier has asserted that the dog
was, perhaps, necessary for the establishment of civilized society, and that a little reflection will convince us that barbarous nations owe much of their
civilization above the brute to the possession of the
dog. He is the friend and companion of his mas-
ter-accompanying him in his walks, his servant aiding him in his hunting, the playmate of his
children, an inmate of his house, protecting it
against all assailants.' "

Strong v. Georgia Railway & Electric Co., 118 Ga. 515, 516–19,
45 S.E. 366, 367–68 (1903).

*   *   *

No tribute to the noble dog is more eloquent than the following of Senator Vest in the Missouri case of *Burden v. Hornsby*:

"The best friend a man has in the world may turn
against him and become his enemy. His son or
daughter that he has reared with loving care may
prove ungrateful. Those who are nearest and dearest
to us, those whom we trust with our happiness and
our good name, may become traitors to our faith.

The money that a man has he may lose. It flies away from him perhaps when he needs it most. A man's reputation may be sacrificed in a moment of ill-considered action. The people who are prone to fall on their knees to do us honor when success is with us may be the first to throw the stone of malice when failure settles its cloud upon our heads. The one absolutely unselfish friend that man can have in this selfish world, the one that never deserts him, the one that never proves ungrateful or treacherous, is his dog. A man's dog stands by him in prosperity and poverty, in health and in sickness. He will sleep on the cold ground, where the winter winds blow and the snow drives fiercely, if he may be only near his master's side. He will kiss the hand that has no food to offer; he will lick the wounds and sores that come in encountering the roughness of the world. He guards the sleep of his pauper master as if he were a prince.

"When all other friends desert, he remains. When riches take wings and reputation falls to pieces, he is as constant in his love as the sun in its journey through the heavens. If misfortune drives the master an outcast in the world, friendless and homeless, the faithful dog asks no higher privilege than that of accompanying him to guard against danger, to fight against his enemies. And when the last scene comes and death takes the master in its embrace, and his body is laid in the ground, no matter if all other friends pursue their way, there by the graveside will be found the noble dog, his head between his paws, his eyes sad, but open in alert watchfulness, faithful and true in death."

J. Seawell, Law Tales for Laymen 127 (1925).

With this background on the legal perspective of dogs as it has evolved throughout our history, we now turn to the issue argued on appeal. Defendant insists the statute is unconstitutional on its face. He contends that, among other things, due process is denied when "any person, adult or child, who while in the company of a dog, which in response to its natural instincts, suddenly and without warning, catches the scent of a deer or a fox and gives chase" is subject to a violation of the criminal law and may be fined. While defendant's argument is intriguing and unique, on the record before us we are not required to reach any constitutional question. A constitutional question will not be passed upon if there is also present some other ground upon which the case may be decided. If the case can be decided on one of two grounds, one involving a constitutional question, the other a question of lesser importance, the latter alone will be determined. The Court will not decide questions of a constitutional nature unless absolutely necessary to a decision of the case.

Here, we are faced at the threshold with the question of the validity of the process. Although counsel do not address this question, it arises on the face of the record.

The process in this case is a uniform traffic citation. Its pertinent parts are as follows:

> *State of North Carolina vs. James E. Wallace*
>
> The undersigned officer has probable cause to believe that on or about 10:20 a.m., the 20th day of Nov. 1979 in the named county, the named defendant did unlawfully and wilfully operate a (motor) vehicle on a (street or highway) . . . By hunting deer with dogs in violation of Senate Bill #391 which prohibits same. . . .
>
> C. W. Swinney
Officer

It is obvious on the face of the citation that it fails to allege a violation of the criminal laws, and is fatally defective. It is the function of a warrant, or citation, to make clear and definite the offense charged so that the investigation may be limited to that offense in order that the proper procedure be followed and the applicable law invoked, and to put the defendant on notice as to what he is charged with and to enable him to make his defense. A warrant must express the charge against defendant in a plain, intelligible and explicit manner and contain sufficient matter to enable the court to proceed to judgment and thus bar another prosecution for the same offense. A cursory examination of the citation in question discloses that it fails to comply with this standard. Likewise, the citation fails to comply with the requirements of N.C.G.S. 15A–302. We hold the citation is fatally defective and the same should be quashed.

As the case is being disposed of on this ground, we do not reach or discuss the alleged constitutional infirmity. It is interesting to note, nevertheless, that the statute in question evidently had its origin in the ancient dog-draw of old forest law. Dog-draw was the manifest deprehension of an offender against venison in a forest, when he was found drawing after a deer by the scent of a hound led in his hand; or where a person had wounded a deer and was caught with a dog drawing after him to receive the same. Manwood, *Forest Law*, 2, c. 8. One way used to prevent dogs from running after deer was the "lawing of dogs," or cutting several claws of the forefeet of dogs.

*   *   *

The case is remanded to the Superior Court of Alamance County with direction that it be remanded to the district court of that county for the entry of an order dismissing the action.

In the following two cases, man's best friend is once again the subject of controversy. These cases are examples of how pets often become such a valuable part of our lives that in times of divorce or even death, owners will go to great lengths to protect or honor their loyal companion.

AKERS
v.
SELLERS

Appellate Court of Indiana, in Banc
May 15, 1944
54 N.E.2d 779, 114 Ind.App. 660

CRUMPACKER, Chief Judge.

This is a controversy over the ownership and possession of a Boston bull terrier dog upon which the appellant, while declining to measure its true value to him in mere money, has placed an arbitrary value of $25. Were we to judge the importance of these proceedings by such a fictitious standard of value we would be inclined to resent this appeal as a trespass on the court's time and an imposition on our patience, of which quality we trust we are possessed to a reasonable degree. But we have in mind Senator Vest's immortal eulogy on the noble instincts of a dog so we approach the question involved without any feeling of injured dignity but with a full realization that no man can be censured for the prosecution of his rights to the full limit of the law when such rights involve the comfort derived from the companionship of man's best friend.

The parties to this litigation were at one time husband and wife. We conclude from the record that their union was not blessed with children, but some seven years ago there came into their lives the Boston terrier which is the subject of this controversy. He was the gift of a doctor of veterinary medicine with whom he had been left to board by a former owner who had never sought his return. What his age may have been at the time is not disclosed, but, assuming that he was then a pup, it is apparent that he is now about to enter the mellow years when those qualities most to be desired in a dog are at their peak, and the natural springtime inclination to roam, common to all males of whatever specie, is on the wane. Despite the tie and cementing influence of this little Boston terrier, the marriage of the parties proved not to have been made in heaven and the appellee sought and obtained a divorce. The court wherein such divorce was decreed, feeling perhaps that the care and custody of the dog of the parties was not an inescapable appendage to their domestic controversy, failed to make any order in reference to the same and the wife, being left in the possession of the domicile on separation from her husband, just naturally came into the custody of the dog. Whether the learned judge who heard the appellant's petition for divorce would have made such disposition of the dog had the matter been called to his attention, we are, of course, unable to say. Whether the interests and desires of the dog, in such a situation, should be the polar star pointing the way to a just and wise decision, or whether the matter should be determined on the brutal and unfeeling basis of legal title, is a problem concerning which we express no opinion. We recognize, however, the tragedy of his consignment to the appellee if, in fact, his love, affection and loyalty are for the appellant. However that may be, the appellant, insisting that legal title and the dog's best interests are in accord and both rest in him, brought this suit in replevin and upon the trial thereof was unsuccessful. The record presents no question for our consideration except that the evidence is insufficient to sustain the decision of the court and that the same is contrary to law. We find evidence tending to prove that the dog in controversy was first given to the appellant and by him, in turn, given to the appellee. This is sufficient to support the decision, and as there is no reason shown why possession should not accompanying ownership such decision is not contrary to law. We feel that had the trial court seen fit to apply Solomon's test and offered to cut the dog in halves, awarding one part to each claimant, the decision might have been for the appellant, as the appellee has failed to show sufficient interest in the controversy, or its subject, to file an answer below or favor us with a brief on appeal. The fact, however, that we may possibly have more confidence in the wisdom of Solomon than we do in that of the trial court hardly justifies us in disturbing its judgment.

Affirmed.

CORSO
v.
CRAWFORD DOG AND CAT HOSPITAL, INC.

Civil Court of the City of New York
March 22, 1979
415 N.Y.S.2d 182, 97 Misc.2d 530

DECISION

SEYMOUR FRIEDMAN, Judge.

The facts in this case are not in dispute.

On or about January 28, 1978, the plaintiff brought her 15 year old poodle into the defendant's premises for treatment. After examining the dog, the defendant recommended euthanasia and shortly thereafter the dog was put to death. The plaintiff and the defendant agreed that the dog's body would be turned over to Bide-A-Wee, an organization that would arrange a funeral for the dog. The plaintiff alleged that the defendant wrongfully disposed of her dog, failed to turn over the remains of the dog to the plaintiff for the funeral. The plaintiff had arranged for an elaborate funeral for the dog including a head stone, an epitaph, and attendance by plaintiff's two sisters and a friend. A casket was delivered to the funeral which, upon opening the casket, instead of the dog's body, the plaintiff found the body of a dead cat. The plaintiff described during the non-jury trial, her mental distress and anguish, in detail, and indicated that she still feels distress and anguish. The plaintiff sustained no special damages.

The question before the court now is two-fold. 1) Is it an actionable tort that was committed? 2) If there is an actionable tort is the plaintiff entitled to damages beyond the market value of the dog?

Before answering these questions the court must first decide whether a pet such as a dog is only an item of personal property as prior cases have held. This court now overrules prior precedent and holds that a pet is not just a thing but occupies a special place somewhere in between a person and a piece of personal property.

As in the case where a human body is withheld, the wrongfully withholding or, as here, the destruction of the dog's body gives rise to an actionable tort.

In ruling that a pet such as a dog is not just a thing I believe the plaintiff is entitled to damages beyond the market value of the dog. A pet is not an inanimate thing that just receives affection it also returns it. I find that plaintiff Ms. Corso did suffer shock, mental anguish and despondency due to the wrongful destruction and loss of the dog's body.

She had an elaborate funeral scheduled and planned to visit the grave in the years to come. She was deprived of this right.

This decision is not to be construed to include an award for the loss of a family heirloom which would also cause great mental anguish. An heirloom while it might be the source of good feelings is merely an inanimate object and is not capable of returning love and affection. It does not respond to human stimulation; it has no brain capable of displaying emotion which in turn causes a human response. Losing the right to memorialize a pet rock, or a pet tree or losing a family picture album is not actionable. But a dog that is something else. To say it is a piece of personal property and no more is a repudiation of our humaneness. This I cannot accept.

Accordingly, the court finds the sum of $700 to be reasonable compensation for the loss suffered by the plaintiff.

Although illegal drug and alien trafficking into the United States is nothing new, the United States Court of Appeals for the Second Circuit was unaware of the "nefarious practice" of rare-bird smuggling until the following case was brought to its attention.

"My favorite opinion is . . . the last decision written by former Circuit Judge William H. Mulligan before his retirement. The opinion captures Judge Mulligan's legendary sense of humor and shows that levity is sometimes appropriate even in the august chambers of a federal circuit court."

—Magistrate Judge, United States District Court

"[W]hat makes this case unique is the exquisiteness of its timing for which divine intervention cannot be easily discounted. . . . It was truly his 'swan song'."

—Magistrate Judge, United States District Court

UNITED STATES

v.

BYRNES

United States Court of Appeals
Second Circuit
March 17, 1981
644 F.2d 107

MULLIGAN, Circuit Judge:

Who knows what evil lurks in the hearts of men? Although the public is generally aware of the sordid trafficking of drugs and aliens across our borders, this litigation alerts us to a nefarious practice hitherto unsuspected even by this rather calloused bench—rare bird smuggling. The appeal is therefore accurately designated as *rara avis*. While Canadian geese have been regularly crossing, exiting, reentering and departing our borders with impunity, and apparently without documentation, to enjoy more salubrious climes, those unwilling or unable to make the flight either because of inadequate wing spans, lack of fuel or fear of buck shot, have become prey to unscrupulous traffickers who put them in crates and ship them to American ports of entry with fraudulent documentation in violation of a host of federal statutes. The traffic has been egregious enough to warrant the empanelling of a special grand jury in 1979 in the Northern District of New York to conduct a broad investigation of these activities. Even the services of the Royal Canadian Mounted Police were mustered to aid the inquiry.

A principal target of the grand jury investigation was Kenneth Clare, a Canadian, who was believed to be in the business of shipping exotic birds into the United States, misrepresenting on import documents the value, the species and even the number of birds in the containers, thus avoiding the payment of United States Customs duties, inspection and quarantine. When one learns that an adult swan stands some four and a half feet tall and is normally ill tempered, the reluctance of a border inspector to make a head count is understandable. In this case Clare even had the audacity to pass off as Canadians, birds whose country of origin was England! Another target of the investigation was a California attorney, Edward R. Fitzsimmons, whose hobbies included the collection of horses, llamas and exotic birds. It was believed that Fitzsimmons and Clare worked together hand or claw in glove.

In February 1975, Fitzsimmons allegedly purchased from Clare four trumpeter swans and two red-breasted geese.[2] The crated birds were brought from Canada through Massena, New York, a Port of Entry in the Northern District of New York. Their entry papers were spurious. The trumpeter swans (cygnus buccinator) were described in the shipping documents as mute swans which are a less valuable variety. The birds were then airlifted to San Francisco by the Flying Tiger Lines where they were picked up by Janet Leslie Cooper Byrnes, the appellant, who was employed as a secretary by Fitzsimmons. Byrnes was a quondam zoologist at the London Zoo and knowledgeable about ornithological matters. When called before the grand jury on February 7, 1979, Byrnes testified that she did pick

---

2. No birds have been indicted and there is no indication in the record that they were even aware of, much less participated in, the criminal activity unearthed by the grand jury. They were at least as innocent as the horses whose jockeys were bribed to discourage their best efforts at Pocono Downs.

up the birds in 1975 but further stated that after driving away from the airport for ten or fifteen minutes, she heard no noises from the crates. She stated that she stopped at a gas station, pried open the crates and discovered that all the birds were dead and in fact so stiff that she assumed they had been dead for some time. (D.O.A.). She promptly drove to a municipal dump where the birds were interred in unconsecrated ground.

By reason of this testimony the appellant was indicted on May 8, 1980 on four counts of false declarations before a grand jury in violation of 18 U.S.C. § 1623. After a three day jury trial before Hon. Neal McCurn, Northern District of New York, Byrnes was convicted on two counts on July 18, 1980. She was sentenced to be committed to the custody of the Attorney General for a period of six months and fined $5,000 on each count. Execution of the prison sentence was suspended and the defendant was placed on probation for a period of one year on each count, the sentences to be served concurrently. This appeal followed.

I.

Appellant does not challenge the sufficiency of the Government's proof to support the conviction. Ida Meffert, who had emigrated from Germany and had obvious difficulty with the English language, was one of four government witnesses brought from California to Syracuse, New York for this momentous trial. She testified that she was a collector of Australian parrots in Hayward, California and described these parrots as "citizens." The court interjected: "A citizen bird?" The witness answered: "Yeah, the whole birds is citizen."[6] More pointedly Mrs. Meffert testified that in February 1975 the appellant delivered four live swans and two live red breasted geese to her pursuant to an arrangement with Fitzsimmons whereby Mrs. Meffert and her husband provided room and board for some of his exotic wildlife. Mrs. Meffert was subjected to a grueling cross examination by counsel for appellant that was

---

6. There are various record references to "citizen" birds which was confusing since those at issue here were aliens. We are persuaded, however, that the word spoken was "psittacines" (parrots) and not citizens. The confusion of the scrivener is understandable.

apparently aimed at her ornithological qualifications.[7] Mrs. Meffert testified that after a few days one of the swans died and she preserved his leg in her freezer to establish his demise.[8]

> "Man comes and tills the field and lies beneath, And after many a summer dies the swan."
>
> *Tithonus*, Alfred Lord Tennyson.

The principal argument on appeal is not that Byrnes had truthfully testified to the grand jury, but rather that her testimony was not "material" within 18 U.S.C. § 1623(a). That statute is violated only when the false statements bear upon issues under investigation by the grand jury. Appellant argues that her testimony that the birds were dead upon arrival and buried rather than delivered to Mrs. Meffert, was totally irrelevant to the grand jury investigation. The District Court rejected this contention and we affirm its finding of materiality.

* * *

Materiality is broadly construed: "Materiality is thus demonstrated if the question posed is such that a truthful answer could help the inquiry, or a false response hinder it, and these

7. On direct examination, the following testimony was given: "Q. Mrs. Meffert, do you recall testifying yesterday about your definition of birds? A. Yes. Q. And do you recall that you said that the swans and geese were not birds? A. Not to me. Q. What do you mean by that, "not to me?" A. By me, the swans are waterfowls." Transcript at 399. Shortly thereafter, Mrs. Meffert was cross examined as follows: "Q. Are sparrows birds? A. I think so, sure. Q. Is a crow a bird? A. I think so. Q. Is a parrot a bird? A. Not to me. Q. How about a seagull, is that a bird? A. To me it is a seagull, I don't know what it is to other people. Q. Is it a bird to you as well or not? A. To me it is a seagull. I don't know any other definition for it. Q. Is an eagle a bird? A. I guess so. Q. Is a swallow a bird? A. I don't know what a swallow is, sir. Q. Is a duck a bird? A. Not to me, it is a duck. Q. But not a bird. A. No, to other people maybe. Q. Where is your husband now, ma'am? A. Up in the room."

8. The difficulty of establishing that swans and geese were birds, a proposition not accepted by Mrs. Meffert, was obviated by a Government stipulation that both were birds.

> "Let the long contention cease! Geese are swans, and swans are geese."
>
> *The Scholar Gypsy, The Last Word*,
> Stanza 2, Matthew Arnold.

The trial judge, perhaps to relieve the tension, observed that while he had enjoyed goose dinners he had never consumed swan—some indication of the limited cuisine available in the Northern District. The swan leg was not offered in evidence as an exhibit.

effects are weighed in terms of potentiality rather than probability. Thus, in applying this gauge to specific situations, it is only the question, at the time of its asking, which is considered. It is of no consequence that the information sought would be merely cumulative . . . or that the matters inquired into were collateral to the principal objective of the grand jury. . . ." *United States v. Berardi*, [629 F.2d 723].

Measured by this broad test it is clear that the appellant's perjury here was material. The grand jury investigation was prolonged and broad in scope. Appellant's argument that it was simply limited to the importation of wildlife and had nothing to do with matters subsequent to importation is not accurate. Fitzsimmons was a target of the investigation and appellant's testimony that he had not received the birds shielded Fitzsimmons from the conspiracy charge relating to his role in the transactions in which he and Clare were allegedly involved. Moreover, had the truth been told Ida Meffert would have been identified months before her role in the matter was actually discovered. Appellant's false testimony clearly impeded and hindered the investigative efforts of the grand jury. Her perjury was therefore material within the meaning of the statute.

II.

Appellant's remaining arguments are even less meritorious. In his opening to the jury, while explaining the background of the case, the prosecutor stated that Kenneth Clare had pleaded guilty to falsifying shipping documents. Appellant immediately moved for a mistrial; Judge McCurn denied the motion, but admonished the jury to disregard the prosecutor's remark, pointing out that "the guilt or innocence of any of these parties is not binding on the young lady." In the three day trial that followed, the Government never mentioned Clare in its case or on summation. In view of the strength of the Government's perjury case and appellant's concession of the sufficiency of evidence to support her perjury, it is apparent that even if any error was committed it was harmless and did not warrant the granting of a new trial.

Finally, appellant urges that the trial judge committed reversible error by not taking judicial notice of Migratory Bird Permit Regulations, 50 C.F.R. Part 21 (1979) which require the registration of trumpeter swans and the obtaining of permits for their possession and disposal. Mrs. Meffert admitted that she had never registered the swans but also stated that she was unaware that any such regulations were in existence. Appellant argues that since they were not registered Mrs. Meffert never possessed the trumpeter swans. The argument is totally unpersuasive. Count II, charging appellant with false testimony that the swans were mute rather than trumpeters, was withdrawn from the jury. Thus, the relevance of the registration was minimal. Furthermore, Mrs. Meffert admitted that the swans weren't registered. Therefore, the point was made and her conceded ignorance of the Migratory Bird regulations hardly establishes that she didn't possess the swans which she didn't consider birds in any event.[9] The existence of the regulations was irrelevant and whether or not Mrs. Meffert violated them would only confuse the issue before the jury. The trial judge has broad discretion in these matters and he committed no abuse of discretion in refusing to take judicial notice of the regulations or submitting them to the jury.

The judgment of conviction is affirmed, justice has triumphed and this is my swan song.

---

9. For a liberal construction of the term "birds," by a Canadian court see *Regina v. Ojibway*, 8 Criminal Law Quarterly 137 (1965–66) (Op. Blue, J.), holding that an Indian who shot a pony which had broken a leg and was saddled with a downy pillow had violated the Small Birds Act which defined a "bird" as "a two legged animal covered with feathers." The court reasoned that the statutory definition "does not imply that only two-legged animals qualify, for the legislative intent is to make two legs merely the minimum requirement. . . . Counsel submits that having regard to the purpose of the statute only small animals 'naturally covered' with feathers could have been contemplated. However, had this been the intention of the legislature, I am certain that the phrase 'naturally covered' would have been expressly inserted just as 'Long' was inserted in the Longshoreman's Act. "Therefore, a horse with feathers on its back must be deemed for the purpose of this Act to be a bird, a fortiori, a pony with feathers on its back is a small bird." Id. at 139.

Should an insurance company be held responsible for the indiscretions of a family pet? The following opinion involves a French poodle by the name of Andre, who used his masters' lovely home as an indoor park when nature called. Instead of training the poodle to appreciate the great outdoors, Andre's owners sued their insurance company for $7,500 in damages under their "floater" provision.

AETNA INSURANCE COMPANY

v.

SACHS

United States District Court, E.D Missouri
Feb. 11, 1960
186 F.Supp. 105

WEBER, District Judge.

This matter arises upon plaintiff insurance company's Complaint for Declaratory Judgment. It seeks determination of liability under its policy No. PPF–Mo 1–242411, issued to defendant January 29, 1956, for a term of 3 years and which policy contained an attached personal property rider. This rider, with a $25 deductible provision, insured certain listed property against loss or damage. The defendant had made a claim against plaintiff for damage caused to carpeting and after plaintiff's complaint was filed he answered and filed a counterclaim in which he sought to recover $7,500 plus damages for vexatious delay and reasonable attorney's fee. The cause was tried before the Court, without a jury.

The law has always been a hard taskmaster and requires of its advocates a serious approach and stern visaged application. When it comes face to face with life, as it unfolds in the drama of the courtroom, the law sometimes reaches its serious, stern results from facts which have been compiled with humor. So—while the end results of the law are deadly serious—there is about the lawyer (and even judges, occasionally) a spark of the humor of life—and a need for it. So let it be with this opinion; for, while the end result is most serious to both plaintiff and defendant, what has brought about the necessity for the end result, is most humorous.

Our factual situation obviously had its inception when defendant obtained the insurance policy from plaintiff. If all had proceeded in the normal course of human events from that point on, this suit would never have been brought, for plaintiff insured against and was prepared for the usual expectancies of fire, wind and rain. But, defendant purchased, and plaintiff issued, the rider, known commonly in the trade as a "floater". Now, "floater" provisions are covered by (and in this instance, rightly so) the rules of "maritime" law, for, the risks are sometimes unusual.

In any event, the policy in question provided generally for damages and loss to the furnishings and personal property of the defendant for reasons other than fire, wind and rain, to-wit, theft and other fortuitous circumstances. What subsequently transpired after issuance brings into play the "floater" provisions of this policy.

Defendant and wife purchased in October 1957 a "french Poodle", which they appropriately and fascinatingly named "Andre". According to defendant, Andre was properly trained and "broke" and life was pleasant for the defendant and his wife and peaceful for the plaintiff until defendant and wife went on a vacation and left Andre at a kennel for the duration. When they returned their first thoughts were of Andre and they promptly brought him back to their chateau, blissful in the reunion. But the home-like serenity was soon shattered, for madam soon spied Andre with his leg hoisted in masculine canine fashion and his purpose had been, and was being, accomplished. Madam did not testify, but defendant said she told him of the occurrence and he promptly surveyed the living room, dining room and hall and found signs of Andre's misfeasance. His next step was to notify his insurance agent and make claim under the "floater" provisions of the policy.

There was some dispute between the parties as to whether proper notice was given and claim made, but the Court is convinced that defendant gave notice within the terms and provisions of the policy and plaintiff cannot escape liability on that point. Plaintiff did send an adjuster to the premises to survey the effects of where Andre, the French Poodle, had popped in, piddled and popped out. In fact, he testified that Andre gave a "command performance" while he was there.

Also, a rug specialist was sent to the premises and he too made a survey. He found spots ranging in diameter from the size of a "dime" to nine inches, and in number from 75 to 80. He testified that one or two could have been repaired, but not that many, for it would have been impossible to match the yarn in the rug and the patches and repairs would have been as obvious as Andre's tell-tale marks. He also said that the spots would have been readily noticeable from the time they dried and that they extended throughout the living room, dining room, hall, stairway and were on the rug, furniture and drapes; which gives rise to the conclusion that Andre had the run of the house.

The owner of the kennel, where Andre spent just two weeks, gave as his opinion that a dog with good habits would not lose them in two weeks; that he properly cared for the dog and had provisions for outside relief facilities for the dogs in his kennels; and, that four to five times a day would be a maximum amount of calls to nature for any dog, including Andre.

Plaintiff brought this declaratory judgment suit to determine its liability for threatened prosecution by the defendant and contended that this was just too many incidents to be liable for. Defendant answered and denied, claiming surprise in Andre's change of habits and further contended that there were but four or five incidents and the rest of the spots were pure dribbles, and he counterclaimed for total loss of carpeting and for damages in the amount of $7,500 therefor.

At the rate of four or five calls per day, at best it would have taken Andre about sixteen days to make all the spots. But, on the theory that each incident is entitled to a dribble or two, it could probably be said, without fear of contradiction, that the spotting represents ten to twelve incidents and probably over a period of a week. In that length of time if the spots had not been seen, they at least should have been recognized by other sensory perception.

A review of the search books to the law reveals no cases in point. Either there never was a poodle as prolific as Andre, or, before such insurance, people caught them, put their nose in it and threw them outside. Thus, we have a case of first impression. The testimony is that Andre met his demise, by truck, some few weeks after his prolific, piddlin' propensities were discovered and he, therefore, can never be made aware of his place in history unless he rests in some Valhalla from whence he can eat, sleep and answer his calls to nature, while still permitted to glance back occasionally to review the results, devastation, chaos and the indecision caused by his handiwork.

The unprecedented problem requires some decision, for the law, right or wrong, must conclude litigation. I would conclude this episode in the following manner:

For one or two occasions of Andre's imprudence we might expect the plaintiff to be liable, even though it is stretching the credulity of any sage of the law to put permission and right upon liability where a person gives a canine pet the right to perambulate and pounce unrestrained throughout the house. Such privileges, even to a poodle, seem more the part of valor than of wisdom, especially where the play pen is a $7,500 rug and expensive furniture and drapes.

The law has always allowed each dog its first bite, for then the owner is put on notice of its dangerous tendencies. I would even go one or two better in incidents such as this and would have allowed recovery for two or three incidents. This would give the insured some opportunity, through sight or smell, to discover the occurrence, prevent its repetition and make claim for that which seems a fortuitous circumstance or event. But, to allow for such prolific indiscretions, ad infinitum, is beyond credulity and borders onto wanton recklessness and disregard for which a person should not be rewarded.

While Andre might not be expected to know the terms and conditions of plaintiff's policy, it seems most fantastic that defendant should be able to contend that Andre's indiscretion was fortuitous. Judge Hand, in *Mellon v. Federal Ins. Co.*, D.C., 14 F.2d 997, loc. cit. 1004, said: "* * *, even in an 'all risk' policy, there must be a fortuitous event—a casualty—to give rise to any liability for insurance."

In the law, "fortuitous" means "by chance" and "by accident". It seems to me that it is just "by accident" that Andre didn't do what he did, much before the alleged occurrence, and, if "by chance" he didn't, it was just too much, and too often, to require plaintiff to pay for it.

One cannot stand by and see damage being done, allow it to be done and then collect for the total loss. In other words, one cannot be present and see a fire when it first originates and at a time when something could be done to extinguish it, then go off and allow the damage to be done and attempt to collect for the total damage. Such conduct constitutes culpable negligence and precludes a recovery.

An insurer is not liable for reckless and inexcusable negligence. Neither is an insurer liable for losses resulting from inherent vice, defect, or infirmity in the subject matter insured. Further, defendant had an obligation under Paragraph 20 of the policy in question to safeguard the property insured thereunder. Under the terms of the policy defendant cannot recover where he discovered, or should have discovered, the damage long before it reached its final extent, in time thereafter to have safeguarded the property and have kept the damage to a minimum.

In the case at bar, defendant allowed and permitted the damage to become so extensive that he is now claiming a total loss, whereas, plaintiff, if liable at all, should have been exposed only to a minimal loss.

I would say that defendant, because of such gross negligence and indiscretion in permitting Andre to roam the house at will, hoisting his leg at random, probably yipping and yiping in his canine Utopia, should not be allowed to recover. Certainly, a dog can be controlled by his master, and while a master cannot expect perfection from a dog, even a poodle, he should be ever aware to keep him from expensive parts of the house where he might do damage with either end. Further, defendant here should not be allowed to collect for a total loss which he himself could have kept at a minimum by the exercise of a little discretion, observance or care.

So, in the Eastern District of Missouri, while we love our dogs, let it be the law that we don't collect for so many puddles made by poodles, even under the "floater" provisions of a policy with "maritime" law as precedent. It is this Court's conclusion that judgment should be entered declaring that plaintiff is not liable under the terms and provisions of its policy of insurance for the damage caused to the carpeting in question under the circumstances proven and existing in this case. Further, that defendant should not be allowed to recover upon his counterclaim against the plaintiff.

In other words, I am saying to the defendant, "You cannot recover"; to the plaintiff, "You may continue your policy in peace"; and to the beloved little French poodle, the proximate cause of this litigation and discourse, I say, "*Paix a toi aussi,* Andre."

* * *

Chapter 2

Crime and Punishment

The definition and punishment of proscribed conduct is at the core of a legal system. One of its most important purposes is to remove "justice" from the hands of the injured person and place it within a structured institution. Crime is the subject of this section but it does not deal with any celebrated criminal cases or, for that matter, with any landmark decisions. It is concerned, rather, with the definition of crime, the power of the government to investigate and prosecute, and the punishment imposed on or suffered by the miscreants.

One may get the impression from reading the saga of Eric Campbell and his treasure trove that in life, things rarely go his way. His history of convictions indicates that he was not very successful in the field of crime. And, his attempt to pay restitution to society was even less successful. Even finding more than $130,000 in cash did not allow Mr. Campbell to move to Easy Street.

In addition to the story that is told by Judge O'Hara, the case has an interesting explication of the law that might, or might not, allow *you* to keep the pirate's treasure when you finally find it.

CAMPBELL

v.

COCHRAN

Superior Court of Delaware
June 5, 1980
416 A.2d 211

O'HARA, Judge.

*   *   *

Procedurally, this mixed bag of criminal and civil motions presents a rather unique situation to the Court. Substantively, they involve novel and complex questions of first impression in this State concerning common law and statutory rights and duties of finders of money. Factually, the events leading up to the instant litigation are so bizarre that one might expect this tale to have been spun from the colorful imagination of Robert Louis Stevenson or Mark Twain. Therefore, due to the thoroughly unique nature of this case, the Court will set out the relevant facts, largely undisputed by the parties, in some detail.

I.

Early in 1977 plaintiff was indicted on multiple charges. Plaintiff entered an agreement with the State whereby he pled guilty to two counts of Burglary Third Degree and one count of misdemeanor Theft and the State dismissed all other charges. On September 7, 1977, plaintiff was sentenced on the above charges to eighteen months imprisonment to be followed by two years probation.

* * *

Plaintiff agreed to work as an informant in certain investigations in return for a reduction in sentence.

* * *

On the evening of December 10, 1977, plaintiff was equipped by the State Police with a hidden radio transmitter on his body. The State Police were interested in obtaining evidence against two individuals. One was Charles Rifon, a friend of plaintiff's, and the other person was an associate of Rifon's who was suspected of dealing in stolen goods, *i.e.*, a "fence." The plan was for plaintiff to get Rifon to set up a meeting with the fence, so that plaintiff could sell a "stolen" typewriter to the fence which had been supplied by the State Police. Due to the limited range of the body transmitter, the officers with whom plaintiff was working had to keep within a quarter to a half mile of plaintiff. Consequently, it was arranged for these officers to follow plaintiff at a reasonable distance in an unmarked car.

On the night in question, plaintiff drove his vehicle to a prearranged meeting place and picked up Rifon at approximately 8:30 P.M. Plaintiff and Rifon then proceeded to drive to a local liquor store. Although Rifon believed they were simply going to buy some beer, plaintiff had previously arranged for the State Police to begin following from this point in their unmarked car. Plaintiff and Rifon, with the officers following, then drove to the vicinity of the fence's home, but for some reason Rifon was reluctant at that time to make direct contact with the fence. Consequently, the two men decided to drive to a secluded area, colorfully known as "Bazoobie Land," apparently to drink their beer and pass the time.

Bazoobie Land can most accurately be described as an unauthorized junk yard. It is located in a relatively remote section of New Castle County and was used generally by persons wanting to dump trash. There is also evidence indicating that Bazoobie Land was a popular dumping ground for thieves who desired to get rid of stolen cars and safes. Rifon, himself, had on more than one occasion abandoned stolen safes in Bazoobie Land after removing the contents.

Plaintiff and Rifon arrived at Bazoobie Land at approximately 11:00 P.M. As they were walking through the area Rifon spotted a safe which he recognized as one he had stolen and then abandoned in the area in 1974. The door to the safe had been removed by Rifon in 1974 at which time he also removed all of the safe's contents. When the safe was found on the night of December 10, 1977, it was lying on its face frozen to the ground so that the inside compartment was concealed from view. Plaintiff hit the safe with a large rock to break it loose from the ground, and the men turned the safe over.

At this point the men discovered a package wedged inside the safe. The packaged was wrapped in green plastic and covered with tape. Although they could not immediately see what was in the package, neither plaintiff nor Rifon was a naive babe in the woods (more accurately, they were not naive babes in Bazoobie Land). It was apparent that the package had been purposely placed in the safe by someone, as Rifon had completely emptied the safe before abandoning it in 1974. Moreover, as both men knew, Bazoobie Land was sometimes frequented by other members of the criminal element. They were, therefore, not anxious to wait around with the package and possibly be discovered themselves. Consequently, the men carried the package to the top of a hill some distance from the safe before attempting to ascertain its contents.

It is important to reiterate here that while these events were occurring, the conversations between plaintiff and Rifon were still being monitored by the State Police officers, who were parked in their car somewhere near Bazoobie Land. Rifon, who was still unaware of the radio transmitter, was apparently talking in an excited manner about the discovery, while plaintiff kept telling Rifon to be quiet.

Upon reaching the top of the hill, plaintiff and Rifon partially tore the package open to see what they had found. Mere words are probably inadequate to describe the amazement of the two men when they discovered that the package contained several bundles of United States currency in $5, $10. $20, $50 and $100 denominations. The money was not new, *i.e.*, the bills were not in serial number sequence, but the bills were not frayed or torn and the package did not appear to have been in the safe for a long time. Rifon began exclaiming excitedly that they were rich. Plaintiff kept telling him to be quiet and suggested that they take the money to a motel room and split it. Plaintiff's words, as recorded by the State Police officers, upon opening the package were as follows:

"Just be quiet. Hear me, just be quiet. Don't say nothing, you just think, and I'll think, we got to get out of here. I got money for a motel room (unintelligable) (sic) we'll split it 50/50 and then we're gone.

"We got $20,000 in cash, we got to go count it and take care of it.

"We got to lay this money out somewhere. We can't cut it up and start spending it. We have to count it, wrap it back up and hide it.

"I want to get out of the Valley."

The men then began to walk back to plaintiff's car, but plaintiff stopped momentarily to pick up the typewriter which the State Police had given him and which he had earlier carried away from the car. While thus engaged and out of Rifon's immediate presence, Campbell spoke to the State Police officers through the hidden transmitter, saying:

"Hang on guys. We hit it big. Bear with me. I repeat bear with me. Don't stop me now."

Plaintiff and Rifon got into plaintiff's car and drove away from Bazoobie Land. As they were leaving the area, plaintiff observed the State Police officers sitting in their car. Plaintiff began driving on Rt. 82 toward Wilmington, and the officers began to follow. However, after a few minutes plaintiff reversed direction and headed north toward the nearby Pennsylvania

State line. The two men continued north until they reached a motel in Chadds Ford, Pennsylvania. After checking into the motel, under an assumed name, and switching off the radio transmitter, plaintiff accompanies Rifon and the money up to their room. The men took the money out of the package and laid it out on a bed. They found that the package contained a total of $136,000 arranged roughly by denomination in one thousand dollar packets. Some of the packets were bound by bank wrappers and others by rubber bands.

After counting the money, plaintiff left the room momentarily, telling Rifon he was going for sodas. While out of the room, plaintiff telephoned the State Police headquarters and left a message for Officer Ford that he and Rifon had found "a lot of money." Plaintiff returned to the room where he and Rifon divided the money equally, each placing his share in a separate pillow case. The men then left the motel and drove back to Delaware. While driving back plaintiff told Rifon about the hidden radio transmitter and the fact that the police had been monitoring them while they were in Bazoobie Land. The two decided to avoid the police for the time being and went to the home of Rifon's girlfriend, arriving at approximately 1:30 A.M. on December 11, 1977.

While at the girlfriend's house, plaintiff and Rifon decided that since the police officers knew they had found some money they would have to turn something over to the State Police. The only figure mentioned while the officers had been monitoring the conversations was $20,000. Figuring that the officers would be suspicious if they turned in precisely $20,000, the two decided to admit to finding $16,000. Plaintiff then telephoned Officer Ford, told him of the discovery, and arranged to meet the officers at a local hotel. Each man took $8,000 to their meeting with the police officers, turned it over, and received a common receipt from the State Police for the total $16,000.

At approximately 6:00 A.M. on December 11, plaintiff and Rifon returned to Bazoobie Land with the officers to show the scene where the money had been found. The police stayed to investigate the scene while plaintiff and Rifon returned to the girlfriend's house to pick up the remainder of the money. Upon reaching the girlfriend's house, Rifon gave one of the pillow cases containing money to plaintiff and shortly thereafter the two men parted company.

Sometime later the same day plaintiff met with his uncle to seek advice on how to proceed but none was forthcoming. Plaintiff then decided to go to his uncle's house and hide his share of the money. While at this house plaintiff again counted the money and found that instead of the $60,000 that was supposed to be in the pillow case, there was only approximately $50,000. He placed this money in a flight bag and secreted it inside a hollow wall in the house.

* * *

After submitting to polygraph tests, first Rifon and then the plaintiff told the police the true amount of the money that they had found. Plaintiff was acquitted of theft charges based on his failure to turn over all of the money immediately.

Despite extensive investigation, defendant has never ascertained the true owner of the money and still retains possession of the funds.

* * *

II.

The basic dispute between plaintiff and defendant centers on the question of which of these parties is entitled to the $58,210 found by plaintiff and turned over to defendant. All three of the instant motions seek a resolution of this basic question.

In the civil action at bar plaintiff claims that he is legally entitled to the money as the finder thereof under either statutory or common law of Delaware. Defendant claims that the common law regarding found money has been entirely preempted by an act of the Legislature, codified at 11 Del.C. § 8307(c), and that pursuant to this statute the money properly belongs in defendant's possession. The pending cross-motions for summary judgment are forthrightly directed at resolving these critical issues.

III.

Although several other issues have been raised by the parties on the cross-motions, the primary issue to be decided is the extent to which 11 Del.C. § 8307(c) has preempted the common law pertaining to rights in found money. As this is a question of first impression, the Court must necessarily examine the historical common law background which preceded enactment of the statute.

A.

* * *

Under the present statute the limitation period is reduced to one year and thereafter the money may become the absolute property of either the finder or the Police Retirement Fund, depending on the circumstances.

Prior to the enactment of these statutes the expressed civil common law in Delaware relating to found property apparently consisted of a single reported decision. In *Clark v. Maloney*, Del.Super., 3 Del. 68 (1840), the court held that "the finder of a chattel, though he does not acquire an absolute property in it, yet has such a property, as will enable him to keep it against all but the rightful owner." The *Clark* formulation was entirely consistent with the general common law rule accepted by the overwhelming majority of jurisdictions in this country, *i.e.*, that a finder has superior title in found goods as against the entire world except for the true owner. Consequently, although *Clark v. Maloney* is the only reported Delaware decision dealing with the subject, it shows an acceptance of the generally held common law principles relating to found property. Therefore, it is to these principles that the Court will initially turn for guidance in deciding the issues presented by the pending cross-motions.

Under the common law all found property, including money, was generally delineated into four categories as defined below:

1. **LOST PROPERTY:** that which the owner has involuntarily parted with through neglect, carelessness or inadvertence and the whereabouts of which is unknown to the owner;

2. **MISLAID PROPERTY:** that which the owner has intentionally laid down in a place where he can again resort to it, and then forgets where he put it;

3. **ABANDONED PROPERTY:** that to which the owner has voluntarily relinquished all right, title, claim and possession, with the intention of terminating his ownership, but without vesting ownership in any other person, and with the intention of not reclaiming any future rights therein; and

4. **TREASURE TROVE:** gold or silver coin or bullion, or money, which has been concealed by the owner in a private place for safekeeping; treasure trove carries the thought of antiquity, *i.e.*, it must have been concealed sufficiently long so as to indicate that the owner is probably dead or unknown. For present purposes, one major distinction between these various characterizations is that only lost property involves an element of involuntariness. The three remaining categories involve voluntary and intentional acts by the true owner in placing the property where it is eventually found by another.

As to the finder's right to possession, the common law held that as against all but the true owner the finder had superior title to lost property or treasure trove. Moreover, the finder of abandoned property who appropriated it to his own possession acquired absolute title thereto. However, the right of possession to mislaid property was held to be in the owner of the premises where such property was found. The finder of such property acquired no right thereto, and the true owner still had supreme title to mislaid property. The true owner's rights in treasure trove, lost or mislaid property continued from the time of the finding until such time as the limitation period expired for actions seeking recovery of the found property from the finder in possession. Absent a statute providing otherwise, the State had no right to found property as against the finder.

The common law also placed certain duties on finders of property. The finder of lost property or treasure trove had no duty to take possession of the found property, but if he chose to do so he had a duty to keep the property safe and return it to the true owner on demand. Moreover, the finder of such property was required to take reasonable steps to find the true owner. The finder of mislaid property was required to turn it over to the owner of the premises where it was found, who then had the duty to protect the property and return it to the true owner. In Delaware, the duty to take reasonable steps to find the true owner of found property was enforced primarily through the criminal law relating to larceny.

B.

Having discussed the common law, it is now appropriate to examine the precise terms of § 8307(c) in order to ascertain its relevance to the instant controversy.

*   *   *

The Court considered the relationship between the statute and the common law in view of the apparent intent of the legislature in enacting the statute.

*   *   *

The practical result of the Court's holdings is that where money is found and delivered into the custody of the State Police, the common law concerning rights to such money is entirely preempted by § 8307(c). However, there is no requirement that found money be delivered to the State Police, and if the State Police do not acquire custody thereof, the common law will control its ultimate disposition. The Court believes that the laudatory purpose behind the statute, *i.e.*, to improve the true owners' chances of recovering their property by encouraging delivery of found money to the State Police, will be served by the decision reached herein, since the finder who does, in fact, deliver found money to the State Police will have an opportunity to acquire absolute title, not merely possession, after only one year, in addition to avoiding (hopefully) prosecution under the theft statute.

IV.

Having delineated the law of the case, the Court must now examine the undisputed material facts to determine whether summary judgment in favor of either party should be granted. Since the question of the ultimate characterization to be given found money is clearly one of fact, it should be reserved for the jury unless the undisputed facts are so conclusive that the Court may pass on the character of the money as a matter of law.

Under the statute, the initial burden is on plaintiff, who does not have possession of the money, to show that he was the finder of the money, that the found money was delivered to and has been in the custody of the State Police for at least one year, and that the true owner has not been located or filed a valid claim for the money within that year. In the case at bar, defendant concedes that undisputed facts establish all of the foregoing elements.

The only material factual dispute between the parties concerns the ultimate characterization of the found money. The basic dispute is that defendant contends the money was "stolen" while plaintiff says it was not. Regarding the initial question as to who must shoulder the burden of proof on this issue, the Court concludes that defendant must show, by a preponderance of the evidence, that the money was stolen before the burden of rebuttal will shift to plaintiff. The Court's conclusion is based simply on the mathematical probability that absent any consideration of the facts in a particular case it is more likely that found money was not stolen than vice versa. Rather than make the finder thereof prove a negative fact, i.e., that the money was not stolen, it is more logical and reasonable to require that defendant affirmatively prove the existence of the disputed fact. In other words, as between a finder and the State Police, § 8307(c) creates a rebuttable presumption that found money was not stolen.

Looking to the facts in this case the Court is unable to conclude as a matter of law that the found money either was or was not stolen. Defendant cites the following facts as proof that the money was stolen:

1. money was found in a "thieves" junkyard;

2. money was found in a previously stolen safe;

3. other stolen property was in the same area, e.g., stripped cars and other safes;

4. the bills were in relatively small denominations and were packaged in denominational order, *i.e.*, $5 bills together, $10 bills together, etc.;

5. the money was found late at night;

6. the failure of the depositor to attempt to claim the full amount of money from the State Police; and

7. the large amount of money in the package.

From this circumstantial evidence defendant insists that the only reasonable inference to be drawn is that the money was stolen. Alternatively, defendant argues that these facts are sufficient to raise a jury issue as to the proper characterization of the found money.

Plaintiff argues that the facts relied upon by defendant are insufficient to overcome his motion for summary judgment. He points to the additional fact that after a standard police computer check by serial number on all the bills only one $10 bill was shown to have been taken in a bank robbery in Philadelphia. Plaintiff also relies on the fact that although nearly one hundred persons made inquiries to the State Police concerning the money, the State Police have been unable to connect the money or any significant portion thereof to a particular theft. Plaintiff contends that these facts compel the conclusion that the found money was not stolen.

On a motion for summary judgment all facts must be viewed in a manner most favorable to the non-moving party, as well as all reasonable inferences which may be drawn from the undisputed facts. While the subsidiary facts upon which the parties herein rely are not disputed, the ultimate fact to be proved, *i.e.*, whether the found money was stolen, is hotly disputed and rests upon inference from the subsidiary facts. The case is a close one, but in the final analysis, at this preliminary stage of the proceedings, the Court is unable to conclude that the only reasonable inferences to be drawn from the undisputed facts conclusively favor plaintiff or defendant. Consequently, summary judgment to either party is inappropriate at this time.

V.

In conclusion and in accordance with the foregoing analysis, the Court has determined that summary judgment to either party should be, and hereby is, denied. The Court has also determined that the pending criminal motion for return of property should also be, and hereby is, denied.

IT IS SO ORDERED.

It is an elementary rule of fairness that a person charged with a crime be given fair written notice of what he or she is accused of doing. But does grammar count? In the next case, it is obvious that the court is sorely tempted to teach the district attorney, or whoever drafted the indictment, a lesson by reversing the conviction, even though it is almost certain that the defendant understood what he was charged with. Still, the drafter must have squirmed as he read the opinion, knowing the delight that it would give his colleagues. Perhaps that was as effective as a reversal would have been.

HENDERSON

v.

STATE

Supreme Court of Mississippi
Feb. 8, 1984
445 So.2d 1364

ROBERTSON, Justice, for the Court:

I.

This case presents the question whether the rules of English grammar are a part of the positive law of this state. If they are, Jacob Henderson's burglary conviction must surely be reversed, for the indictment in which he has been charged would receive an "F" from every English teacher in the land.

Though grammatically unintelligible, we find that the indictment is legally sufficient and affirm, knowing full well that our decision will receive of literate persons everywhere opprobrium as intense and widespread as it will be deserved.

II.

On May 15, 1982, the Maaco Paint Shop in Jackson, Mississippi, was burglarized. Jacob Henderson was arrested immediately thereafter, four items of stolen merchandise still in his possession.

On July 6, 1982, Henderson was formally charged with business burglary in violation of Miss.Code Ann. § 97–17–33 (1972) in an indictment returned by the Hinds County Grand Jury. The indictment further charged that Henderson was a recidivist within the meaning of Miss.Code Ann. § 99–19–81 (Supp.1983). Henderson entered a plea of not guilty to all charges.

On February 9, 1983, this case was called for trial in the Circuit Court of Hinds County. In due course, the jury found Henderson guilty on the principal charge of burglary.

III.

A.

The primary issue presented on this appeal regards the legal adequacy of the indictment under which Henderson has been tried, convicted and sentenced. That indictment, in pertinent part, reads as follows:

> The Grand Jurors for the State of Mississippi, . . . upon their oaths present: That Jacob Henderson . . . on the 15th day of May, A.D., 1982.

> The store building there situated, the property of Metro Auto Painting, Inc., . . . in which store building was kept for sale or use valuable things, to-wit: goods, ware and merchandise unlawfully, feloniously and burglariously did break and enter, with intent the goods, wares and merchandise of said Metro Auto Painting then and there being in said store building unlawfully, feloniously and then and there being in said store building burglariously to take, steal and carry away; And

>> One (1) Polaroid Land Camera,
>> One (1) Realistic AM/FM Stereo Tuner
>> One (1) Westminster AM/FM radio
>> One (1) Metal Box and contents thereof,

> . . .

the property of the said Metro Auto Painting then
and there being in said store building did then and
there unlawfully, feloniously and burglariously take,
steal and carry away the aforesaid property, he, the
said Jacob Henderson, having been twice previously
convicted of felonies, to-wit: . . . .

The remainder of the indictment charges Henderson with being
a recidivist.

Henderson, no doubt offended, demurred. In support, he
presented an expert witness, Ann Dreher, who had been a
teacher of English for nine years. Ms. Dreher testified that,
when read consistent with accepted rules of English grammar,
the indictment did not charge Jacob Henderson with doing
anything; rather it charged that goods, ware and merchandise
broke and entered the paint store. The trial judge overruled
the objection and the motion, but not without reservation.
He stated:

[T]his same objection has been made numerous
times. It is one of Mr. Hailey's pets. [B]ut as far as
I know no one has elected to appeal and I'm going
to follow the decision whether it is grammatically
correct or not. I have repeatedly begged for six years
or five years for the district attorney not to use this
form. It is very poor English. It is impossible English. . . . In addition to being very poor English,
it also charges him with the crime of larceny, which
is not necessary to include in an indictment for burglary. I never did understand the reason for that.
I again ask the district attorney not to use this form.
It's archaic. Even Shakespeare could not understand
the grammatical construction of this indictment.
But the objection will be overruled. Maybe it will
take a reversal on a case of a similar nature where
there is a serious offense as this one is by the fact
that he is indicted as a habitual to get the district
attorney's attention.

B.

1.

In the trial court and on this appeal, Henderson insists that the meaning of the indictment may be obtained only within the strait jacket of accepted rules of grammatical construction of the English language. From this point of view, we are asked to examine the indictment and concentrate on the words ". . . unlawfully, feloniously and burglariously did break and enter. . . ." Who, we are asked, when the rules of good grammar are employed, did this alleged breaking and entering?

There are two possible answers (again, looking at the indictment as would an English teacher). "Goods, ware and merchandise" are the most obvious choice. Those nouns proximately precede the verb(s) "did break and enter" (separated only by the familiar string of adverbs "unlawfully, feloniously and burglariously"—the district attorney, like other lawyers, never uses one word when two or three will do just as well). Thus read, the indictment charges that Goods, ware and merchandise, not Jacob Henderson, burglarized the Maaco Paint Shop on May 15, 1982.

More properly, however, the words "Goods, ware and merchandise" are seen as the tail end of a largely unintelligible effort to describe something else: the store building. A perceptive English grammarian would conclude that it is "the store building there situated. . . ." which is charged with the burglary, for those words seem to constitute the subject of the nonsensical non-sentence we are charged to construe.

Even so, whether the indictment charges that "Goods, ware and merchandise" or "The store building there situated" . . . "unlawfully, feloniously and burglariously did break and enter. . . ." matters not to Jacob Henderson. His point is merely that the indictment does not charge that he did the breaking and entering.

Were this a Court of nine English teachers, Henderson no doubt would prevail.

The indictment does contain at the outset the charge "That Jacob Henderson . . . on the 15th day of May, A.D., 1982." We have another non-sentence. The unmistakable period after

1982 is used by astute defense counsel to nail down the point—that the indictment fails to charge that Jacob Henderson did anything on May 15, 1982. Again, we must concede that grammatically speaking counsel is correct. The period after 1982 grammatically precludes the possibility that the indictment charges that Jacob Henderson did break and enter. Either the words "did break and enter" would have to precede the period, or the name Jacob Henderson would have to appear following it. Neither is the case.

Recognizing that the period is important, the State argues that in reality the indictment consists of one long sentence, written albeit in legalese instead of English. The State argues that "the period grammatically disjoined the first part of the sentence from the second", conceding that we are indeed confronted with "a patently inappropriate period". This, of course, prompts Henderson to analogize the state's argument to Lady Macbeth's famous "Out damned spot! Out, I say!"[1] W. Shakespeare, Macbeth, Act V, sc. 1, line 38. The retort would be telling in the classroom or in a court of the literati. Alas, it has meager force in a court of law.

2.

With no little temerity, we insist that the correct statement of the question before this Court is: Does the indictment conform to the requirements of Rule 2.05, Uniform Criminal Rules of Circuit Court Practice.

For better or for worse, nothing in Rule 2.05 requires any adherence to correct grammatical form. We know of no constitutional or natural law that might supplement Rule 2.05 with the rules of good grammar.

Rule 2.05 states that "formal or technical words are not necessary". Correct grammar, however desirable, is similarly unnecessary. So long as from a fair reading of the indictment taken as a whole the nature and cause of the charge against the accused are clear, the indictment is legally sufficient.

---

1. It cannot be gainsaid that all the perfumes of Arabia would not eviscerate the grammatical stench emanating from this indictment. Cf. W. Shakespeare, Macbeth, Act V, sc. 1, lines 56–57.

The instant indictment, however inartfully worded, clearly charges Jacob Henderson with the crime of business burglary. It informs Henderson that the burglary is alleged to have occurred on May 15, 1982. The indictment names the business burglarized as Maaco Paint Shop operated by Metro Auto Painting, Inc. It charges that the crime occurred within the First Judicial District of Hinds County. Further, the indictment identifies the items of property said to have been stolen in the course of the burglary.

Viewing the indictment under Rule 2.05, we find it legally adequate. It provides Henderson with a "written statement of the essential facts constituting the offense charged" in language which is "plain, concise and definite", albeit grammatically atrocious. Beyond that, the indictment notified Henderson of "the nature and cause of the accusation against him".

Establishment of a literate bar is a worthy aspiration. 'Tis without doubt a consummation devoutly to be wished. Its achievement, however, must be relegated to means other than reversal of criminal convictions justly and lawfully secured.

The assignment of error is rejected.

* * *

AFFIRMED.

Even in 1959, a $10 fine was not considered a lot of money. In fact, the Kentucky appellate courts were not permitted to waste their time on cases involving a fine of less than $20. But the United States Supreme Court was persuaded to hear this next case. Of course, it wasn't the money—it was the principle.

❖–❖–❖–❖–❖

THOMPSON

v.

CITY OF LOUISVILLE

Supreme Court of the United States
March 21, 1960
80 S.Ct. 624, 362 U.S. 199, 4 L.Ed.2d 654

Mr. Justice BLACK delivered the opinion of the Court.

Petitioner was found guilty in the Police Court of Louisville, Kentucky, of two offenses—loitering and disorderly conduct. The ultimate question presented to us is whether the charges against petitioner were so totally devoid of evidentiary support as to render his conviction unconstitutional under the Due Process Clause of the Fourteenth Amendment. Decision of this question turns not on the sufficiency of the evidence, but on whether this conviction rests upon any evidence at all.

The facts as shown by the record are short and simple. Petitioner, a longtime resident of the Louisville area, went into the Liberty End Cafe about 6:20 on Saturday evening, January 24, 1959. In addition to selling food the cafe was licensed to sell beer to the public and some 12 to 30 patrons were present during the time petitioner was there. When petitioner had been in the cafe about half an hour, two Louisville police officers came in on a 'routine check.' Upon seeing petitioner 'out there on the floor dancing by himself,' one of the officers, according to his testimony, went up to the manager who was sitting on a stool nearby and asked him how long petitioner had been in there and if he had bought anything. The officer testified that upon being told by the manager that petitioner had been there 'a little over a half-hour and that he had not bought anything,' he accosted Thompson and 'asked him what was his reason for being in there and he said he was waiting on a bus.' The officer then informed petitioner that he was under arrest and took him outside. This was the arrest for loitering. After going outside, the officer testified, petitioner 'was very argumentative—he argued with us back and forth and so then we placed a disorderly conduct charge on him.' Admittedly the disorderly conduct conviction rests solely on this one sentence description of petitioner's conduct after he left the cafe.

The foregoing evidence includes all that the city offered against him, except a record purportedly showing a total of 54 previous arrests of petitioner. Before putting on his defense, petitioner moved for a dismissal of the charges against him on the ground that a judgment of conviction on this record would deprive him of property and liberty without due process of law under the Fourteenth Amendment in that (1) there was no evidence to support findings of guilt and (2) the two arrests and prosecutions were reprisals against him because petitioner had employed counsel and demanded a judicial hearing to defend himself against prior and allegedly baseless charges by the police. This motion was denied.

Petitioner then put in evidence on his own behalf, none of which in any way strengthened the city's case. He testified that he bought, and one of the cafe employees served him, a dish of macaroni and a glass of beer and that he remained in the cafe waiting for a bus to go home. Further evidence showed without dispute that at the time of his arrest petitioner gave the officers his home address; that he had money with him, and a bus schedule showing that a bus to his home would stop within half a block of the cafe at about 7:30; that he owned two unimproved lots of land; that in addition to work he had done for others, he had regularly worked one day or more a week for the same family for 30 years; that he paid no rent in the home where he lived and that his meager income was sufficient to meet his needs. The cafe manager testified that petitioner had frequently patronized the cafe, and that he had never told petitioner that he was unwelcome there. The manager further testified that on this very occasion he saw petitioner 'standing there in the middle of the floor and patting his foot,' and that he did not at any time during petitioner's stay there object to anything he was doing. There is no evidence that anyone else in the cafe objected to petitioner's shuffling his feet in rhythm with the music of the

jukebox or that his conduct was boisterous or offensive to anyone present. At the close of his evidence, petitioner repeated
his motion for dismissal of the charges on the ground that
a conviction on the foregoing evidence would deprive him of
liberty and property without due process under the Fourteenth
Amendment. The court denied the motion, convicted him of
both offenses, and fined him $10 on each charge. A motion
for new trial, on the same grounds, also was denied, which
exhausted petitioner's remedies in the police court.

Since police court fines of less than $20 on a single charge
are not appealable or otherwise reviewable in any other Kentucky court, petitioner asked the police court to stay the judgments so that he might have an opportunity to apply for
certiorari to this Court (before his case became moot) to review
the due process contentions he raised. The police court suspended judgment for 24 hours during which time petitioner
sought a longer stay from the Kentucky Circuit Court. That
court, after examining the police court's judgment and transcript, granted a stay concluding that 'there appears to be merit'
in the contention that 'there is no evidence upon which conviction and sentence by the Police Court could be based' and
that petitioner's Federal Constitutional claims are substantial
and not frivolous.' On appeal by the city, the Kentucky Court
of Appeals held that the Circuit Court lacked the power to
grant the stay it did, but nevertheless went on to take the
extraordinary step of granting its own stay, even though petitioner had made no original application to that court for such
a stay. Explaining its reason, the Court of Appeals took occasion to agree with the Circuit Court that petitioner's 'federal
constitutional claims are substantial and not frivolous.' The
Court of Appeals then went on to say that petitioner

> 'appears to have a real question as to whether he
> has been denied due process under the Fourteenth
> Amendment of the Federal Constitution, yet this
> substantive right cannot be tested unless we grant
> him a stay of execution because his fines are not
> appealable and will be satisfied by being served in
> jail before he can prepare and file his petition for
> certiorari. Appellee's substantive right of due process
> is of no avail to him unless this court grants him
> the ancillary right whereby he may test same in the
> Supreme Court.'

Our examination of the record presented in the petition for certiorari convinced us that although the fines here are small, the due process questions presented are substantial and we therefore granted certiorari to review the police court's judgments.

The city correctly assumes here that if there is no support for these convictions in the record they are void as denials of due process. The pertinent portion of the city ordinance under which petitioner was convicted of loitering reads as follows:

> 'It shall be unlawful for any person * * *, without visible means of support, or who cannot give a satisfactory account of himself, * * * to sleep, lie, loaf, or trespass in or about any premises, building, or other structure in the City of Louisville, without first having obtained the consent of the owner or controller of said premises, structure, or building; * * *'
> § 85–12, Ordinances of the City of Louisville.

In addition to the fact that petitioner proved he had 'visible means of support,' the prosecutor at trial said 'This is a loitering charge here. There is no charge of no visible means of support.' Moreover, there is no suggestion that petitioner was sleeping, lying or trespassing in or about this cafe. Accordingly he could only have been convicted for being unable to give a satisfactory account of himself while loitering in the cafe, without the consent of the manager. Under the words of the ordinance itself, if the evidence fails to prove all three elements of this loitering charge, the conviction is not supported by evidence, in which event it does not comport with due process of law. The record is entirely lacking in evidence to support any of the charges.

Here, petitioner spent about half an hour on a Saturday evening in January in a public cafe which sold food and beer to the public. When asked to account for his presence there, he said he was waiting for a bus. The city concedes that there is no law making it an offense for a person in such a cafe to 'dance,' 'shuffle' or 'pat' his feet in time to music. The undisputed testimony of the manager, who did not know whether petitioner had bought macaroni and beer or not but who did see the patting, shuffling or dancing, was that petitioner was welcome there. The manager testified that he did not at any time during petitioner's stay in the cafe object to anything petitioner was doing and that he never saw petitioner do anything that would cause any objection. Surely this is implied consent, which the city admitted in oral argument satisfies the ordinance. The arresting officer admitted that there was nothing in any way 'vulgar' about what he called petitioner's 'ordinary dance,' whatever relevance, if any, vulgarity might have to a charge of loitering. There simply is no semblance of evidence from which any person could reasonably infer that petitioner could not give a satisfactory account of himself or that he was loitering or loafing there (in the ordinary sense of the words) without 'the consent of the owner or controller' of the cafe.

Petitioner's conviction for disorderly conduct was under § 85–8 of the city ordinance which, without definition, provides that '(w)hoever shall be found guilty of disorderly conduct in the City of Louisville shall be fined * * *.' etc. The only evidence of 'disorderly conduct' was the single statement of the policeman that after petitioner was arrested and taken out of the cafe he was very argumentative. There is no testimony that petitioner raised his voice, used offensive language, resisted the officers or engaged in any conduct of any kind likely in any way to adversely affect the good order and tranquillity of the City of Louisville. The only information the record contains on what the petitioner was 'argumentative' about is his statement that he asked the officers 'what they arrested me for.' We assume, for we are justified in assuming, that merely 'arguing' with a policeman is not, because it could not be, 'disorderly conduct' as a matter of the substantive law of Kentucky. Moreover, Kentucky law itself seems to provide that if a man wrongfully arrested fails to object to the arresting officer, he waives any right to complain later that the arrest was unlawful.

Thus we find no evidence whatever in the record to support these convictions. Just as 'Conviction upon a charge not made would be sheer denial of due process,' so is it a violation of due process to convict and punish a man without evidence of his guilt.

The judgments are reversed and the cause is remanded to the Police Court of the City of Louisville for proceedings not inconsistent with this opinion.

Reversed and remanded.

The Upper Peninsula of Michigan was the setting for one of the most intriguing cases in fiction, the murder prosecution of *Anatomy of a Murder*. The UP is also the setting for what might have been one of the most mundane federal prosecutions ever. That mundane prosecution, however, raised one of the most basic issues in criminal law, the issue of "intent." And that is why a case involving some discarded bomb casings ended up in the United States Supreme Court.

"As a marriage of imagination, sound scholarship and technical skill in an opinion, I think Morissette can stand as the best we have any right to expect."

—Professor, University of California at Davis

MORISSETTE
v.
UNITED STATES

Supreme Court of the United States
Jan. 7, 1952
72 S.Ct. 240, 342 U.S. 246, 96 L.Ed. 288

Mr. Justice JACKSON delivered the opinion of the Court.

This would have remained a profoundly insignificant case to all except its immediate parties had it not been so tried and submitted to the jury as to raise questions both fundamental and far-reaching in federal criminal law, for which reason we granted certiorari.

On a large tract of uninhabited and untilled land in a wooded and sparsely populated area of Michigan, the Government established a practice bombing range over which the Air Force dropped simulated bombs at ground targets. These bombs consisted of a metal cylinder about forty inches long and eight inches across, filled with sand and enough black powder to cause a smoke puff by which the strike could be located. At various places about the range signs read 'Danger—Keep Out— Bombing Range.' Nevertheless, the range was known as good deer country and was extensively hunted.

Spent bomb casings were cleared from the targets and thrown into piles 'so that they will be out of the way.' They were not sacked or piled in any order but were dumped in heaps, some of which had been accumulating for four years or upwards, were exposed to the weather and rusting away.

Morissette, in December of 1948, went hunting in this area but did not get a deer. He thought to meet expenses of the trip by salvaging some of these casings. He loaded three tons of them on his truck and took them to a nearby farm, where they were flattened by driving a tractor over them. After expending this labor and trucking them to market in Flint, he realized $84.

Morissette, by occupation, is a fruit stand operator in summer and a trucker and scrap iron collector in winter. An honorably discharged veteran of World War II, he enjoys a good name among his neighbors and has had no blemish on his record more disreputable than a conviction for reckless driving.

The loading, crushing and transporting of these casings were all in broad daylight, in full view of passers-by, without the slightest effort at concealment. When an investigation was started, Morissette voluntarily, promptly and candidly told the whole story to the authorities, saying that he had no intention of stealing but thought the property was abandoned, unwanted and considered of no value to the Government. He was indicted, however, on the charge that he 'did unlawfully, wilfully and knowingly steal and convert' property of the United States of the value of $84, in violation of 18 U.S.C. § 641, 18 U.S.C.A. § 641, which provides that 'whoever embezzles, steals, purloins, or knowingly converts' government property is punishable by fine and imprisonment. Morissette was convicted and sentenced to imprisonment for two months or to pay a fine of $200. The Court of Appeals affirmed, one judge dissenting.

On his trial, Morissette, as he had at all times told investigating officers, testified that from appearances he believed the casings were cast-off and abandoned, that he did not intend to steal the property, and took it with no wrongful or criminal intent. The trial court, however, was unimpressed, and ruled: '(H)e took it because he thought it was abandoned and he knew he was on government property. * * * That is no defense. * * * I don't think anybody can have the defense they thought the property was abandoned on another man's piece of prop-

erty.' The court stated: 'I will not permit you to show this
man thought it was abandoned. * * * I hold in this case that
there is no question of abandoned property.' The court refused
to submit or to allow counsel to argue to the jury whether
Morissette acted with innocent intention. It charged: 'And I
instruct you that if you believe the testimony of the government in this case, he intended to take it. * * * He had no
right to take this property. * * * (A)nd it is no defense to claim
that it was abandoned, because it was on private property. * * *
And I instruct you to this effect: That if this young man took
this property (and he says he did), without any permission
(he says he did), that was on the property of the United States
Government (he says it was), that it was of the value of one
cent or more (and evidently it was), that he is guilty of the
offense charged here. If you believe the government, he is
guilty. * * * The question on intent is whether or not he intended to take the property. He says he did. Therefore, if you
believe either side, he is guilty.' Petitioner's counsel contended,
'But the taking must have been with a felonious intent.' The
court ruled, however: 'That is presumed by his own act.'

The Court of Appeals suggested that 'greater restraint in
expression should have been exercised', but affirmed the conviction because, 'As we have interpreted the statute, appellant
was guilty of its violation beyond a shadow of doubt, as evidenced even by his own admissions.' Its construction of the
statute is that it creates several separate and distinct offenses,
one being knowing conversion of government property. The
court ruled that this particular offense requires no element of
criminal intent. This conclusion was thought to be required
by the failure of Congress to express such a requisite and this
Court's decisions in *United States v. Behrman*, 258 U.S. 280, 42
S.Ct. 303, 66 L.Ed. 619, and *United States v. Balint*, 258 U.S.
250, 42 S.Ct. 301, 66 L.Ed. 604.

I.

In those cases this Court did construe mere omission from
a criminal enactment of any mention of criminal intent as
dispensing with it. If they be deemed precedents for principles
of construction generally applicable to federal penal statutes,
they authorize this conviction. Indeed, such adoption of the
literal reasoning announced in those cases would do this and
more—it would sweep out of all federal crimes, except when
expressly preserved, the ancient requirement of a culpable state

of mind. We think a resumé of their historical background is convincing that an effect has been ascribed to them more comprehensive than was contemplated and one inconsistent with our philosophy of criminal law.

The contention that an injury can amount to a crime only when inflicted by intention is no provincial or transient notion. It is as universal and persistent in mature systems of law as belief in freedom of the human will and a consequent ability and duty of the normal individual to choose between good and evil. A relation between some mental element and punishment for a harmful act is almost as instinctive as the child's familiar exculpatory 'But I didn't mean to,' and has afforded the rational basis for a tardy and unfinished substitution of deterrence and reformation in place of retaliation and vengeance as the motivation for public prosecution. Unqualified acceptance of this doctrine by English common law in the Eighteenth Century was indicated by Blackstone's sweeping statement that to constitute any crime there must first be a 'vicious will.' Common-law commentators of the Nineteenth Century early pronounced the same principle, although a few exceptions not relevant to our present problem came to be recognized.

Crime, as a compound concept, generally constituted only from concurrence of an evil-meaning mind with an evil-doing hand, was congenial to an intense individualism and took deep and early root in American soil. As the state codified the common law of crimes, even if their enactments were silent on the subject, their courts assumed that the omission did not signify disapproval of the principle but merely recognized that intent was so inherent in the idea of the offense that it required no statutory affirmation. Courts, with little hesitation or division, found an implication of the requirement as to offenses that were taken over from the common law. The unanimity with which they have adhered to the central thought that wrongdoing must be conscious to be criminal is emphasized by the variety, disparity and confusion of their definitions of the requisite but elusive mental element. However, courts of various jurisdictions, and for the purposes of different offenses, have devised working formulae, if not scientific ones, for the instruction of juries around such terms as 'felonious intent,' 'criminal intent,' 'malice aforethought,' 'guilty knowledge,' 'fraudulent intent,' 'wilfulness,' 'scienter,' to denote guilty knowledge, or 'mens rea,' to signify an evil purpose or mental culpability. By use or combination of these various tokens, they have sought to protect those who were not blameworthy in mind from conviction of infamous common-law crimes.

However, the *Balint* and *Behrman* offenses belong to a category of another character, with very different antecedents and origins. The crimes there involved depend on no mental element but consist only of forbidden acts or omissions. This, while not expressed by the Court, is made clear from examination of a century-old but accelerating tendency, discernible both here and in England, to call into existence new duties and crimes which disregard any ingredient of intent. The industrial revolution multiplied the number of workmen exposed to injury from increasingly powerful and complex mechanisms, driven by freshly discovered sources of energy, requiring higher precautions by employers. Traffic of velocities, volumes and varieties unheard of came to subject the wayfarer to intolerable casualty risks if owners and drivers were not to observe new cares and uniformities of conduct. Congestion of cities and crowding of quarters called for health and welfare regulations undreamed of in simpler times. Wide distribution of goods became an instrument of wide distribution of harm when those who dispersed food, drink, drugs, and even securities, did not comply with reasonable standards of quality, integrity, disclosure and care. Such dangers have engendered increasingly numerous and detailed regulations which heighten the duties of those in control of particular industries, trades, properties or activities that affect public health, safety or welfare.

While many of these duties are sanctioned by a more strict civil liability, lawmakers, whether wisely or not, have sought to make such regulations more effective by invoking criminal sanctions to be applied by the familiar technique of criminal prosecutions and convictions. This has confronted the courts with a multitude of prosecutions, based on statutes or administrative regulations, for what have been aptly called 'public welfare offenses.' These cases do not fit neatly into any of such accepted classifications of common-law offenses, such as those against the state, the person, property, or public morals. Many of these offenses are not in the nature of positive aggressions or invasions, with which the common law so often dealt, but are in the nature of neglect where the law requires care, or inaction where it imposes a duty. Many violations of such regulations result in no direct or immediate injury to person or property but merely create the danger or probability of it which the law seeks to minimize. While such offenses do not threaten the security of the state in the manner of treason, they may be regarded as offenses against its authority, for their occurrence impairs the efficiency of controls deemed essential to the social order as presently constituted. In this respect, whatever the intent of the violator, the injury is the same, and the consequences are injurious or not according to fortuity. Hence, legislation applicable to such offenses, as a matter of policy, does not specify intent as a necessary element. The accused, if he does not will the violation, usually is in a position to prevent it with no more care than society might reasonably expect and no more exertion than it might reasonably exact from one who assumed his responsibilities. Also, penalties commonly are relatively small, and conviction does not grave damage to an offender's reputation. Under such considerations, courts have turned to construing statutes and regulations which make no mention of intent as dispensing with it and holding that the guilty act alone makes out the crime. This has not, however, been without expressions of misgiving.

* * *

Neither this Court nor, so far as we are aware, any other has undertaken to delineate a precise line or set forth comprehensive criteria for distinguishing between crimes that require a mental element and crimes that do not. We attempt no closed definition, for the law on the subject is neither settled nor static. The conclusion reached in the *Balint* and *Behrman* cases has our approval and adherence for the circumstances to which it was there applied. A quite different question here is whether we will expand the doctrine of crimes without intent to include those charged here.

Stealing, larceny, and its variants and equivalents, were among the earliest offenses known to the law that existed before legislation; they are invasions of rights of property which stir a sense of insecurity in the whole community and arouse public demand for retribution, the penalty is high and, when a sufficient amount is involved, the infamy is that of a felony, which, says Maitland, is '* * * as bad a word as you can give to man or thing.' State courts of last resort, on whom fall the heaviest burden of interpreting criminal law in this country, have consistently retained the requirement of intent in larceny-type offenses. If any state has deviated, the exception has neither been called to our attention nor disclosed by our research.

Congress, therefore, omitted any express prescription of criminal intent from the enactment before us in the light of an unbroken course of judicial decision in all constituent states of the Union holding intent inherent in this class of offense, even when not expressed in a statute. Congressional silence as to mental elements in an Act merely adopting into federal statutory law a concept of crime already so well defined in common law and statutory interpretation by the states may warrant quite contrary inferences than the same silence in creating an offense new to general law, for whose definition the courts have no guidance except the Act. Because the offenses before this Court in the *Balint* and *Behrman* cases were of this latter class, we cannot accept them as authority for eliminating intent from offenses incorporated from the common law. Nor do exhaustive studies of state court cases disclose any well-considered decisions applying the doctrine of crime without intent to such enacted common-law offenses, although a few deviations are notable as illustrative of the danger inherent in the Government's contentions here.

The Government asks us by a feat of construction radically to change the weights and balances in the scales of justice. The purpose and obvious effect of doing away with the requirement of a guilty intent is to ease the prosecution's path to conviction, to strip the defendant of such benefit as he derived at common law from innocence of evil purpose, and to circumscribe the freedom heretofore allowed juries. Such a manifest impairment of the immunities of the individual should not be extended to common-law crimes on judicial initiative.

The spirit of the doctrine which denies to the federal judiciary power to create crimes forthrightly admonishes that we should not enlarge the reach of enacted crimes by constituting them from anything less than the incriminating components contemplated by the words used in the statute. And where Congress borrows terms of art in which are accumulated the legal tradition and meaning of centuries of practice, it presumably knows and adopts the cluster of ideas that were attached to each borrowed word in the body of learning from which it was taken and the meaning its use will convey to the judicial mind unless otherwise instructed. In such case, absence of contrary direction may be taken as satisfaction with widely accepted definitions, not as a departure from them.

We hold that mere omission from § 641 of any mention of intent will not be construed as eliminating that element from the crimes denounced.

* * *

Of course, the jury, considering Morissette's awareness that these casings were on government property, his failure to seek any permission for their removal and his self-interest as a witness, might have disbelieved his profession of innocent intent and concluded that his assertion of a belief that the casings were abandoned was an afterthought. Had the jury convicted on proper instructions it would be the end of the matter. But juries are not bound by what seems inescapable logic to judges. They might have concluded that the heaps of spent casings left in the hinterland to rust away presented an appearance of unwanted and abandoned junk, and that lack of any conscious deprivation of property or intentional injury was indicated by Morissette's good character, the openness of the taking, crushing and transporting of the casings, and the candor with which it was all admitted. They might have refused to brand Morissette as a thief. Had they done so, that too would have been the end of the matter.

Reversed.

It is by now well established that the local constabulary cannot simply walk up to a "suspicious" character on Main Street, detain him, ask him to empty his pockets and direct him to the stationhouse. But what if the Main Street is not in your home town but in Disney World? And what if the constable is not a duly appointed official but a privately employed security person with a Mickey Mouse badge?

UNITED STATES

v.

FRANCOEUR

United States Court of Appeals
Fifth Circuit
Feb. 25, 1977
547 F.2d 891

TUTTLE, Circuit Judge:

This appeal of the three appellants, each on several counts of an indictment charging them with having passed counterfeit $50 bills at Disney World in Florida, and having conspired to do so, raises principally the question whether the conduct of the security personnel of the privately-operated amusement park is to be equated with, and to be given the same effect as, actions by Government officials in the application of Fourth Amendment protection.

There is no issue on this appeal as to the sufficiency of the evidence for the conviction of the three defendants. The grounds of the appeal relate to the appellants' claim that they were detained, questioned, and viewed for identification purposes in a manner which, if carried on by either state or federal officials, would have amounted to a violation of their Fourth Amendment rights.

Briefly stated, a Disney World employee alerted a Mr. Morgan to the fact that several $50 counterfeit bills had been cashed on the morning in question. Morgan promptly sought to notify various outlets for merchandise, separately run throughout the park. He personally saw a transaction in which

Francoeur took an article from the China Shop at a time when he observed a $50 bill with the critical serial number lying on the counter in his immediate presence. Morgan followed Francoeur and observed him meet appellant Pacheco in what was known as the Artist's Alleyway. He followed the two on to the Main Street where they made a couple of moves that increased Morgan's suspicions, turning and retracing their steps toward the alleyway. Morgan then stopped long enough to call a Mr. Schmidt, a Walt Disney World security officer, at about which time appellant Pizio joined Pacheco and Francoeur. Schmidt followed the defendants until they reached the Train Station. There, they were stopped by Schmidt who identified himself and showed his badge (the insignia of Walt Disney World, a design of a globe with Mickey Mouse ears on top). He told them to keep their hands out of their pockets; that he wanted to talk with them; that they should not run; and that they should follow him to the Disney Security Office. Without objection, Schmidt testified at the trial at about this time, Pacheco went through some motions which Schmidt "assumed" represented an effort by Pacheco to hand a folded Disney World guidebook to Pizio but that Pizio moved away "like he didn't want to have anything to do with it."

After the three defendants were moved to a room in the Disney Security Office, Schmidt examined the Disney guidebook obtained from Pacheco and found that between the pages were nine crisp $50 counterfeit bills all with the critical serial number. He asked the three men to empty their pockets, which they did. Among the articles turned over were three Eastern Airline tickets, carbon copies dated the same day from Boston to Orlando, in the names of Kramer, Sullivan and Sousa, the names that the three men gave to the security officers when they were being questioned. Pacheco also gave up the key to Room No. 1220 in one of the hotels in the compound serving Disney World and the receipts for the payment for the room in the names of Sousa, Creamer and Sullivan. Pacheco also had nine packets of genuine currency, each packet containing bills folded just once and each containing less than $50. Without objection, Schmidt testified: "It was in nine little packets. It was all together like if you went in and got change for a larger bill and you kept all of that change in one pocket. The stacks weren't taken out in your tens or your twenties or whatever, and put together. It was just packets of money like change from a bill."

While in custody, which we may assume for the purpose of this issue, would have amounted to forcible detention if the defendants had sought to leave over the protest of the security officials, they were placed before a one-way mirror and groups of sales persons were permitted to look at each of them individually in an effort to identify any or all of them as persons who had passed $50 bills to such sales persons during the day. Some one or other of the sales persons identified each of the three defendants as having passed such a bill or more. Thereupon, the Secret Service officials took over and filed formal charges, and obtained a search warrant for the search of the hotel room. There, or in the security office, they found a key which fit a suitcase found in the hotel room, which contained some $48,000 in counterfeit $50 bills with the same serial number.

All of the activities through the identification procedures were performed by Disney World security personnel and before special agents of the Secret Service arrived at the scene.

The appellants do not contest the validity of the arrest or of the issuance of the search warrant except to the extent that they were the result of the actions of the Disney World security personnel which we may assume, for the purpose of this discussion, would have violated the defendants' constitutional rights if carried out by governmental officials.

As has been recognized since *Burdeau v. McDowell*, 256 U.S. 465, 41 S.Ct. 574, 65 L.Ed. 1048 (1921) the Fourth Amendment gives protection only against unlawful governmental action.
* * *

In *United States v. Mekjian*, we said: "Where no official of the federal government has any connection with a wrongful seizure, or any knowledge of it until after the fact, the evidence is admissible. (Citations omitted)." 505 F.2d 1320 at 1327.

This same principle has been announced in *United States of America v. Lamar & Aaron* (5th Cir. 1977), 545 F.2d 488, 490: "Thus, if a search is conducted by a private individual, for purely private reasons, it does not fall within the protective ambit of the Fourth Amendment, *United States v. Maxwell* (5th Cir. 1973), 484 F.2d 1350, 1352."

Recognizing this principle, appellants say that, nevertheless, the security personnel of Disney World in this case are in truth and in fact "government" officials. This they seek to do under some such principle as announced by the Supreme Court in *Marsh v. Alabama*, 326 U.S. 501, 66 S.Ct. 276, 90 L.Ed. 265 (1946). In *Marsh*, the Court held that even though the town in question was totally a company-owned town, the fact that it was wide open to public access, and contained all of the necessary adjuncts and amenities of an ordinary town, a person could not be denied the right guaranteed under the First Amendment of freedom of speech on the streets of the company town. Of course, the most obvious difference between this case and *Marsh* is that Disney World is not an open town fully accessible and available to all commerce. This private property is an amusement park to which admission is charged. Moreover, there is no showing that it has all of the facilities ordinarily identified with a community in which persons live and carry on their business. No one is permitted into the outer gates of Disney World except by consent of the owners.

If the owners of this amusement park impose in an illegal manner on their clientele, such imposition, if in violation of statutes forbidding trespass, assault, false arrest, or any other offense, would subject the owners to a civil suit on behalf of the injured person. Such illegal conduct would not, however, give them the protection of the Fourth Amendment and the exclusionary rule which has developed from it. The exclusionary rule, itself, was adopted by the courts because it was recognized that it was only by preventing the use of evidence illegally obtained by public officials that a curb should be put on over-zealous activities of such officials. The Supreme Court has in no instance indicated that it would apply the exclusionary rule to cases in which evidence has been obtained by private individuals in a manner not countenanced if they were acting for state or federal government.

*   *   *

The judgments are AFFIRMED.

This case features an officer with an apparently unusual talent—one which the defendant doesn't quite believe. The court, however, has no reason to doubt the officer's ability or veracity.

UNITED STATES
v.
SENTOVICH

United States Court of Appeals
Eleventh Circuit
June 4, 1982
677 F.2d 834

JOHNSON, Circuit Judge:

The ubiquitous DEA Agent Paul Markonni once again sticks his nose into the drug trade. This time he is on the scent of appellant Mitchell Sentovich's drug courier activities. We now learn that among Markonni's many talents is an olfactory sense we in the past attributed only to canines. Sentovich argues that he should have been able to test, at a magistrate's hearing on issuance of a search warrant, whether Markonni really is the human bloodhound he claims to be. Sentovich's claims, however, have more bark than bite. In fact, they have not a dog's chance of success. Zeke, Rocky, Bodger and Nebuchadnezzar, and the drug dogs of the southeast had best beware. Markonni's sensitive proboscis may soon put them in the dog pound.

I.

An anonymous telephone caller told a Florida Sheriff's department that three males carrying seven suitcases full of marijuana would leave the Fort Myers airport at seven the next morning. The next day local police, proving they had their noses to the grindstone, telephoned Atlanta police detective James Burkhalter and informed him that they had dogged Sentovich and two other men, Mark Diefenthaler and Randall Alander, at the airport. The men had purchased tickets for flights from Fort Myers to Montana, via Atlanta. Police located a cart with luggage to be put on the flight to Atlanta. Not having Drug Enforcement Agency Agent Paul Markonni about, they had to fall back on a mere canine, Rocky, with 50–60 hours training in marijuana detection, who sniffed the bags on the cart as well as other bags nearby. Rocky alerted strongly to two bags belonging to Diefenthaler. Police detained Diefenthaler. Alander, without being asked to do so, left the plane and proceeded to a security lounge. Before the plane left, police found and seized seven pieces of luggage, including two carry-on bags, belonging to the two men. Sentovich, showing what a dog-eat-dog world this is, abandoned the men to their fate and flew on to Atlanta with his two suitcases and shoulder-type bag.

Burkhalter informed the Drug Enforcement Agency (DEA) of the information he had received. Agent Paul Markonni had the airline on whose flight Sentovich had arrived in Atlanta nose around and locate Sentovich's bags. Markonni, who stated in an affidavit that he had smelled marijuana more than 100 times over the past eleven years, applied his proboscis to the three bags and alerted to two of them because of the odor of marijuana. Not willing to have Sentovich depart from under his very nose, Markonni told Burkhalter of his discovery. Burkhalter stopped Sentovich as he was boarding a flight to Montana and asked him to consent to a search. Sentovich initially consented but, after talking to an attorney, changed his mind and refused to allow a search.

Markonni doggedly went to obtain a search warrant for the two bags that smelled of marijuana. He presented to a magistrate an affidavit containing the information obtained from Florida police and stating that he had detected the nose-tickling odor of marijuana emanating from the luggage. The magistrate issued the warrant after refusing to have the bags taken to the courthouse to be smelled by him or by another neutral party and after refusing to allow counsel for Sentovich to cross-examine Markonni. The counsel asked to be allowed to be present when the bags were opened. Markonni advised that counsel could be present but that he would not allow counsel to ride with him to the airport and would open the bags immediately. Markonni returned to the airport. Before defense counsel arrived, he opened the two bags in which he had detected the odor and found marijuana in them. Sentovich was convicted of possession of marijuana with intent to distribute, in violation of 21 U.S.C.A. § 841(a)(1).

II.

Sentovich argues that he should have been able to cross-examine Markonni before a search warrant was issued. Unless some compelling reason requires an ex parte hearing, he asserts that a police officer will be able to obtain a warrant too dog-cheaply unless the hearing on whether to issue a search warrant is adversarial. The Supreme Court has ruled otherwise. "To mandate an evidentiary hearing (with respect to a request for a search warrant), the challenger's attack must be more than conclusory and must be supported by more than a mere desire to cross-examine. There must be allegations of deliberate false-hood or of reckless disregard for the truth, and those allegations must be accompanied by an offer of proof. . . . Allegations of negligence or innocent mistake are insufficient." *Franks v. Delaware*, 438 U.S. 154, 171, 98 S.Ct. 2674, 2684, 57 L.Ed.2d 667 (1978). Sentovich asserts that cross-examination would have provided an opportunity to test Markonni's ability to discern the odor of marijuana. Neither on appeal nor below does he allege that Markonni deliberately lied or recklessly disregarded the truth in stating that he nosed out marijuana. Without a claim of such doggery, the magistrate was on the nose in finding that no adversarial hearing was necessary.

Sentovich next asserts that the magistrate should have ordered the bags to be brought to the court or that Markonni should have awaited the arrival of Sentovich's counsel before opening the bags. Because of the absence of third-party confirmation, he argues that important evidence was destroyed. Sentovich suggests several remedies: exclusion of the alleged odor of the luggage from a determination of whether probable cause for the warrant existed, suppression of the evidence of the marijuana discovered in the bags, or dismissal of the indictment.

* * * Since there was no allegation of deliberate falsehood or reckless disregard of the truth by Markonni, there was no reason for the magistrate to hold a hearing allowing third-party confirmation of Markonni's sense of smell. There was also no misconduct by Markonni in failing to delay opening the luggage until Sentovich's counsel arrived at the airport. Police with a search warrant simply need not await the arrival of counsel before executing that warrant. Moreover, the inability of counsel to smell marijuana would have no bearing on the validity of the warrant. Even if Markonni was wrong in thinking that he smelled marijuana, his misstatement would invalidate the warrant only if it was intentional or made in deliberate disregard of the truth. We note again that Sentovich never alleges any malodorous motive or activity by Markonni that was intentional or in reckless disregard of the truth.

Sentovich did seek dismissal of the indictment against him because of the alleged destruction of the evidence of the odor of the marijuana. At the very least, Sentovich must make some showing of the materiality of the evidence the government suppressed. The standard for determining materiality varies somewhat with the situation at issue. Here, however, we need not inquire into the exact applicable standard. Whatever the standard may be, Sentovich has not met it. The odor of the marijuana—as opposed to the marijuana itself—was of no relevance to Sentovich's conviction.

Markonni emerges with his nose unbloodied and his tail wagging. Sentovich's claims are without merit. Having also reviewed the evidence, we find it sufficient for his conviction.

The judgment of the district court is AFFIRMED.

What goes through people's minds when they plan a crime? One would think that there would be a well thought-out plan, including contingencies and alibis. But in some cases, it is obvious that very little went through the criminal's mind. Here we have a presumably intelligent man who, after making a smuggling device out of a T–shirt, packed up the remnants and brought them along for the customs inspector to find.

"Forget the law, I like the facts. . . . Discussion of this case always causes me to ask my Criminal Procedure class whether or not they think there might be a class of criminal defendants who are 'too stupid to possess constitutional rights?' "

—Professor, University of Pittsburgh

UNITED STATES

v.

HAVENS

Supreme Court of the United States
May 27, 1980
100 S.Ct. 1912, 446 U.S. 620, 64 L.Ed.2d 559

Mr. Justice WHITE delivered the opinion of the Court.

The petition for certiorari filed by the United States in this criminal case presented a single question: whether evidence suppressed as the fruit of an unlawful search and seizure may nevertheless be used to impeach a defendant's false trial testimony, given in response to proper cross-examination, where the evidence does not squarely contradict the defendant's testimony on direct examination.

I.

Respondent was convicted of importing, conspiring to import, and intentionally possessing a controlled substance, cocaine. According to the evidence at his trial, Havens and John McLeroth, both attorneys from Ft. Wayne, Ind., boarded a flight from Lima, Peru, to Miami, Fla. In Miami, a customs officer searched McLeroth and found cocaine sewed into make-shift pockets in a T–shirt he was wearing under his outer cloth-ing. McLeroth implicated respondent, who had previously cleared customs and who was then arrested. His luggage was seized and searched without a warrant. The officers found no drugs but seized a T–shirt from which pieces had been cut that matched the pieces that had been sewn to McLeroth's T–shirt. The T–shirt and other evidence seized in the course of the search were suppressed on motion prior to trial.

Both men were charged in a three-count indictment, but McLeroth pleaded guilty to one count and testified against Havens. Among other things, he asserted that Havens had sup-plied him with the altered T–shirt and had sewed the makeshift pockets shut. Havens took the stand in his own defense and denied involvement in smuggling cocaine. His direct testimony included the following:

> "Q. And you heard Mr. McLeroth testify earlier as to something to the effect that this material was taped or draped around his body and so on, you heard that testimony?
>
> "A. Yes, I did.
>
> "Q. Did you ever engage in that kind of activity with Mr. McLeroth and Augusto or Mr. McLeroth and anyone else on that fourth visit to Lima, Peru?
>
> "A. I did not." App. 34.

On cross-examination, Havens testified as follows:

> "Q. Now, on direct examination, sir, you testified that on the fourth trip you had absolutely nothing to do with the wrapping of any bandages or tee shirts or anything involving Mr. McLeroth; is that correct?
>
> "A. I don't—I said I had nothing to do with any wrapping or bandages or anything, yes. I had nothing to do with anything with McLeroth in connection with this cocaine matter.

* * *

"Q. And your testimony is that you had nothing to do with the sewing of the cotton swatches to make pockets on that tee shirt?

"A. Absolutely not.

"Q. Sir, when you came through Customs, the Miami International Airport, on October 2, 1977, did you have in your suitcase Size 38–40 medium tee shirts?" *Id.*, at 35. An objection to the latter question was overruled and questioning continued:

"Q. On that day, sir, did you have in your luggage a Size 38–40 medium man's tee shirt with swatches of clothing missing from the tail of that tee shirt?

"A. Not to my knowledge.

* * *

"Q. Mr. Havens, I'm going to hand you what is Government's Exhibit 9 for identification and ask you if this tee shirt was in your luggage on October 2nd, 1975 [sic]?

"A. Not to my knowledge. No." *Id.*, at 46.

Respondent Havens also denied having told a Government agent that the T–shirts found in his luggage belonged to McLeroth.

On rebuttal, a Government agent testified that Exhibit 9 had been found in respondent's suitcase and that Havens claimed the T–shirts found in his bag, including Exhibit 9, belonged to McLeroth. Over objection, the T–shirt was then admitted into evidence, the jury being instructed that the rebuttal evidence should be considered only for impeaching Havens' credibility.

The Court of Appeals reversed, relying on *Agnello v. United States*, 269 U.S. 20, 46 S.Ct. 4, 70 L.Ed. 145 (1925), and *Walder v. United States*, 347 U.S. 62, 74 S.Ct. 354, 98 L.Ed. 503 (1954). The court held that illegally seized evidence may be used for impeachment only if the evidence contradicts a particular statement made by a defendant in the course of his direct examination. We reverse.

II.

* * *

In our view, however, a flat rule permitting only statements on direct examination to be impeached misapprehends the underlying rationale of *Walder, Harris* [v. New York, 401 U.S. 222, 91 S.Ct. 643 (1971)] and [Oregon v.] *Hass* [420 U.S. 714, 95 S.Ct. 1215 (1975)]. These cases repudiated the statement in Agnello that no use at all may be made of illegally obtained evidence. Furthermore, in *Walder*, the Court said that in *Agnello*, the Government had "smuggled in" the impeaching opportunity in the course of cross-examination. The Court also relied on the statement in *Agnello, supra*, at 35, 46 S.Ct., at 7, that Agnello had done nothing "to justify cross-examination in respect of the evidence claimed to have been obtained by the search." The implication of Walder is that Agnello was a case of cross-examination having too tenuous a connection with any subject opened upon direct examination to permit impeachment by tainted evidence.

In reversing the District Court in the case before us, the Court of Appeals did not stop to consider how closely the cross-examination about the T–shirt and the luggage was connected with matters gone into in direct examination. If these questions would have been suggested to a reasonably competent cross-examiner by Havens' direct testimony, they were not "smuggled in"; and forbidding the Government to impeach the answers to these questions by using contrary and reliable evidence in its possession fails to take account of our cases, particularly *Harris* and *Hass*. In both cases, the Court stressed the importance of arriving at the truth in criminal trials, as well as the defendant's obligation to speak the truth in response to proper questions. We rejected the notion that the defendant's constitutional shield against having illegally seized evidence used against him could be "perverted into a license to use perjury by way of a defense, free from the risk of confrontation with prior inconsistent utterances." Both cases also held that the deterrent function of the rules excluding unconstitutionally obtained evidence is sufficiently served by denying its use to the government on its direct case. It was only a "speculative possibility" that also making it unavailable to the government for otherwise proper impeachment would contribute substantially in this respect.

Neither *Harris* nor *Hass* involved the impeachment of assertedly false testimony first given on cross-examination, but the reasoning of those cases controls this one. There is no gainsaying that arriving at the truth is a fundamental goal of our legal system. We have repeatedly insisted that when defendants testify, they must testify truthfully or suffer the consequences. This is true even though a defendant is compelled to testify against his will. It is essential, therefore, to the proper functioning of the adversary system that when a defendant takes the stand, the government be permitted proper and effective cross-examination in an attempt to elicit the truth. The defendant's obligation to testify truthfully is fully binding on him when he is cross-examined. His privilege against self-incrimination does not shield him from proper questioning. He would unquestionably be subject to a perjury prosecution if he knowingly lies on cross-examination. In terms of impeaching a defendant's seemingly false statements with his prior inconsistent utterances or with other reliable evidence available to the government, we see no difference of constitutional magnitude between the defendant's statements on direct examination and his answers to questions put to him on cross-examination that are plainly within the scope of the defendant's direct examination. Without this opportunity, the normal function of cross-examination would be severely impeded.

We also think that the policies of the exclusionary rule no more bar impeachment here than they did in *Walder, Harris,* and *Hass.* In those cases, the ends of the exclusionary rules were thought adequately implemented by denying the government the use of the challenged evidence to make out its case in chief. The incremental furthering of those ends by forbidding impeachment of the defendant who testifies was deemed insufficient to permit or require that false testimony go unchallenged, with the resulting impairment of the integrity of the factfinding goals of the criminal trial. We reaffirm this assessment of the competing interests, and hold that a defendant's statements made in response to proper cross-examination reasonably suggested by the defendant's direct examination are subject to otherwise proper impeachment by the government, albeit by evidence that has been illegally obtained and that is inadmissible on the government's direct case, or otherwise, as substantive evidence of guilt.

* * *

We reverse the judgment of the Court of Appeals and remand the case to that court for further proceedings consistent with this opinion.

As the next three cases indicate, the punishment resulting from criminal behavior is often not just that imposed by the court. In fact, the collateral consequences or the nonjudicial punishment may be the harsher. Take, for example, the man who lost not only his freedom but, apparently, the consideration of his wife. There are "wrongs" that the courts simply cannot remedy.

COLON
v.
COLON

United States District Court, W.D. New York
Jan. 17, 1985
600 F.Supp. 814

TELESCA, District Judge.

Plaintiff, Alfredo Colon, instituted this civil rights action pursuant to 42 U.S.C. Section 1983 against his wife, Robin Colon, "in her personal individual capacity" for alleged violations of his constitutional rights. According to the complaint, "The plaintiff alleges that his wife has violated all the agreements implement [sic] in their marriage licence [sic]. His wife refuses to write him while in prison or to communicate with him by telephone, visits, etc.".

The facts alleged by plaintiff are admittedly moving, but they most certainly do not amount to a violation of any rights protected by the United States Constitution. The First Amendment unquestionably protects the right of a prison inmate to receive mail, but only if there is someone outside the prison who is interested in writing to him.

Plaintiff's wife may someday be moved to write or call him, perhaps out of a sense of natural affection, or in recognition of the sacred intimacy they share through the bonds of marriage. (The likelihood of that prospect may be diminished, however, now that plaintiff has sued her for a total of $200,000 in compensatory and punitive damages.) Although her conscience may one day compel Robin Colon to write to her husband, the Constitution will never do so. On the contrary, the Constitution guarantees that defendant need never write or call anyone against her will. The right of freedom of thought protected by the First Amendment "includes both the right to speak freely and the right to refrain from speaking at all". Criminal defendants are not the only Americans who enjoy the celebrated constitutional "right to remain silent".

A District Court is empowered by 28 U.S.C. Section 1915(d) to dismiss sua sponte a pro se civil rights complaint which is frivolous on its face. The Court of Appeals for this Circuit has cautioned that "a federal judge should not dismiss a prisoner's pro se, in forma pauperis claim as frivolous unless statute or controlling precedent forecloses the pleading, liberally construed." Such is the case here, even if all the allegations of plaintiff's complaint are construed liberally in his favor. Accordingly, plaintiff's complaint is dismissed.

If Mr. Colon despaired of ever again hearing from his wife, maybe he would like to change places with Mr. Silva, the defendant in this next case. On the other hand, if Judge Jenkins is correct, Mr. Silva might some day envy Mr. Colon. The language of the opinion may be somewhat dated, but the underlying idea is timeless.

Judge Jenkins finds "humor in a situation without demeaning the litigants."

—Judge, United States District Court

STATE

v.

SILVA

Supreme Court of Tennessee
March 6, 1972
477 S.W.2d 517

ERBY L. JENKINS, Special Judge.

The defendant below, Gene Silva, was convicted in the Criminal Court of Williamson County in a non-jury trial of violating T.C.A. § 37–270, by contributing to the delinquency of a minor and was sentenced to six months in the county jail or workhouse and was fined $50.00.

The indictment under which he was convicted charged that the defendant, Gene Silva, on the 8th day of January, 1970, unlawfully did contribute to or encourage the delinquency of a certain child, to-wit: one Diane Fowler, then and there under the age of eighteen years, by aiding or abetting or encouraging the said child in the commission of an act of delinquency, to-wit: 'The said Gene Silva attempted to persuade the said Diane Fowler to check into a motel room with him, they not being Married.'

Section 37–270 of Tennessee Code Annotated provided in part as follows:

> 'Any adult who shall contribute to or encourage the delinquency of a child whether by aiding or abetting or encouraging the said child in the commission of an act of delinquency or by participating as a principal with the child in an act of delinquency or by aiding the child in concealing an act of delinquency following its commission shall be guilty of a misdemeanor . . .'

The defendant made a motion for a new trial which was overruled, and appealed to the Court of Criminal Appeals, which court in a split decision reversed the judgment of the Criminal Court of Williamson County and dismissed the case, and this Court has granted certiorari.

The defendant below, a twenty-nine year old married man in the bloom of youth, with two children, prior to and at the time of the inception of his troubles, was the solicitor for a so-called charitable organization known as Mission Workers Organization.

In the conduct of his business, he employed one Diane Fowler, fifteen years of age, who according to the record, shook or rattled a tambourine around the streets and in front of business houses mostly during the long holidays before Christmas when the average person is in a giving mood.

On the day and date in question, the defendant picked up Diane, she being out of school on account of snow, and drove to a combination motel-restaurant near Franklin, parked in front of said place, and was seen by a witness who said 'they were hugging and kissing, and that sort of thing.' The defendant had earlier overpaid Diane to the extent of about ten dollars, it appearing in the record that Diane was to receive one-third of what she collected, and we think it can be more or less assumed that the defendant, Gene Silva, in the operation of this so-called charitable business and in the red-tape of the administration thereof took his fair share of the offerings, and thus, charity in this instance began at home. Anyway, it is apparent from the record that the solicitors were to benefit more financially and otherwise than the needy children that they were allegedly collecting for.

Be that as it may, on said date, the defendant, after picking up Miss Fowler, attended to some business in Nashville and drove to the Roberson Motel in Williamson County, and parked in front of its restaurant, it being a combination motel and restaurant, and after 'hugging and kissing' for some thirty minutes, borrowed ten dollars from her and entered the motel, rented a room and purchased two cokes to go.

As heretofore stated, while the two of them were parked in front of the motel, they were observed by the principal of the Franklin Junior High School, who was apparently out of school also on account of snow. It could be said that he was of a suspicious nature, but nevertheless this conduct aroused his suspicion, as it should, and he called the sheriff whose deputy and a highway patrolman arrived and asked Miss Fowler if anything was wrong, and she replied that there was not. During this time, Gene Silva, who was on the inside in the act of renting a room, saw the officers, and according to witnesses, became nervous, left his change, went to his automobile and drove off, and was apprehended by the officers some ways off who arrested him and placed him in jail. He called his wife from jail and she, at that time, took a dim view of the situation.

On the trial of the case, the State, of necessity, used Diane Fowler as a State's witness and she was, to say the least, not sympathetic with the State's case, and we have some misgivings about her conduct in front of the motel as well as her testimony. She testified that she told the defendant three times that 'she wasn't going in there,' and '. . . you know, I didn't know what to say or do, I just sat there.' She testified that the defendant made her no proposition, but the trial judge was justified in taking her testimony with a grain of salt. As a matter of fact, the learned trial judge disbelieved both Gene Silva and Miss Fowler, and for good cause.

*   *   *

The court ruled that the state was not bound by Fowler's testimony, even though it had called her as its witness, and that the state could introduce evidence that contradicted her testimony.

*   *   *

This defendant was not convicted on the testimony of Miss Fowler alone, but also on the testimony of the school principal, the testimony of officers and other witnesses, and also by surrounding facts and circumstances. Incidentally, in this time when people close their eyes to open crimes, we need more citizens of prying proclivities and urgent speech, and we commend the school principal for his conduct in this case.

When this defendant parked in front of the combination motel-restaurant and began hugging and kissing this fifteen year old girl in wide open daylight and where witnesses could observe him, he was sorely tempted and the passion that possessed him had conquered his reason and swayed his judgment, and in this blinded state he went to the motel clerk and rented a room, and bought two cokes. At that time, his mind and thoughts were far from his hearthstone, and his testimony that he was renting this room for himself and his wife, who was then many cold snowy miles away from him, is too thin to believe, for it is apparent from the record that the signs point toward his guilty intentions, and his conduct in front of the motel was not that of the true and faithful husband and father, for at the moment he had forgotten the wife of his bosom when temptation beset him. It is not clear whether Diane tempted him or he tempted her, or whether they just tempted each other.

Be that as it may, this ridiculous excuse of renting a room for himself and his wife is unbelievable. It must be remembered that at the time the defendant was renting the room, his wife was in Nashville at home with the children, unaware of his so-called plans to take her out for the night, and that to accomplish his stated purpose he would have had to drive home and tell his wife of his plans; she would have had to ready herself for the occasion, obtain a baby sitter, and they then would have driven back to the Roberson Motel, covering a total distance of more than thirty miles in rough winter weather, consuming at least three hours in time. Human experience teaches us that by this time his ardor would have subsided and his blood run cold.

However, he was apparently either a good father and husband, or a good salesman, for by trial time his wife had either forgiven him of his indiscretions or believed in his innocence for she gave aid and comfort to him in that she swore that at times they did go to a motel room to find surcease from the workaday world of taking care of two children. We must say this is not the usual way of married life as we have observed it, but she rose to his defense as good wives often do when 'we are in trouble.'

The Court does not condemn her for coming to the aid of her beleaguered husband, the defendant, but takes a rather clouded view of this angle of the defense because we think that it is rather unusual that a man would be 'hugging and kissing' another woman, borrow money from her, and then enter a motel and rent a room for himself and his wife. When passion rules, concern for the woman at hand is the usual pattern, and it is not suddenly and without temptation or provocation transferred from one to the other, especially when the other is many miles distant and it is cold and snowy outside. The learned trial judge had a right to disbelieve this testimony.

We, therefore, reverse the action of the Court of Criminal Appeals and sustain the judgment entered by the Criminal Court of Williamson County. However, since it appears that the defendant works regularly, and from the record, at trial time, had the confidence, love and affection of his wife, we would suggest to the Court below that it modify its judgment and put the defendant on probation so that he can continue to make a living for his family. We believe that the ends of justice will be met if the case is handled in this manner. We base this suggestion to the trial court under the authority of *Stanley v. State*, 171 Tenn. 406, 104 S.W.2d 819 (1937).

In making this suggestion, we believe the State has had its day in court. We know the defendant has had more time in court than he wants. To place him on probation would not be too merciful. He has suffered the humiliation of a trial for a would-be sin of the flesh, and had to seek refuge behind the petticoats of an angry wife who publicly forgave him, but whatever is done by the courts cannot restore the peace and harmony of that happy marriage, for if the pattern of wifely conduct runs true to form, he will throughout his natural life be reminded of the time she saved him from jail. When the members of this Court have passed to their respective rewards, whether upwards or downwards, the defendant will in all probability still be reminded of this unfortunate incident for it is a woman's right never to forget. She may think that she has forgiven him, and when she reminds him of his waywardness, she will not be fussing, only 'telling him.'

And if perchance the defendant should ever rise to high office, such as Justice of the Peace, a Deacon in the church, or a member of an appellate court, he will until death brings him blessed relief hear 'if it hadn't been for me, you'd been a jail bird.' Six months in jail would be a small price to pay for his sudden heat of passion, for he will all his married life remain suspect in her eyes, and as the shadows of life lengthen and his hair grows grey and he has more children and then grandchildren, he could hear the ever-present theme of 'remember when I saved you from jail!' Jail in his declining years could be a sanctuary from an ever remembering and never forgiving wife. The prisoner of Chillon could become a kindred spirit.

A convict stays in jail for a stated time, is released, and aside from the stigma of prison, he is free, but a convict husband must forever bear the shackles of guilt, and no matter how hard he works, how much he accomplishes, how much he does for his partner in marriage, or how high he rises in the esteem of his fellows, he will remain a convict to her, and he will only escape temporarily each day while at work making a living.

This defendant has in the eyes of the law done wrong, but not enough in this instance to be jailed, and the least the trial judge can do is to relieve him of his temporary sentence, and remember that he is forever and eternally on probation to his wife, who will be his wife, his warden and parole officer all wrapped up in one. What a sad fate for any poor mortal to face. Whenever he is late from work and not home 'on the dot,' he can envision his wife wrinkling her brow in a gathering storm and nursing her wrath to keep it warm. This problem was recognized long ago, in Proverbs XX:19, where it is said, 'it is better to dwell in a corner of the housetop than with a brawling woman in a wide house.'

In his twilight years, after a life of toil, failure or success, when he is entitled to dream dreams and see visions, remember parts of a pleasant past and contemplate a place among the Blessed when he passes from this green earth to a better land, and after he no longer remembers the name of Diane, much less her shape, form or figure, his musings will no doubt be interrupted by the shrill voice of his wife, warden and probation officer, 'What are you thinking about—that woman the sheriff caught you with down in Franklin?'

We do not have the power to restore the defendant's matrimonial tranquility, would that we could; all we can do is make the suggestion of probation to the trial judge with the hope that he understands life and can foresee the bleak and lacerated future of the defendant.

The action of the Court of Criminal Appeals is reversed and the judgment of the trial court is sustained with the suggestion that a petition for probation be entertained as set out herein.

In this case, both Mr. and Mrs. Flowers apparently wished to maintain contact while he was in prison. The nature of the contact which they wished to maintain, however, made that impossible. Although some penal institutions have allowed conjugal visits, they are a definite minority.

In the Matter of FLOWERS

United States District Court, E.D. Wisconsin
Oct. 24, 1968
292 F.Supp. 390

GRUBB, Senior District Judge.

Hugh Edward Flowers, an inmate of the Wisconsin State Prison, has submitted a seventh application attacking the validity of his detention. In this purported complaint under the Civil Rights Statutes, brought in the name of Dorothy M. and Hugh Edward Flowers, it is contended that the enforced celibacy under the detention in the custodial institution constitutes impairment of the obligations under the marriage contract between the plaintiffs, who request compensatory damages in the amount of eight million dollars.

The application fails to state an actionable claim for various reasons. Foremost among these is that marriage is a social relation subject to the police power of the state and is not considered a contract within the constitutional protection against impairment. Further, in this instance the applicant, by his own act, has impaired his ability to perform the obligations of the marriage, thus precluding himself from reliance on the constitutional provisions.

Now, therefore, it is ordered that leave to proceed in forma pauperis be, and it is hereby denied.

This is a death penalty case in which no one's life was at stake. A district attorney sought a declaratory judgment as to whether the death penalty violated the Declaration of Rights in the Massachusetts Constitution. The court said that it contravened the prohibition against cruel and unusual punishment because it was unacceptably cruel under contemporary standards of decency and was administered with arbitrariness and discrimination. It is Justice Liacos's concurring opinion that was referred to us and which we print here.

DISTRICT ATTORNEY for
the SUFFOLK DISTRICT
v.
WATSON

Supreme Judicial Court of Massachusetts
Oct. 28, 1980
411 N.E.2d 1274, 381 Mass. 648

LIACOS, Justice (concurring).

* * *

I write to amplify my reasons for joining in the conclusion of the court that "the death penalty, with its full panoply of concomitant physical and mental tortures, is impermissibly cruel under art. 26 when judged by contemporary standards of decency."

The imposition of the death penalty is disguised by the language and technique of abstraction. "Indeed, no one dares speak directly of the ceremony. Officials and journalists who have to talk about it, as if they were aware of both its provocative and its shameful aspects, have made up a sort of ritual language, reduced to stereotyped phrases. Hence we read at breakfast time in a corner of the newspaper that the condemned 'has paid his debt to society' or that he has 'atoned' or that 'at five a.m. justice was done.' " A. Camus, Reflections on the Guillotine, in Resistance, Rebellion, and Death 132

(1960). Consistent with the views of Camus, of authorities cited elsewhere in this opinion, and of the majority, are the experiences described by Henry Arsenault, a convicted murderer sentenced to death in this Commonwealth. Arsenault is presently an inmate at the Massachusetts Correctional Institution at Norfolk and has submitted a brief pro se as amicus curiae. His brief tells his story.

For over two years, Henry Arsenault "lived on death row feeling as if the Court's sentence were slowly being carried out." Arsenault could not stop thinking about death. Despite several stays, he never believed he could escape execution. "There was a day to day choking, tremulous fear that quickly became suffocating." If he slept at all, fear of death snapped him awake sweating. His throat was clenched so tight he often could not eat. His belly cramped, and he could not move his bowels. He urinated uncontrollably. He could not keep still. And all the while a guard watched him, so he would not commit suicide. The guard was there when he had his nightmares and there when he wet his pants. Arsenault retained neither privacy nor dignity. Apart from the guards he was alone much of the time as the day of his execution neared.

And on the day of the execution, after three sleepless weeks and five days' inability to eat, after a night's pacing the cell, he heard the warden explain the policy of the Commonwealth- no visitors, no special last meal, and no medication. Arsenault asked the warden to let him walk to the execution on his own. The time came. He walked to the death chamber and turned toward the chair. Stopping him, the warden explained that the execution would not be for over an hour. Arsenault sat on the other side of the room as the witnesses filed in behind a one-way mirror. When the executioner tested the chair, the lights dimmed. Arsenault heard other prisoners scream. After the chaplain gave him last rites, Arsenault heard the door slam shut and the noise echoing, the clock ticking. He wet his pants. Less than half an hour before the execution, the Lieutenant Governor commuted his sentence. Arsenault's legs would not hold him up. Guards carried him back to his cell. He was trembling uncontrollably. A doctor sedated him. And he was moved off death row.

"That capital punishment is horrible and cruel is the reason for its existence." C. Darrow, A Comment on Capital Punishment, quoted in Attorneys for the NAACP Legal Defense and Educational Fund, A Cruel and Unusual Punishment, in Voices Against Death 264, 283 (P. Mackey ed. 1976). The raw terror and unabating stress that Henry Arsenault experienced was torture; torture in the guise of civilized business in an advanced and humane polity. This torture was not unique, but merely one degrading instance in a legacy of degradation. The ordeals of the condemned are inherent and inevitable in any system that informs the condemned person of his sentence and provides for a gap between sentence and execution. Whatever one believes about the cruelty of the death penalty itself, this violence done the prisoner's mind must afflict the conscience of enlightened government and give the civilized heart no rest.

Death is the "king of terrors." *Job* 18:14. Aristotle called death "the most terrible of all things; for it is the end, and nothing is thought to be any longer either good or bad for the dead." Aristotle, Nicomachean Ethics, Book III, c. 6, 64 (D. Ross trans. 1969). Fear of death is natural and universal in human experience.[8] It resides in our inability to imagine our own nonexistence We imagine the manner of death and the corpse[10] or, perhaps in hopes of finding consolation, we envision the continuing life of the soul.[11] So deep is the fear of death and the corresponding desire for transcendence that

---

8. Aristotle, Nicomachean Ethics, Book III, c. 7, 65 (D. Ross trans. 1969) ("What is terrible is not the same for all men; but we say there are things terrible even beyond human strength. These, then, are terrible to every one . . .").

10. "Ay, but to die, and go we know not where;
To lie in cold obstruction and to rot;
This sensible warm motion to become
A kneaded clod; and the delighted spirit
To bathe in fiery floods, or to reside In thrilling region of
thick-ribbed ice;
To be imprison'd in the viewless winds,
And blown with restless violence round about
The pendent world. . . ."

W. Shakespeare, Measure for Measure, Act III, Scene i.

11. Such thoughts, of course, are not invariably comforting: "(T)he dread of something after death—The undiscover'd country from whose bourn No traveller returns. . . ." W. Shakespeare, Hamlet, Act III, Scene i. See generally J. Choron, Death and Western Thought (1963).

Christian thought attributes death to the fall of Adam,[12] and the New Testament proclaims Christ's victory over death. *1 Corinthians* 15:20, 26.

Psychiatrists have observed that terror of death is at the root of much mental disease. "The anxiety neuroses, the various phobic states, even a considerable number of depressive suicidal states and many schizophrenias amply demonstrate the ever-present fear of death which becomes woven into the major conflicts of the given psychopathological conditions." We instinctively hold to life. "The weariest and most loathed worldly life, That age, ache, penury and imprisonment, Can lay on nature is a paradise, To what we fear of death."[13]

The condemned must confront this primal terror directly, and in the most demeaning circumstances. A condemned man knows, subject to the possibility of successful appeal or commutation, the time and manner of his death. His thoughts about death must necessarily be focused more precisely than other people's. He must wait for a specific death, not merely expect death in the abstract. Apart from cases of suicide or terminal illness, this certainty is unique to those who are sentenced to death. The State puts the question of death to the condemned person, and he must grapple with it without the consolation that he will die naturally or with his humanity intact. A condemned person experiences an extreme form of debasement.

A sociologist has identified the ideal characteristics of the modern "humane" practice of capital punishment. The treatment of the condemned and the execution itself can be described as "stark, impersonal, solemn, unemotional, privatized," unlike the raucous spectacles of earlier times. Not all recent executions accomplish these objectives. Indeed, grotesque descriptions of electrocutions, both bungled and successful, indicate that the method presently used falls far short of its goal. Shortcomings aside, however, the result of this

---

12. See, e. g., J. Milton, Paradise Lost, Book I, Lines 2–3.

13. W. Shakespeare, Measure for Measure, Act III, Scene i.

attempt at "humane" execution is to go far toward concealing the fact and significance of the event: that a human being has been put to death. Thus, writers have remarked on the anomaly of hiding from the public a practice ostensibly designed to deter crime.

Less frequently observed is the effect of these policies upon the condemned. The death sentence itself is a declaration that society deems the prisoner a nullity, less than human and unworthy to live. But that negation of his personality carries through the entire period between sentence and execution. "(I)n Death Row, organized and controlled in grim caricature of a laboratory, the condemned prisoner's personality is subjected to incredible stress for prolonged periods of time."[21] The condemned person is generally isolated, allowed few visitors, limited in permissible activities, and kept under close guard. The execution occurs within prison walls in a small room before witnesses whom the prisoner may not be able to see. The prisoner wears prison clothes. He is allowed to say little, if anything, and is often blindfolded. An anonymous executioner puts him to death at an odd hour. The mode of execution ideally causes little commotion to inform the witnesses that a person has died. And the body is not displayed. In this context, the prisoner has only the most meager opportunities to assert his shattered dignity, and few persons ever see any gesture he chooses to make. Under the circumstances it is virtually impossible to die a noble or courageous or self-respecting death.[24]

"(W)hat man experiences at such times," Camus wrote, "is beyond all morality. . . . Having to face an inevitable death, any man, whatever his convictions, is torn asunder from head to toe. The feeling of powerlessness and solitude of the condemned man, bound up and against the public coalition that demands his death, is in itself an unimaginable punishment. . . . (I)t would be better for the execution to be public.

21. West, Psychiatric Reflections on the Death Penalty, in Voices Against Death 290–291 (P. Mackey ed.1976).

24. Contrast the death of Socrates, who died for an idea after conversation with an audience of friends and disciples, at a time of his choosing, and out of sight of officials other than the man who prepared the hemlock. See Plato, Phaedo, in Plato: The Collected Dialogues 40, especially 41–43 and 95–98 (E. Hamilton & H. Cairns, eds.1961).

The actor in every man could then come to the aid of the terrified animal and help him cut a figure, even in his own eyes. But darkness and secrecy offer no recourse. In such a disaster, courage, strength of soul, even faith may be disadvantages. As a general rule, a man is undone by waiting for capital punishment well before he dies. Two deaths are inflicted on him, the first being worst than the second, whereas he killed but once. Compared to such torture, the penalty of retaliation seems like a civilized law" (footnote omitted). A. Camus, *supra* at 155–156.

* * *

The purpose of the cruel or unusual punishment prohibition is to guarantee a measure of human dignity even to the wrongdoers of our society. The Massachusetts Constitution recognizes that there are some punishments so abhorrent, so offensive to evolved standards of decency, that no justification can support their employment. Inflicting upon a person the terror of death in a definite manner is such a punishment. My views would not change if stays on death row were made more pleasant, killing techniques less painful, or removal from death row more swift. This is a punishment antithetical to the spiritual freedom that underlies the democratic mind. What dignity can remain for the government that countenances its use?

Fyodor Dostoyevsky was sentenced to die for discussing Utopian Socialist ideas. Arrayed with his coprisoners, he saw three men bound to stakes and blindfolded before the firing squad. Just as the commanding officer was about to shout "Fire!" an official waved his white handkerchief to stop the execution and inform them that the Czar had commuted the men's sentences. "Standing before the firing squad he was so certain of the imminence of death that he felt more dead than alive at the abrupt proclamation of the Czar's clemency; when he finally recovered his senses it was to find himself in irons and on his way to Siberia. There he . . . had to submit to treatment so inhuman that only glimpses of it can be caught in his later work . . . ." Thus, Dostoyevsky wrote from experience when he discussed the fate of the condemned. In *The Idiot*, Prince Myshkin hears the suggestion that the guillotine is painless. He contends that a painless execution may be harder for the condemned than torture. "(T)he chief and the worst pain is perhaps not inflicted by wounds, but by your certain knowledge that in an hour, in ten minutes, in half a minute, now, this moment your soul will fly out of your body, and that you will be a human being no longer, and that that's certain—the main thing is that it is certain. Just when you lay your head under the knife and you hear the swish of the knife as it slides down over your head—it is just that fraction of a second that is the most awful of all. . . . To kill for murder is an immeasurably greater evil than the crime itself. . . . (H)ere all . . . last hope, which makes it ten times easier to die, is taken away for certain; here you have been sentenced to death, and the whole terrible agony lies in the fact that you will most certainly not escape, and there is no agony greater than that. Take a soldier and put him in front of a cannon in battle and fire at him and he will still hope, but read the same soldier his death sentence for certain, and he will go mad or burst out crying. Who says that human nature is capable of bearing this without madness? Why this cruel, hideous, unnecessary, and useless mockery? . . . It was of agony like this and of such horror that Christ spoke. No, you can't treat a man like that!"

Chapter 3
What's the Question?

Our judicial system was established more than 200 years ago with the specific goal of carrying out the administration of justice. That goal continues today as federal and state courts around the country are called upon each day to interpret laws and resolve legal questions. Sometimes the questions appear to be very complex, yet may be fairly straightforward. At other times, the reverse is true: the questions seem to be quite basic but in reality are extremely complicated. In this chapter we will discover how the courts have resolved a variety of disputes and have answered some of the more interesting legal questions such as "What is chicken?", "What is a 'What'?" and "Is a girdle a burglar's tool?"

If someone told you that a person was recently arrested at a popular department store in possession of a burglar's tool and stolen merchandise, you might envision that the person wore dark clothing and gloves and possessed a lock pick or crowbar and a black bag to stash the loot in. That mental image, however, may be the result of watching too many old television shows such as *It Takes a Thief* or *Mission Impossible.* Would you picture the person wearing a girdle? The following case involves a young girl who wore a girdle to stash her loot in while shoplifting at Macy's department store. The question for the court was, is a girdle a "burglar's tool"?

"[This is] a case which stretched the limits of statutory analysis to answer the foundational question: 'Is a girdle a "burglar's tool" ' within the elastic meaning of New York Penal Law?"

—Professor, Northern Illinois University

In the Matter of CHARLOTTE K., Age 15

Family Court, Richmond County, New York
April 21, 1980
427 N.Y.S.2d 370, 102 Misc.2d 848

DANIEL D. LEDDY, Jr., Judge.

Is a girdle a burglar's tool or is that stretching the plain meaning of Penal Law Sec. 140.35? This elastic issue of first impression arises out of a charge that the respondent shoplifted certain items from Macy's Department Store by dropping them into her girdle.

Basically, Corporation Counsel argues that respondent used her girdle as a Kangaroo does her pouch, thus adapting it beyond its maiden form.

The Law Guardian snaps back charging that with this artificial expansion of Sec. 140.35's meaning, the foundation of Corporation Counsel's argument plainly sags. The Law Guardian admits that respondent's tight security was an attempt to evade the store's own tight security. And yet, it was not a tool, instrument or other article adapted, designed or commonly used for committing or facilitating offenses involving larceny by physical taking. It was, instead, an article of clothing, which, being worn under all, was, after all, a place to hide all. It was no more a burglar's tool than a pocket, or maybe even a kangaroo's pouch.

The tools, instruments or other articles envisioned by Penal Law Sec. 140.35 are those used in taking an item and not in hiding it thereafter. They are the handy gadgets used to break in and pick up, and not the bags for carrying out. Such is the legislative intent of this section, as is evident from the Commission Staff Comments on the Revised Penal Law of 1965. Title I, Article 140, N Sec. 140.35, which reads in relevant part: "The new section, by reference to instruments involving larceny . . . expands the crime to include possession of numerous other tools, such as those used for breaking into motor vehicles, stealing from public telephone boxes, tampering with gas and electric meters, and the like."

The Court has decided this issue mindful of the heavy burden that a contrary decision would place upon retail merchants. Thus is avoided the real bind of having customers check not only their packages, but their girdles too, at the department store's door.

The Court must also wonder whether such a contrary decision would not create a spate of unreasonable bulges that would let loose the floodgates of stop and frisk cases, with the result of putting the squeeze on court resources already overextended in this era of trim governmental budgets.

Accordingly, the instant allegation of possession of burglar's tools is dismissed.

For deer hunters, this case may be the ultimate lesson in humility. Defendant shot an adult male deer in a National Forest but was charged with shooting a "fawn." The district court judge defended the actions of the defendant in a compassionate opinion that could have been used in part as a eulogy for the deceased.

"This decision has more subtle humor than has been espoused by most federal judges in their entire lives."

—Judge, United States Bankruptcy Court

UNITED STATES
v.
DOWDEN

United States District Court, W.D. Louisiana
April 5, 1956
139 F.Supp. 781

DAWKINS, Jr., Chief Judge.

A tiny tempest in a tinier teapot has brought forth here all the ponderous powers of the Federal Government, mounted on Clydesdale in hot pursuit of a private citizen who shot a full-grown deer in a National Forest.

Not content with embarrassing defendant by this prosecution, and putting him to the not inconsiderable expense of employing counsel, the Government has compounded calumny by calling the poor dead creature a "fawn". Otherwise fully equipped with all the accouterments of virile masculinity, the deceased, alas, was a "muley". Unlike other young bucks, who could proudly preen their points in the forest glades or the open meadows, this poor fellow was foredoomed to hide his head in shame: by some queer quirk of Nature's caprice, he had no horns, only "nubbins", less than an inch in length.

Instead of giving him a quiet, private interment and a "requiescat in pace", which decency should have dictated as his due, the Government has filed his blushing head in evidence for all to see. Pointing to the lack of points, to prove its point, it now insists that, whatever his status may have been in other climes, in Louisiana our departed friend is officially puerile.

All this—requiring the services of five game agents, two biologists, the opposing attorneys, the United States Marshal and three Deputies, the Clerk, Court Reporter, and a Federal Judge who is a little tired of such matters—stems at least partly from the failure of the Louisiana Legislature to reckon wisely with the exceptional or unusual.

* * *

Federal law requires that persons hunting on federal land obey state hunting laws.

The Louisiana Statutes Annotated—Revised Statutes, Title 56:124(1), stipulate, in pertinent part:

"No person shall:

"(1) Take any *fawn (a deer with horns less than three inches long)* or any doe (a female wild deer), at any time; or a wild deer at any time when driven to the high lands by overflow or high water." (Emphasis supplied.)

Evidently relying on some uncanny prescience instead of his eyesight for his judgment of the deer, or perhaps having trusted to luck—which was with him—or a proper profile view, defendant slew the animal at some forty paces in the Kisatchie National Forest on December 10, 1953. Soon the law had him in its clutches, but because the authorities obviously were unsure of their ground, formal charges were not filed here until February 24, 1955. Meanwhile, a State Grand Jury, having jurisdiction over the heinous offense, had refused to indict. Trial in this Court has been delayed until now by slightly weightier matters and by several continuances engendered by fruitless efforts of counsel to stipulate the facts.

Finally and inexorably, jury trial having been formally waived and that expense at least avoided, Nimrod's case has been heard and he is found not wanting:

1. The object of our inspection was not less than sixteen
    months, nor more than eighteen months, old. His teeth
    told the tale.

2. He was no doe, or psuedo-doe. *All* witnesses agree on
    this.

3. Except for his unfortunate looks, which he couldn't
    help, he was "all man". He could have and may have
    become the father of a fawn.

4. He weighed some 90 to 100 pounds on his cloven
    hooves, and 57 pounds dressed, or rather, undressed.
    Deer on Government lands apparently aren't as well
    nourished, and don't grow as large, as elsewhere.

5. Biologically he was a buck, not a fawn, who in strictly
    female company would have had to bow to no critic.
    His handicap actually was one only upon having to
    fight for the affections of the distaff side. What he
    lacked in weapons, he could have made up for in celer-
    ity, dexterity or finesse.

In all *important* respects, therefore, notwithstanding the
Louisiana Legislature, which may be forgiven for its ignorance,
Buck has been grossly slandered. He never should have been
dubbed arbitrarily as a "fawn". He was no baby and was not
even a sissy.

It necessarily follows that if Buck is not guilty, neither is
Alvin, who is acquitted and discharged *sine die.*

Over the years, children have been entertained by Weebles that Wobble, Willie Wonka (and the Chocolate Factory) and Where's Waldo. But in 1987, there was a dispute as to whether children would have the opportunity to enjoy "Whats" and "Wuzzles." The following case answered the intriguing questions surrounding the dispute: "Just what's a 'What', what's the similarity between a 'What' and a 'Wuzzle', and 'Wuzzle' we do about it?"

SELMON

v.

HASBRO BRADLEY, INC.

United States District Court, S.D. New York
Sept. 16, 1987
669 F.Supp. 1267

GOETTEL, District Judge:

Once upon a time, in lands far, far away, lived strange but cuddly creatures that became involved in a struggle for identity. In "Whatland," which is just a few miles north of Fairyland, lived the "Whats." In the "Land of Wuz" lived the "Wuzzles." We don't know where "Wuz" was, but we are told we could get there if we "snuzzle a Wuzzle." It appears that for a time, never the two did meet. But one day the creators of the "Whats" discovered the "Wuzzles" and were astonished to learn that "Whats" and "Wuzzles" had certain similarities. Most specifically, it seems each "What" and "Wuzzle" had the names and characteristics of two different animals combined into one. In "Whatland," there was "Me-ouse" (a mouse and cat combined), "Wissh" (a walrus and seal), "Ch-uck" (a chicken and duck), "Skeet" (a skunk and parakeet), "Pea-tur" (a peacock and turkey), "Gir-itch" (a giraffe and ostrich), "Leo-Lamo" (a lion and lamb), and "Beav-aire" (a beaver and bear). The "Wuzzles" included "Moosel" (a moose and seal), "Butterbear" (a butterfly and bear), "Hoppopotamus" (a rabbit and hippopotamus), "Eleroo" (an elephant and Kangaroo), "Rhinokey" (a rhinoceros and monkey), and "Bumblelion" (a bumblebee and lion).

Our story now moves to its sad conclusion. The creators of the "Whats," who were protected by copyright, were outraged and thought that the creators of the "Wuzzles" had stolen their idea. A lawsuit broke out, with the plaintiffs, creators of the "Whats," alleging violation of the federal copyright laws and unjust enrichment. The defendants, creators of the "Wuzzles," have moved for summary judgment, as well as attorney's fees and sanctions under 17 U.S.C. § 505 of the Copyright Act, 28 U.S.C. § 1927, and Rule 11 of the Federal Rules of Civil Procedure for plaintiffs' pursuit of allegedly frivolous and vexatious litigation.

This battle on high between creators has filtered down to us in this "What"-less and "Wuzzle"-less Land of White Plains. The questions before us are really quite simple: "Just what's a "What," what's the similarity between a "What" and a "Wuzzle," and "Wuzzle" we do about it?"

I. Facts

Plaintiffs, doing business as Engrav-it, created eight fanciful characters they called "Whats" (described above) from "Whatland." The characters were created by combining characteristics and names from two different animals into one. On September 24, 1984, plaintiffs registered the "Whats" characters, short storylines in poetic form about the characters, and a brief overview entitled "What's What in Whatland" with the federal copyright office.

On September 21, 1984, plaintiffs sent copies of this material with a cover letter to defendant Hasbro Bradley, Inc. (Hasbro) and Walt Disney World of Florida. A similar package was sent later to defendant Walt Disney Productions of California (Disney). Each ultimately wrote back to plaintiffs and returned the submission.

The facts further reveal that as early as 1982, Disney was working on a project called "Jumble Isle," which involved characters similar in concept to plaintiffs' "Whats." "Jumble Isle" was registered for copyright protection on April 18, 1984, well before plaintiffs' submission. In May of 1984, Disney broached with Hasbro the idea of marketing a line of "Jumble Isle" toys. It was discovered that Hasbro already was working on its own, very similar project. The defendants agreed to join forces and collaborate on what became the "Wuzzles" project.

Six "Wuzzles" (described above), complete with storylines, were registered for copyright protection in January of 1985 and were introduced officially to the public at the February 1985 Annual Toy Fair in New York City. Although defendants' creative work on this initial introduction was substantially complete by September 21, 1984, which both parties agree is the earliest possible date that defendants could have become aware of plaintiffs' works, it appears that not all details had been finalized. The best that can be said as to this point is that the facts are unclear. Whatever, it is clear that six additional "Wuzzles" were introduced in 1986, well after the time defendants had received plaintiffs' unsolicited submissions. The additional "Wuzzles" included: "Tycoon" (a tiger and raccoon combined), "Pandeaver" (a panda and beaver), "Skowl" (a skunk and owl), "Piggypine" (a pig and porcupine), "Woolrus" (a walrus and lamb), and "Koalakeet" (a koala and parakeet). The line was discontinued in 1987.

When plaintiffs became aware that Disney/Hasbro was marketing the "Wuzzles" line, they commenced this action.

* * *

The Copyright Claim

As this Court recently stated, the central thrust of the Copyright Act is protecting tangible expressions of ideas. To sustain an action for copyright infringement, a plaintiff must prove (1) a valid copyright and (2) the unauthorized copying of the copyrighted work. Defendants here do not dispute that plaintiffs have a valid copyright, although plaintiffs themselves seem somewhat unsure as to just what is protected by that copyright.

Direct evidence of copying is rarely available, and none has been presented here. Copying, however, may be inferred (and at this stage, we must draw any reasonable inferences in the plaintiffs' favor) by showing (1) that defendants had "access" to the copyrighted material, and (2) that defendants' work bears a "substantial similarity" to that material. It is important to underscore that there must be at least an arguable showing as to both prongs of this test if plaintiffs are to survive this motion for summary judgment.

With respect to access, both defendants offered affidavits asserting that none of their creative people see unsolicited submissions. Hasbro produced evidence that, as a matter of course, when unsolicited submissions are received in the mailroom they are forwarded immediately to the legal department for return to the sender(s). It claims that at no time do its creative people "peek" at or become aware of unsolicited submissions. In his September 29 letter returning plaintiffs' submission, Hasbro's Corporate Secretary advised that "present policy does not permit us to accept outside submissions . . . due to the heavy volume of material sent and the possibility of conflict with our own research program." It is clear that Hasbro has taken steps to try to insulate itself from suits such as it is now forced to defend. Further, despite the fact that it was Hasbro's Corporate Secretary and not its legal department that answered plaintiffs' inquiry, it appears that Hasbro generally complied with its own policy, especially given the short turnaround time between submission and return.

Disney, however, was less careful. Plaintiffs maintain that on or about October 3, Al Stratton, Merchandise Buyer for Disney World in Florida, telephoned plaintiffs, acknowledged receipt, and asked if the "Whats" were trademarked. Although plaintiffs' submission was returned via Stratton letter dated October 10, the letter advises that Stratton would keep a copy of the submission on file "in the event it could be used in the future," and further states that the plaintiffs' submission "has been discussed and reviewed by the appropriate Buyers and Managers in our Merchandising Division." Plaintiffs later forwarded a similar package to defendant Disney Productions of California, but it was returned immediately.

Disney World is a wholly-owned subsidiary of Disney Productions. The question turns on the possibility that plaintiffs' submission to Disney World, which apparently had been "discussed and reviewed," could have found its way "upstream" to Disney Productions, which was then collaborating with Hasbro on the "Wuzzles" project.

Alternatively, defendants argue that only access gained "prior to the creation of defendant's work" can support an inference of copying. We are referred to no Second Circuit cases on point, but it would seem to follow, ipso facto, that if access is gained following a project's completion, access becomes irrelevant. The undisputed facts clearly reveal that, by September

21, the defendants virtually had completed all creative work on the "Wuzzles" project. Hasbro began working on the project in the fall of 1983. In March of 1984, with the concept considerably refined, an outside marketing firm was retained to conduct a market survey. Also in March, Hasbro's research and design department presented the engineering department with a preliminary package, including final drawings and sewing patterns for the toys. Six of the characters then presented (three with slight modification later on) were to become the six toys actually introduced in 1985. On May 11, 1984, the engineering department issued a "final takeover package" (FTP) for the project that included specifications in minute detail for each of the characters. In June of 1984, Hasbro executives flew to the Far East to select fabrics and meet with vendors who would produce the toys. In July, Carnival Enterprises was retained to develop a storyline for the "Wuzzles" from the "Land of Wuz," and preliminary storylines were submitted on July 12. All of this preparatory work had been completed before the plaintiffs mailed their package on September 21, 1984.

Plaintiffs argue that defendants' work, although substantially complete, was not finalized until after plaintiffs' submission. As evidence of this contention, they argue that three of the characters originally contained in the May 1984 FTP were modified before market introduction in 1985, and that those changes were made after September 21. It is clear that "Spotopotamus," "Seal-A-Saurus," and "Ring-A-Rang-A-Tang," all characters in the May FTP, were changed at some time to become "Hoppopotamus," "Moosel," and "Rhinokey," respectively. Exactly when those changes occurred is unclear.

*   *   *

[M]aterial facts as to both prongs of the copying test (access and substantial similarity) must be in issue if plaintiffs are to survive a summary judgment motion. The rationale for this requirement seems clear—even if defendants had access to copyrighted material, if substantial similarity between defendants ultimate product and the copyrighted material cannot be shown, no inference of copyright infringement can be justified and access is rendered irrelevant. The record on this issue leaves no room for doubt.

The copyright laws protect "only the work's particular expression of an idea, not the idea itself." *Eden Toys, Inc. v. Marshall Field & Co.*, 675 F.2d 498, 500 (2d Cir.1982). In determining whether copying of a particular, copyrighted expression may be inferred, the general test for substantial similarity is "whether the average lay observer would recognize the alleged copy as having been appropriated from the copyrighted work." *Warner Bros.*, 654 F.2d at 208 (quoting *Ideal Toy Corp. v. Fab-Lu Ltd.*, 360 F.2d 1021, 1022 (2d Cir.1966)). When the infringement involves cartoon-like characters, as here, courts have considered "not only the visual resemblance but also the totality of the characters' attributes and traits [in determining] the extent to which the allegedly infringing character captures the 'total concept and feel' of the copyrighted character." *Warner Bros., Inc. v. American Broadcasting Co.*, 720 F.2d 231, 241 (2d Cir.1983) (citations omitted). Although we find some conceptual similarity between plaintiffs' and defendants' creations, we do not find substantial similarity in the particular expressions of those ideas, nor do we find that defendants' "Wuzzles" capture the "total concept and feel" of plaintiffs' works.

First and foremost, no "Wuzzle" is comprised of the same two animals comprising any particular "What." In our view, the most similar combinations are the "Beav-aire," a "What" combining a bear with a beaver, and the "Pandeaver," a "Wuzzle" combining a panda with a beaver. The names, however, are not substantially similar, and the artistic renditions are thoroughly dissimilar. The fact that both combine a bear, or, more accurately, a bear-like character (a panda looks like a bear but is actually a member of the raccoon family), with a beaver does not, standing alone, render these characters substantially similar.

* * *

With respect to the storylines, plaintiffs make a broad assortment of generalizations as to the similarities between the storyline concepts. Again, although the storyline concepts are similar, the specific content is not. First, because the "Wuzzle" and "What" characters are completely different, it follows that the storylines about each character must, by necessity, be somewhat different. Second, the "Whats" storylines are in poetic form; the "Wuzzles" storylines are not. Third, defendants offered affidavits attesting that storylines typically are introduced with stuffed characters of this sort. Not only is this eminently ascertainable through common experience, but plaintiffs have offered nothing of substance to suggest it isn't so. Again, plaintiffs have not "cornered the market" with respect to the storyline concept by virtue of their copyright. It is only the particulars of their copyrighted storylines that are protected, and there are not substantial similarities between the "Whats" and "Wuzzles" storylines.

* * * We will not belabor the obvious. Suffice it to say that we find no artistic similarities between the works.

*   *   *

Is an airplane a "vehicle"? In other words, can a "vehicle" fly? The United States Supreme Court had the opportunity to pilot that question with respect to a stolen airplane that was transported across state lines.

"[The McBoyle opinion] is a model of conciseness and precision, demonstrating that a legal analysis of an issue can be written tersely without sacrificing its analytical soundness."

—Professor, University of Pittsburgh

McBOYLE
v.
UNITED STATES

United States Supreme Court
March 9, 1931
51 S.Ct. 340, 283 U.S. 25, 75 L.Ed. 816

Mr. Justice HOLMES delivered the opinion of the Court.

The petitioner was convicted of transporting from Ottawa, Illinois, to Guymon, Oklahoma, an airplane that he knew to have been stolen, and was sentenced to serve three years' imprisonment and to pay a fine of $2,000. The judgment was affirmed by the Circuit Court of Appeals for the Tenth Circuit. A writ of certiorari was granted by this Court on the question whether the National Motor Vehicle Theft Act applies to aircraft. That Act provides: 'Sec. 2. That when used in this Act: (a) The term 'motor vehicle' shall include an automobile, automobile truck, automobile wagon, motor cycle, or any other self-propelled vehicle not designed for running on rails.* * * Sec. 3. That whoever shall transport or cause to be transported in interstate or foreign commerce a motor vehicle, knowing the same to have been stolen, shall be punished by a fine of not more than $5,000, or by imprisonment of not more than five years, or both.'

Section 2 defines the motor vehicles of which the transportation in interstate commerce is punished in Section 3. The question is the meaning of the word 'vehicle' in the phrase 'any other self-propelled vehicle not designed for running on rails.' No doubt etymologically it is possible to use the word to signify a conveyance working on land, water or air, and sometimes legislation extends the use in that direction. * * * But in everyday speech 'vehicle' calls up the picture of a thing moving on land. * * * So here, the phrase under discussion calls up the popular picture. For after including automobile truck, automobile wagon and motor cycle, the words 'any other self-propelled vehicle not designed for running on rails' still indicate that a vehicle in the popular sense, that is a vehicle running on land is the theme. It is a vehicle that runs, not something, not commonly called a vehicle, that flies. Airplanes were well known in 1919 when this statute was passed, but it is admitted that they were not mentioned in the reports or in the debates in Congress. It is impossible to read words that so carefully enumerate the different forms of motor vehicles and have no reference of any kind to aircraft, as including airplanes under a term that usage more and more precisely confines to a different class. The counsel for the petitioner have shown that the phraseology of the statute as to motor vehicles follows that of earlier statutes of Connecticut, Delaware, Ohio, Michigan and Missouri, not to mention the late Regulations of Traffic for the District of Columbia, none of which can be supposed to leave the earth.

Although it is not likely that a criminal will carefully consider the text of the law before he murders or steals, it is reasonable that a fair warning should be given to the world in language that the common world will understand, of what the law intends to do if a certain line is passed. To make the warning fair, so far as possible the line should be clear. When a rule of conduct is laid down in words that evoke in the common mind only the picture of vehicles moving on land, the statute should not be extended to aircraft simply because it may seem to us that a similar policy applies, or upon the speculation that if the legislature had thought of it, very likely broader words would have been used.

Judgment reversed.

When most people talk about "traffic," they are referring to the frustrating conditions that they encounter on the highways and byways during their commute to and from work or school. However, as we shall see, "traffic" does not always pertain to the congestion of cars and buses. In the following case, the court was asked to determine whether a mule constitutes traffic.

STATE
v.
JACKSON

Court of Appeals of Kansas
July 11, 1980
613 P.2d 398, 5 Kan.App.2d 152

FOTH, Chief Judge:

The issue in this case is whether an animal constitutes "traffic" subject to police regulation. If so, the owner of the animal in this case was guilty of refusing to comply with the lawful order of an officer directing traffic, in violation of K.S.A. 8–1503, and was properly fined $25.00. If an animal is not traffic, and the statute deals only with vehicular traffic, then the defendant owner is not guilty and must prevail in his appeal.

The animal involved here was named Frieda. Frieda's mother apparently had an impeccable equine pedigree indeed, the events of the case suggest origins in the hunt country of Maryland or Virginia, with strains of hunter, Morgan, or perhaps saddle-bred in her background. Unfortunately, like many young ladies of breeding she made a love match far below her station. Her mate may have had charm, and clearly had animal magnetism, but he was also indisputably a jackass. Frieda, the product of this unhappy union, was a mule.

She was no ordinary mule, however. Although genealogy and geography had conspired together to deprive her of her rightful heritage, Frieda could not be content with a mule's customary plodding fate shackled to a plow or wagon, with no hope of pleasure in youth or even progeny to comfort her in old age. Encouraged by her owner and by a coonhound named Buck—reportedly valued at $1500—Frieda took up that nocturnal ritual known as coon-hunting. She was an apt pupil. From her father she had inherited a surefootedness which proved advantageous on rough and rocky ground. From her mother she had acquired talents which, with a little practice, enabled her to clear a four-foot fence with ease. It was this latter ability that precipitated the case at bar.

It was in April of 1979, while returning from one of her favorite evening outings, that Frieda had her present brush with the law. It was almost midnight and Frieda, tired from the chase, was riding in the back of her owner's pickup, swaying gently between the stock racks and looking forward to spending the rest of the night peacefully in her pasture on the banks of the Verdigris River. Buck was in the cab with their mutual owner, the defendant. They had proceeded up the River Road to a point less than half a mile from Frieda's pasture when they encountered a police barricade and Deputy Lee Coltharp of the Montgomery County sheriff's office.

Coltharp advised defendant that that portion of the River Road was restricted and no unauthorized traffic could go through. The sheriff's office was dragging the river for a reported drowning victim, and the area contained a command center in a large tent, portable generators and flood lights, and numerous official vehicles. Although he had been allowed through some six hours earlier when he had picked Frieda up, this time the defendant was ordered to turn around and go back. He protested that doing so would mean eight or ten miles of driving to reach the nearby pasture, but Coltharp was adamant; it was "Sheriff's orders."

Defendant pulled his truck just past the barricade and off the road as if to turn around. Instead, he parked, got out, and signaled to Frieda. Obediently, Frieda jumped out of the truck. Before Coltharp could react, defendant mounted and rode off into the night, up the River Road, through the restricted area, to the pasture. There Frieda made her last jump of the night, over the fence and into the familiar safety of her home grounds.

Defendant returned down the River Road afoot, again through the restricted area, to his truck and the waiting Buck. Also waiting was Deputy Coltharp, citation in hand. The citation was later replaced by a complaint, charging a violation of K.S.A. 8–1503: "No person shall willfully fail or refuse to comply with any lawful order or direction of any police officer or fireman invested by law with authority to direct, control or regulate traffic."

Defendant was convicted after trial to the court, and appeals contending that the statute is directed only at vehicular traffic, and not at jumping mules and pedestrians. The contention must fail.

The statute under which the charge was made is part of the uniform act to regulate traffic on the highways, enacted as Laws 1974, ch. 33. Definitions of the terms used in that act are now found in Article 14 of Chapter 8 of the statutes, and include K.S.A. 8–1477:

"'Traffic' means pedestrians, ridden or herded animals, vehicles and other conveyances either singly or together while using any highway for purposes of travel."

Thus both Frieda when ridden up the highway and defendant when walking back down the highway were "traffic" subject to police traffic control. There being no contention that the police order forbidding access to the River Road was not "lawful," defendant's violation of the order contravened the statute.

Trial counsel for the defendant urged to the trial court that the incident should be regarded as an essentially humorous affair, not deserving of criminal sanction. The argument is repeated in the brief on appeal. The trial court rebuffed that suggestion, and so do we. The untrammeled passage of civilians through an area marked off for police investigation has a potential for mischief which is obvious. Although all participants except Frieda may have exhibited a certain amount of stubbornness the law did not require Deputy Coltharp to make an exception for the defendant and Frieda.

Affirmed.

Colonel Sanders may have appreciated the issues involved in this next dispute.

"Why I like this case: For starters, my grandmother would understand it perfectly. That is, it belies the misconception that legal writing must be magical, opaque, incantatory code. . . . [L]anguage is complex, elusive, vague and ambiguous, making the lawyer's job literally impossible: Even if you manage, miraculously, to say exactly what you mean, you have only the slightest chance of conveying that meaning intact to another. That is not to say that attempts at precision are irrelevant, but rather that they are essential."

—Professor, University of Missouri, Kansas City

FRIGALIMENT IMPORTING CO.

v.

B.N.S. INTERNATIONAL SALES CORP.

United States District Court S.D. New York
Dec. 27, 1960
190 F.Supp. 116

FRIENDLY, Circuit Judge.

The issue is, what is chicken? Plaintiff says "chicken" means a young chicken, suitable for broiling and frying. Defendant says "chicken" means any bird of that genus that meets contract specifications on weight and quality, including what it calls "stewing chicken" and plaintiff pejoratively terms "fowl". Dictionaries give both meanings, as well as some others not relevant here. To support its, plaintiff sends a number of volleys over the net; defendant essays to return them and adds a few serves of its own. Assuming that both parties were acting in good faith, the case nicely illustrates Holmes' remark "that the making of a contract depends not on the agreement of two minds in one intention, but on the agreement of two sets of external signs—not on the parties having meant the same thing but on their having said the same thing." The Path of the

Law, in Collected Legal Papers, p. 178. I have concluded that plaintiff has not sustained its burden of persuasion that the contract used "chicken" in the narrower sense.

* * *

This action is for breach of warranty under two contracts involving the sale of fresh frozen chicken.

* * *

Since the word "chicken" standing alone is ambiguous, I turn first to see whether the contract itself offers any aid to its interpretation. Plaintiff says the 1½–2 lbs. birds necessarily had to be young chicken since the older birds do not come in that size, hence the 2½–3 lbs. birds must likewise be young. This is unpersuasive—a contract for "apples" of two different sizes could be filled with different kinds of apples even though only one species came in both sizes. Defendant notes that the contract called not simply for chicken but for "US Fresh Frozen Chicken, Grade A, Government Inspected." It says the contract thereby incorporated by reference the Department of Agriculture's regulations, which favor its interpretation; I shall return to this after reviewing plaintiff's other contentions.

The first hinges on an exchange of cablegrams which preceded execution of the formal contracts. The negotiations leading up to the contracts were conducted in New York between defendant's secretary, Ernest R. Bauer, and a Mr. Stovicek, who was in New York for the Czechoslovak government at the World Trade Fair. A few days after meeting Bauer at the fair, Stovicek telephoned and inquired whether defendant would be interested in exporting poultry to Switzerland. Bauer then met with Stovicek, who showed him a cable from plaintiff dated April 26, 1957, announcing that they "are buyer" of 25,000 lbs. of chicken 2½–3 lbs. weight, Cryovac packed, grade A Government inspected, at a price up to 33 cents per pound, for shipment on May 10, to be confirmed by the following morning, and were interested in further offerings. After testing the market for price, Bauer accepted, and Stovicek sent a confirmation that evening. Plaintiff stresses that, although these and subsequent cables between plaintiff and defendant, which laid the basis for the additional quantities under the first and for all of the second contract, were predominantly in German, they used the English word "chicken"; it claims this was done because it understood "chicken" meant young chicken whereas the German word, "Huhn," included both "Brathuhn" (broilers) and "Suppenhuhn" (stewing chicken), and that defendant, whose officers were thoroughly conversant with German, should have realized this. Whatever force this argument might otherwise have is largely drained away by Bauer's testimony that he asked Stovicek what kind of chickens were wanted, received the answer "any kind of chickens," and then, in German, asked whether the cable meant "Huhn" and received an affirmative response. *   *   *

Plaintiff's next contention is that there was a definite trade usage that "chicken" meant "young chicken." Defendant showed that it was only beginning in the poultry trade in 1957, thereby bringing itself within the principle that "when one of the parties is not a member of the trade or other circle, his acceptance of the standard must be made to appear" by proving either that he had actual knowledge of the usage or that the usage is "so generally known in the community that his actual individual knowledge of it may be inferred." 9 Wigmore, Evidence (3d ed.§1940) 2464. Here there was no proof of actual knowledge of the alleged usage; indeed, it is quite plain that defendant's belief was to the contrary. *   *   *

Plaintiff endeavored to establish such a usage by the testimony of three witnesses and certain other evidence. Strasser, resident buyer in New York for a large chain of Swiss cooperatives, testified that "on chicken I would definitely understand a broiler." However, the force of this testimony was considerably weakened by the fact that in his own transactions the witness, a careful businessman, protected himself by using "broiler" when that was what he wanted and "fowl" when he wished older birds. Indeed, there are some indications, dating back to a remark of Lord Mansfield, *Edie v. East India Co.*, 2 Burr. 1216, 1222 (1761), that no credit should be given "witnesses to usage, who could not adduce instances in verification." 7 Wigmore, Evidence (3d ed. 1940) While Wigmore thinks this goes too far, a witness' consistent failure to rely on the alleged usage deprives his opinion testimony of much of its effect. Niesielowski, an officer of one of the companies that had furnished the stewing chicken to defendant, testified that "chicken" meant "the male species of the poultry industry. That could be a broiler, a fryer or a roaster", but not a stewing chicken; however, he also testified that upon receiving defendant's inquiry for "chickens", he asked whether the desire was for "fowl or frying chickens" and, in fact, supplied fowl, although taking the precaution of asking defendant, a day or two after plaintiff's acceptance of the contracts in suit, to change its confirmation of its order from "chickens," as defendant had originally prepared it, to "stewing chickens." Dates, an employee of Urner-Barry Company, which publishes a daily market report on the poultry trade, gave it as his view that the trade meaning of "chicken" was "broilers and fryers." In addition to this opinion testimony, plaintiff relied on the fact that the Urner-Barry service, the Journal of Commerce, and Weinberg Bros. & Co. of Chicago, a large supplier of poultry, published quotations in a manner which, in one way or another, distinguish between "chicken," comprising broilers, fryers and certain other categories, and "fowl," which, Bauer acknowledged, included stewing chickens. This material would be impressive if there were nothing to the contrary. However, there was, as will now be seen.

Defendant's witness Weininger, who operates a chicken eviscerating plant in New Jersey, testified "Chicken is everything except a goose, a duck, and a turkey. Everything is a chicken, but then you have to say, you have to specify which category you want or that you are talking about." Its witness Fox said that in the trade "chicken" would encompass all the various classifications. Sadina, who conducts a food inspection service, testified that he would consider any bird coming within the classes of "chicken" in the Department of Agriculture's regulations to be a chicken. The specifications approved by the General Services Administration include fowl as well as broilers and fryers under the classification "chickens." Statistics of the Institute of American Poultry Industries use the phrases "Young chickens" and "Mature chickens," under the general heading "Total chickens." and the Department of Agriculture's daily and weekly price reports avoid use of the word "chicken" without specification.

*   *   *

Defendant makes a further argument based on the impossibility of its obtaining broilers and fryers at the 33 cents price offered by plaintiff for the 2½–3 lbs. birds. There is no substantial dispute that, in late April, 1957, the price for 2½–3 lbs. broilers was between 35 and 37 cents per pound, and that when defendant entered into the contracts, it was well aware of this and intended to fill them by supplying fowl in these weights. It claims that plaintiff must likewise have known the market since plaintiff had reserved shipping space on April 23, three days before plaintiff's cable to Stovicek, or, at least, that Stovicek was chargeable with such knowledge. It is scarcely an answer to say, as plaintiff does in its brief, that the 33 cents price offered by the 2½–3 lbs. "chickens" was closer to the prevailing 35 cents price for broilers than to the 30 cents at which defendant procured fowl. Plaintiff must have expected defendant to make some profit—certainly it could not have expected defendant deliberately to incur a loss.

Finally, defendant relies on conduct by the plaintiff after the first shipment had been received. On May 28 plaintiff sent two cables complaining that the larger birds in the first shipment constituted "fowl." Defendant answered with a cable refusing to recognize plaintiff's objection and announcing "We have today ready for shipment 50,000 lbs. chicken 2½–3 lbs. 25,000 lbs. broilers 1½–2 lbs.," these being the goods procured for shipment under the second contract, and asked immediate answer "whether we are to ship this merchandise to you and whether you will accept the merchandise." * * * Defendant argues that if plaintiff was sincere in thinking it was entitled to young chickens, plaintiff would not have allowed the shipment under the second contract to go forward, since the distinction between broilers and chickens drawn in defendant's cablegram must have made it clear that the larger birds would not be broilers. However, plaintiff answers that the cables show plaintiff was insisting on delivery of young chickens and that defendant shipped old ones at its peril. * * *

When all the evidence is reviewed, it is clear that defendant believed it could comply with the contracts by delivering stewing chicken in the 2½–3 lbs. size. Defendant's subjective intent would not be significant if this did not coincide with an objective meaning of "chicken." Here it did coincide with one of the dictionary meanings, with the definition in the Department of Agriculture Regulations to which the contract made at least oblique reference, with at least some usage in the trade, with the realities of the market, and with what plaintiff's spokesman had said. Plaintiff asserts it to be equally plain that plaintiff's own subjective intent was to obtain broilers and fryers; the only evidence against this is the material as to market prices and this may not have been sufficiently brought home. In any event it is unnecessary to determine that issue. For plaintiff has the burden of showing that "chicken" was used in the narrower rather than in the broader sense, and this it has not sustained.

This opinion constitutes the Court's findings of fact and conclusions of law. Judgment shall be entered dismissing the complaint with costs.

More than half of American households have one or more pets, and the numbers are steadily increasing. Most of those pets have four legs, are cuddly and respond to names such as Max or Patches. However, canines and felines are not for everyone. In the next two scenarios, the Courts of Appeals of Minnesota and North Carolina were asked to decide whether a rooster, two goats and a pony were considered livestock or pets—according to city ordinance.

STATE
v.
NELSON

Court of Appeals of Minnesota
May 4, 1993
499 N.W.2d 512

SCHUMACHER, Judge.

Tammie Nelson appeals her conviction under a Maplewood zoning ordinance, arguing that her pet rooster is not livestock prohibited by the ordinance. We reverse.

FACTS

Nelson keeps Jerry, an eight-year-old adult rooster, at her Maplewood residence as a pet. Jerry is housed in a cage in Nelson's yard and is prone to herald the breaking of dawn each day with a resounding cock-a-doodle-doo. The city alleges that neighbors have frequently complained about the rooster's crowing.[1] In June of 1992, Nelson was cited by the city's environmental health officer for violation of Maplewood, Minn. Zoning Ordinance § 36–66(c)(1) (1988), which prohibits the

---

1. This is not Jerry's, nor his owner's, first appearance before this tribunal. In 1987, this court upheld Nelson's misdemeanor conviction for keeping her rooster in violation of a St. Paul ordinance. The earlier adjudication is not relevant here because the St. Paul ordinance, unlike the Maplewood code, expressly prohibited the keeping of a chicken without a permit.

"raising or handling of livestock or animals causing a nuisance." The ordinance also provides that violations are misdemeanor offenses.

At trial, the environmental health officer was the only witness called by the prosecution. Nelson testified on her own behalf. The trial court found Nelson guilty of violating the ordinance and imposed a fine of $100, which was stayed provided Jerry was removed from the city within 10 days. Nelson admits that Jerry does, in fact, perform each morning in conformity with his nature but claims that the statute does not apply to her pet rooster because he is neither livestock nor an animal causing a nuisance under the ordinance.

ISSUE

Did the trial court correctly determine that Nelson's keeping a rooster as a pet violates Maplewood, Minn. Zoning Ordinance § 36–66(c)(1) (1988)?

ANALYSIS

The interpretation of a zoning ordinance is a question of law which this court reviews de novo.

The ordinance in dispute clearly prohibits (1) all livestock, and (2) any animal causing a nuisance. We acknowledge that a crowing rooster may well constitute a nuisance, but at trial the city expressly waived this issue and prosecuted its case solely on a theory that, under the ordinance, a rooster is livestock as a matter of law.

Since "livestock" is not defined in the ordinance, Maplewood relies on a dictionary definition of the term as "domestic animals kept for use on a farm or raised for sale and profit." Webster's New Twentieth Century Dictionary 1059 (2d ed. 1979). Other authorities have also defined livestock broadly enough to encompass roosters.

At least as commonly, however, the term livestock is defined as separate from chickens. Minnesota's own statutes consistently define "livestock" as "cattle, sheep, swine, horses, mules and goats." When the legislature intends to reach chickens, it uses the term poultry, often in conjunction with live-stock. Clearly the lawmakers of this state understand livestock to be a category of animal distinct from poultry.

Other state statutes also define livestock to include four-legged animals, but not chickens or other poultry.

Because the meaning of livestock is not entirely certain, we turn to rules of construction to resolve the ambiguity. Minnesota courts have often recognized that because zoning ordinances restrict common law rights, they should be strictly construed against the governmental unit and in favor of property owners. In light of this principle, we give "livestock" a less inclusive meaning than does the city and conclude that the term as used in the Maplewood Zoning Ordinance does not reach chickens or other poultry.

Our conclusion is further supported by the fact that the ordinance expressly establishes that violations will be misdemeanors and therefore punishable by up to $700 in fines and 90 days incarceration. The criminal consequences which attend violations of the ordinance also obligate us to construe its provisions strictly in favor of the accused.

Nelson should not bear the penal consequences of an ordinance the terms of which are reasonably capable of different meanings. Because a pet rooster does not plainly fall under the definition of livestock as used in the ordinance, we reverse Nelson's conviction.

DECISION

We reverse the trial court and hold that a pet rooster does not clearly constitute livestock for purposes of sustaining a conviction under the Maplewood Zoning Ordinance.

Reversed.

TOWN OF ATLANTIC BEACH
v.
YOUNG

Court of Appeals of North Carolina
Aug. 3, 1982
293 S.E.2d 821, 58 N.C.App. 597

WHICHARD, Judge.

I.

Plaintiff municipality enacted an ordinance which prohibited the keeping "within the town limits [of] livestock, animals, or poultry other than house pets." The ordinance specified that its prohibition included, inter alia, horses and goats.

Defendant, in response to plaintiff's request for admission, acknowledged that she kept two goats and one pony on her premises. While she denied that her premises were within plaintiff's town limits, the only record evidence was to the contrary.

By this action plaintiff sought, pursuant to the above ordinance, a permanent injunction "directing defendant to remove all animals other than specified domestic house pets from her premises." The trial court denied plaintiff's motion for summary judgment, and granted defendant's.

Plaintiff appeals.

II.

One ground for defendant's motion for summary judgment was: The animals the defendant keeps on her premises, according to the affidavit attached hereto, are house pets which are permitted under the Town Ordinance. The plaintiff does not allege in its Complaint that the animals are not house pets, and no discovery has indicated they are anything other than house pets. Whether defendant's animals are "house pets" requires two determinations: (1) the legal question of the meaning of "house pets" as used in the ordinance, and (2) the specific facts which invoke application of this legal definition.

Absent evidence of a contrary intent, the words of an ordinance are presumed to have their common and ordinary meaning. The common meaning of "pet" is "a domesticated animal kept for pleasure rather than utility." Webster's International Dictionary 1689 (3d ed. 1968). We thus construe the exception in the ordinance for "house pets" to encompass all domesticated animals kept for pleasure in or around a house.

The facts material to the determination whether defendant's animals are "house pets" are the following: (1) the kind of animals they are, (2) the reason for which they were kept, and (3) the place where they were kept. Defendant has shown by affidavit that (1) her animals are two goats and a pony, which we find are "domesticated" animals, *i.e.*, ones that "live and breed in a tame condition," Webster's, *supra*, at 671; (2) they are kept as "pets," and thus are for pleasure rather than utility; and (3) they are kept within the walls of her house.

> G.S. 1A–1, Rule 56(e), in part provides: When a motion for summary judgment is made and supported as provided in this rule [*i.e.*, by pleadings, depositions, answers to interrogatories, admissions on file, or affidavits], an adverse party may not rest upon the mere allegations 'or denials of his pleading, but his response, by affidavits or as otherwise provided in this rule, must set forth specific facts showing that there is a genuine issue for trial. If he does not so respond, summary judgment, if appropriate, shall be entered against him.

Defendant demonstrated the facts necessary to make the legal determination that her animals were "house pets" within the meaning of the ordinance. Plaintiff then had the burden to respond, by affidavit or other evidentiary matter, to show contrary material facts, and that there thus was a genuine issue for trial. * * *

Plaintiff failed to offer any evidentiary matter in opposition to defendant's affidavit. There thus was no genuine issue for trial. A motion for summary judgment must be granted where "there is no genuine issue as to any material fact and . . . any party is entitled to a judgment as a matter of law." G.S. 1A–1, Rule 56(c). By applying the legal definition of "house pets" as used in the ordinance to the undisputed facts, we hold that defendant's animals fell within the ordinance's exception for "house pets," and that defendant thus was entitled to judgment as a matter of law.

* * *

V.

Plaintiff commenced this action for the purpose of getting defendant's goats. Defendant's obtaining a summary judgment against plaintiff may, instead, get plaintiff's goat.

We hold the grant of defendant's motion for summary judgment proper. Denial of plaintiff's motion for summary judgment therefore was equally proper. Plaintiff's assignment of error to the grant of defendant's motion and the denial of its motion is overruled, and the judgment is

Affirmed.

Chapter 4
Going to Extremes

The opinions in this chapter do not share a common subject matter, and the cases do not involve the same area of the law. What brings them together is that each features a party who has gone to extraordinary lengths to accomplish something. In some cases, that extreme action is why the party is in court. In other cases, it is the fact that the party is in court, or the relief the party is seeking, that represents an extreme measure. From the employee who risks his life to save his employer to the employer who takes an employee's dental plate to enforce its rights, from someone who sues the devil to someone who sues himself, here are people who have definitely gone to the extreme.

"While I have no doubt that Judge Weber decided this case in a legally correct fashion, I cannot help but wonder what if? Had the judge gone beyond a technical application of the Federal Rules of Civil Procedure, might there not have been an opportunity to do a world of good? How much suffering in this world could the judge have averted if only an appropriate injunction had been issued by the United States District Court for the Western District of Pennsylvania?"

—Professor, Dickinson School of Law

UNITED STATES ex rel. MAYO
v.
SATAN AND HIS STAFF

United States District Court, W. D. Pennsylvania
Dec. 3, 1971
54 F.R.D. 282

WEBER, District Judge.

Plaintiff, alleging jurisdiction under 18 U.S.C. § 241, 28 U.S.C. § 1343, and 42 U.S.C. § 1983 prays for leave to file a complaint for violation of his civil rights in forma pauperis. He alleges that Satan has on numerous occasions caused plaintiff misery and unwarranted threats, against the will of plaintiff, that Satan has placed deliberate obstacles in his path and has caused plaintiff's downfall.

Plaintiff alleges that by reason of these acts Satan has deprived him of his constitutional rights.

We feel that the application to file and proceed in forma pauperis must be denied. Even if plaintiff's complaint reveals a prima facie recital of the infringement of the civil rights of a citizen of the United States, the Court has serious doubts that the complaint reveals a cause of action upon which relief can be granted by the court. We question whether plaintiff may obtain personal jurisdiction over the defendant in this judicial district. The complaint contains no allegation of residence in this district. While the official reports disclose no case where this defendant has appeared as defendant there is an unofficial account of a trial in New Hampshire where this defendant filed an action of mortgage foreclosure as plaintiff. The defendant in that action was represented by the preeminent advocate of that day, and raised the defense that the plaintiff was a foreign prince with no standing to sue in an American Court. This defense was overcome by overwhelming evidence to the contrary. Whether or not this would raise an estoppel in the present case we are unable to determine at this time.

If such action were to be allowed we would also face the question of whether it may be maintained as a class action. It appears to meet the requirements of Fed.R. of Civ.P. 23 that the class is so numerous that joinder of all members is impracticable, there are questions of law and fact common to the class, and the claims of the representative party is typical of the claims of the class. We cannot now determine if the representative party will fairly protect the interests of the class.

We note that the plaintiff has failed to include with his complaint the required form of instructions for the United States Marshal for directions as to service of process.

For the foregoing reasons we must exercise our discretion to refuse the prayer of plaintiff to proceed in forma pauperis.

It is ordered that the complaint be given a miscellaneous docket number and leave to proceed in forma pauperis be denied.

"Redfearn was accused of using the threat of snakes as a means of evicting a tenant from Redfearn's apartment complex. Redfearn had unsuccessfully attempted to evict the tenant and ultimately devised a scheme to claim that snakes had been placed in the apartment to get rid of mice. Redfearn drove to the apartment complex in a truck having a sign on it that read "exterminating service" and placed signs at the apartment complex warning of dangerous snakes. He used a loudspeaker to advise tenants in the apartment complex that the snakes were being placed in the apartment complex to get rid of mice. Needless to say, the tenant promptly moved out of the apartment."

—Judge, Texas State Court

REDFEARN

v.

STATE

Court of Appeals of Texas
Aug. 25, 1987
738 S.W.2d 28

CORNELIUS, Chief Justice.

Jerry Redfearn was convicted of making a terroristic threat. The sufficiency of the evidence is not challenged, and Redfearn's only contention on appeal is that the charging instrument, the information, states no offense against the laws of the State. We disagree and affirm the conviction.

Redfearn was charged under Tex.Penal Code Ann. § 22.07 (Vernon Supp.1987), which in relevant part provides as follows:

(a) A person commits an offense if he threatens to commit any offense involving violence to any person or property with intent to:

* * *

(3) prevent or interrupt the occupation or use of a building; room; place of assembly; place to which the
public has access; place of employment or occupation; aircraft, automobile, or other form of conveyance; or other public place; . . . .

The information states that Redfearn:

[D]id then and there intentionally threaten to commit an offense involving violence to Henry Washington, namely assault Henry Washington by telling
Henry Washington that Defendant had on said date
released snakes in the building located at 1806 West
Main Street in Clarksville, Texas where Henry Washington then and there resided, with intent to interrupt the occupation of said building by Henry
Washington.

The offense involving violence which Redfearn is accused
of threatening is an assault upon Henry Washington. *Assault*,
defined by Tex.Penal Code Ann. § 22.01(a)(1) (Vernon
Supp.1987), requires that a person intentionally, knowingly or
recklessly cause bodily injury to another. *Bodily injury* is defined
as "physical pain, illness, or any impairment of physical condition." Tex.Penal Code Ann. § 1.07(a)(7) (Vernon 1974).

Redfearn contends that as a matter of law the act of telling
someone of the release of snakes into his residence cannot constitute a threat of imminent bodily injury. He bases this contention upon the argument that a simple allegation of the
release of *snakes*, as opposed to *dangerous and/or poisonous
snakes*, cannot constitute a threat of imminent bodily injury.
We disagree.

In *Garrett v. State*, 619 S.W.2d 172 (Tex.Crim.App.1981),
it was held that an assault may be accomplished through the
use of an animate or inanimate object, and that an assault
may be had through the use of a dog, such as the Doberman
pinscher involved in that case, which was not alleged to be
dangerous. Certainly a threat to release snakes into a person's
residence, whether or not the snakes are stated to be poisonous,
is calculated to raise a reasonable apprehension of bodily harm

on the part of the person threatened. The information thus states an offense even though the snakes are not alleged to be poisonous.

It is also argued that the information states no offense because the statement was that snakes had been placed in the building rather than that they would be placed there. This argument reveals a misunderstanding of the nature of the offense of terroristic threat. It is the threat of harm—not the threat of a sterile act—that constitutes the offense. Implicit in the statement that snakes had been placed in the building was the threat of future harm from those snakes. It is similar to a statement that a time bomb had been placed in the building. The act of placing the bomb was in the past, but the threat is of future harm. Indeed, cases construing similar statutes as that involved here have held that the threat need not be in any particular form or even in words at all, but may be made by acts, innuendo or suggestions. Acts which have been held to constitute threats include the burning of a cross on a victim's property, shooting a gun at a police officer, and a statement that a bomb had been placed in the victim's place of business. The test is what is reasonably communicated to the victim. It is clear that the statement here communicated to the victim a reasonable apprehension of future violence.

For the reasons stated, the judgment of the trial court is affirmed.

BLEIL, Justice, dissenting.

Jerry Redfearn was charged with and tried for the offense of threatening to assault Washington by threatening him with bodily injury. The trial court instructed the jury that "[a] person commits the offense of assault if the person intentionally threatens another with imminent bodily injury." The majority, tacitly agreeing with Redfearn that a threat to assault by threat is not an offense, says that an assault can be committed in ways other than by threatening bodily injury and affirms his conviction for an offense for which he was not tried. Were justice a game I might cry "foul." As it is not, I enter my dissent to today's decision, which is both erroneous and fundamentally unfair.

The information filed against Redfearn in the County Court of Red River County charged an offense under Tex.Penal Code Ann. § 22.07(a) (Vernon Supp.1987). That statute provides that a person commits an offense "if he threatens to commit any offense involving violence to any person. . . ." What offense involving violence does the information allege that Redfearn *threatened to commit*? None.

To determine if the information charges him with an offense under Section 22.07(a), first the meaning of the word threaten must be ascertained. No definition is given in the statute; therefore, we are required to give the word "threaten" its plain meaning according to common usage.

Webster's New College Dictionary defines "threat" as: 1. an indication of something impending; 2. an expression of intention to inflict evil, injury, or damage; 3. something that threatens. Black's Law Dictionary defines "threat" as: A declaration of intention or determination to inflict punishment, loss, or pain on another, or to injure another by the commission of some unlawful act.

*   *   *

The first sentence in the Practice Commentary under Section 22.07 provides, "[t]his section is directed toward those who seek to cause terror or public inconvenience by threatening to *commit* crimes of violence." (emphasis added). The State charged Redfearn with having told Washington that he "had on said date released snakes in the building. . . ." That statement certainly was not a threat to commit an offense involving violence, it merely related his past actions. Nor was it the classic threat in which the defendant intends to "execute his threat," to put his words into action. Indeed, the statement by Redfearn can under no reasonable construction be termed a "threat" to do anything. Further, assuming he had threatened Washington in some manner, the threat did not involve any future act on Redfearn's part as required by the statute. The statute specifically uses the future tense to describe the commission of the offense involving violence.

When the common meaning is applied to the language of the information filed against Redfearn, the conclusion logically follows that the offense of terroristic threat is not stated. Conduct such as that alleged to have been committed by this defendant cannot be condoned. Perhaps the information did charge an offense under one or more of the provisions of Title 18 of the United States Code (Crimes and Criminal Procedure). Or, perhaps the alleged conduct constitutes an assault or reckless conduct under Tex.Penal Code Ann. § 22.01 (Vernon Supp.1987) or § 22.05 (Vernon 1974). But, no matter how bad the conduct alleged may be, it cannot logically be said to be a threat by Redfearn "to commit any offense involving violence."

The majority's comparison of the allegations against Redfearn to a statement that a "time bomb had been placed in the building" underscores its misunderstanding of the requirement of a threat of some future action *on the part of a defendant.* Placing a time bomb in a building would be committing several offenses but it would not be a *threat* to commit an offense involving violence under Section 22.07.

* * *

During the course of a spelling bee, contest officials determined that the word "horsy" could be spelled either h–o–r–s–y OR h–o–r–s–e–y. As a result, two students were allowed to move on to the countywide spelling bee. Who would have guessed that the decision would become the root of a lawsuit reaching the California Court of Appeal? Obviously not Associate Justice Gilbert. His advice to the plaintiff (and to his parents and attorney) was "it's not that you won or lost . . . but how you play the game."

McDONALD, a Minor
v.
SCRIPPS NEWSPAPER

Court of Appeal
Second District
April 12, 1989
As Modified May 10, 1989
257 Cal.Rptr. 473, 210 Cal.App.3d 100

GILBERT, Associate Justice.

Question—When should an attorney say "no" to a client?

Answer—When asked to file a lawsuit like this one.

Master Gavin L. McDonald did not win the Ventura County Spelling Bee. Therefore, through his guardian ad litem,[1] he sued. Gavin alleges that contest officials improperly allowed the winner of the spelling bee to compete. Gavin claimed that had the officials not violated contest rules, the winner "would not have had the opportunity" to defeat him. The trial court wisely sustained a demurrer to the complaint without leave to amend.

---

1. We do not hold Gavin responsible.

We affirm because two things are missing here—causation and common sense. Gavin lost the spelling bee because he spelled a word wrong. Gavin contends that the winner of the spelling bee should not have been allowed to compete in the contest. Gavin, however, cannot show that but for the contest official's allowing the winner to compete, he would have won the spelling bee.

In our puzzlement as to how this case even found its way into court, we are reminded of the words of a romantic poet.

"The [law] is too much with us; late and soon,
Getting and spending, we lay waste our powers:
Little we see in Nature that is ours;
We have given our hearts away, a sordid boon!"

(Wordsworth, The World Is Too Much With Us (1807) with apologies to William Wordsworth, who we feel, if he were here, would approve.)

FACTS

Gavin was a contestant in the 1987 Scripps Howard National Spelling Bee, sponsored in Ventura County by the newspaper, the Ventura County Star-Free Press. The contest is open to all students through the eighth grade who are under the age of sixteen. Gavin won competitions at the classroom and school-wide levels. This earned him the chance to compete against other skilled spellers in the county-wide spelling bee. The best speller in the county wins a trip to Washington D.C. and a place in the national finals. The winner of the national finals is declared the national champion speller.

Gavin came in second in the county spelling bee. Being adjudged the second best orthographer in Ventura County is an impressive accomplishment, but pique overcame self-esteem. The spelling contest became a legal contest.

We search in vain through the complaint to find a legal theory to support this metamorphosis. Gavin alleges that two other boys, Stephen Chen and Victor Wang, both of whom attended a different school, also competed in the spelling contest. Stephen had originally lost his school-wide competition to Victor. Stephen was asked to spell the word "horsy." He spelled it "h–o–r–s–e–y." The spelling was ruled incorrect. Victor spelled the same word "h–o–r–s–y." He then spelled another word correctly, and was declared the winner.

Contest officials, who we trust were not copy editors for the newspaper sponsoring the contest, later discovered that there are two proper spellings of the word "horsy," and that Stephen's spelling was correct after all.

Contest officials asked Stephen and Victor to again compete between themselves in order to declare one winner. Victor, having everything to lose by agreeing to this plan, refused. Contest officials decided to allow both Victor and Stephen to advance to the county-wide spelling bee, where Gavin lost to Stephen.

Taking Vince Lombardi's aphorism to heart, "Winning isn't everything, it's the only thing," Gavin filed suit against the Ventura County Star-Free Press and the Scripps Howard National Spelling Bee alleging breach of contract, breach of implied covenant of good faith and fair dealing, and intentional and negligent infliction of emotional distress.

In his complaint, Gavin asserts that contest officials violated spelling bee rules by allowing Stephen Chen to compete at the county level. He suggests that had Stephen not progressed to the county-wide competition, he, Gavin, would have won. For this leap of faith he seeks compensatory and punitive damages.

The trial court sustained Scripps' demurrer without leave to amend because the complaint fails to state a cause of action. The action was dismissed, and Gavin appeals.

DISCUSSION

Gavin asserts that he has set forth the necessary elements of a cause of action for breach of contract, and that these elements are: "(1) The contract; (2) Plaintiff's performance; (3) Defendant's breach; (4) Damage to plaintiff. 4 *Witkin*, California Procedure, *Pleading*, § 464 (3rd Ed.1985)."

Gavin's recitation of the law is correct, but his complaint wins no prize. He omitted a single word in the fourth element of an action for breach of contract, which should read "damage to plaintiff *therefrom*." Not surprisingly, the outcome of this case depends on that word. A fundamental rule of law is that "whether the action be in tort or contract compensatory damages cannot be recovered unless there is a causal connection between the act or omission complained of and the injury sustained."

The erudite trial judge stated Gavin's shortcoming incisively. "I see a gigantic causation problem. . . ." Relying on the most important resource a judge has, he said, "common sense tells me that this lawsuit is nonsense."

Even if Gavin and Scripps had formed a contract which Scripps breached by allowing Stephen Chen to compete at the county level in violation of contest rules, nothing would change. Gavin cannot show that he was injured by the breach. Gavin lost the spelling bee because he misspelled a word, and it is irrelevant that he was defeated by a contestant who "had no right to advance in the contest."

Gavin argues that had the officials "not violated the rules of the contest, Chen would not have advanced, and would not have had the opportunity to defeat" Gavin. Of course, it is impossible for Gavin to show that he would have spelled the word correctly if Stephen were not his competitor. Gavin concedes as much when he argues that he would not have been damaged if defeated by someone who had properly advanced in the contest. That is precisely the point.

Gavin cannot show that anything would have been different had Stephen not competed against him. Nor can he show that another competitor would have also misspelled that or another word, thus allowing Gavin another opportunity to win. "It is fundamental that damages which are speculative, remote, imaginary, contingent, or merely possible cannot serve as a legal basis for recovery." (*Earp v. Nobmann* (1981) 122 Cal.App.3d 270, 294, 175 Cal.Rptr. 767.)

*   *   *

The third cause of action, paragraph 29, states that plaintiff has suffered humiliation, indignity, mortification, worry, grief, anxiety, fright, mental anguish, and emotional distress, not to mention loss of respect and standing in the community. These terms more appropriately express how attorneys who draft complaints like this should feel.

A judge whose prescience is exceeded only by his eloquence said that ". . . Courts of Justice do not pretend to furnish cures for all the miseries of human life. They redress or punish gross violations of duty, but they go no farther; they cannot make men virtuous: and, as the happiness of the world depends upon its virtue, there may be much unhappiness in it which human laws cannot undertake to remove." (*Evans v. Evans* (1790) Consistory Court of London.) Unfortunately, as evidenced by this lawsuit, this cogent insight, although as relevant today as it was nearly 200 years ago, does not always make an impression on today's practitioner.

In *Shapiro v. Queens County Jockey Club* (1945) 184 Misc. 295, 53 N.Y.S.2d 135, plaintiff's horse was the only horse to run the full six furlongs in the sixth race at Aqueduct Race Track after racing officials declared a false start. A half hour later the sixth race was run again, and plaintiff's horse came in fifth out of a total of six.

The *Shapiro* court held that plaintiff had no cause of action against the race track. Plaintiff could not support the theory that his horse would have won the second time around if all the other horses had also run the six furlongs after the false start. Plaintiff was not content to merely chalk up his loss to a bad break caused by the vicissitudes of life. The lesson to be learned is that all of us, like high-strung horses at the starting gate, are subject to life's false starts. The courts cannot erase the world's imperfections.

The Georgia Supreme Court in *Georgia High School Ass'n v. Waddell* (1981) 248 Ga. 542, 285 S.E.2d 7, decided it was without authority to review the decision of a football referee regarding the outcome of the game. The court stated that the referee's decision did not present a justiciable controversy. Nor does the decision of the spelling bee officials present a justiciable controversy here.

Our decision at least keeps plaintiff's bucket of water from being added to the tidal wave of litigation that has engulfed our courts.

Sanctions—a close call

Causation has been counsel's nemesis. Its absence makes Gavin's quest for "justice" an illusory one. The lack of causation in the complaint is the cause for dismissal of the complaint. Counsel could not show us or the trial court how an amendment could cure the complaint. The lesson should have been learned at the trial court. As the law disregards trifles, so, too, one should not trifle with the Court of Appeal. The filing of an appeal here, for a case so trivial, and so lacking in merit, makes it a likely candidate for sanctions.

To counsel's credit, we are convinced that he did not prosecute this appeal for an improper motive or to delay the effect of an adverse judgment. He, therefore, at least avoids two criteria set forth in *In re Marriage of Flaherty* (1982) 31 Cal.3d 637, 183 Cal.Rptr. 508, 646 P.2d 179. This case, however, lacks merit, and we cannot conceive of a reasonable attorney who would disagree with this appraisal.

Falling within a criterion of *Flaherty*, however, does not in and of itself compel sanctions. The *Flaherty* court warned that "any definition must be read so as to avoid a serious chilling effect on the assertion of litigants' rights on appeal. . . . An appeal that is simply without merit is not by definition frivolous and should not incur sanctions. Counsel should not be deterred from filing such appeals out of a fear of reprisals."

It is creative and energetic counsel who from time to time challenge existing law and question past policies. This insures that the law be a living and dynamic force. Although noble aims were not advanced here, we are mindful of the caution in *Flaherty* that the borderline between appeals that are frivolous and those that simply have no merit is vague, and that punishment should be used sparingly "to deter only the most egregious conduct." We therefore decline to impose sanctions, but we hope this opinion will serve as a warning notice for counsel to be discerning when drawing the line between making new law or wasting everyone's time.

Advice to Gavin and an aphorism or two

Gavin has much to be proud of. He participated in a spelling bee that challenged the powers of memory and concentration. He met the challenge well but lost out to another contestant. Gavin took first in his school and can be justifiably proud of his performance.

It is this lawsuit that is trivial, not his achievement. Our courts try to give redress for real harms; they cannot offer palliatives for imagined injuries.

Vince Lombardi may have had a point, so did Grantland Rice—It's "not that you won or lost . . . but how you play the game"?

As for the judgment of the trial court, we'll spell it out. A–F–F–I–R–M–E–D. Appellant is to pay respondent's costs on appeal.

This may be one of those situations that seems funny as long as it didn't happen to you. Even allowing for the fact that the case is from the '60s, the damage award seems quite small compared to the millions of dollars awarded in the '90s to someone who is burned by hot coffee at a fast-food restaurant.

JONES
v.
FISHER, *et al.*

Supreme Court of Wisconsin
April 1, 1969
166 N.W.2d 175, 42 Wis.2d 209

This is an assault and battery action brought by the plaintiff-respondent, Aleta I. Jones, for compensatory and punitive damages against Jerome Paul Fisher and Clara Belle Fisher, his wife, defendants-appellants.

The defendants were the owners and operators of a nursing home in Middleton, Wisconsin. The plaintiff, age twenty-six, married but separated, started to work for the defendants as a nurse's aide in December of 1966. She cared for the home residents during the night hours, set up and gave medication, prepared and served breakfast and had some clean-up duties in the kitchen. Until the incident in question the relationship between the parties had been cordial and friendly. The defendants regarded her as a good employee and were personally fond of her.

In September, 1967, the plaintiff was told by her dentist that her teeth were in bad condition. She needed an upper plate but complained to Mrs. Fisher about the cost of her dental work. The Fishers volunteered and did loan her $200 to apply on her dental expenses. All but $10 of the proceeds of the loan was paid to the dentist.

Shortly after she obtained the upper plate she quit working for the Fishers. About a week or more after she quit, on November 6, 1967, at noon, she returned to the nursing home to get her check in the amount of $48 for her last week's work. Mrs. Fisher tried to convince the plaintiff to return to work at the nursing home. The plaintiff refused. Mr. Fisher entered the conversation and inquired when she was going to repay the $200. She told him he could take $20 out of the $48 check and that she would pay the balance at the rate of $20 per month. He told her that was not satisfactory and that she would have to pay the entire amount in three days or leave the upper plate for security. She refused to agree to these conditions. She was told to leave the teeth and an argument ensued. There is a dispute as to whether the Fishers used profane and indecent language toward her. She attempted to run out of the room. Mr. Fisher seized her arms and forced them in back of her. The evidence is unclear as to whether she was forced onto his lap or into a crouched position; if she kicked at Mr. Fisher; or if she threatened to kill him. In any event, Mrs. Fisher grabbed at her face and mouth and extracted the upper plate. Mr. Fisher released her and she immediately ran out of the house. The affray was less than fifteen minutes. At the trial she testified that her arms and her back hurt while she was being held and that her mouth, which was sore because the teeth did not fit properly, hurt when Mrs. Fisher took her plate out. She had no bruises nor scratches. She testified that she was in fear and was humiliated and embarrassed.

After she left the rest home she walked about a block to a drugstore where she called her subsequent employer and asked him to call his lawyer. She then walked another block to the police station and reported the incident to two police officers. One of the officers went to the Fisher nursing home, obtained the teeth, returned to the station and gave Mrs. Jones her teeth. She testified she suffered humiliation, embarrassment and shame at the drugstore and at the police station and that she had these same emotions for about a week which made it difficult to sleep. She did not see a doctor or take any prescriptive medicine.

The jury found that both defendants had committed an assault and battery on her and awarded compensatory damages of $1,000 and punitive damages of $2,500 as to each defendant.

The trial court denied the defendants' motions after verdict and ordered judgment in the amount of $6,000, plus costs.

Defendants appeal.

BEILFUSS, Justice.

The defendants raise four issues:

1. Are the compensatory damages excessive?

2. Are the punitive damages excessive?

3. Was it error to require the defendants to testify as to their net income for 1966 and 1967?

4. Was it error to permit plaintiff's counsel to read portions of her adverse examination into evidence before the jury?

The jury awarded the plaintiff $1,000 compensatory damages. Compensatory damages are to compensate the injured party for his actual damages and not as punishment of the defendant. If there is personal injury the award should include compensation for loss of earnings, pain and suffering, and permanent or future disability if such appears. The award can also include compensation for mental suffering such as humiliation, shame, embarrassment, and fear. Granted, mental suffering is many times difficult to evaluate in terms of monetary awards, nevertheless, it is compensable.

Considering the testimony and other proof in the record most favorable to the plaintiff, we find that plaintiff was subjected to a painful physical assault for a very few minutes at the most. She testified her arms and back hurt while she was held and that the soreness of her mouth was aggravated when the teeth were taken. There was no objective physical evidence of injury. She did not consult a physician, nor use prescriptive medicine. Her physical injury was nominal. She testified that she was nervous, humiliated and scared during the altercation at the nursing home, at the drugstore, the police station, and for about a week thereafter and still (at the time of trial) thinks about it. She was without her teeth for, at the most, an hour. Understandably she could suffer humiliation and shame during this period. Conceivably she could continue to suffer these emotions for some time thereafter, but her symptoms were all subjective and not supported by any medical testimony nor any other corroborating evidence. The lack of medical testimony or other corroborating evidence is not fatal to her claim for past suffering but it would have done much to add credence to her almost minimal testimony of her subjective emotions.

I

We are of the opinion that the jury could (they are not required to do so) award punitive damages based upon the facts before them. The conduct of Mr. and Mrs. Fisher was illegal, outrageous and grossly unreasonable. It may be as appellants contend that they erroneously thought they had a right to take the teeth as security for their loan. Even so, it was grossly unreasonable to use the tactics they did and subject the plaintiff to this outrage.

The principal problem that confronts us is whether the damages awarded are excessive.

Punitive damages are assessed not to compensate the injured party but as a punishment to the wrongdoer and as a deterrent to others.

The evidence reveals that the defendants' own property was worth approximately $75,000, subject to a mortgage of $41,000, leaving an equity of about $34,000. Their net income for the years 1966 and 1967 was about $24,000 per year. It appears as though the nursing home operation was a joint venture between Mr. and Mrs. Fisher. In contrasting the punitive awards with the wealth of the defendants we must either assume the award was $5,000 or consider that each owned one-half of the wealth of the parties.

In viewing the wealth of the defendants, the character and extent of their acts, and the probable motivation, and then applying the standard of punishment and deterrence, the court is of the unanimous opinion that the assessment of $2,500 as punitive damages to each defendant was excessive.

Having determined the punitive damages are excessive, we apply the Powers rule and give the plaintiff the option of accepting a reduced reasonable amount or a new trial on damages.

* * *

The Court next determines that any error in having a portion of plaintiff's deposition read to the jury was harmless.

* * *

Judgment reversed, and cause remanded with directions. The appellants are entitled to costs on this appeal.

ROBERT W. HANSEN, Justice (dissenting).

The majority opinion sustains the collecting of punitive damages in a case involving a one hour deprivation of dentures. Next may come the case approving such added damages for the near-identical deed of toupee-snatching. We do not minimize the unpleasantness of an hour spent without newly acquired dentures, nor of an hour spent without the adornment of a substitute headpiece. We agree that compensatory damages for the deprivation and humiliation involved are justified. We do not agree that the added penalty of punitive or vindictive damages is also warranted in such instance. We would hold that the public interest does not require nor ought the public policy permit the awarding of punishment damages in this type of situation.

The road that has brought us to the present state of affairs in regard to punitive damages in Wisconsin courts is a long one, paved with good intentions. Over 100 years ago, this court decreed that a plaintiff under certain circumstances could be awarded extra damages to punish the defendant in addition to those that compensated the plaintiff. Early attacks upon the wisdom of this idea were repulsed. Such punishment damages have been awarded in this state in cases involving batteries, trespass to realty, libel and slander, seduction, breach of promise, alienation of affections and other categories of tort action. We find, however, no cases where victims of rapes, robberies, burglaries, forgeries or highway accidents have been given similar retributive awards.

WHAT IS THE BASIS?

What is the justification in certain situations for permitting a tort-plaintiff to recover money beyond the compensatory damages established? It has been said that such punitive awards are permitted in most jurisdictions '* * * as a punishment to the defendant and as a warning and example to deter him and others from committing like offenses in the future.' Can it seriously be contended that such underlying justification is present in the case before us? Would not the recollection of the compensatory damages paid render very unlikely a repetition by the husband and wife here involved of the offense of denture detention? Would not the $1,000 compensatory damage award, standing alone, be a sufficient deterrent to others who might be tempted to hold dentures as security for an unpaid loan? Are we dealing here with a propensity to grab, and hold upper plates that is marked either by a high rate of recidivism or contagion? Is there here present a situation that justifies the heavy-handed use of punishment to deter? We think not, particularly because we do not deal with a matter of plaintiff's rights, but the question of what the public interest requires and what the public policy should permit.

WHAT ARE THE LIMITS?

While the roadway to punitive awards has been around a long time, it always has had limits since such punishment awards were first approved. It has often been said that to warrant the imposition of punitory damages, it must appear that the wrong was inflicted 'under circumstances of aggravation, insult, or cruelty, with vindictiveness and malice.' The road was widened with the holding that, where actual malice was not present, it would be enough that there be 'wanton or reckless disregard of plaintiff's rights.' In a comparatively recent case, the road limits broadened, with this court approving, this statement:

"Where the defendant's wrongdoing has been intentional and deliberate, and has the character of outrage frequently associated with crime, all but a few courts have permitted the jury to award in the tort action 'punitive' or 'exemplary' damages, or what is sometimes called 'smart money.'" Prosser, *Laws of Torts*, 2d., p. 9, sec. 2.

Unless malice is equated with momentary loss of temper or is to be presumed from an act of poor judgment, there is no element of malevolence or vindictiveness present here. The bicuspid corpus delicti is present only because of an interest-free loan made by defendants to plaintiff. Granted that they expected her to remain in their employ and to pay them back from her earnings, goodwill, not illwill is evidenced by the transaction, the advancing of the $200 to pay the dentist.

Conceding that the taking of the upper plate which belonged to the plaintiff, even if paid for by the defendants, was an invasion of her rights, can it be termed 'wanton or reckless?' It is evident that there was a mutually cordial, supportive and agreeable relationship between the old couple and the young lady who worked for them in their nursing home, almost up to the incident here involved. It was the lady's decision, loan unpaid, to go to work for someone else that precipitated a change in the relationship. Is this flareup of emotions, this shift in mood, this disappointment of expectations on the part of the employing couple a foundation for a finding of wanton and reckless disregard of the rights of another. If so, the most trivial of altercations and mildest of scuffles dons the garment of wantonness or recklessness.

Given the unfortunate escalation of unpleasantness in the argument of the parties, can its climax, the grabbing of the dentures, be found to have the 'character of outrage frequently associated with crime?' If the police had been called to stop the argument, instead of being called to get the plate back, would they have made an arrest? If they had, would a district attorney have issued a state warrant for battery, or even for disorderly conduct, on the basis of what had taken place? If he had, would a misdemeanor court have considered the situation here to involve violation of a criminal statute or as a falling-out among friends to be settled by an apology and a handshake? Is this the type of situation that Prosser contemplated when he wrote of an 'outrage frequently associated with crime?' We think it falls short of being that. Certainly, if punitive damages are to be imposed 'in view of the enormity of the crime,' this is no situation justifying their imposition. We do not attach great weight to the fact that the denture-deprived plaintiff went to the police to get her denture back, not to get a warrant. This is an unfortunate but predictable concomitant of placing the weapon of punishment to deter in private hands. Why should the plaintiff seek a warrant when her case would not be aided by the securing of a public sanction or penalty prior to or in addition to the private retribution she was seeking?

We have grave doubts about the public policy involved in thus placing in private hands the use of punishment to deter. Some observers challenge the right or efficacy of even the state using punishment as punishment to deter. At least in the public administration of criminal justice there are clearly defined crimes, clearly delineated penalties, constitutional protections and in-built restraints.

However, we need not challenge the whole idea of placing the right to seek retribution, in addition to compensation, in private hands, to challenge the applicability of such concept in the case before us. Whether or not it operates to deter scalpings, it ought not be used in the effort to deter toupee dislodgings. The concept of punitive damages, it has been said, is 'not a favorite of the law,' should be 'exercised with great caution,' and properly be 'confined within the narrowest limits.' This case, it appears to the writer, is well beyond the limits.

So we would sustain the admittedly high award of $1,000 for compensatory damages, as including every ounce of hurt and humiliation that can be placed upon the scales, and strike the awards for punitive damages as not being warranted by the facts of this case.

Plaintiffs with preposterous claims of injury or creative, as well as remunerative, prayers for relief are not uncommon. Even so, this case is extreme on both counts. As you might guess, relief is sought from that most popular of deep-pockets defendants—the federal government.

KAZMAIER
v.
CENTRAL INTELLIGENCE AGENCY, *et al.*

United States District Court, E.D. Wisconsin
April 11, 1983
562 F.Supp. 263

MYRON L. GORDON, Senior District Judge.

John Wesley Kazmaier, the plaintiff in this action, seeks leave of the court to proceed in forma pauperis. The complaint states that federal jurisdiction is based on 28 U.S.C. § 1983; because there is no such statute, it appears that Mr. Kazmaier may have intended to refer to 42 U.S.C. § 1983. Named as defendants are the Central Intelligence Agency (CIA), the Federal Bureau of Investigation (FBI), the United States Department of Justice, and the United States government.

The complaint sets forth in great detail the alleged wrongdoings of the defendants. Generally stated, Mr. Kazmaier claims that the CIA has subjected him to brainwashing and torture attacks since 1965 through the use of satellite beams, portable dental laser equipment, and other such means. The other defendants are alleged to have failed to investigate these incidents. As a result of these attacks, he contends that his high school career was ruined, he was prevented from receiving his college degree, his right ankle was broken, and he suffered tremendous agony. He seeks $7,308,089,250,000.00 in damages, employment as the director and assistant director of the FBI, protection from assassins, authorization to carry concealed weapons, and other forms of relief.

In several letters to the court, Mr. Kazmaier has "ordered" me to provide him with ridiculously large sums of money as loans or advances against his future court award. He has also "ordered" me to send him immediately a list of items, including:

"1. A 25 layer Kevlar bullet-proof vest with protection of both front and rear of body.

2. A 357 magnum caliber revolver in a right hand shoulder holster, preferably with a four inch barrel.

3. A selective-fire Beretta 9mm type 92 pistol in a left-hand shoulder holster.

4. An Uzi Submachine gun caliber 9mm with 5 large magazines, in a soft side case with a zipper top.

5. An M–16 rifle with 5 large magazines, caliber .223.

6. A .380 or .32 ACP caliber Gatling gun with one or more medium or large ammo-pak magazines. This gun is a multiple-barrel high speed gun capable of a high rate of fire, and it has an accurate range of 50 yards.

7. A United States Marshals Service Badge and I.D. set.

8. A bullet-proof car, such as a bullet-proof Lincoln Continental four door model from Ford Motor Company."

Based on the allegations of the complaint, the nature of the relief sought, and the contents of Mr. Kazmaier's letters, I find that this proposed lawsuit falls easily into the "frivolous" category. I will not grant the plaintiff permission to pursue this action without payment of fees, pursuant to 28 U.S.C. § 1915. Furthermore, the plaintiff has filed a nearly identical complaint in case no. 82–C–1384, now pending before Honorable John W. Reynolds, and he has paid the filing fee in that case. I see no reason to encourage duplication of judicial efforts, especially in a case as this one.

Therefore, IT IS ORDERED that the plaintiff's motion for leave to proceed in forma pauperis be and hereby is denied.

Love is a powerful emotion. And hate spawned by love may be stronger yet, for it can lead to the most wicked of actions. As a matter of law, this case is about insurance. But, as a matter of fact, it is about love and hate.

GULLEDGE
v.
ATLANTIC COAST LIFE INSURANCE COMPANY

Supreme Court of South Carolina
March 1, 1971
179 S.E.2d 605, 255 S.C. 472

LITTLEJOHN, Justice:

The defendant issued its accidental death insurance policy to Linda Faye Gulledge (also referred to as Linda Faye Gulledge Larrymore). She died April 9, 1967. The defendant refused to pay, and this action alleging accidental death was brought by her beneficiary.

The complaint alleges that Linda Faye Gulledge 'was killed by an automobile which death was the result of an accident and plaintiff is entitled to collect from the defendant the sum of Three Thousand and no/100 ($3000.00) Dollars plus interest under the terms of said policy.'

The answer alleges, first, that the death of the insured 'was not an accident within the meaning of the instant policy' and alleges secondly, that the 'death of Linda Faye Gulledge Larrymore resulted, at least in part, from her engaging in activities constituting a violation of statutory law, and that under paragraph No. 19 of the defendant's policy the contribution of such activities to her death bars the benefit of said policy.'

After all evidence had been submitted the trial judge directed a verdict in favor of the plaintiff, holding, in effect, that the only reasonable inference to be drawn from the whole of the testimony was that the insured died as a result of an accident within the terms of the policy, and that death did not result from a violation of statutory laws or municipal ordinances. We affirm that ruling.

The facts giving rise to this action are not in dispute. Thomas Wilkerson and Mary Wilkerson were husband and wife. The insured, Linda Faye Gulledge, became romantically involved with Mr. Wilkerson. She had announced her intention to marry Mr. Wilkerson, and had on occasion telephoned Mrs. Wilkerson to apprise her of that fact.

On April 9, 1967, the insured was riding in her mother's automobile with a young man named Jackie Horne. They rode by the Wilkerson home. A short time thereafter they observed a car following them. It continued to follow them down a dirt road and pulled up along side; both cars stopped. Mrs. Wilkerson was in the other car; she got out and came over to the car where the insured and Jackie Horne were sitting. After talking a few minutes Mrs. Wilkerson got out of the car of the insured and went back to her own car, ostensibly to get and show the insured and Jackie a letter. Instead of returning with a letter she came back with a pistol and shot both of them. After they were shot, both got out of the car. Horne scuffled with Mrs. Wilkerson and took the gun, which he placed in his back pocket. A little later Mrs. Wilkerson grabbed the gun out of his pocket and shot both of them again. Both the injured parties ended up in the road. Mrs. Wilkerson got in her car and ran over both of them. Horne survived; it is agreed that the cause of the insured's death was being run over by the automobile.

We think the plaintiff made a prima facie case by proof of the existence of the insurance policy, and proof that the insured died as result of being run over by the automobile. The burden of proof then shifted to the defendant to show that the insured should have foreseen that her own conduct would bring about serious bodily injury or death, or show that the death was a result of a violation of statutory law or ordinance by the insured.

The appellant presents two questions for determination by this court. The first: Did the defendant present evidence from which a reasonable inference can be drawn that the insured should have foreseen that her own conduct would result in serious bodily harm or death to herself.

Injuries are regarded as accidental unless it can be said that they are a natural or probable result of the insured's action, reasonably foreseeable by the insured or by a reasonably prudent person in the same position.

* * *

The conduct of the insured was improper, but we do not think that the conduct, as disclosed by the preponderance of the evidence in the record, was such that it can be said that the injury and death should have been foreseen. Accordingly, the death was accidental within the meaning of the policy. We think the evidence on this issue gave rise to a question of law only, and we cannot say that the trial judge erred in directing a verdict.

The second question arises because of a provision in the policy which reads as follows:

"Moreover, this Policy shall not cover and no indemnity shall be paid hereunder for accident or sickness resulting wholly or partly from any of the following causes or conditions:

* * *

"f. Any violation of statutory laws or Municipal ordinance;"

In oral argument counsel implies that the insured was guilty of adultery, but upon questioning, admitted that the evidence did not support such a finding. Accordingly, as a matter of law the defendant has failed to submit evidence tending to prove death resulting from violation of a statutory law or a city ordinance.

We conclude that the trial judge properly directed a verdict in favor of the plaintiff.

Affirmed.

"The court is required for the purpose of its decision to accept the facts as pleaded as true, even though they may have struck the court—as they have always struck me—as implausible. It seems much more likely that Webb just lost his balance, and McGowin (who was in fact Webb's employer) felt enough sympathy for his misfortune to help him financially."

—Professor, New York University School of Law

WEBB

v.

McGOWIN, *et al.*

Court of Appeals of Alabama
Nov. 12, 1935
168 So. 196, 27 Ala.App. 82

BRICKEN, Presiding Judge.

* * *

A fair statement of the case presenting the questions for decision is set out in appellant's brief, which we adopt.

"On the 3d day of August, 1925, appellant while in the employ of the W. T. Smith Lumber Company, a corporation, and acting within the scope of his employment, was engaged in clearing the upper floor of mill No. 2 of the company. While so engaged he was in the act of dropping a pine block from the upper floor of the mill to the ground below; this being the usual and ordinary way of clearing the floor, and it being the duty of the plaintiff in the course of his employment to so drop it. The block weighed about 75 pounds.

"As appellant was in the act of dropping the block to the ground below, he was on the edge of the upper floor of the mill. As he started to turn the block loose so that it would drop to the ground, he saw J. Greeley McGowin, testator of the defendants, on the ground below and directly under where the block would have fallen had appellant turned it loose. Had he turned it loose it would have struck McGowin with such force as to have caused him serious bodily harm or death. Appellant could have remained safely on the upper floor of the mill by turning the block loose and allowing it to drop, but had he done this the block would have fallen on McGowin and caused him serious injuries or death. The only safe and reasonable way to prevent this was for appellant to hold to the block and divert its direction in falling from the place where McGowin was standing and the only safe way to divert it so as to prevent its coming into contact with McGowin was for appellant to fall with it to the ground below. Appellant did this, and by holding to the block and falling with it to the ground below, he diverted the course of its fall in such way that McGowin was not injured. In thus preventing the injuries to McGowin appellant himself received serious bodily injuries, resulting in his right leg being broken, the heel of his right foot torn off and his right arm broken. He was badly crippled for life and rendered unable to do physical or mental labor.

"On September 1, 1925, in consideration of appellant having prevented him from sustaining death or serious bodily harm and in consideration of the injuries appellant had received, McGowin agreed with him to care for and maintain him for the remainder of appellant's life at the rate of $15 every two weeks from the time he sustained his injuries to and during the remainder of appellant's life; it being agreed that McGowin would pay this sum to appellant for his maintenance. Under the agreement McGowin paid or caused to be paid to appellant the sum so agreed on up until McGowin's death on January 1, 1934. After his death the payments were continued to and including January 27, 1934, at which time they were discontinued. Thereupon plaintiff brought suit to recover the unpaid installments accruing up to the time of the bringing of the suit.

"The material averments of the different counts of the original complaint and the amended complaint are predicated upon the foregoing statement of facts."

In other words, the complaint as amended averred in substance: (1) That on August 3, 1925, appellant saved J. Greeley McGowin, appellee's testator, from death or grievous bodily harm; (2) that in doing so appellant sustained bodily injury crippling him for life; (3) that in consideration of the services rendered and the injuries received by appellant, McGowin agreed to care for him the remainder of appellant's life, the amount to be paid being $15 every two weeks; (4) that McGowin complied with this agreement until he died on January 1, 1934, and the payments were kept up to January 27, 1934, after which they were discontinued.

The action was for the unpaid installments accruing after January 27, 1934, to the time of the suit.

The principal grounds of demurrer to the original and amended complaint are: (1) It states no cause of action; (2) its averments show the contract was without consideration; (3) it fails to allege that McGowin had, at or before the services were rendered, agreed to pay appellant for them; (4) the contract declared on is void under the statute of frauds.

1. The averments of the complaint show that appellant saved McGowin from death or grievous bodily harm. This was a material benefit to him of infinitely more value than any financial aid he could have received. Receiving this benefit, McGowin became morally bound to compensate appellant for the services rendered. Recognizing his moral obligation, he expressly agreed to pay appellant as alleged in the complaint and complied with this agreement up to the time of his death; a period of more than 8 years.

Had McGowin been accidentally poisoned and a physician, without his knowledge or request, had administered an antidote, thus saving his life, a subsequent promise by McGowin to pay the physician would have been valid. Likewise, McGowin's agreement as disclosed by the complaint to compensate appellant for saving him from death or grievous bodily injury is valid and enforceable.

Where the promisee cares for, improves, and preserves the property of the promisor, though done without his request, it is sufficient consideration for the promisor's subsequent agreement to pay for the service, because of the material benefit received.

In *Boothe v. Fitzpatrick*, 36 Vt. 681, the court held that a promise by defendant to pay for the past keeping of a bull which had escaped from defendant's premises and been cared for by plaintiff was valid, although there was no previous request, because the subsequent promise obviated that objection; it being equivalent to a previous request. On the same principle, had the promisee saved the promisor's life or his body from grievous harm, his subsequent promise to pay for the services rendered would have been valid. Such service would have been far more material than caring for his bull. Any holding that saving a man from death bodily harm is not a material benefit sufficient to uphold a subsequent promise to pay for the service, necessarily rests on the assumption that saving life and preservation of the body from harm have only a sentimental value. The converse of this is true. Life and preservation of the body have material, pecuniary values, measurable in dollars and cents. Because of this, physicians practice their profession charging for services rendered in saving life and curing the body of its ills, and surgeons perform operations. The same is true as to the law of negligence, authorizing the assessment of damages in personal injury cases based upon the extent of the injuries, earnings, and life expectancies of those injured.

In the business of life insurance, the value of a man's life is measured in dollars and cents according to his expectancy, the soundness of his body, and his ability to pay premiums. The same is true as to health and accident insurance.

It follows that if, as alleged in the complaint, appellant saved J. Greeley McGowin from death or grievous bodily harm, and McGowin subsequently agreed to pay him for the service rendered, it became a valid and enforceable contract.

2. It is well settled that a moral obligation is a sufficient consideration to support a subsequent promise to pay where the promisor has received a material benefit, although there was no original duty or liability resting on the promisor. * * *

The case at bar is clearly distinguishable from that class of cases where the consideration is a mere moral obligation or conscientious duty unconnected with receipt by promisor of benefits of a material or pecuniary nature. Here the promisor received a material benefit constituting a valid consideration for his promise.

3. Some authorities hold that, for a moral obligation to support a subsequent promise to pay, there must have existed a prior legal or equitable obligation, which for some reason had become unenforceable, but for which the promisor was still morally bound. This rule, however, is subject to qualifi-

cation in those cases where the promisor, having received a material benefit from the promisee, is morally bound to compensate him for the services rendered and in consideration of this obligation promises to pay. In such cases the subsequent promise to pay is an affirmance or ratification of the services rendered carrying with it the presumption that a previous request for the service was made.

[Based upon earlier court decisions], McGowin's express promise to pay appellant for the services rendered was an affirmance or ratification of what appellant had done raising the presumption that the services had been rendered at McGowin's request.

4. The averments of the complaint show that in saving McGowin from death or grievous bodily harm, appellant was crippled for life. This was part of the consideration of the contract declared on. McGowin was benefited. Appellant was injured. Benefit to the promisor or injury to the promisee is a sufficient legal consideration for the promisor's agreement to pay.

5. Under the averments of the complaint the services rendered by appellant were not gratuitous. The agreement of McGowin to pay and the acceptance of payment by appellant conclusively shows the contrary.

*   *   *

The Court also determined that the contract was not void under the statute of frauds, which requires that certain contracts be in writing.

Based on the foregoing, the court held that appellant's complaint should be heard before a jury.

The absurdity of this case is only heightened by the fact that Mr. Lodi appeared pro se both as plaintiff and as defendant.

"I particularly enjoy the last paragraphs on costs recoverable!"

—Professor, San Francisco School of Law

Oreste LODI

v.

Oreste LODI

Court of Appeal, Third District
Oct. 22, 1985
As Modified Nov. 7, 1985
219 Cal.Rptr. 116, 173 Cal.App.3d 628

SIMS, Associate Justice.

This case started when plaintiff Oreste Lodi sued himself in the Shasta County Superior Court.

In a complaint styled "Action to Quiet Title Equity," plaintiff named himself, under the title "Oreste Lodi, Beneficiary," as defendant. The pleading alleges that defendant Lodi is the beneficiary of a charitable trust, the estate of which would revert to plaintiff Lodi, as "Reversioner," upon notice. Plaintiff attached as Exhibit A to his complaint a copy of his 1923 New York birth certificate, which he asserts is the "certificate of power of appointment and conveyance" transferring reversioner's estate to the charitable trust. Plaintiff Lodi goes on to allege that for 61 years (*i.e.*, since plaintiff/defendant was born), defendant has controlled the estate, that plaintiff has notified defendant of the termination of the trust by a written "Revocation of all Power" (which apparently seeks to revoke his birth certificate), but that defendant "intentionally persist [sic] to control said estate. . . ." Plaintiff requested an order that he is absolutely entitled to possession of the estate, and terminating all claims against the estate by any and all persons "claiming" under defendant.[1]

The complaint was duly served by plaintiff Lodi, as "Reversioner," upon himself as defendant/beneficiary. When defendant/beneficiary Lodi failed to answer, plaintiff/reversioner Lodi had a clerk's default entered and thereafter requested entry of a default judgment. At the hearing on the entry of a default judgment, the superior court denied the request to enter judgment and dismissed the complaint.[2]

In this court, appellant and respondent are the same person. Each party has filed a brief.

The only question presented is whether the trial court properly dismissed the complaint even though no party sought dismissal or objected to entry of judgment as requested.

As is obvious, the complaint states no cognizable claim for relief. Plaintiff's birth certificate did not create a charitable trust; consequently, there was no trust which could be terminated by notice. In the arena of pleadings, the one at issue here is a slam-dunk frivolous complaint.

We conclude the trial court was empowered to strike or dismiss the complaint by section 436 of the Code of Civil Procedure which provides in pertinent part: "The court may, upon a motion . . . or at any time in its discretion, and upon terms it deems proper: . . . [¶] (b) Strike out all or any part of any pleading not drawn or filed in conformity with the laws of this state, a court rule, or an order of the court."

Section 425.10 provides in pertinent part: "A complaint . . . shall contain . . . the following: [¶] A statement of the facts constituting the cause of action, in ordinary and concise language."

---

1. The purpose of plaintiff's action is not entirely clear. However, we note plaintiff caused a complimentary copy of his complaint to be served upon the Internal Revenue Service. It may be that plaintiff hoped to obtain a state court judgment that, he thought, would be of advantage to him under the Internal Revenue Code.

2. The minute order indicates that the court also suggested to plaintiff/reversioner/defendant/beneficiary that he seek the assistance of legal counsel.

* * *

Here, plaintiff's complaint fails to state facts showing a primary right by plaintiff or a primary duty devolving on defendant or a wrong done by defendant. The complaint therefore fails to state facts constituting a cause of action as required by section 425.10. Consequently, the complaint was not drawn in conformity with the laws of this state and was thus properly subject to the court's own motion to strike under section 436, subdivision (b).

We need not consider whether the court's power under this statute should be exercised where plaintiff seeks leave to amend. Here, so far as the record before us shows, plaintiff made no such request nor is any prospect of saving the pleading by amendment apparent. The trial court therefore properly struck and dismissed the complaint on its own motion.

In the circumstances, this result cannot be unfair to Mr. Lodi. Although it is true that, as plaintiff and appellant, he loses, it is equally true that, as defendant and respondent, he wins! It is hard to imagine a more even handed application of justice. Truly, it would appear that Oreste Lodi is that rare litigant who is assured of both victory and defeat regardless of which side triumphs.

We have considered whether respondent/defendant/beneficiary should be awarded his costs of suit on appeal, which he could thereafter recover from himself. However, we believe the equities are better served by requiring each party to bear his own costs on appeal.

The judgment (order) is affirmed. Each party shall bear his own costs.

Chapter 5
Let the Games Begin

Although baseball has traditionally been referred to as the "national pastime," it is fairly safe to say that sports in general have become America's favorite pastime. Whether one is a spectator or a participant, and whether it is football, basketball, tennis or golf, most Americans love competition. From time to time, however, the competition moves from the playing field into the courtroom. There, athletes, team owners and fans find their opponents are no longer referred to by name or mascot, but are assigned the title plaintiff or defendant.

The stated reasons may vary, but the basic scenario is all too familiar to many sports fans, who will identify with Justice Lane's conclusion.

Due to potential delays in finishing the renovation of their stadium, the New York Yankees informed the city of New York in November of 1982 that the 1983 home opening series against the Detroit Tigers would be played in Denver's Mile High Stadium instead of in New York. The city immediately commenced a court action and moved for a preliminary injunction to prevent the Yankees from entering into any agreement with Denver to change the venue of the opening series.

"One never knows when incidental knowledge will become useful and significantly legal."

—Adjunct Professor, Seton Hall University School of Law

❖–❖–❖–❖–❖

CITY OF NEW YORK
v.
NEW YORK YANKEES

Supreme Court, New York County
Jan. 10, 1983
458 N.Y.S.2d 486, 117 Misc.2d 332

RICHARD S. LANE, Justice:

*   *   *

With the season only a few months off the motion may be the whole ball game.

Sometime after the extensive renovations to the Stadium undertaken by the City as the cornerstone of the 1972 lease with the Yankees, it was discovered there were certain structural flaws in the stands in lines abutting on left field and right field. Temporary repairs were made for several years; permanent repairs were scheduled to be made between the close of the

1982 season and the opening of the 1983 season; and plans and specifications were drafted, all with the participation and approval of the Yankees.

Came July 30, 1982 and the Deputy Commissioner of Parks wrote to the Yankees expressing confidence that the goal of completion prior to the beginning of the 1983 season could be achieved, but also expressing a caveat as follows:

> "However, in view of the magnitude of the project and the small time frame we would consider it prudent to establish a contingency schedule for Yankee games to be played at the Stadium during the early part of the season. While we will attempt to provide for contingencies in the contract itself, since a large part of the work will be accomplished in the winter it is conceivable that inclement weather and other unforeseeables may negatively affect our schedule.

> "We would appreciate any thoughts and assistance you can give us in this connection. If you have any questions, please don't hesitate to call me."

The City contends, and the Yankees on argument concede, that there had been ongoing discussions between the parties about problems created by the proposed construction work, and that this letter was written at the request of the Yankees as the basis for consultation with the Tigers and with the American League.

The Summer passed without any response from the Yankees to this July 30th letter. Meanwhile the plans and specifications were put out for bid, and a contract was let calling for completion by February 28. The contract included unusual provisions for overtime and enclosing the affected areas to protect against any interruption of the work as a result of adverse weather. In addition it was now understood with the contractor, as apparently it was not in the earlier discussions between the parties, that the playing field itself would not be affected in any way, thus saving about five weeks. The Yankees were fully briefed on this progress in early September.

Came October 8, 1982 and the Yankees at last replied to the July 30th letter requesting a guarantee of completion in a timely manner and an indemnification against any loss of revenue if the Stadium should not be available for opening day. The City's initial reaction was affirmative. However, on October 12 while the City's formal answer was allegedly awaiting the approval of the Corporation Counsel, the Yankees spelled out that the guarantee would have to extend to no debris or litter in view of fans and no seats unavailable on opening day. Scrapping the proposed guarantee and indemnification, if indeed it had ever been drafted, the Commissioner of Parks instead wrote personally to Mr. Steinbrenner on October 19, 1982. He adverted to the history of cooperation between them and to all of the efforts being made to assure timely completion, and suggested that, in the worst case, only 1000 to 2000 seats would be unavailable for which the Yankees would be compensated by abatement of rent pursuant to the lease.

Again there was no immediate response from the Yankees. Some three weeks later came the bombshell call about Denver.

There can be no dispute that playing in Denver would violate Section # 4.7 of the Lease requiring all home games to be played in the Stadium through the year 2002.

Is such violation justified in any way by the pas de deux between the parties during the Summer and early Fall.

The first possibility that comes to mind is anticipatory breach by the City. But clearly that possibility has to be rejected.

*   *   *

Commendably recognizing the weakness of the anticipatory breach theory, the Yankees place greater reliance on the doctrine of waiver and estoppel. But these are equally tenuous reeds. Since there is no suggestion of any fraud or negligent misrepresentation by the City true estoppel or "estoppel in pais" is not involved here. *   *   *

Nor may the City be charged with laches. It commenced this action within days after learning of the Yankees' intentions.

Accordingly the Court finds a strong likelihood of eventual success by the City in this action.

The Court also finds that the equities weigh on the side of the City. Viewed as objectively as possible it would appear that Mr. Steinbrenner, ignoring the good faith efforts by the City to satisfy his needs, was grabbing a pretext to take his team to greener pastures—*i.e.* a larger stadium and a populace with an unfulfilled yearning for major league baseball. Tending to demonstrate that concern about the conditions of the Stadium was not his only motivation are the following: a) He waited passively throughout the entire summer while the risk of non-availability of the Stadium was at its highest; b) He escalated his demand when it appeared that the City was about to give him the guarantee and indemnification he requested; c) He chose to negotiate with cities seeking a major league franchise while ignoring the obvious solutions—Shea Stadium or Tiger Stadium in Detroit; and d) In November looking forward, if the Stadium might not be ready on April 11, how could he assume that it would be ready on April 15?

Furthermore, to allow the Yankees to proceed to contract with Denver might open a real Pandora's Box. It would leave the Yankees with conflicting contract obligations. It would invite litigation in Colorado as well as New York with results in doubt throughout the winter not to mention the nightmare of possibly opposite results.

Finally the Court easily finds a threat of irreparable injury to the City. Much more is at stake than merely the loss of direct and indirect revenue to the City.

The Yankee pin stripes belong to New York like Central Park, like the Statue of Liberty, like the Metropolitan Museum of Art, like the Metropolitan Opera, like the Stock Exchange, like the lights of Broadway, etc. Collectively they are "The Big Apple". Any loss represents a diminution of the quality of life here, a blow to the City's standing at the top, however narcissistic that perception may be.

"Big deal" argue the Yankees. We open in Seattle anyhow on April 5. We will have a New York opening with all the traditional hoopla on April 15. And it's only three games we are talking about * * *. However it is the symbolism of the act not the quantity which counts. Any reduction in the number of home games, especially if it involves the home opening games eagerly awaited by the real fans after a long winter in the hot stove league, erodes the ties of loyalty between the people of the City and their team. Dare one whisper the dreaded words: "The Denver Yankees".

No money damages can measure or assuage this kind of harm.

Taking major league baseball on tour, Mr. Steinbrenner, is an idea whose time has not yet come. Perhaps it will come in due course. As the New York Times editorialized recently: "And however the Court rules in this case, fans accustomed to seeing players shift venue every season, had better get ready for the day when the whole team calls the whole country home.". But if and when it does come, it should be institutionalized by the League so that no home stadium contracts are violated.

The motion for a preliminary injunction is granted.

The opinions of Justice Michael Musmanno of the Pennsylvania Supreme Court are legendary among those who have attended law school in the last 40 years. His wit and hyperbole, especially in dissent, have delighted students as much as they may have irritated his colleagues. He seemed especially passionate about personal injury cases, as the next opinion will demonstrate.

Although golf is not considered a contact sport, there are hazards on the golf course besides sand and water. Because the dissenting opinion of Justice Musmanno lays out the facts of this case, we will not repeat the details of this unfortunate accident.

TAYLOR
v.
CHURCHILL VALLEY COUNTY CLUB

Supreme Court of Pennsylvania
April 24, 1967
228 A.2d 768, 425 Pa. 266

MUSMANNO, Justice (dissenting opinion)

Richard L. Taylor, 20 years of age, was employed as a caddy at the Churchill Valley Country Club in Allegheny County. His duties seemed innocuous enough. His job was to carry golf clubs, hand the proper one, more or less, to the player for whom he caddied, follow the flight of the balls lofted by the player and then search in bushes, ponds, sand, and other intended or unintended terrain for the released burrowing missile.

As harmless, tranquil, and serene as a golf course may seem to the casual observer, it can, on occasion, become as dangerous as a pocket in jungle battle in Vietnam. On July 5, 1959, while occupying a little bridge in the middle of the golf course, young Richard found himself amid a fusillade of fiercely driven golf balls. One of them hit him in the head with the impact of a bullet, fracturing his skull and rendering him hors de combat for a long period of time.

He brought suit against the Churchill Valley Country Club and was non-suited. He appealed, and this Court affirms the non-suit, stating that the plaintiff did not prove any negligence. Negligence is simply the failure to do what may be reasonably anticipated to be necessary to avoid injuring others. Did the defendant do all that was necessary, in the circumstances, to save the plaintiff from harm?

I am not a golf player, as is the writer of the Majority Opinion who, I am informed, is exceedingly skillful and graceful on the golf links. Thus, I do not know from personal experience what I lose in not having the fun of breathing the refreshing breezes of a country club, enjoying the intoxicating ecstasy of a 'double eagle,' and reveling in the salubrious effects of tramping over beautiful greenswards and by enchanting lakes. But, despite that absence of personal golf experience, I am sufficiently acquainted with the nature of the game, and am helplessly exposed to the enthusiastic garrulity which accompanies all meetings of golfers to such an extent that I must perforce realize that, mixed in with the felicity of the sport, goes considerable hazard apart from the over-indulging temptations of the 19th hole.

The young plaintiff in this case was compelled to take up a position at a bridge over a creek, there to observe the trajectory of golf spheroids being driven by players on the 17th hole. Possessed, like all normal human beings, with only one pair of eyes and thus being able to look only in one direction at a time, he failed to see the golfer, who, standing at a point about 45 yards in front of the 17th teeing ground, struck with such a fancy swing that the hard rubber pellet, traveling with the force of a cannon ball, but with the indecision of a temperamental bee gathering scattered honey, landed on the head of the caddy who had to be wary of other golfers also firing at and about the bridge with their hooking, slicing and dubbing shots.

Richard Taylor averred in his Complaint that Churchill Valley County Club was negligent in not having erected at this Fort Sumter of its golf course a screen which would receive and accommodate the erratic bombardment of the less artistic golfers. He stated also that the defendant was negligent in requiring him to take up a position in the direct line of fire of the 17th hole sharpshooters; further, that the defendant was negligent in the manner in which it laid out the golf course, namely, that the area separating the 15th and 17th fairways was so narrow that the caddies were unable to stay at a safe and sufficient distance from the mortar fire of the golfers driving desperately toward the refreshments of the 19th hole.

A professional golfer testified that there was no screen at the 17th hole, although one reared its protecting expanse at the 18th tee, this plainly demonstrating that the defendant was fully aware of the necessity for screens at the more dangerous sectors of the teeing and putting battlefront. He testified further that he had seen protective screens at other well-maintained golf links.

Thus, it seems to me that it became a clear question of fact for the jury to determine whether the defendant had maintained its golf grounds in accordance with the highest standards of safety generally recognized in this game, which has been declared the sport of kings and the ruination of many a conference because of the absence therefrom of expected bankers, lawyers and business men.

After being hit by a golf ball on the Churchill Valley Country Club golf course, the plaintiff came into Court and was hit again, this time with the mashie iron of a non-suit, even before he had a chance to drive on to the green of a jury deliberation. Being forced into the sand trap of a non-suit, the plaintiff was denied an opportunity to enter into the fairway of his litigation. I believe this is not a fair way to dispose of a suit in trespass.

Accordingly, I yell 'Fore!' and dissent.

This case takes us back to the days before free agency in major league sports. It was definitely a harbinger of things to come. The case involves the antitrust challenge of Curt Flood, an all-star player at the time, to major league baseball's "reserve clause," which bound a player to the same team year after year. The Supreme Court adhered to its 1922 decision in *Federal Baseball Club v. National League* that baseball is exempt from antitrust laws, and thus ruled against Flood.

It is because of Justice Blackmun's essay on the national pastime that the opinion was commended to us. However, it may also be of interest to note the difference in compensation of Mr. Flood in the 1960s and the multimillion-dollar salaries of ballplayers today—a result of the adoption of free agency.

(As an aside, in his first years on the high court, Justice Blackmun voted so frequently with his fellow Minnesotan, Chief Justice Warren Burger, that the two were sometimes referred to as the "Minnesota Twins.")

"The first page or so of Flood *clearly shows that the decision was written more as a tribute to our 'national pastime' than as a reasoned legal analysis of a hotly contested issue. The author of the opinion, Justice Blackmun, is a confirmed baseball fanatic. . . . Interestingly, the Justice had more trouble getting the other justices to agree on a list of baseball's greatest players than to vote in favor of his curious analysis.*

"[Flood] represents a wonderful slice of sports and legal Americana."

—Adjunct Professor, William Mitchell College of Law
and Hamline University School of Law

FLOOD

v.

KUHN, *et al.*

June 19, 1972

92 S.Ct. 2099, 407 U.S. 258, 32 L.Ed.2d 728

Mr. Justice BLACKMUN delivered the opinion of the Court.

* * *

The Game

It is a century and a quarter since the New York Nine defeated the Knickerbockers 23 to 1 on Hoboken's Elysian Fields June 19, 1846, with Alexander Jay Cartwright as the instigator and the umpire. The teams were amateur, but the contest marked a significant date in baseball's beginnings. That early game led ultimately to the development of professional baseball and its tightly organized structure.

The Cincinnati Red Stockings came into existence in 1869 upon an outpouring of local pride. With only one Cincinnatian on the payroll, this professional team traveled over 11,000 miles that summer, winning 56 games and tying one. Shortly thereafter, on St. Patrick's Day in 1871, the National Association of Professional Baseball Players was founded and the professional league was born.

The ensuing colorful days are well known. The ardent follower and the student of baseball know of General Abner Doubleday; the formation of the National League in 1876; Chicago's supremacy in the first year's competition under the leadership of Al Spalding and with Cap Anson at third base; the formation of the American Association and then of the Union Association in the 1880's; the introduction of Sunday baseball; interleague warfare with cut-rate admission prices and player raiding; the development of the reserve 'clause'; the emergence in 1885 of the Brotherhood of Professional Ball Players, and in 1890 of the Players League; the appearance of the American League, or 'junior circuit,' in 1901, rising from the minor Western Association; the first World Series in 1903, disruption in 1904, and the Series' resumption in 1905; the short-lived Federal League on the majors' scene during World War I years; the troublesome and discouraging episode of the 1919 Series; the home run ball; the shifting of franchises; the expansion of the leagues; the installation in 1965 of the major league draft of potential new players; and the formation of the Major League Baseball Players Association in 1966.

Then there are the many names, celebrated for one reason or another, that have sparked the diamond and its environs and that have provided tinder for recaptured thrills, for reminiscence and comparisons, and for conversation and anticipation in-season and off-season: Ty Cobb, Babe Ruth, Tris Speaker, Walter Johnson, Henry Chadwick, Eddie Collins, Lou Gehrig, Grover Cleveland Alexander, Rogers Hornsby, Harry Hooper, Goose Goslin, Jackie Robinson, Honus Wagner, Joe McCarthy, John McGraw, Deacon Phillippe, Rube Marquard, Christy Mathewson, Tommy Leach, Big Ed Delahanty, Davy Jones, Germany Schaefer, King Kelly, Big Dan Brouthers, Wahoo Sam Crawford, Wee Willie Keeler, Big Ed Walsh, Jimmy Austin, Fred Snodgrass, Satchel Paige, Hugh Jennings, Fred Merkle, Iron Man McGinnity, Three-Finger Brown, Harry and Stan Coveleski, Connie Mack, Al Bridwell, Red Ruffing, Amos Rusie, Cy Young, Smokey Joe Wood, Chief Meyers, Chief Bender, Bill Klem, Hans Lobert, Johnny Evers, Joe Tinker, Roy Campanella, Miller Huggins, Rube Bressler, Dazzy Vance, Edd Roush, Bill Wambsganss, Clark Griffith, Branch Rickey, Frank Chance, Cap Anson, Nap Lajoie, Sad Sam Jones, Bob O'Farrell, Lefty O'Doul, Bobby Veach, Willie Kamm, Heinie Groh, Lloyd and Paul Waner, Stuffy McInnis, Charles Comiskey, Roger Bresnahan, Bill Dickey, Zack Wheat, George Sisler, Charlie Gehringer, Eppa Rixey, Harry Heilmann, Fred Clarke, Dizzy Dean, Hank Greenberg, Pie Traynor, Rube Waddell, Bill Terry, Carl Hubbell, Old Hoss Radbourne, Moe Berg, Rabbit Maranville, Jimmie Foxx, Lefty Grove. The list seems endless.

And one recalls the appropriate reference to the 'World Serious,' attributed to Ring Lardner, Sr.; Ernest L. Thayer's 'Casey at the Bat';[4] the ring of 'Tinker to Evers to Chance';[5] and all the other happenings, habits, and superstitions about and around baseball that made it the 'national pastime' or, depending upon the point of view, 'the great American tragedy.'[6]

The Petitioner

The petitioner, Curtis Charles Flood, born in 1938, began his major league career in 1956 when he signed a contract with the Cincinnati Reds for a salary of $4,000 for the season. He had no attorney or agent to advise him on that occasion. He was traded to the St. Louis Cardinals before the 1958 season. Flood rose to fame as a center fielder with the Cardinals during

---

4. Millions have known and enjoyed baseball. One writer knowledgeable in the field of sports almost assumed that everyone did until, one day, he discovered otherwise:

'I knew a cove who'd never heard of Washington and Lee,
Of Caesar and Napoleon from the ancient jamboree,
But, bli'me, there are queerer things than anything like that,
For here's a cove who never heard of 'Casey at the Bat'!
. . .
'Ten million never heard of Keats, or Shelley, Burns or Poe;
But they know 'the air was shattered by the force of Casey's blow';
They never heard of Shakespeare, nor of Dickens, like as not,
But they know the somber drama from old Mudville's haunted lot.
'He never heard of Casey! Am I dreaming? Is it true?
Is fame but windblown ashes when the summer day is through?
Does greatness fade so quickly and is grandeur doomed to die
That bloomed in early morning, ere the dusk rides down the sky?'

'He Never Heard of Casey' Grantland Rice,
The Sportlight, New York Herald Tribune,
June 1, 1926, p. 23.

5. 'These are the saddest of possible words,
'Tinker to Evers to Chance.'
Trio of bear cubs, and fleeter than birds,
'Tinker to Evers to Chance.'
Ruthlessly pricking our gonfalon bubble,
Making a Giant hit into a double—
Words that are weighty with nothing but trouble:
'Tinker to Evers to Chance.''

Franklin Pierce Adams, Baseball's Sad Lexicon.

6. George Bernard Shaw, The Sporting News, May 27, 1943, p. 15, col. 4.

---

the years 1958–1969. In those 12 seasons he compiled a batting
average of .293. His best offensive season was 1967 when he
achieved .335. He was .301 or better in six of the 12 St. Louis
years. He participated in the 1964, 1967, and 1968 World Series. He played errorless ball in the field in 1966, and once
enjoyed 223 consecutive errorless games. Flood has received
seven Golden Glove Awards. He was co-captain of his team
from 1965–1969. He ranks among the 10 major league out-
fielders possessing the highest lifetime fielding averages.

Flood's St. Louis compensation for the years shown was:

1961	$13,500	(including a bonus for signing)
1962	$16,000	
1963	$17,500	
1964	$23,000	
1965	$35,000	
1966	$45,000	
1967	$50,000	
1968	$72,500	
1969	$90,000	

These figures do not include any so-called fringe benefits or
World Series shares.

But at the age of 31, in October 1969, Flood was traded
to the Philadelphia Phillies of the National League in a multi-
player transaction. He was not consulted about the trade. He
was informed by telephone and received formal notice only
after the deal had been consummated. In December he complained to the Commissioner of Baseball and asked that he
be made a free agent and be placed at liberty to strike his
own bargain with any other major league team. His request
was denied.

* * *

Flood declined to play for Philadelphia in 1970, despite
a $100,000 salary offer, and he sat out the year. After the season
was concluded, Philadelphia sold its rights to Flood to the
Washington Senators. Washington and the petitioner were able
to come to terms for 1971 at a salary of $110,000. Flood started
the season but, apparently because he was dissatisfied with his
performance, he left the Washington club on April 27, early
in the campaign. He has not played baseball since then.

The Present Litigation

Judge Cooper, in a detailed opinion, first denied a preliminary injunction, 309 F.Supp. 793 (S.D.N.Y.1970), observing on the way:

> 'Baseball has been the national pastime for over one hundred years and enjoys a unique place in our American heritage. Major league professional baseball is avidly followed by millions of fans, looked upon with fervor and pride and provides a special source of inspiration and competitive team spirit especially for the young.
>
> 'Baseball's status in the life of the nation is so pervasive that it would not strain credulity to say the Court can take judicial notice that baseball is everybody's business. To put it mildly and with restraint, it would be unfortunate indeed if a fine sport and profession, which brings surcease from daily travail and an escape from the ordinary to most inhabitants of this land, were to suffer in the least because of undue concentration by any one or any group on commercial and profit considerations. The game is on higher ground; it behooves every one to keep it there.' * * *

Trial to the court took place in May and June 1970. An extensive record was developed. In an ensuing opinion, 316 F.Supp. 271 (S.D.N.Y.1970), Judge Cooper first noted that:

> "Plaintiff's witnesses in the main concede that some form of reserve on players is a necessary element of the organization of baseball as a league sport, but contend that the present all-embracing system is needlessly restrictive and offer various alternatives which in their view might loosen the bonds without sacrifice to the game. . . .
>
> "Clearly the preponderance of credible proof does not favor elimination of the reserve clause. With the sole exception of plaintiff himself, it shows that even plaintiff's witnesses do not contend that it is wholly undesirable; in fact they regard substantial portions meritorious. . . ."

*   *   *

The Court has emphasized that since 1922 baseball, with full and continuing congressional awareness, has been allowed to develop and to expand unhindered by federal legislative action. Remedial legislation has been introduced repeatedly in Congress but none has ever been enacted. The Court, accordingly, has concluded that Congress as yet has had no intention to subject baseball's reserve system to the reach of the antitrust statutes. This, obviously, has been deemed to be something other than mere congressional silence and passivity.

*   *   *

We continue to be loath, 50 years after Federal Baseball and almost two decades after *Toolson*[v. New York Yankees, Inc., 346 U.S. 356, 74 S.Ct. 78 (1953)], to overturn those cases judicially when Congress, by its positive inaction, has allowed those decisions to stand for so long and, far beyond mere inference and implication, has clearly evinced a desire not to disapprove them legislatively.

*   *   *

We repeat for this case what was said in *Toolson*:

'Without re-examination of the underlying issues, the (judgment) below (is) affirmed on the authority of *Federal Baseball Club of Baltimore v. National League of Professional Baseball Clubs, supra,* so far as that decision determines that Congress had no intention of including the business of baseball within the scope of the federal antitrust laws.' 346 U.S., at 357, 74 S.Ct., at 79.

And what the Court said in *Federal Baseball* in 1922 and what it said in *Toolson* in 1953, we say again here in 1972: the remedy, if any is indicated, is for congressional, and not judicial, action.

The judgment of the Court of Appeals is affirmed.

Julia Patton, an Ohio homeowner, wasn't going to take it anymore. Julia was fed up with the proclivity of golfers to misplay their tee shots on the 15th hole at Westwood Country Club. Stray golf balls landed on her "demesne," broke her windows, and even struck her daughter in the leg. As a result, she sued the country club. On appeal, the Court of Appeals of Ohio gave Julia a golf lesson on why "the average golfer does not always hit the ball straight."

PATTON

v.

The WESTWOOD COUNTRY CLUB CO.

Court of Appeals of Ohio, Cuyahoga County
May 15, 1969
247 N.E.2d 761, 18 Ohio App.2d 137

CORRIGAN, Judge

*   *   *

The record reflects that The Westwood Country Club Company was formed as a private club in 1913. One year later the members constructed a nine-hole golf course on the club premises. Nine additional holes were added in 1924. * * *

In 1955, Julia Patton purchased a parcel of land immediately adjacent to the fairway of the Westwood Country Club's fifteenth hole. She built a home on this lot in 1956. Julia Patton's back yard abuts the Westwood Country Club premises on the south, or right side, of the fifteenth fairway approximately one hundred eighty yards east or off the tee. From the center of that portion of the fairway which is adjacent to the rear edge of Julia Patton's north property line there is a distance of about one hundred twenty-five feet. Other homes, located on both sides of Julia Patton's property, abut along the entire length of Westwood's three hundred seventy-five-yard fifteenth hole. None of these neighbors joined in this lawsuit, nor did any of them testify.

The gravamen of Julia Patton's complaint concerns the alleged proclivity of some golfers who play the fifteenth hole at Westwood to misplay their tee shots onto her demesne. According to testimony presented at the trial, stray golf balls from the Westwood premises have landed on Julia Patton's grounds on numerous occasions since 1956, and have broken windows on several occasions. In addition, a daughter of Julia Patton, one Angela, testified that she was struck on the leg by a golf ball in 1957, and a second daughter testified to several near misses.

The bill of exceptions reveals that Julia Patton knew of the location of Westwood Country Club when the purchased her lot in 1955 and when she built her home and moved into it during Easter week 1956. And it further shows that her deceased husband and her sons have played golf in the past, and that one daughter took golf lessons. Her testimony reflects that in July 1957, when Julia Patton was in her yard, a golf ball 'went right over my head, and then it hit the side of my house, and then landed at my foot.' The condition Julia Patton complains of has really existed since she built the house and moved into it, according to the record. Her daughter Angela said that golf balls had landed on the Julia Patton property as early as 1956, and she also testified, in reply to a question as to whether the situation has remained constant or has worsened, that the situation has remained constant during the golf season.

It is generally known that the average golfer does not always hit the ball straight. One less than the Mosaic decalogue, the adjurations enjoined by acroamatic golf professionals, upon the millions of votaries of the royal and ancient sport, in interpreting the esoteric principles of the golf swing are: don't slice, hook, push, pull, sky, sclaff, smother, top or shank.

The literature of the sport fills countless library shelves, on sub-topics ranging from proper mental attitudes by some of the game's more recondite gurus to tracts on putting styles perfected during the winter season before glowing fireplaces on deeppiled Royal Kermanshah rugs by preserved old codgers.

Julia Patton's jeremiad over Westwood's golfers may be related chiefly to one of those faults forbidden to the initiated of the links, namely, that of slicing by right handers. The root of this evil is the propensity to hit the ball with a club face that is open at impact, usually from the outside in. Some few confirmed slicers allow for it by aiming all shots to the left, and the resulting curve to the right lands the ball at the desired spot in the fairway. One nationally known amateur, Judge Don C. Miller, of Notre Dame's famed 'Four Horsemen,' employs such an educated slice regularly. It is a matter of common knowledge that he can curl a drive around a *Thujopsis dolobrata* one hundred and fifty yards out and split the fairway ahead of it. This is one of his things of life. An uneducated slice apparently is a thing of life for some Westwood members or guests.

There seem to be just three other forbidden shot possibilities that could reach Julia Patton's estate from Westwood's fifteenth tee. The first of these is the push which occurs when the right-handed player hits the ball with an open face while the club is still moving from inside out. It is generally a straight ball that goes to the right of the target. Since the center of the fifteenth fairway is one hundred and twenty-five feet from the northern boundary of the Patton property, such a push on the part of Westwood's fine players would probably be a rarity landing on the Patton plot.

The two other *verboten* hits that might reach our complainant's private preserve would necessarily be directed thereto by left-handed golfers. In order of importance, they are hooks and pulls. Hooking is hitting with a closed face, and this really is a venial golf sin. It is considered the good player's error. The hook for the southpaw curves to the right, and in the pull the left-handed player hits the ball straight to the right of the target. The record before us does not demonstrate how many left-handed golfers play Westwood in a season.

Upon consideration of the facts, the trial judge found in favor of Westwood Country Club, denying plaintiff's plea for temporary and permanent injunctions.

Plaintiff, appellant herein, raises three assignments of error as follows:

(1) The judgment is contrary to law.

(2) The judgment is against the weight of the evidence.

(3) Other errors occurring at trial.

Instead of treating each assignment of error separately, plaintiff in her brief establishes two central issues which she then discusses. These issues are: (1) whether hitting golf balls onto plaintiff's property constitutes a private nuisance; and, if so, (2) whether plaintiff is entitled to injunctive relief from such nuisance.

Under a broad definition of the term 'nuisance,' the activity of defendant's erring golfers could be included. In Black's Law Dictionary (4th Ed., 1951), nuisance is defined as: 'That which annoys and disturbs one in possession of his property, rendering its ordinary use or occupation physically uncomfortable to him.' Also, there is authority to the effect that golf balls driven onto adjoining premises can be considered a nuisance.

Assuming for the moment that hitting golf balls onto plaintiff's premises comes within the definition of a private nuisance, the next consideration is whether the complained of activity should be enjoined under the circumstances of this case. The trial court relied heavily on the well-known defense that plaintiff 'came to the nuisance.' * * * Plaintiff contends that she was not aware of the situation initially due to the fact that the golf ball problem has grown gradually worse over the years. There is some evidence in the record, contributed by plaintiff and her daughters, to support this contention. There is considerable evidence, from plaintiff's witnesses and others, that the condition has remained stable. This latter body of evidence speaks eloquently of the quality of play of Westwood's membership and, in turn, of the quality of instruction of the professional staff. Thus, the trial judge, who was in a position to hear the witnesses and evaluate their testimony, cannot be said to have found against the manifest weight of the evidence when he determined that the golf ball hazard had not increased substantially between the years 1956 and 1967.

In comparing the equities of the situation, it should be noted that no one on the Patton premises has been struck by a golf ball since 1957. Also, in 1963 Westwood Country Club did attempt to appease plaintiff by changing the sprinkling system on the fifteenth fairway, by moving the fairway farther away from the Patton premises, and by planting twenty pine trees opposite plaintiff's lot. The cost of these changes was approximately $2,000. Finally, the trial court had for consideration the testimony of defendant's golf expert that the changes to the fifteenth hole proposed by plaintiff's expert would cost approximately $25,000; would ruin the character of the hole; and would not decrease the golf hazard to neighboring homeowners. Therefore, there was strong evidence in the record in support of the trial court's decision.

*   *   *

For the reasons stated the judgment of the Common Pleas Court is affirmed in favor of The Westwood Country Club and against Julia Patton.

Ever since Jackie Robinson signed with the Brooklyn Dodgers, sports and social issues have been intertwined. The next two cases in this chapter reflect that development. The first case deals with the rights of student-athletes at a state university to express their opinion during a university-sponsored event. The second case deals with the rights of a sports organization to determine who may and may not participate in an open competition for women.

WILLIAMS, *et al.*
v.
EATON, *et al.*

United States Court of Appeals
Tenth Circuit
Oct. 31, 1972
468 F.2d 1079

A few days prior to a football game between the University of Wyoming and Brigham Young University, one of the fourteen black players on the Wyoming team informed the head coach that the black players intended to wear armbands during the game in protest of the religious beliefs of the Mormon Church, which they believed to be racially discriminatory. The coach responded by ordering that no armbands were to be worn during the game. One day prior to the game, all fourteen black players approached the head coach wearing black armbands and insisted that they be allowed to wear them during the football game. After some discussion, the coach dismissed those players from the team.

The student-athletes then brought this civil rights action against the state of Wyoming , the president of the University of Wyoming, its board of trustees, the head coach of the football team and the athletic director. The case was dismissed by the trial court, and this appeal followed.

HOLLOWAY, Circuit Judge.

* * *

We believe the controlling issues on this appeal are as follows:

(1) whether findings of fact 14 and 15 made by the trial court, dealing with the purpose of the athletes in seeking to wear the armbands and the position they took thereon, are clearly erroneous; (2) whether the determination by the Board of Trustees of the University refusing to permit the athletes to wear the armbands on the field during the game was a reasonable and lawful ruling or regulation under the principles of *Tinker v. Des Moines Independent School District*, 393 U.S. 503, 89 S.Ct. 733, 21 L.Ed.2d 731, and similar cases.

We do not treat certain additional propositions forcefully argued for the athletes on this appeal. Arguments are made that the football coaching rule against participation generally by the athletes in demonstrations was invalid. However, we feel that questions concerning the rule need not be decided. The original dismissal of the athletes by Coach Eaton for violation of the rule was not the end of the matter. Later the controversy was considered by the Trustees and President Carlson at a conference with the athletes and the athletic officials. It was found by the trial court that the decision of the Trustees to sustain the dismissal of the athletes was made after this conference during which the athletes insisted on the right to wear the armbands during the game. And it was further found that the Trustees' decision was made on the ground that permitting the wearing of the armbands would be in violation of the constitutional mandate requiring complete neutrality on religion. Therefore our decision focuses on the lawfulness of the Trustees' action.

Findings 14 and 15 and the purpose
of the athletes in seeking to wear the armbands

The plaintiffs challenge findings 14 and 15 of the trial court, arguing that they are clearly erroneous under the test of *United States v. United States Gypsum Co.*, 333 U.S. 364, 395, 68 S.Ct. 525, 92 L.Ed. 746.[3]

*   *   *

We are satisfied that the record supports the challenged findings and that they are not clearly erroneous.

First Amendment principles under
Tinker v. Des Moines Independent School District

Both plaintiffs and defendants rely on the principles stated in the *Tinker* case and similar decisions. The plaintiffs argue that they come within its bounds of freedom of expression recognized therein as applying to students in different places, including the playing field. On the other hand the defendants say that their actions were within the exceptions stated in the opinion. We feel the controlling guidelines from the *Tinker* case are the following:

> "A student's rights, therefore, do not embrace merely the classroom hours. When he is in the cafeteria, or on the playing field, or on the campus during the authorized hours, he may express his opinion, even on controversial subjects like the conflict in Vietnam, if he does so without 'materially and substantially interfer[ing] with the requirements of appropriate discipline in the operation of the school' and without colliding with the rights of others. *   *   * But conduct by the student, in class or out of it, which for any reason—whether it stems from time, place, or type of behavior—materially

3. Findings of fact 14 and 15 were as follows: "14. [T]here is no merit in the contention raised by the Plaintiffs in their complaint filed herein that one of the purposes of the black armband display was that of protesting against the alleged cheap shots and name-calling charged to members of the Brigham Young University football team; on the contrary, the Court finds that such allegation is without merit and that the sole and only purpose in the armband display was that of protesting against alleged religious beliefs of the Church of Jesus Christ of Latter-Day Saints. *   *   *"15. That, taking all of the evidence and facts adduced by the parties into consideration, the Court finds that each of the Plaintiffs refused to play football as a member of the University of Wyoming football team unless and until the Defendant, Lloyd Eaton, was removed from his position as Head Football Coach of the Universty of Wyoming."

disrupts class work or involves substantial disorder or invasion of the rights of others is, of course, not immunized by the constitutional guarantee of freedom of speech. * * *"

* * *

". . . The Constitution says that Congress (and the States) may not abridge the right to free speech. This provision means what it says. We properly read it to permit reasonable regulation of speech-connected activities in carefully restricted circumstances. But we do not confine the permissible exercise of First Amendment rights to a telephone booth or the four corners of a pamphlet, or to supervised and ordained discussion in a school classroom." [citations omitted]

393 U.S. at 512, 513, 89 S.Ct. at 740.

The trial court concluded that had the defendants, as governing officials of the University of Wyoming, permitted display of the armbands, their actions would have been violative of the First Amendment establishment clause and its requirement of neutrality on expressions relating to religion, citing *School District of Abington v. Schempp,* 374 U.S. 203, 83 S.Ct. 1560, 10 L.Ed.2d 844, and similar cases. The Court further grounded its conclusions on the provisions of the Wyoming Constitution guaranteeing the free exercise and enjoyment of religion and worship without discrimination or preference.

". . . The government is neutral, and, while protecting all [religious opinions and sects], it prefers none, and it disparages none." *Id.* at 215, 83 S.Ct. at 1567. Thus stemming from state and federal law there is strong support for a policy restricting hostile expressions against religious beliefs of others by representatives of a state or its agencies. We feel that the Trustees' decision was a proper means of respecting the rights of others in their beliefs, in accordance with this policy of religious neutrality.

The plaintiffs vigorously deny that there would have been state action or a violation of the First Amendment principles on religion by permitting the armband display. Without deciding whether approval of the armband display would have involved state action or a violation of the religion clauses, we are persuaded that the Trustees' decision was lawful within the limitations of the *Tinker* case itself. Their decision protected against invasion of the rights of others by avoiding a hostile expression to them by some members of the University team. It was in furtherance of the policy of religious neutrality by the State. It denied only the request for the armband display by some members of the team, on the field and during the game. In these limited circumstances we conclude that the Trustees' decision was in conformity with the *Tinker* case and did not violate the First Amendment right of expression of the plaintiffs.

We do not base our holding on the presence of any violence or disruption. There was no showing or finding to that effect and the trial court's conclusions of law state that the denial of the right to wear the armbands during the game ". . . was not predicated upon the likelihood of disruption, although such a demonstration might have tended to create disruption." Instead the trial court referred only to the mandate of complete neutrality in religion and religious matters as the basis for the court's ruling.

We hold that the trial court's findings and this record sustain the Trustees' decision as lawful, made for the reasons found by the trial court, as a reasonable regulation of expression under the limited circumstances involved, in accord with the principles of the *Tinker* case on free speech.

Affirmed.

In the late 1970s, the controversial case involving Dr. Renee Richards touched upon emotional issues related to sexuality, gender and discrimination. The question before the court was whether the United States Tennis Association could, under New York law, require a professional tennis player who had undergone a sex reassignment operation to take a sex-determination test. While the legal and moral implications of the controversy are not ignored, much of the court's discussion focuses on the medical question of whether Dr. Richards is a female.

RICHARDS

v.

UNITED STATES TENNIS ASSOCIATION, *et al.*

Supreme Court of New York
Aug. 16, 1977
400 N.Y.S.2d 267, 93 Misc.2d 713

ALFRED M. ASCIONE, Justice.

Plaintiff, Dr. Renee Richards, nee Richard H. Raskind, an opthalmologist physician licensed to practice in the State of New York, underwent a sex reassignment operation about two years ago, at the age of 41, "at which time", Dr. Richards avers, "for all intents and purposes, I became a female, psychologically, socially and physically, as has been attested to by my doctors." Dr. Richards says that, "I underwent this operation after many years of being a transsexual, a woman trapped inside the body of a man."

As Dr. Richard H. Raskind, plaintiff was an accomplished male tennis player, and in 1974 ranked third in the East and thirteenth nationally in the men's 35–and-over tennis. Since the sex reassignment operation in 1975, plaintiff has entered nine women's tennis tournaments and has won two tournaments and finished as runner-up in three. Most recently, Dr. Richards, now 43 years of age, reached the finals of the

Women's singles at the Mutual Benefit Life Open played on August 7, 1977 at the Orange Town Tennis Club in South Orange, New Jersey.

Claiming a violation of the New York State Human Rights Law (Section 297(9) of the New York State Executive Law) and the 14th Amendment to the U. S. Constitution, Plaintiff now seeks a preliminary injunction against the defendants, the United States Tennis Association (USTA), United States Open Committee (USOC) and the Women's Tennis Association (WTA) "so that I shall be allowed to qualify and/or participate in the United States Open Tennis Tournament, as a woman in the Women's Division." The U.S. Open, the USTA's National Championships, is to begin on August 25, 1977, at the West Side Tennis Club, Forest Hills, New York.

Dr. Richards says that she is prevented from qualifying and/or participating in the U.S. Open as a woman in the Women's Division since defendants require that she take a sex-chromatin test (aka the Barr body test) to determine whether she is a female, "which test," she says, "is recognized to be insufficient, grossly unfair, inaccurate, faulty and inequitable by the medical community in the United States for purposes of excluding individuals from sports events on the basis of gender." Plaintiff argues that the criteria for such a test is arbitrary and capricious and does not have a rational basis.

Furthermore, plaintiff claims that she is prevented from qualifying and/or participating in the U.S. Open due to defendant Women's Tennis Association's failure to rank plaintiff as a woman tennis professional, a necessary prerequisite for qualification and participation in the U.S. Open.

The Barr body test or sex-chromatin test, determines the presence of a second x chromosome in the normal female; a male has a y chromosome instead, as set forth in detail below.

The sex-chromatin test was first employed by the International Olympic Committee in connection with the 1968 Olympics. The USTA first required a sex determination test for women in connection with the 1976 U.S. Open, after plaintiff applied to play in women's singles in the Open in July 1976. Plaintiff demanded that USTA waive the test requirement, which request was rejected by the USTA. However, apparently, plaintiff failed to appear at a qualifying site and, in effect, withdrew her application, rendering academic the question of the test for 1976.

The record is clear that USTA's and USOC's decision to require a sex-determination test for the 1976 U.S. Open, the National Championships, was a direct result of plaintiffs application to the 1976 U.S. Open, and plaintiff's frank presentation of her medical situation in a personal letter to the chairman of the U.S. Open, Mike Blanchard.

Apparently, until August 1976, there had been no sex determination test in the 95–year history of the USTA National Championships, other than a simple phenotype test (observation of primary and secondary sexual characteristics). It also seems that the USTA has not required the sex-chromatin test for sanctioned tournaments other than the U.S. Open. The USTA permits each Tournament Committee to make its own determination as to whether to use the chromatin test.

Eugene Scott, Tournament Chairman, of the Mutual Benefit Life Open held in South Orange, New Jersey, in which Dr. Richards played and reached the finals, avers in an affidavit submitted in support of plaintiff's application:

"I have invited Dr. Renee Richards to play in my tournament and, in fact, she has done so. I extended the invitation to Dr. Richards as a woman because as a tennis tournament chairman based on the information afforded to me, I recognize her as a woman.

I rejected reliance solely on the Barr body test and instead chose to rely on the Phenotype test which concerns itself with the observation of primary and secondary sexual characteristics . . ."

According to defendants, their primary concern in instituting the chromatin test is that of insuring fairness. They claim that there is a competitive advantage for a male who has undergone "sex-change" surgery as a result of physical training and development as a male. As stated by George W. Gowen for defendant USTA:

"We have reason to believe that there are as many as 10,000 transsexuals in the United States and many more female impersonators or imposters. The total number of such persons throughout the world is not known. Because of the millions of dollars of prize money available to competitors, because of nationalistic desires to excel in athletics, and because of world-wide experiments, especially in the iron curtain countries, to produce athletic stars by means undreamed of a few years ago, the USTA has been especially sensitive to its obligation to assure fairness of competition among the athletes competing in the U.S. Open, the leading international tennis tournament in the United States. The USTA believes that the Olympic type sex determination procedures, are a reasonable way to assure fairness and equality of competition when dealing with numerous competitors from around the world. The USTA believes the question at issue transcends the factual background or medical history of one applicant."

The defendants have submitted the affidavit of Dr. Daniel Federman, professor and chairman of the Department of Medicine, Stanford University School of Medicine, in support of the applicability of the Barr body test for the determination of sexual identity. Since Dr. Federman conducted no physical examination of plaintiff and he relied solely on a review of the moving papers and supporting affidavits submitted by Dr. Richards, his affidavit is therefore limited in its probative value to a general consideration of the applicability of the Barr test. It is Dr. Federman's opinion that the Barr body test reliably and inexpensively ($15.00) determines the presence of a second x chromosome in the "normal female". He says:

"The cells of a normal female contain 22 pairs of chromosomes which are identical to those of a normal male. In addition, there is a pair of sex chromosomes. In the female, there are two like structures, two x-chromosomes. In the male, the sex chromosomes are unlike a larger x and a smaller y."

Dr. Federman says that the y chromosome is related to physical characteristics in the normal male that affect an individual's competitive athletic ability. The y chromosome controls the development of the testes, the source of the larger amounts of androgen (the male sex hormone) produced by the male relative to the female:

> "At puberty, the presence in the male of the y chromosome plus the much higher ratio of androgens to estrogens (the female sex hormone) results, on the average, in greater height, different body proportions, and a higher muscle mass than in the female. In the adult male beyond puberty, neither the removal of the testes by sex reassignment surgery, nor any subsequent treatment with estrogen can affect the individuals achieved height or skeletal structure. Removal of the testes plus ingestion of estrogens can reduce male strength, but any such effect is partial and depends upon continued ingestion of estrogen to be sustained."

*   *   *

The Barr body test is generally administered by having the individual rinse the mouth and obtaining a sample of cells by scraping the inner lining of the cheek. The sample is then transferred to a slide. Dye is applied and the smear is examined under a microscope. Dr. Federman describes the procedure:

> "The examiner typically counts 100 or 200 cells and records the percentage of the cells which show an oval concentration of dye next to the surrounding border of the nucleus of the cell. This heavy concentration of dye reveals the presence of a second x-chromosome."

However, Dr. Federman points out, the Barr body test does not determine the presence or absence of a y chromosome. Individuals with chromosomal defects may not therefore be definitively classified by the Barr body test alone. The Karyotype test, involving blood sampling and culture, will, though it is more expensive ($150.00–$300.00) and takes at least one week for the test results.

The Women's Tennis Association (WTA) has submitted an affidavit in opposition from Jerry Diamond, its executive director. Mr. Diamond, avers that the WTA maintains a computerized system to rank both professional and amateur women tennis players."

> "Weighted results from all WTA approved events are entered into the system in order to determine the rank of each woman player. The WTA approved tournament administer the Barr body test and that only those individuals who pass the Barr body test be allowed to participate in the tournament. The WTA will not knowingly enter into its ranking system the results of a tournament which has not utilized the Barr body test as a condition for participation in the tournament or which admits a participant who has failed the test."

Also submitted in opposition are affidavits of women's professional tennis players Francoise Durr, Janet Newberry and Kristien K. Shaw, each stating that based on her experience, "the taller a player is the greater advantage the player has . . . similarly, the stronger a player is, the greater advantage the player has, assuming like ability."

In another affidavit, Vicki Berner, Director of Women's Tennis for the USTA, formerly the number one ranked women's singles player from Canada, and then Tour Director in charge of players, asserts that she has been unable to find a record of any woman player over age 40 who has had such a successful competitive record as plaintiff, a record unparalleled in the history of women's professional tennis.

The record shows that on June 27, and July 1, 1977, Dr. Richards went to the Institute of Sports Medicine and Athletic Trauma at Lenox Hill Hospital, selected by defendants USTA and USOC to conduct the sex determination tests for the 1977 U.S. Open. The Barr test was administered but "the results . . . are ambiguous" * * *

It does not appear that plaintiff returned for further testing and, accordingly, defendants have not qualified plaintiff to play in the U.S. Open.

What is a transsexual? A transsexual is an individual anatomically of one sex who firmly believes he belongs to the other sex. This belief is so strong that the transsexual is obsessed with the desire to have his body, appearance and social status altered to conform to that of his "rightful" gender. They are not homosexual. They consider themselves to be members of the opposite sex cursed with the wrong sexual apparatus. They desire the removal of this apparatus and further surgical assistance in order that they may enter into normal heterosexual relationships. On the contrary, a homosexual enjoys and uses his genitalia with members of his own anatomical sex. Medical Science has not found any organic cause or cure (other than sex reassignment surgery and hormone therapy) for transsexualism, nor has psychotherapy been successful in altering the transsexual's identification with the other sex or his desire for surgical change.

*   *   *

Dr. Granato [plaintiff's surgeon] states, that prior to and after the sex reassignment operation, Dr. Richards underwent endocrinological testing and administration of female hormones so as to change Dr. Richards' endocrinological hormonal balance to that of a woman. The removal of the testes, the main source of androgen (male hormones), decreases tremendously the male hormones in the blood and results in a decreased muscular mass, the structure of the muscle/fat ratio of the male is changed to a feminine type, together with the development of the breasts.

Dr. Granato sees no unfair advantage for Dr. Richards "when competing against other women. Her muscle development, weight, height and physique fit within the female norm." (Dr. Richards is 6'2 tall and weighs 147 lbs.) Dr. Granato's professional conclusion is that, except for reproduction, Dr. Richards should be considered a woman, classified as a female and allowed to compete as such.

Dr. Leo Wollman, states that he has treated over 1700 transsexual patients including plaintiff. It is his view that Dr. Richards should be considered a female. The Barr test, would classify Dr. Richards as a male and despite the fact that the chromosomes may appear to be that of a man, if she has the external genital appearance, the internal organ appearance, gonadal identity, endocrinological makeup and psychological and social development of a female, she would be considered a female by any reasonable test of sexuality.

*   *   *

Dr. Money's professional conclusion, based on 26 years of professional experience as a psychoendocrinologist, is that a person such as Dr. Renee Richards should be classified as female and for anyone in the medical or legal field to find otherwise is completely unjustified. Dr. Money also believes that Dr. Richards will have no unfair advantage when competing against other women. He says that her muscle development, weight, height and physique fit within the female norm.

Measured by all the factors, including chromosomal structure, Dr. Money asserts that Dr. Richards should be classified as female and that would be a widely held conclusion of medicine today.

Finally, plaintiff submits the affidavit of women's tennis professional star Billie Jean King, holder of hundreds of titles including Wimbledon and the U.S. Open, and who defeated male tennis professional Bobby Riggs on national television, in support of plaintiff's application. Billie Jean King states that she and Dr. Richards were doubles teammates in one tournament and that she participated in two tournaments in which Dr. Richards played. It is Billie Jean King's judgment that, "she (plaintiff) does not enjoy physical superiority or strength so as to have an advantage over women competitors in the sport of tennis."

In this court's view, the requirement of defendants that this plaintiff pass the Barr body test in order to be eligible to participate in the women's singles of the U.S. Open is grossly unfair, discriminatory and inequitable, and violative of her rights under the Human Rights Law of this state (Executive Law, Article 15, Sections 290, et seq.). It seems clear that defendants knowingly instituted this test for the sole purpose of preventing plaintiff from participating in the tournament. The only justification for using a sex determination test in athletic competition is to prevent fraud, i.e., men masquerading as women, competing against women.

This court rejects any such suggestion as applied to plaintiff. This court is totally convinced that there are very few biological males, who are accomplished tennis players, who are also either preoperative or post-operative transsexuals.

When an individual such as plaintiff, a successful physician, a husband and father, finds it necessary for his own mental sanity to undergo a sex reassignment, the unfounded fears and misconceptions of defendants must give way to the overwhelming medical evidence that this person is now female.

This court is not striking down the Barr body test, as it appears to be a recognized and acceptable tool for determining sex. However, it is not and should not be the sole criterion, where as here, the circumstances warrant consideration of other factors.

Section 290, subd. 3, of the Executive Law of this State, declares that the State has the responsibility to act to assure that every individual within this State is afforded an equal opportunity to enjoy a full and productive life and that the failure to provide such equal opportunity, whether because of discrimination, prejudice, intolerance or inadequate education, training, housing or health care not only threatens the rights and proper privileges of its inhabitants but menaces the institutions and foundation of a free democratic state and threatens the peace, order, health, safety and general welfare of the state and its inhabitants.

Section 296 declares that it shall be an unlawful discriminatory practice for an employee because of age, race, creed, color, national origin, sex or disability, or marital status of any individual to refuse to hire or employ or to bar or to discharge from employment such individual or to discriminate against such individual in compensation or in terms, conditions or privileges of employment.

As indicated, this court finds defendants and each of them in violation of plaintiff's rights under the Human Rights Law and, accordingly, pursuant to section 297, subd. 9 thereof, plaintiff's application for a preliminary injunction is granted in all respects.

Chapter 6

Our Creative Judiciary

Words are the basic tools of the law. From legislators who write the law, to attorneys who argue the law and judges who interpret the law, a vast vocabulary is used to communicate within the legal system. In each instance, it is critical that words be chosen carefully when preparing legal documents in order to convey to others precisely what is intended. For judges authoring an opinion, this can be extremely challenging; they are required to interpret complex laws as they apply to a variety of unique circumstances. But in the hands of a wordsmith, the English language can be molded into marvelous prose that can be appreciated by lawyers and non-lawyers alike.

In this chapter we present some of the best creative writing by the courts. These judicial craftspersons have used their knowledge of the language to create powerful arguments, vivid imagery, delightful whimsy and shameless puns.

"During the early seventies, Dade County, Florida, passed an ordinance designed to ban phosphates and other pollutants from washing products sold within the county. Of course, it was attacked by every major manufacturer of such products.

"At the time, I was serving as a U.S. District Judge on that court and the case was assigned to me. After many hearings and much study, I decided that under the Home Rule Amendments to the Florida Constitution, Dade County had very broad authority in the area and that the federal statutes dealing with labeling, etc. would not prevent local authorities from imposing stricter standards designed to protect the waters from pollution. The ruling was not without controversy and was immediately appealed.

"While the case was on appeal and during the period the ordinance was in effect, I returned home one Saturday after a round of golf and met my wife in the driveway. She inquired as to my availability to watch over our three young children for the afternoon. Somewhat surprised by her request, I responded in the affirmative; and, unfortunately also asked her where she was going. Her reply was forceful and direct. 'Since your brilliant ruling in the soap case, Ft. Lauderdale (50 miles from our home) is the closest place I can go to buy Tide to wash your dirty clothes,' she responded. She was off in a cloud of dust.

"A few months later the United States Court of Appeals for the old Fifth Circuit issued its ruling. [My wife's] position prevailed; I was reversed. Judge John Brown's special concurrence is my favorite judicial opinion."

—Judge, United State Court of Appeals

"I have a special reason for loving such opinion as Judge Brown was a close, personal friend of mine and I have a hard time determining which is greater, his brilliance as a jurist or his magnificent sense of humor. Often times, we can tell more about a great man by some aside from his main vocation. I can just see the twinkle in his eye when he penned that humorous concurring opinion."

—Judge, United States District Court

CHEMICAL SPECIALTIES MANUFACTURERS ASSOCIATION, INC.

v.

CLARK, *et al.*

United States Court of Appeals
Fifth Circuit
July 12, 1973
482 F.2d 325

PER CURIAM:

On March 30, 1971, the Board of County Commissioners of Dade County, Florida adopted an ordinance amending its Municipal Code by adding Section 24–44. That ordinance, as now modified, required that every product within the definition of detergent or synthetic detergent must bear a label showing the ingredients of the product, listed in descending order of their presence by weight. CSMA consists of manufacturers and marketers of products falling within the scope of the ordinance. Their basic premise is that Congress preempted this field of regulation through the 1966 Amendments to the Federal Hazardous Substances Act (FHSA), 15 U.S.C.A. § 1261. Thus, they seek a declaratory judgment that the Dade County ordinance is invalid.

*   *   *

In its analysis, the court recognized that although this was an area usually subject to state regulation, federal law is supreme whenever there is a conflict between federal and state law. It acknowledged that state regulations often supplement federal law and thereby extend or increase the degree of regulation. In this case, however, Congress had attached a preemption clause to the 1966 amendment that prohibited any further state or local government regulation. As a result, the court held that the Dade County ordinance requiring the warning label must yield to the federal law.

* * *

JOHN R. BROWN, Chief Judge (concurring):

As soap, now displaced by latter day detergents is the grist of Madison Avenue, I add these few comments in the style of that street to indicate my full agreement with the opinion of the Court and to keep the legal waters clear and phosphate-free.

As *Proctor* of this dispute between the representative of many manufacturers of household detergents and the Board of Commissioners of Metropolitan Dade County, Florida, who have promulgated regulations which seek to control the labeling of such products sold within their jurisdiction (largely to discourage use which pollutes their waters), the Court holds that Congress has specifically preempted regulatory action by Dade County. Clearly, the decision represents a *Gamble* since we risk a *Cascade* of criticism from an increasing *Tide* of ecology-minded citizens. Yet, a contrary decision would most likely have precipitated a *Niagara* of complaints from an industry which justifiably seeks uniformity in the laws with which it must comply. Inspired by the legendary valor of *Ajax*, who withstood Hector's lance, we have *Boldly* chosen the course of uniformity in reversing the lower Court's decision upholding Dade County's local labeling laws. And, having done so, we are *Cheered* by the thought that striking down the regulation by the local jurisdiction does not create a void which is detrimental to consumers, but rather merely acknowledges that federal legislation has preempted this field with adequate labeling rules.

Congress, of course, has the *Cold Power* to preempt. Of the three situations discussed by the Court, the first (direct conflict) is easy, for it is *Crystal Clear* that the state law must yield. The third, in which the ordinance may supplement the federal law and thereby extend or increase the degree of regulation, is more troublesome. For where Congress has chosen to fashion a regulatory scheme that is only the *Head and Shoulders*, but has not opted to regulate every aspect of the area, the states have implied power to flesh out the body. It is where Congress fails to clearly signify, with an appropriate preemption clause, its intent to fully occupy the area regulated that the problem arises. With some *Joy*, the Court finds there is such a clause.

Concerning the precautionary labeling aspect, this is *SOS* to consumers. If we *Dash* to the heart of the question, it is apparent, as the Court points out, that the 1966 Amendments to FHSA indicate an explicit congressional purpose to preempt state regulation of the labeling of these substances. Undoubtedly, this unequivocal congressional *Salvo* was directed at such already existing regulations as those of the Fire Department of New York City relating to pressurized containers. Indeed, Congress intended to wield its *Arm and Hammer* to *Wisk* away such local regulations and further, to preclude the growing *Trend* toward this proliferation of individual community supervision. Its purpose was at least two-fold: (i) to put day-to-day responsibility in the hands of local government, but (ii) at the same time to impose detailed identical standards to eliminate confusion or overlapping.

With this clear expression of congressional intent to create some form of preemption, the only thing remaining was whether the meaning of the term "precautionary labeling" is sufficiently broad to embrace the words of the Dade County ordinance, *Vel* non. In making this determination, the Court is furnished with a *Lever* by our *Brothers* of the Second Circuit. And so we hold. This is all that need be said. It is as plain as *Mr. Clean* the proper *Action* is that the Dade County Ordinance must be superseded, as *All* comes out in the wash.

Unless you are planning on participating in Spain's annual "running of the bulls," the thought of being charged by a large, horned, adult male bovine is not only extremely frightening, but also can be physically disabling. In the following case, Mrs. Bosley had the grave misfortune of having her neighbor's 1,500–pound Hereford bull charge after her, and the good fortune of having her loyal cattle dog save the day.

BOSLEY

v.

ANDREWS

Supreme Court of Pennsylvania
June 4, 1958
142 A.2d 263, 393 Pa. 161

Defendant's cattle strayed onto plaintiffs' farm and injured their crops, for which the jury gave plaintiffs a verdict of $179.99. Mrs. Mary Louise Bosley, the wife-plaintiff, sought to recover damages for a heart disability that resulted from her fright and shock upon being chased by a Hereford bull owned by the defendant. However, the bull did not strike or touch the plaintiff, and she suffered no physical injury. Thus, the Superior Court sustained the entry of a nonsuit and the Supreme Court affirmed.

The following is the articulate dissent of Justice Musmanno, which lays out the facts with a touch of humor, yet demonstrates his compassion for the plaintiff's injuries. It may be of interest to note that in 1970, the Supreme Court of Pennsylvania overruled the court's decision, thus siding with Justice Musmanno.

MUSMANNO, Justice (dissenting).

Like those human beings who believe that fame and fortune always lie in some land distant from their own, the cows of the Dale Andrews farm in West Salem, Mercer County, were not satisfied to browse and chew their cuds in their own pasture. They were certain that in the fields across the highways which bordered their owner's domain, the grass was greener, the earth fresher, the trees shadier, and the skies above bluer. Thus from time to time they would leave their own preserves and invade the Bosley farm on the other side of the road where, with the spirit of bovine buccaneers, they devoured their neighbor's corn and wheat, destroyed his vegetable gardens, knocked over young peach trees, damaged the apple orchard, mangled berry bushes, and eventually departed, leaving behind them a wide swath of ruin destruction. They sometimes went away of their own accord, but frequently they had to be driven back to their home territory by the Bosleys.

On the morning of April 10, 1950, at about 9 o'clock, they ambled over to the Bosley farm to breakfast in the fields which were the scene of former invasions but before they reached the regurgitation stage, Mrs. Evelyn Turner (married daughter of the Bosleys), assisted by a trained cattle dog, which was half collie and half of indeterminate breed, headed them off and sent them mooing back to their own pastures. By noon, however, they forgot their defeat of the morning and decided to visit the Bosleys for lunch. This time they came, eight of them, with reinforcements. They brought along their boy friend, a 1500–pound Hereford white-faced bull.

Inspirited and encouraged by their horned escort, the female bovines overran the peach trees and apple orchard when Mrs. Turner, who was in the field with her 6–year old son and the dog, sounded the alarm to her mother, Mrs. Bosley, then in the house. Mrs. Turner at once rang up the Andrews on the telephone to tell them to call off their cloven-hoofed trespassers, and then hurried outside to assist her daughter, not knowing of the presence of Mr. Hereford. Mr. Hereford and Mrs. Bosley saw each other at the same time. Mrs. Bosley screamed, and the truculent Hereford lowered his head to charge. Terror-stricken, Mrs. Bosley tried to run, but, as in a bad dream one cannot flee although disaster is at one's heels, she froze to the spot. As she later described the agonizing moment:

> 'I turned around and looked, and he was coming at me with his head down, and I started to run, but I thought I could not get my legs to go and I choked up and I collapsed, and momentarily, I thought he was going to get me, I could just even feel that he was on top of me.'

In the meantime, the collie-mongrel dog, who was to become the unwreathed hero of the episode, bounded into the space between the bull and the terror-stricken woman. The bull then, as dull-witted as his brothers in the shouting arenas of Spain who pursue an innocuous red rag, took after the dog, and Mrs. Bosley was saved from a leaden-footed torreador's end.

After managing some five stumbling steps, Mrs. Bosley fainted. Upon regaining consciousness, her daughter was rubbing her wrists and her grandson was crying: 'Nan, Nan, are you breathing?' From this point she was helped to the barn some 150 feet away where she remained for half an hour. From here she was assisted to a milk house between the barn and the family dwelling. Finally she was taken home where she was at once put to bed. A doctor was summoned and he found her suffering from 'an attack of coronary insufficiency and some heart failure.'

Following ten days' confinement to bed she was taken to the Greenville Hospital where she remained 17 days. Since then her health has never been good. She suffers sinking spells and blackouts, she is weak and exhausted, she has become a periodical guest of clinics and hospitals. It is the medical opinion of Dr. G. H. Diehl, who treated her from the day of the bull episode, that the angina pectoris, with which she is at present afflicted, was precipitated by 'the running, the chasing and the fear that was caused when the bull chased her.' It is his opinion further that Mrs. Bosley 'will probably always have angina pectoris and cardiac insufficiency in the future.'

Oliver H. Bosley, husband to Mrs. Mary Bosley, and Mrs. Bosley in her own right, brought suit in trespass against Dale Andrews on three counts: (1) for damages done to Bosley's crops, (2) for injuries to Mrs. Bosley, and (3) for expenses incurred by Mr. Bosley on account of his wife's injuries. The plaintiffs recovered a verdict on the first count, but the Trial Judge directed a verdict for the defendant on the second and third counts. The plaintiffs appealed to the Superior Court which affirmed the action of the lower Court by a 4 to 3 vote; and the plaintiffs, by obtaining an allocatur, appealed to this Court which has affirmed the decision of the Superior Court.

The Majority Opinion of this Court states at the outset that Mrs. Bosley 'sought to recover damages for a heart disability which resulted from her fright and shock upon being chased by a Hereford bull owned by defendant.' The Majority thus admits that Mrs. Bosley's heart disability is a result of the fright and shock caused by the aggressiveness of the defendant's bull. Although the bull was about 25 feet away from Mrs. Bosley when she first beheld him charging toward her, she ran some 'five steps' before she collapsed. Allowing for at least two feet for each step, it becomes evident that the bull was within 10 to 15 feet of Mrs. Bosley before his course was diverted. It is enough merely to visualize a snorting, charging bull with impaling horns only a dozen feet away, to grasp at once the magnitude of Mrs. Bosley's fright and the extent of the terror to which she was subjected.

Although there is evidence that Mrs. Bosley did suffer from arteriosclerosis prior to April 10, 1950, it was the charge by the bull which, as another doctor (Dr. Ernstene) testified, 'constituted the trigger mechanism that brought the symptoms into clinical prominence.' The defendant's attorney, in cross-examining Dr. Ernstene, asked if some other shock might not have brought on the heart attack. Specifically, he asked if an automobile accident, or sudden death in the family, might not have been capable of precipitating a heart attack such as Mrs. Bosley experienced. The doctor answered these questions in the affirmative, thus strengthening the plaintiff's case, instead of weakening it.

* * *

The Majority says:

> 'To allow recovery for fright, fear, nervous shock, humiliation, mental or emotional distress—with all the disturbances and illnesses which accompany or result therefrom—where there has been no physical injury or impact, would open a Pandora's box.'

What is in Pandora's box which would apply to cases of this character? The Majority does not specify, but presumably it fears that from Pandora's box there would issue forth what it recounts in the immediately following sentence, namely:

> 'A plaintiff might be driving her car alertly or with her mind preoccupied, when a sudden or unexpected or exceptionally loud noise of an automobile

> horn behind or parallel with her car, or a sudden
> loud and unexpected fire engine bell or siren, or
> a sudden unexpected frightening buzz-sawing noise,
> or an unexpected explosion from blasting or dyna-
> miting, or an unexpected nerve-wracking noise pro-
> duced by riveting on a street, or the shrill and
> unexpected blast of a train at a spot far from a cross-
> ing, or the witnessing of a horrifying accident,
> [which was caused by the negligence of the defen-
> dant], or the approach of a car near or over the
> middle line, even though it is withdrawn to its own
> side in ample time to avoid an accident, or any one
> of a dozen other every-day events, can cause or ag-
> gravate fright or nervous shock or emotional distress
> or nervous tension or mental disturbance.'

I would say that a woman who could run the gamut of
such a potential succession of blasts, shrills, dynamitings,
nerve-wracking rivetings, explosions, buzzings, horn blowings,
siren wailings and bell tollings, and emerge alive at the end—a
trip more fraught with wild excitement and adventure than
Vice President Nixon's journey through South America—should
be compensated in some fashion, if not in a lawsuit, at least
by public subscription.

The great fear of the Majority seems to be that if we should
allow the plaintiff in this case to submit her case to a jury,
and, incidentally, that is all she is seeking, the courts would
be besieged with 'faked' cases. The majority prophesies with
alarm:

> 'For every wholly genuine and deserving claim,
> there would likely be a tremendous number of il-
> lusory or imaginative or 'faked' ones.'

But are our courts so naive, are they so gullible, are they
so devoid of worldly knowledge, are they so childlike in their
approach to realities that they can be deceived and hood-
winked by claims that have no factual, medical, or legalistic
basis? If they are, then all our proud boasts of the worthiness
of our judicial system are empty and vapid indeed.

The Majority's apprehension that if we should allow the
instant case to go to a jury for factual determination, the Courts
would be engulfed in a tidal wave of lawsuits, is to look upon

a raindrop and visualize an inundation. Many jurisdictions now permit recovery where physical disablement tortiously caused is not made manifest through visible trauma, and I have seen no report that in those States the Courts are awash in trumped-up cases. Many States at one time followed the non-liability doctrine but later abandoned it. * * *

The Majority Opinion says that:

> 'The rule is long and well established in Pennsyl-vania that there can be no recovery of damages for injuries resulting from fright or nervous shock or mental or emotional disturbances or distress, unless they are accompanied by physical injury or physical impact.'

It is true that this Court has consistently denied recovery in the type of cases described in this quotation, but that does not mean that, consonant with law, reason, and justice, it should continue to do so. *Stare decises* is the viaduct over which the law travels in transporting the precious cargo of justice. Prudence and a sense of safety dictates that the piers of that viaduct should be examined and tested from time to time to make certain that they are sound, strong and capable of sup-porting the weight above. One of the piers supposedly uphold-ing the span of non-liability is the case of *Huston v. Freemansburg Borough*, 212 Pa. 548, 61 A. 1022, 1023, 3 L.R.A., N.S., 49, cited in the Majority Opinion. A review of that alleged authority will reveal it to be made up of something less than the durable masonry which should be the foundation of any jurisprudential structure in America. Chief Justice Mitchell, who wrote the Opinion in that case, said:

> 'In the last half century the ingenuity of counsel, stimulated by the cupidity of clients and encouraged by the prejudices of juries, has expanded the action for negligence until it overtops all others in fre-quency and importance; but it is only in the very end of that period that it has been stretched to the effort to cover so intangible, so untrust-worthy, so illusory, and so speculative a cause of action as mere mental disturbance. It requires but a brief judicial experience to be convinced of the large proportion of exaggeration, and even of actual fraud, in the ordinary action for physical injuries from negli-

gence; and if we opened the door to this new invention the result would be great danger, if not disaster, to the cause of practical justice.'

With all the respect that one naturally holds for the jurists of the past, I cannot generate any veneration for this intemperate out burst. On the contrary, I believe that it should be repudiated and condemned. It amounts to an unjust attack on our whole judicial system. It lays under suspicion every attorney at the bar, casts a shadow on every plaintiff litigant, and shamelessly condemns juries as being motivated by unworthy intentions. Fifty-three years have passed since Mitchell's philippic, but, despite his dire prophecies, there is no report of disaster in those States which allow recovery for mental and nervous disorders caused by tort, even though unaccompanied by physical injury.

* * *

I have said that this Court has been consistent in refusing recovery in this type of case. I must modify that statement somewhat. There has been an occasion or two when a ray of wholesome and humane inconsistency broke through the dark clouds of illogical consistency. * * *

But even if we were to assume the absolute correctness in law and justice of this Court's decisions which in the past have denied liability for mental and nervous conditions not connected with physical fracture and laceration, this would not be to say that such liability cannot be proclaimed today. It could well be that conditions have changed and, therefore, the whole problem should be re-evaluated, especially in view of the tremendous progress which has been made in the fields of mental, cardiac, and neurological research. With highly sensitive equipment and with accurately developed laboratory formulae, plus a profounder knowledge in the whole cyclopedia of health versus disease, doctors and scientists no longer stand helpless before the problem of determining the causation of abnormal behavior in man. And if that increased knowledge decreases the possibility of fraudulent claims evading the argus-eyed vigilance of court and jury, there should be a change in the judicial attitude toward the type of claim under consideration.

*   *   *

It seems to me that it is a violation of the living spirit of the law to adhere to an ancient rule which has no pragmatic application to realities of today. A precedent, in law, in order to be binding, should appeal to logic and a genuine sense of justice. What lends dignity to the law founded on precedent is that, if analyzed, the particularly cited case wields authority by the sheer force of its self-integrated honesty, integrity, and rationale. A precedent can not, and should not, control, if its strength depends alone on the fact that it is old, but may crumble at the slightest probing touch of instinctive reason and natural justice. With such criteria in mind, it is difficult to understand how this Court can allow damages for mental and nervous disability if incurred at the same time that a finger is bruised, but will deny compensation of any kind to the victim who sustains no outer mutilation but will be invalidated for life because his inner mechanism has been shattered beyond repair.

In the case of *Potere v. City of Philadelphia*, 380 Pa. 581, 589, 112 A.2d 100, 104, the plaintiff was driving a truck in Philadelphia when the street caved in beneath him, over an open tunnel. The cab of his truck suspended momentarily at the edge of the abyss, allowing him to escape to safety before the truck fell. His physical injuries were slight but the terror he experienced as he teetered between escape and a possible fatal drop into the tunnel brought on an anxiety neurosis, for which he claimed and received damages at the hands of the jury. The defendant City of Philadelphia complained that the plaintiff was not entitled to recovery for the anxiety neurosis. This court affirmed the verdict and, speaking through Justice Chidsey, said:

> 'It has been well established that in the absence of physical injury or physical impact, mental or emotional distress is not the subject of legal redress. * * * However, where, as here, a plaintiff sustains bodily injuries, even though trivial or minor in character, which are accompanied by fright or mental suffering directly traceable to the peril in which the defendant's negligence placed the plaintiff, then mental suffering is a legitimate element of damages.'

If, in the *Potere* case, the jury could trace the connection between the plaintiff's neurosis and his fear of falling in the tunnel, why may it not trace the connection between Mrs. Bosley's heart disablement and the fear which overwhelmed her when she expected that any moment she might be gored by the defendant's bull?

What is the difference, in point of liability, on the part of a railroad company, between a case where a passenger's arm is cut in a train wreck, and a case where a passenger suffers a broken heart valve as a result of the fear he experienced in expecting death as a car passed over him? Is the negligence and responsibility of the tortfeasor any less marked toward the living man than to the dead man's family when, after the throb of the overturned locomotive has ceased and the hissing of the punctured air brakes has faded away, there lie on the ground, next to one another, the body of a stark dead passenger and the body of a living passenger, unconscious, but unblemished by a single scratch? To determine liability by what follows rather than by what precedes and accompanies a catastrophe is like concluding that no earthquake has occurred because no one was killed even though the earth gaped and the houses danced as if doing a grisly quadrille.

The crux of this Court's position is that in cases where the plaintiff suffered no physical laceration, bruise, or abrasion, it is difficult to discover false claims. But is it not equally as difficult to uncover false claims where the mental or nervous disturbance is not physiologically connected with the bruise or laceration? In the *Potere* case, the plaintiff's sprained ankle and bruised elbow had nothing to do with his anxiety neurosis. As the jury had to determine whether the disablement in Potere's nervous system was caused by his fear of falling, could it not in this case have decided whether Mrs. Bosley's heart disablement was precipitated by her fear of being gored to death? Injury to the heart is a physical injury and not merely a mental or emotional vagary.

The heart has been so excessively the subject of poetic rhapsodizing that it would seem we may have lost sight of the fact that it is objectively a physical organ with mechanical functions as rigidly followed as the metallic movements of the village pump. Mrs. Bosley's ailment is not to be equated with intangible grieving or sentimental lamenting. Her heart condition is as much a matter of muscle and tissue as traumatic neuritis. However, while Mrs. Bosley's condition is tangible and palpable, it was caused by a force which did not touch her except through operation of the mind. But that does not mean that the application of the distant force was any less realistic. When a person whitens with fear, blushes with shame, shivers from apprehension, or petrifies with horror, there is no immediate bodily contact with the force which produces those definite physical reactions. But can we say that there is no actual bond between the emotion-creating phenomenon and the organism of the person who responds to the phenomenon? To answer that question in the negative would be to deny the most elementary certainties of human experience.

What provokes laughter? Is laughing not the result of a mental appraisement? But laughter itself is not mental. Abdominal, facial, and labial muscles, vocal cords, larynx and pharynx must all operate and coordinate in order to produce a hearty guffaw. What are tears? Except when they are concomitant with torture or whipping, they are the result purely of intangible thought. One thinks of a lost relative, a departed friend, a tragic event, and a saline solution forms in the eyes. A great deal of physical machinery goes into action to manufacture those drops of water, and it would be sheer perversity to say that there is no connection between the item of grief and distillation of the resulting tears.

Can laughter and weeping ever be physically injurious? It is no figure of speech that people have actually laughed themselves to death. It is no rhetorical exaggeration to say that people have died of weeping and grief. There is, therefore, an objective linking—of cause and effect—between outer phenomenon and physical reaction. Thus, if one can die with laughing, perish with weeping and freeze from fear, how can it be said that there is no tie of contact between the terror of immediate death caused by the charging of a ferocious beast and a heart ailment which contemporaneously occurs and thereafter unceasingly continues?

One can think of many situations where a person could be gravely injured by a trespassing force which in no way physically touched him. For instance, the violent displacement of air caused by an explosion negligently performed could deafen a passerby who would most assuredly be entitled to recover from the trespasser even though he could show no outer lesion on his person. Instruments and expert examination would attest to ruptured eardrums. How would such evidence differ from the evidence presented by the doctors in this case, which was medical proof that the plaintiff had suffered organic damage to the heart?

The blinding light of an explosion improperly managed could ruin the eyesight of one fortuitously in the area. Certainly there would be no merit to a defense in such a case which argued that there was no actual impact between the blasted materials and the eyes of the blinded person.

The nervous system is peculiarly susceptible to non-tangible excitation, and it is not to be denied that the wrecking of nerve ganglia can often be more disabling than the breaking of bones or the tearing of flesh. And where it is definitively established that such injury and suffering were proximately caused by an act of negligence, why should the tortfeasor not be liable in damages? Is law so lacking in the cognizance of natural science that it is incapable of following the fiery trajectory of the intangible bolt of lightning which blasts the towering tree?

This Court finds difficulty in attaching liability to the defendant in this case because of the gap between the bull's nose and Mrs. Bosley's prostrate body, which measured no more than 10 to 15 feet. If the animal's charging horns had advanced closer and had just grazed, without seriously harming Mrs. Bosley, then, according to the *Potere* case, she would be entitled to recover. This all produces in the law a heterogeneous pattern which did not escape Judge Ervin of the Superior Court, who, in his powerful dissenting opinion when that tribunal passed on this controversy, said:

> 'There can be no doubt that the plaintiff could have recovered if the bull had caught up with her and had butted her, even gently, and there can be no doubt that she would have recovered, not merely for the bruises resulting from being gently butted, but also for any heart condition which resulted from her emotional excitement. Likewise, there can be no doubt that if, in running away from the bull, she had fallen and had damaged her eye by running a weed into it, she could have recovered for that damage. To say that when she runs from the same trespassing bull and falls and suffers a heart attack,

she cannot recover for the heart injury is making a distinction which cannot be justified.' [135 A.2d at Page 109.]

To carry Judge Ervin's splendid argument a little further, suppose that Mrs. Bosley had already had an injured foot or even a rheumatic leg prior to April 10, 1950, but the strain of running away from the bull aggravated that condition. Would this Court, under its previous rulings, not have to hold, in such a situation, that she would be entitled to recover for what she suffered because of the aggravation of a previous condition? And, in that event, what would be the difference between a previously existing arteriosclerosis and a previously existing rheumatic leg?

The paradoxical law which the appellate Courts of Pennsylvania are now laying down, for lower Courts to follow, goes even further than either Judge Ervin or I have indicated. The Majority holds here that Mr. Bosley may not recover for the damages he sustained as the result of the fright and resulting heart disability suffered by his wife. However, under present law, if Mr. Bosley owned a horse which had been frightened, but not physically injured by the defendant's bull, he could recover for any loss in value of his horse occasioned by the fright. * * *

I would not recommend that the Supreme Court of Pennsylvania change one of its rules which is venerable with age, if it were one which appeals to reason, fairness, and justice. But when the rule defended by the Majority stands on such slippery ground as has been indicated in this case, should we not look to other jurisdictions to see how they are treating the same problem? The Majority Opinion does not lift binoculars to look across our borders into other States. It does not even apply spectacles to the Restatement on Torts. Section 436(2) of that magnificent compendium of legal principles states:

'If the actor's conduct is negligent as creating an unreasonable risk of causing bodily harm to another otherwise than by subjecting him to fright, shock or other similar and immediate emotional disturbance, the fact that such harm results solely from the internal operation of fright or other emotional disturbance does not protect the actor from liability.'

*   *   *

In conclusion I would say that the Majority Opinion has concentrated its argument principally on the proposition that it would be unwise to allow recoveries for mental and nervous disorders following fear, fright, and shock. However, the plaintiff is not claiming damages because of any mental or nervous ailment. At the risk of tiresome repetition I must repeat that she is asking for a verdict as the result of physical damage done to her heart. The fact that the heart is locked in one's breast does not make it inaccessible to doctors nor unfelt by its owner. Thus, in considering the nature and the extent of the plaintiff's disability we are dealing with something very tangible and very concrete.

*   *   *

Since the doctors have stated categorically that Mrs. Bosley's heart disability is the direct result of the bull's aggression, and since it is conceded that the bull's presence on the Bosley property constitutes an almost wanton trespass, it is inexplicable how this Court can legally dispose of a controversy which is peculiarly one for a jury's determination. The explanation offered in the Majority Opinion does not explain. To say that to grant what the law allows in this case might create an untoward situation in other cases is like saying that the fountain of justice should be boarded up because of the possibility that someone might drown in its salutary waters.

I would have the fountain flowing at all times, assured that the established safeguards of the law will keep away those who would defile its pure and refreshing essence just as those same safeguards are prepared, if not shackled, to hold responsible those who allow ferocious animals to roam at large to the hurt and grievous loss of the innocent and the unsuspecting, in the tranquil enjoyment of their homes, their gardens, and the prospect of a safe and cloudless future.

In recapitulation I wish to go on record that the policy of non-liability announced by the Majority in this type of case is insupportable in law, logic, and elementary justice—and I shall continue to dissent from it until the cows come home.

On April 16, 1978, two army buddies decided to get away from their base and enjoy the sights and sounds of Nashville, Tennessee. Their ultimate goal on that spring afternoon, however, was "to get bombed." That goal became a double-edged sword for the Classic Cat II, which was the establishment where they chose to spend most of their time—and money. As a result of the soldiers' good time, the Classic Cat II had its license suspended and the owner found herself in the midst of a court battle.

The METROPOLITAN GOVERNMENT OF NASHVILLE AND DAVIDSON COUNTY, et al.

v.

MARTIN, d/b/a Classic Cat II

Supreme Court of Tennessee
July 2, 1979
584 S.W.2d 643

The Metropolitan Beer Permit Board of Nashville and Davidson County suspended the beer permit of Classic Cat II, pursuant to two citations. In the first citation, the Beer Board supposedly charged the Classic Cat II with an assortment of Metropolitan Code violations, such as filing false statements in the permit application and refusing to allow a police officer to enter the establishment. However, due to the fact that there were major procedural flaws and inadequate proof of the violations in the first citation, the lower court reversed the 60–day suspension and the Supreme Court affirmed.

HENRY, Chief Justice.

* * *

The Second Citation

The second citation was properly certified by the Beer Board and is included in the record. It charges the permittee with allowing "an[y] intoxicated person to loiter on or about the premises," on April 14, 1978.

All the proof was directed to activities occurring on April 16, 1978; however, counsel makes no issue of this discrepancy. Therefore, we do not treat it as being of critical significance. It is but another of many instances of sloppy Beer Board procedure.

The proof presented to the Beer Board was meager and marginal. If there were no other proof in the record we unhesitatingly would affirm the Trial Judge and hold that the Beer Board acted arbitrarily; however, upon the De novo hearing before the Trial Judge additional proof was presented which places the matter in an entirely different light.

Before the Trial Court the Beer Board presented the deposition of the "loitering drunk" and his cohort and companion. This proof was not presented to the Beer Board.

He is a member of the regular army stationed at Fort Campbell. He and his companion, another soldier, arrived in Nashville in the early afternoon of April 16, 1978 and took a room at a local motel.

About mid-afternoon they wended their way to the Classic Cat II, where they stayed several hours imbibing seven and sevens, [Seagrams and 7–up] "[m]aybe 10 to 15." Thereafter, they left, bought a bottle of Seagrams V.O. and settled down to some serious drinking—"drinking out of the bottle."

Around 9:30 or 10:00 p.m. they returned to the Classic Cat and the seven and sevens. While he denies that his first 10–15 drinks caused him to be "smashed," he admits that after his interlude with Seagrams V.O. and after topping that off with more seven and sevens, he was drunk.

He says that every time he drinks "hard liquor" he gets drunk or tries to. He admits that he was in Nashville to get "bombed," and that he went to the Classic Cat to get drunk and "watch the women." Of course, he denies that he has a drinking problem; he says he just likes to drink.

They apparently remained at the Classic Cat for some two or three hours on their second visit.

When we analyze this soldier's actions in terms of his stated intention "to get bombed," the conclusion is inevitable that success crowned his efforts. While he lolled, loafed, and loitered about the Classic Cat satisfying his lickerish craving for liquor by lapping up lavish libations, he fell from his chair, clutching his drink in his hand, into the waiting hands of vice squad officer McElhaney, who helped him up and took him to jail.

We subject his conduct to the most liberal standard that has come to the attention of the author of this opinion.

> Not drunk is he who from the floor
> Can rise alone and still drink more;
> But drunk is he, who prostrate lies,
> Without the power to drink or rise.[3]

This soldier fails the test. He was drunk—openly, visibly, notoriously, gloriously and uproariously drunk.

The Classic Cat II violated one of the great commandments by which "beer joints" must live. In summary and in short, in paraphrase and in idiom, the law "don't allow no [drunken] hanging around" beer establishments.

We do not deal with an isolated case of a drunk who came in from the cold and was drunk on arrival, or with a customer who consumed beer and became intoxicated as a result of that consumption under circumstances where the management reasonably could not be expected to realize that the customer

---

3. Thomas L. Peacock, The Misfortunes of Elphin (1827) Translated from the Welsh.

had reached the point of intoxication. We deal purely and simply with permitting a drunk to "hang around" a beer joint under circumstances that were known, or should have been known to the permittee, or her employees.

We find no reported cases wherein the courts have attempted to define the offense of drunken loitering about premises where beer was sold. However, *Hopper v. State*, 194 Tenn. 600, 253 S.W.2d 765 (1952) deals with an analogous prohibition against permitting minors to loiter about such premises. There, this Court quoted with approval the definition of "loitering" as contained in a decision of the Connecticut Supreme Court:

> To be slow in moving; to delay; to linger; to be dilatory; to spend time idly; to saunter; to lag behind. 194 Tenn. at 601, 253 S.W.2d at 766.

We approve these definitions; they accord with the common understanding of the term "loiter" or "loitering."

Appellants' assignment number IV is sustained and the action of the Beer Board in suspending Classic Cat II's license for a period of thirty (30) days is upheld.

Appellants assign as error the Trial Court's ruling that Metropolitan Code Section 5–1–23(k), which makes it unlawful to permit an intoxicated person to loiter on or about premises where beer is sold, is unconstitutionally vague.

It is well settled that municipalities, in the exercise of their police power, are given wide discretion in regulating the sale of intoxicating beverages.

Although an ordinance must "give a person of ordinary intelligence fair notice that his contemplated conduct is forbidden by the statute," *United States v. Harriss*, 347 U.S. 612, 617, 74 S.Ct. 808, 812, 98 L.Ed. 989, 996 (1954), the United States Supreme Court has stated that laws governing regulated activities are not subject to the same degree of scrutiny as laws applicable to the general population:

> In the field of regulatory statutes governing business activities, where the acts limited are in a narrow category, greater leeway is allowed. . . .

> The poor among us, the minorities, the average householder are not in business and not alerted to the regulatory schemes of vagrancy laws; and we assume they would have no understanding of their meaning and impact if they read them. *Papachristou v. City of Jacksonville*, 405 U.S. 156, 162–63, 92 S.Ct. 839, 843, 31 L.Ed.2d 110, 115–16 (1972).

The ordinance in question applies only to beer permit holders and their employees. The sale of beer is a regulated business in which the permit holders are cognizant of the regulatory scheme and aware of its impact.

As noted above, the definition of "loiter" approved in previous cases reflects the common understanding of the term. We therefore hold that in the context of this regulatory scheme, the ordinance is not unconstitutionally vague, under either the state or federal constitution.

This cause is remanded to the Circuit Court at Nashville for appropriate action as to the 30–day suspension of the permit of the Classic Cat II.

Affirmed in part; reversed in part; remanded.

"The Zim *decision grew out of a complex series of contractual disputes between science educator and author Herbert Zim and his publisher, Western Publishing Co., concerning royalties, bonuses, and arrangements for the revision of Zim's phenomenally successful series of 'Golden Guides.' While Zim's author, Judge Irving L. Goldberg, is much celebrated for his humor and distinctive literary style, the Zim case is special even within the Goldberg oeuvre in its extended development of biblical themes (drawing on the creation story at the beginning of* Genesis, *the* Exodus *narratives, and elements of the Passover Seder ceremony)."*

—Associate Professor, University of Wisconsin–Madison

ZIM

v.

WESTERN PUBLISHING COMPANY

United States Court of Appeals
Fifth Circuit
June 2, 1978
573 F.2d 1318

GOLDBERG, Circuit Judge:

I

In the beginning, Zim created the concept of the Golden Guides. For the earth was dark and ignorance filled the void. And Zim said, let there be enlightenment and there was enlightenment. In the Golden Guides, Zim created the heavens (STARS) (SKY OBSERVER'S GUIDE) and the earth. (MINERALS) (ROCKS and MINERALS) (GEOLOGY).

And together with his publisher, Western, he brought forth in the Golden Guides knowledge of all manner of living things that spring from the earth, grass, herbs yielding seed, fruit-trees yielding fruits after their kind, (PLANT KINGDOM) (NON-FLOWERED PLANTS) (FLOWERS) (ORCHIDS) (TREES), and Zim saw that it was good. And they brought forth in the Golden Guides knowledge of all the living moving creatures that dwell in the waters, (FISHES) (MARINE MOLLUSKS) (POND LIFE), and fowl that may fly above the earth. (BIRDS) (BIRDS OF NORTH AMERICA) (GAMEBIRDS). And Zim saw that it was good. And they brought forth knowledge in the Golden Guides of the creatures that dwell on dry land, cattle, and creeping things, (INSECTS) (INSECT PESTS) (SPIDERS), and beasts of the earth after their kind. (ANIMAL KINGDOM). And Zim saw that it was very good.

II

Then there rose up in Western a new Vice-President who knew not Zim. And there was strife and discord, anger and frustration, between them for the Golden Guides were not being published or revised in their appointed seasons. And it came to pass that Zim and Western covenanted a new covenant, calling it a Settlement Agreement. But there was no peace in the land. Verily, they came with their counselors of law into the district court for judgment and sued there upon their covenants.

And they put upon the district judge hard tasks. And the district judge listened to long testimony and received hundreds of exhibits. So Zim did cry unto the district judge that he might remember the promises of the Settlement Agreement. And the district judge heard Zim's cry, but gave judgment for Western. Yea, the district judge gave judgment to Western on a counterclaim as well. Therefore, Zim went up out of the court of the district judge.

III

And Zim spake unto the Court of Appeals saying, make a sacrifice of the judgment below. And the judges, three in number, convened in orderly fashion to recount the story of the covenants and to discuss and answer the four questions which Zim brought before them.

*   *   *

IV

A. Parol Evidence

And the parties came before the district judge for an accounting of the royalties of Zim. Under Sections 3 and 4 of the 1970 Settlement Agreement, Zim was entitled to payments of royalties and bonuses for books in the "Golden Guide Series." * * *

The parties agree that Zim is to earn royalties and bonuses only on those books "published or to be published or distributed by Western. . . ." They disagree sharply, however, on the correct construction of "Western." Zim offered parol evidence, the testimony of the attorney who represented him during the contract negotiations, to support his view that "Western" means not only Western Publishing Co., the defendant here, but its affiliates and subsidiaries as well. The district judge excluded the testimony on the grounds that "Western" was unambiguous as a matter of law in view of the first recital in the contract. There the parties to the contract were stated to be Zim and "Western Publishing Co., Inc. (a Wisconsin Corporation), its successors and assigns, herein referred to as 'Western' . . ." In the district court's view, the contract provided its own definition of "Western" and that definition was not itself subject to ambiguity, i.e., Western Publishing Co., Inc. (a Wisconsin Corporation), its successors and assigns, meant that jural entity and none other. Zim contends that this ruling denies him his "day in court" and is inconsistent with the Wisconsin parol evidence rule.

*   *   *

The law in Wisconsin appears to be that parol evidence is not admissible to contradict or vary the terms of an agreement, but may be considered in interpreting an ambiguous term. * * *

The ultimate aim of all contract interpretation is to ascertain the intent of the parties. If this intent can be determined with reasonable certainty from the face of the contract itself, there is no need to resort to extrinsic evidence. If, however, the language of the contract is ambiguous, then the court is not restricted to the face of the instrument in ascertaining intent, but may consider extrinsic evidence. Words or phrases in a contract are ambiguous when they are reasonably susceptible of more than one meaning.

*   *   *

In the case at bar, the parties made an effort in the written instrument to define the term whose meaning they now contest. They defined "Golden Guides" by reference to another term, "Western," the meaning of which the agreement also provides explicitly. "Western," the recitals tell us, is to stand for "Western Publishing Co., Inc., (A Wisconsin Corporation) its successors and assigns." Western Publishing Co., Inc. (a Wisconsin Corporation), is a definite entity, created by the law and legally distinct from separately incorporated affiliates or subsidiaries. *   *   *

Here, then, counseled parties made a deliberate effort to define a crucial term in the agreement. They defined that term in words with a quite definite legal significance. When they wished to give that term some special meaning different from its definition in the agreement, they so provided in unmistakable terms. We think the district court was correct in its conclusion that the intent of the parties was unambiguously evidenced by the writing itself. Under Wisconsin law, the parol evidence was properly excluded.

B. The Contract Claims

Zim next contends that Western breached the 1970 Settlement Agreement by publishing revised versions of two of the Golden Guides, STARS and SKY OBSERVER'S GUIDE, without his approval. Zim bases his claim on Subsection 6.5 of the contract.

> Subsection 6.5—Zim releases to Western all Zim's right, interest and claim under all programs heretofore agreed upon or now under way for the revision of books published prior to the date hereof. It is agreed, however, that Western will not publish any revision, change, correction, alteration or updating of any book published prior to October 1, 1970 on which Zim is entitled to a royalty or bonus, without Zim's prior approval.

It is undisputed that both STARS and SKY OBSERVER'S GUIDE had been published prior to October 1, 1970. It is also undisputed that projects for the revision of both books were "under way" when the contract was executed. It is also undisputed that Western failed to obtain Zim's approval of the revisions prior to publication of the revised versions of the books. Zim vigorously contends that these facts establish a breach of contract by Western and that he was entitled to damages and an injunction against further publication without his approval.

Western counters by pointing out that the district judge found that Western had submitted all proposed changes to Zim for his approval, but that Zim "unreasonably withheld" his approval of the changes. Western contends that Zim's failure to make a meaningful response to the proposed changes excuses Western's publication of the revisions.

* * *

Zim's power of approval under subsection 6.5 cannot, however, be construed to be an unlimited power to prevent publication of revised versions of the Guides covered by 6.5. Zim bargained for the retention of his power to exercise his judgment as a science educator with enormous experience in the presentation of material in the Golden Guides format. That judgment, once exercised, was to be decisive; Western could not publish revisions of which Zim disapproved. Nonetheless, justice and fairness considered in the light of the parties interests here require that Zim's power not extend to holding Western hostage to dilatoriness, obstructionism, or greed. Zim's retained power to disapprove changes, therefore, has to be exercised within a reasonable time and in a reasonable manner, i.e., in a manner which makes it possible for Western to rework the manuscript in order to obtain his approval. * * *

[W]e have no hesitation in concluding that Zim failed to exercise his power of disapproval within the time and in the manner required, and in so doing effectively waived his right to reject the proposed revisions. Zim's approval conditioned on execution of a new contract was an abusive use of his power and an attempt to reform the Settlement Agreement. This is not to say that Zim was not honestly motivated by a desire to maintain and improve the quality of SKY OBSERVER'S GUIDE. It is to say, however, that conditioning his approval in this manner was beyond the scope of his contractual power. Zim's failure to exercise his power properly operated to authorize Western's publication of the revised work. The district court's holding as to SKY OBSERVER'S GUIDE must be affirmed.

The situation with STARS is quite different. Although proposed revisions were sent to Zim in 1972, a final set of revisions was first sent to Zim in September of 1974. Western at that time demanded that Zim examine the revisions and report within sixty days his approval or disapproval together with suggested changes. Western stated that it would consider his suggestions and advise him whether the changes would be made. Western stated it would then ask Zim whether he wished to be shown as co-author, original project editor, or have his name removed entirely from the book. Western proceeded to publish the book notwithstanding Zim's express disapproval communicated within the sixty day period.

It is apparent that Western breached the agreement here. Western's 1974 letter confused Zim's rights under subsections 6.4 and 6.5 of the agreement. Zim's prior approval of the revised version of STARS was a prerequisite to lawful publication by Western, absent waiver by Zim. Since there had been no waiver as to STARS, Western's publication of the book without Zim's approval constituted a breach of contract.

*   *   *

C. The Tort Claims

The third count of Dr. Zim's complaint alleged an unauthorized and wrongful appropriation of Zim's name, a claim sounding in tort under Florida law. Zim's claim again grows out of the publication of revised revisions of STARS and SKY OBSERVER'S GUIDE. Zim's name appeared on the spine of both books even though he never approved the revisions. Moreover, Zim's initials appeared beneath a foreword added to STARS which expressed his gratitude to the authors hired by Western to revise the book. Zim never approved this foreword either.

*   *   *

We have already concluded, however, that Western was entitled under the contract to publish SKY OBSERVER'S GUIDE without Zim's actual approval in view of Zim's default. Western's right under the contract to publish the book in these circumstances operates as an authorization sufficient to privilege Western's use of Zim's name as a matter of tort law as well.

Just the opposite result obtains with respect to STARS. Paradoxically, if repeatedly in this case, he who observes the skies does not see the STARS. Western's use of Zim's name in STARS was unauthorized by the contract and was, therefore, tortious. Although Zim failed to prove any actual damages from the publication of the revised version of STARS, under Florida law, nominal damages, at least are recoverable; the plaintiff need not plead or prove actual damages. We must, therefore, reverse the district court and remand for an award of nominal damages.

D. Western's Counterclaim

* * *

Western's counterclaim is premised on an erroneous construction of the relevant provisions of the contract. As we read subsection 6.6, Western made an unconditional, undivided promise to pay $67,200 for the set of releases executed by Zim in subsections 6.1–6.5. Western's obligation to pay this sum was in no way conditioned on publication of all twenty books listed in subsection 6.4. * * *

The fact that Western decided not to publish three of the books means only that Western's gamble will not pay off as handsomely as it might have. The cost of obtaining the releases will not be reduced by the theoretical maximum. That is no warrant, however, for reducing the absolute obligation to pay Zim $67,200 as promised in subsection 6.6.

V

And when the judges of the Court of Appeals had passed through the wilderness of *Zim*, they recapitulated the history of their journey.

The ruling of the district judge regarding parol evidence on the meaning of "Western" is AFFIRMED. The court's conclusion that Western did not breach the Settlement Agreement or commit a tort by publishing the revised version of SKY OB-SERVER'S GUIDE is also AFFIRMED. We REVERSE, however, the court's conclusion that Western committed no breach of the contract by publishing the revised version of STARS. We REMAND for a determination and award of nominal damages for the breach of contract, for a determination of the propriety of injunctive relief against future breaches, for a determination and award of nominal damages to Zim for the tort committed by Western by using Zim's name on STARS without his authorization, and for reconsideration of the award of costs against Zim. We REVERSE the judgment for Western on its counterclaim. And it therefore shall come to pass that the district judge shall write another chapter in the chronicle of Zim.

"The [following] case is my favorite opinion for a variety of reasons: First of all, it is a lower trial court case in which the sitting judge recognized the importance of the case to the litigants, despite the fact that it was a seemingly minor dispute, and took the time and trouble to write an opinion; indeed, not only did he write an opinion, but it was a thoughtful, considerate and appropriately humorous one, articulating a fair and reasoned result. . . . As we hurtle towards the end of this century, the law could clearly use more such wit and wisdom."

—Professor, University of Maryland School of Law

LOUISIANA LEASING COMPANY

v.

SOKOLOW, et al.

Civil Court of the City of New York
Jan. 7, 1966
266 N.Y.S.2d 447, 48 Misc.2d 1014

DANIEL E. FITZPATRICK, Justice.

This is a proceeding to remove the respondents from the premises of the petitioner upon the ground that they are objectionable tenants. The applicable clauses in the lease between the parties contain the following:

> "15. No Tenant shall make or permit any disturbing noises in the building by himself, his family, servants, employees, agents, visitors and licensees, nor do or permit anything by such persons that will interfere with the rights, comforts or convenience of other tenants."

Paragraph 9 of said lease states in part as follows:

> "9. Tenant and Tenant's family, servants, employees, agents, visitors, and licensees shall observe faithfully and comply strictly with the Rules and Regulations set forth on the back of this lease, * * *. Tenant

agrees that any violation of any of said Rules and
Regulations by Tenant or by a member of Tenant's
family, or by servants, or employees, or agents, or
visitors, or licensees, shall be deemed a substantial
violation by Tenant of this lease and of the Ten-
ancy."

The landlord alleges that the noise from respondents' apartment is destroying the peace and quiet of the new tenants
immediately underneath them. The claim is and the proof attempted to establish that the noise is of such a character as
to constitute a violation of the provisions of the lease set out
above. The respondents have been in possession over two and
one-half years and their lease runs until December 31, 1966.
It is significant that the respondents over that period gave no
evidence of being objectionable until the new tenants, the
Levins, moved in last October. From the court's opportunity
to observe them, both the respondents and the tenants below
seem to be people who under other circumstances would be
congenial and happy neighbors. It is unfortunate that they
have had to come to court to face each other in an eye-ball
to eye-ball confrontation.

The respondents are a young couple with two small children, ages 4 and 2. It was admitted by them that the children
do run and play in their apartment, but they say that they
keep shoes off their feet when at home. The father says that
he does walk back and forth at various times when at home,
particularly to the refrigerator during the TV commercials and,
also, to other areas of the apartment as necessity requires, but
denies that he does this excessively or in a loud or heavy manner. They maintain that whatever noises emanate from their
apartment are the normal noises of everyday living.

The tenants below, the Levins, are a middle-aged couple
who go to business each day. They are like many others of
our fellow citizens, who daily go forth to brave the vicissitudes
of the mainstream of city life. At the end of the toilsome day,
like tired fish, they are only too happy to seek out these quiet
backwaters of the metropolis to recuperate for the next day's
bout with the task of earning a living. They have raised their
own child and are past the time when the patter of little feet
overhead is a welcome sound. They say they love their new
apartment and that it is just what they have been looking for
and would hate to have to give it up because of the noise

from above. Mrs. Levin is associated with the publisher of a teen-age magazine and realizes that she is in a bind between her desire for present comfort and the possible loss of two future subscribers. She consequently hastens to add that she loves children and has no objection to the Sokolows because of them—that it is solely the noise of which she complains. So we have the issue.

The landlord's brief states that in its "view, the conduct that is even more objectionable than the noise, is the uncooperative attitude of the Tenants". This observation is probably prompted by testimony to the effect that Mr. Sokolow, one of the upstairs tenants, is reported to have said "This is my home, and no one can tell me what to do in my own home". This is a prevalent notion that stems from the ancient axiom that a man's home is his castle.

The difficulty of the situation here is that Mr. Sokolow's castle is directly above the castle of Mr. Levin. That a man's home is his castle is an old Anglo-legal maxim hoary with time and the sanction of frequent repetition. It expressed an age when castles were remote, separated by broad moors, and when an intruder had to force moat and wall to make his presence felt within. The tranquillity of the King's Peace, the seclusion of a clandestine romance and the opportunity, like Hamlet, to deliver a soliloquy from the ramparts without fear of neighborly repercussions were real. Times however change, and all change is not necessarily progress as some sage has perceptively reminded us. For in an era of modernity and concentrated urban living, when high-rise apartment houses have piled castle upon castle for some twenty or more stories in the air, it is extremely difficult to equate these modern counterparts with their drawbridged and turreted ancestors. The builders of today's cubicular confusion have tried to compensate for the functional construction by providing lobbies in Brooklyn Renaissance that rival in decor the throne room at Knossos. They have also provided built-in air-conditioning, closed circuit television, playrooms and laundromats. There are tropical balconies to cool the fevered brow in the short, hot northern summer; which the other nine months serve as convenient places to store the floor mop and scrub pail. On the debit side they also contain miles of utility and sanitary piping which convey sound throughout the building with all the gusto of the mammoth organ in the Mormon Tabernacle at Salt Lake City. Also, the prefabricated or frugally plastered walls have their molecules so critically near the separation level that they oppose almost no barrier at all to alien sounds from neighboring apartments. This often forces on into an embarrassingly auditory intimacy with the surrounding tenants. Such are the hazards of modern apartment house living. One of my brother justices, the Honorable Harold J. Crawford, has opined that in this day in our large cities it is fruitless to expect the solitude of the sylvan glen. In this we concur. Particularly so, when we consider that all of us are daily assaulted by the "roaring traffic's boom", the early-morning carillon of the garbage cans and the determined whine of homing super-sonic jets. Further, children and noise have been inseparable from a time whence the mind of man runneth not to the contrary. This Court, therefore, is not disposed to attempt anything so schizophrenic at this late date.

Weighing the equities in this difficult controversy, the court finds that the Sokolows were there first, with a record as good tenants. The Levins underneath seem to be good tenants also. This was attested to by the superintendent who was called upon to testify. He made the understatement of the year when he said, "I kept out of the middle of this fight. It's near Christmas and this is no time for me to fight with tenants"—a piece of homely pragmatism which would have gladdened the heart of William James.

In his own crude way the superintendent may have suggested the solution to this proceeding. This is a time for peace on earth to men of good will. As the court noted above, they are all nice people and a little mutual forbearance and understanding of each other's problems should resolve the issues to everyone's satisfaction.

The evidence on the main question shows that in October the respondents Sokolow were already in a fixed relationship to the landlord. The Levins, on the other hand, were not—their position was a mobile one. They had the opportunity to ascertain what was above them in the event they decided to move in below. They elected to move in and afterwards attempted to correct the condition complained of. Since upon the evidence the overhead noise has been shown to be neither excessive nor deliberate, the court is not constrained to flex its muscles and evict the respondents. Upon the entire case the respondents are entitled to a final order dismissing the petition.

Here is one for self-proclaimed "movie buffs." In the late 1980s, a civil antitrust action was brought against Syufy Enterprises, a fast-growing movie theater chain in Las Vegas, Nevada. The district court found that the defendant did not have monopoly power in the nation's gambling capital and the government appealed. On appeal, Circuit Judge Kozinski authored the majority opinion, clearly stating the role of antitrust laws in a free economy. However, it is not just a well-written opinion. According to a Brigham Young University Law Review article, "The *Syufy* Rosetta Stone," 1992 B.Y.U. L. Rev. 457, Judge Kozinski either intentionally or coincidentally incorporated more than 200 movie titles into his opinion. Can you locate them? (Note: Due to editing, there are approximately 130 movie titles in this version.)

UNITED STATES

v.

SYUFY ENTERPRISES, *et al.*

United States Court of Appeals
Ninth Circuit
May 9, 1990
903 F.2d 659

KOZINSKI, Circuit Judge:

Suspect that giant film distributors like Columbia, Paramount and Twentieth Century-Fox had fallen prey to Raymond Syufy, the canny operator of a chain of Las Vegas, Nevada, movie theatres, the United States Department of Justice brought this civil antitrust action to force Syufy to disgorge the theatres he had purchased in 1982–84 from his former competitors. The case is unusual in a number of respects: The Department of Justice concedes that moviegoers in Las Vegas suffered no direct injury as a result of the allegedly illegal transactions; nor does the record reflect complaints from Syufy's bought-out competitors, as the sales were made at fair prices and not precipitated by any monkey business; and the supposedly oppressed movie companies have weighed in on Syufy's side. The Justice Department nevertheless remains intent on rescuing this platoon of Goliaths from a single David.

After extensive discovery and an 8½ day trial, the learned district judge entered comprehensive findings of fact and conclusions of law, holding for Syufy. He found, *inter alia*, that Syufy's actions did not injure competition because there are no barriers to entry—others could and did enter the market—and that Syufy therefore did not have the power to control prices or exclude the competition. While Justice raises a multitude of issues in its appeal, these key findings of the district court present the greatest hurdle it must overcome.

Facts

Gone are the days when a movie ticket cost a dime, popcorn a nickel and theatres had a single screen: This is the age of the multiplex. With more than 300 new films released every year—each potentially the next Batman or E.T.—many successful theatres today run a different film on each of their six, twelve or eighteen screens. The multiplex offers something for everyone: Moviegoers can choose from a wider selection of films; theatre operators are able to balance profits and losses from blockbusters and flops, and to reduce manpower by consolidating concession islands; the producers, of course, like having the extra screens on which to display their wares.

Raymond Syufy understood the formula well. In 1981, he entered the Las Vegas market with a splash by opening a six-screen theatre. Newly constructed and luxuriously furnished, it put existing facilities to shame. Syufy's entry into the Las Vegas market caused a stir, precipitating a titanic bidding war.[1]

1. Film distributors do not hand out prints for free; they sell exhibition licenses. These licenses normally specify a percentage of weekly house receipts, known as license fees, payable by the theatre owner to the distributor. Where more than one theatre in a given area volunteers to pay the license fee for a particular film, the distributor has several options: It can license the film to more than one theatre in the area; it can award the film to a particular theatre with which it has an ongoing relationship; or it can let them all bid for exclusive exhibition rights. Where the distributor adopts the competitive bidding approach, as virtually all distributors did in Las Vegas prior to October 1984, the high bid usually includes a guarantee—a minimum fee payable to the distributor even if the film bombs.

As bidding in Las Vegas grew more fierce, guarantee amounts went over the top. Too often, the bids were so high that theatre owners ran up substantial losses. The industry refers to these as busted guarantees, meaning that because the film did less business than was expected, the theatre was trapped into paying the higher guarantee amount instead of the percentage of box office it had negotiated. Occasionally, guarantees in Las Vegas were so high that they exceeded the gate at a particular theatre.

Soon, theatres in Las Vegas were paying some of the highest license fees in the nation, while distributors sat back and watched the easy money roll in.

It is the nature of free enterprise that fierce, no holds barred competition will drive out the least effective participants in the market, providing the most efficient allocation of productive resources. And so it was in the Las Vegas movie market in 1982. After a hard fought battle among several contenders, Syufy gained the upper hand. Two of his rivals, Mann Theatres and Plitt Theatres, saw their future as rocky and decided to sell out to Syufy. While Mann and Plitt are major exhibitors nationwide, neither had a large presence in Las Vegas. Mann operated two indoor theatres with a total of three screens; Plitt operated a single theatre with three screens. Things were relatively quiet until September 1984; in September, Syufy entered into earnest negotiations with Cragin Industries, his largest remaining competitor. Cragin sold out to Syufy midway through October, leaving Roberts Company, a small exhibitor of mostly second-run films, as Syufy's only competitor for first-run films in Las Vegas.

It is these three transactions—Syufy's purchases of the Mann, Plitt and Cragin theatres—that the Justice Department claims amount to antitrust violations. As government counsel explained at oral argument, the thrust of its case is that "you may not get monopoly power by buying out your competitors."

Discussion

Competition is the driving force behind our free enterprise system. Unlike centrally planned economies, where decisions about production and allocation are made by government bureaucrats who ostensibly see the big picture and know to do the right thing, capitalism relies on decentralized planning—millions of producers and consumers making hundreds of millions of individual decisions each year—to determine what and how much will be produced. Competition plays the key role in this process: It imposes an essential discipline on producers and sellers of goods to provide the consumer with a better product at a lower cost; it drives out inefficient and marginal producers, releasing resources to higher-valued uses; it promotes diversity, giving consumers choices to fit a wide array of personal preferences; it avoids permanent concentrations of economic power, as even the largest firm can lose market share to a feistier and hungrier rival. If, as the metaphor goes, a market economy is governed by an invisible hand, competition is surely the brass knuckles by which it enforces its decisions.

When competition is impaired, producers may be able to reap monopoly profits, denying consumers many of the benefits of a free market. It is a simple but important truth, therefore, that our antitrust laws are designed to protect the integrity of the market system by assuring that competition reigns freely. While much has been said and written about the antitrust laws during the last century of their existence, ultimately the court must resolve a practical question in every monopolization case: Is this the type of situation where market forces are likely to cure the perceived problem within a reasonable period of time? Or, have barriers been erected to constrain the normal operation of the market, so that the problem is not likely to be self-correcting? In the latter situation, it might well be necessary for a court to correct the market imbalance; in the former, a court ought to exercise extreme caution because judicial intervention in a competitive situation can itself upset the balance of market forces, bringing about the very ills the antitrust laws were meant to prevent.

It is with these observations in mind that we turn to the case before us. Perhaps the most remarkable aspect of this case is that the accused monopolist is a relatively tiny regional entrepreneur while the alleged victims are humongous national corporations with considerable market power of their own. While this is not dispositive—it is conceivable that a little big man may be able to exercise monopoly power locally against large national entities—chances are it is not without significance. Common sense suggests, and experience teaches, that monopoly power is far more easily exercised by larger, economically more powerful entities against smaller, economically punier ones, than vice versa.

Also of significance is the government's concession that Syufy was only a monopsonist, not a monopolist.[4] Thus, the government argues that Syufy had market power, but that it

4. Monopsony is defined as a "market situation in which there is a single buyer or a group of buyers making joint decisions. Monopsony and monopsony power are the equivalent on the buying side of monopoly and monopoly power on the selling side." R. Lipsey, P. Steiner & D. Purvis, *Economics* 976 (7th ed. 1984).

exercised this power only against its suppliers (film distributors), not against its consumers (moviegoers). This is consistent with the record, which demonstrates that Syufy always treated moviegoers fairly: The movie tickets, popcorn, nuts and the Seven-Ups cost about the same in Las Vegas as in other, comparable markets. While it is theoretically possible to have a middleman who is a monopolist upstream but not downstream, this is a somewhat counterintuitive scenario. Why, if he truly had significant market power, would Raymond Syufy have chosen to take advantage of the big movie distributors while giving a fair shake to ordinary people? And why do the distributors, the alleged victims of the monopolization scheme, think that Raymond Syufy is the best thing that ever happened to the Las Vegas movie market?

The answers to these questions are significant because, like all antitrust cases, this one must make economic sense.Keeping in mind that competition, not government intervention, is the touchstone of a healthy, vigorous economy, we proceed to examine whether the district court erred in concluding that Syufy does not, in fact, hold monopoly power. There is universal agreement that monopoly power is the power to exclude competition or control prices. The district court determined that Syufy possessed neither power. As the government's case stands or falls with these propositions, the parties have devoted much of their analysis to these findings. So do we.

1. Power to Exclude Competition

It is true, of course, that when Syufy acquired Mann's, Plitt's and Cragin's theatres he temporarily diminished the number of competitors in the Las Vegas first-run film market. But this does not necessarily indicate foul play; many legitimate market arrangements diminish the number of competitors. It would be odd if they did not, as the nature of competition is to make winners and losers. If there are no significant barriers to entry, however, eliminating competitors will not enable the survivors to reap a monopoly profit; any attempt to raise prices above the competitive level will lure into the market new competitors able and willing to offer their commercial goods or personal services for less.

Time after time, we have recognized this basic fact of economic life:

> A high market share, though it may ordinarily raise an inference of monopoly power, will not do so in a market with low entry barriers or other evidence of a defendant's inability to control prices or exclude competitors.

There is nothing magic about this proposition; it is simple common sense, embodied in the Antitrust Division's own Merger Guidelines:

> If entry into a market is so easy that existing competitors could not succeed in raising price for any significant period of time, the Department is unlikely to challenge mergers in that market.

*   *   *

We bypass as surplusage the hundreds of pages of expert and lay testimony that support the district court's finding, and focus instead only on a single—to our minds conclusive—item. Immediately after Syufy bought out the last of his three competitors in October 1984, he was riding high, having captured 100% of the first-run film market in Las Vegas. But this utopia proved to be only a mirage. That same month, a major movie distributor, Orion, stopped doing business with Syufy, sending all of its first-run films to Roberts Company, a dark horse competitor previously relegated to the second-run market. Roberts Company took this as an invitation to step into the major league and, against all odds, began giving Syufy serious competition in the first-run market. Fighting fire with fire, Roberts opened three multiplexes within a 13–month period, each having six or more screens. By December 1986, Roberts was operating 28 screens, trading places with Syufy, who had only 23. At the same time, Roberts was displaying a healthy portion of all first-run films. In fact, Roberts got exclusive exhibition rights to many of its films, meaning that Syufy could not show them at all.

By the end of 1987, Roberts was showing a larger percentage of first-run films than was the Redrock multiplex at the time Syufy bought it. Roberts then sold its theatres to United Artists, the largest theatre chain in the country, and Syufy continued losing ground. It all boils down to this: Syufy's acquisitions did not short circuit the operation of the natural market forces; Las Vegas' first-run film market was more competitive when this case came to trial than before Syufy bought out Mann, Plitt and Cragin.

The Justice Department correctly points out that Syufy still has a large market share, but attributes far too much importance to this fact. In evaluating monopoly power, it is not market share that counts, but the ability to maintain market share. Syufy seems unable to do this. In 1985, Syufy managed to lock up exclusive exhibition rights to 91% of all the first-run films in Las Vegas. By the first quarter of 1988, that percentage had fallen to 39%; United Artists had exclusive rights to another 25%, with the remaining 36% being played on both Syufy and UA screens.

Syufy's share of box office receipts also dropped off, albeit less precipitously. In 1985, Syufy raked in 93% of the gross box office from first-run films in Las Vegas. By the first quarter of 1988, that figure had fallen to 75%. The government insists that 75% is still a large number, and we are hardpressed to disagree; but that's not the point. The antitrust laws do not require that rivals compete in a dead heat, only that neither is unfairly kept from doing his personal best. Accordingly, the government would do better to plot these points on a graph and observe the pattern they form than to focus narrowly on Syufy's market share at a particular time. The numbers reveal that Roberts/UA has steadily been eating away at Syufy's market share: In two and a half years, Syufy's percentage of exclusive exhibition rights dropped 52% and its percentage of box office receipts dropped 18%. During the same period, Roberts/UA's newly opened theatres evolved from absolute beginners, barely staying alive, into a big business.

The government concedes that there are no structural barriers to entry into the market: Syufy does not operate a bank or similar enterprise where entry is limited by government regulation or licensing requirements. Nor is this the type of industry, like heavy manufacturing or mining, which requires onerous front-end investments that might deter competition from all but the hardiest and most financially secure investors. Nor do we have here a business dependent on a scarce commodity, control over which might give the incumbent a substantial structural advantage. Nor is there a network of exclusive contracts or distribution arrangements designed to lock out potential competitors. To the contrary, the record discloses a rough-and-tumble industry, marked by easy market access, fluid relationships with distributors, an ample and continuous supply of product, and a healthy and growing demand. It would be difficult to design a market less susceptible to monopolization.

Confronted with this record and the district court's clear findings, the government trots out a shopworn argument we had thought long abandoned: that efficient, aggressive competition is itself a structural barrier to entry. According to the government, competitors will be deterred from entering the market because they could not hope to turn a profit competing against Syufy. In the words of government counsel:

> There is no legal barrier. There is no law that says you can't come into this market, it's not that kind of barrier. . . . But, the fact of mere possibility in the literal sense, is not the appropriate test. Entry, after all, must, to be effective to dissipate the monopoly power that Syufy has, entry must hold some reasonable prospect of profitability for the entrant, or else the entrant will say, as Mann Theatres said . . . this is not an attractive market to enter. There will be shelter. And the reason is very clear. You have to compete effectively in this market. And witness after witness testified you would need to build anywhere from 12 to 24 theatres, which is a very expensive and time consuming proposition. *And, you would then find yourself in a bidding war against Syufy.*

The notion that the supplier of a good or service can monopolize the market simply by being efficient reached high tide in the law 44 years ago in Judge Learned Hand's opinion in *United States v. Aluminum Co. of Am.*, 148 F.2d 416 (2d Cir.1945). In the intervening decades the wisdom of this notion has been questioned by just about everyone who has taken a close look at it.

The argument government counsel presses here is a close variant of *Alcoa:* The government is not claiming that Syufy monopolized the market by being too efficient, but that Syufy's effectiveness as a competitor creates a structural barrier to entry, rendering illicit Syufy's acquisition of its competitors' screens. We hasten to sever this new branch that the government has caused to sprout from the moribund *Alcoa* trunk.

It can't be said often enough that the antitrust laws protect competition, not competitors. As we noted earlier, competition is essential to the effective operation of the free market because it encourages efficiency, promotes consumer satisfaction and prevents the accumulation of monopoly profits. When a producer is shielded from competition, he is likely to provide lesser service at a higher price; the victim is the consumer who gets a raw deal. This is the evil the antitrust laws are meant to avert. But when a producer deters competitors by supplying a better product at a lower price, when he eschews monopoly profits, when he operates his business so as to meet consumer demand and increase consumer satisfaction, the goals of competition are served, even if no actual competitors see fit to enter the market at a particular time. While the successful competitor should not be raised above the law, neither should he be held down by law.

The Supreme Court has accordingly distanced itself from the *Alcoa* legacy, taking care to distinguish unlawful monopoly power from "growth or development as a consequence of a superior product, business acumen, or historic accident," *United States v. Grinnell Corp.*, 384 U.S. 563, 571, 86 S.Ct. 1698, 1704, 16 L.Ed.2d 778 (1966), which is off limits to the enforcer of our antitrust laws. If a dominant supplier acts consistent with a competitive market—out of fear perhaps that potential competitors are ready and able to step in—the purpose of the antitrust laws is amply served. We make it clear today, if it was not before, that an efficient, vigorous, aggressive competitor is not the villain antitrust laws are aimed at eliminating. Fostering an environment where businesses fight it out using the weapon of efficiency and consumer goodwill is what the antitrust laws are meant to champion. As the Second Circuit has said: "We fail to see how the existence of good will achieved through effective service is an impediment to, rather than the natural result of, competition." *United States v. Waste Mgmt., Inc.*, 743 F.2d 976, 984 (2d Cir.1984).

But we need not rely on theory alone in rejecting the government's argument. The record here conclusively demonstrates that neither acquiring the screens of his competitors nor working hard at better serving the public gave Syufy deliverance from competition. Immediately following the disappearance of Mann, Plitt and Cragin, Roberts took up the challenge, aggressively competing with Syufy for first-run films—and with considerable success. United Artists, with substantial resources at its disposal and nationwide experience in running movie theatres, considered the market sufficiently open that it bought out Roberts in 1987. We see no indication that competition suffered in the Las Vegas movie market as a result of Syufy's challenged acquisitions. The district court certainly had ample basis in the record for its finding that Syufy lacked the power to exclude competitors. Indeed, on this voluminous record we are hard-pressed to see how the district court could have come to the other conclusion.

2. Power to Control Prices

The crux of the Justice Department's case is that Syufy, top gun in the Las Vegas movie market, had the power to push around Hollywood's biggest players, dictating to them what prices they could charge for their movies. The district court found otherwise. This finding too has substantial support in the record.

Perhaps the most telling evidence of Syufy's inability to set prices came from movie distributors, Syufy's supposed victims. At the trial, distributors uniformly proclaimed their satisfaction with the way the Las Vegas first-run film market operates; none complained about the license fees paid by Syufy. Columbia's President of Domestic Distribution testified that "Syufy paid a fair amount of film rental" that compared favorably with other markets. A representative of Buena Vista, a division of Disney, testified that Syufy had never refused to accept its standard terms. Particularly damaging to the government's case was the testimony of the former head of distribution for MGM/UA that his company "never had any difficulty . . . in acquiring the terms that we thought were reasonable,"explaining that the license fees Syufy paid "were comparable or better than any place in the United States. And in most cases better." Indeed, few if any of the distributors were willing to say anything to support the government's claim.

The documentary evidence bears out this testimony. Syufy has at all times paid license fees far in excess of the national average, even higher than those paid by exhibitors in Los Angeles, the Mecca of Moviedom. In fact, Syufy paid a higher percentage of his gross receipts to distributors in 1987 and 1988 than he did during the intensely competitive period just before he acquired Cragin's Redrock.

While successful, Syufy is in no position to put the squeeze on distributors. The one time he tried there was an immediate backlash. In 1984, about seven days after allegedly acquiring its monopoly, Syufy informed Orion Releasing Group that he had cold feet about The Cotton Club and would not honor the large guarantees he had contracted for, only to see his gambit backfire. Orion sued Syufy for breach of contract, licensed the film to Roberts and cut Syufy off cold turkey. To this day, Orion refuses to play its films in any Syufy theatre, in Las Vegas or elsewhere. Accordingly, Syufy lost the opportunity to exhibit top moneymakers like Robocop, Platoon, Hannah and Her Sisters and No Way Out. The district court found no evidence that Orion considered Roberts/UA's theatres a less than adequate substitute for Syufy's.

Because he needs plenty of first-run films to fill his many screens (22 at the time of trial; 34 now), Syufy is vulnerable. Distributors like Orion have substantial leverage over Syufy and they know it. One witness, the President of Domestic Distribution for Columbia, testified at length about the power he and other distributors wield over Syufy:

> . . . [W]ith Syufy having 23 first-run screens, he could not get into a two and a half percent fight with Columbia; he had so many mouths to feed in those theatres, that he was more or less compelled to pay national suggested terms for films. . . . .

> . . . He could have tried [to dictate terms], but he wouldn't have gotten away with it, your Honor. He was very vulnerable. My point is that he was very vulnerable in that market. He could not—he needed the flow of product to fill those screens, and to take on—to get into a fight with the distributor over terms, or film rentals paid to a distributor, would create an attitude where we could sell [to] his opposition and he'd be egregiously hurt.

*   *   *

. . . [H]e was his own competition, your Honor. He had created such a large amount of screens that he was—he was himself—he was himself vulnerable. As I described before, if he would have pressed, and if he would have come to Jimmie Spitz and said, "I'm not going to pay you this percentage for the film," I would have said, "Fine, Ray, we'll stay out of the marketplace." He couldn't afford—he has to— he has to have film in his theatres. And that's the leverage that this company had with Mr. Syufy. ([T]estimony of James Spitz).

After hours of such testimony, the judge quite rightly concluded that Syufy did not have the power to control license fees. This evidence, moreover, reveals the trap in the oftmade assumption that, by virtue of being a leviathan, a company will automatically have the power to wield a big stick with which to push around suppliers, customers and competitors. While size no doubt provides significant business advantages, it can also have very substantial drawbacks, such as increased management costs and other diseconomies of scale.

More fundamentally, in a free economy the market itself imposes a tough enough discipline on all market actors, large and small. Every supplier of goods and services is integrated into an endless chain of supply and demand relationships, making it dependent on the efficiency and goodwill of upstream suppliers, as well as the patronage of customers. Absent structural constraints that keep competition from performing its levelling function, few businesses can dictate terms to customers or suppliers with impunity. It's risky business even to try. As Syufy learned in dealing with Orion and his other suppliers, a larger company often is more vulnerable to a squeeze play than a smaller one. It is for that reason that neither size nor market share alone suffice to establish a monopoly. Without the power to exclude competition, large companies that try to throw their weight around may find themselves sitting ducks for leaner, hungrier competitors. Or, as Syufy saw, the tactic may boomerang, causing big trouble with suppliers.

On this record, we have no basis for overturning the district court's finding that Syufy lacked the power to set the prices he paid his suppliers. As with the district court's finding as to Syufy's power to exclude competition, we believe the record here lent itself to only one sensible conclusion.

*   *   *

Conclusion

The judgment of the district court is affirmed.

Once again, Justice Musmanno is the author of an extremely powerful and thought-provoking dissenting opinion. However, this time the case does not involve a personal injury, per se, but a moral injury to our society.

"Throughout his distinguished career, Justice Musmanno often found himself at odds with the position taken by the majority of his Court, but never shrunk from his responsibilities or his convictions. . . . I make this selection not as an endorsement of the result Justice Musmanno reached, but to honor a jurist whose extraordinary vision and unshrinking dedication to the cause of justice is an inspiration to all who are fortunate enough to don judicial robes."

—Judge, Pennsylvania State Court

COMMONWEALTH of Pennsylvania
v.
DELL PUBLICATIONS, INC., *et al.*

Supreme Court of Pennsylvania
Sept. 29, 1967
233 A.2d 840, 427 Pa. 189

A complaint was brought by the district attorney of Philadelphia County to enjoin the sale and distribution of an allegedly obscene book entitled Candy. The Court of Common Pleas issued an injunction after finding the book obscene, and defendants appealed. The Supreme Court reversed the lower court, holding that although the book had the requisite prurient appeal, it did not go beyond customary limits of candor as measured by contemporary community standards and had at least a modicum of social value so that it could not be proscribed as obscene.

MUSMANNO, Justice (dissenting).

The Supreme Court of Pennsylvania had an opportunity in this case to unlimber some heavy artillery in fighting for American morality; it had unlimited freedom to pour devastating fire into the forces that would destroy the very foundations of decency, purity and wholesome conduct upon which our American society is founded; it had the clearest chance to draw from the armory of the law the weapons which would beat back those who, for greed and lucre, would poison the minds of the youth of our Commonwealth. The Supreme Court, however, did none of these things. The Majority of this Court retired from the field of battle without firing a shot. It did more. It encouraged the foul foe to smash more effectively at the bastions of American decency; it unfurled a flag of impeccability and authority over the invading filthy battalions; it supplied to each hoodlum in the putrid expeditionary force a bar of Ivory Soap which made him, according to the Majority's reasoning, $99\frac{1}{2}\%$ Pure!

I disassociate myself, as far as I can, intellectually, jurisprudentially, and philosophically, from the decision of this Court in this case.

Here was a case where this Court could have declared that the book under consideration was so devoid of literary merit, so odious in its presentation of its immoral theme, so obviously designed to appeal to the baser animalism of man, that its sale and distribution should be outlawed in Pennsylvania. Whom would such a decision have hurt or offended? No one but those who are heaping up sordid dollars, as a rake gathers up rotten leaves in an abandoned and unseeded garden.

The Majority Opinion says that "[o]ur decision in this case, * * * should not, in any manner, be construed as an approval of 'Candy'." How else can it be construed? The Majority's statement is like saying that the Court does not approve of a snake entering a nursery but forbids anyone to build a fence around the nursery to keep the serpent out. I reject as untenable the pious statement that the Majority does not approve of "Candy" when the Opinion oleaginously oozes with praise of this filthy book. It points out that "Candy" sold over $2\frac{1}{2}$ million copies in the hard cover edition. How does that establish that it is not obscene? There are millions of persons who use narcotics which admittedly are ruinous to health. Does that say that narcotics should be sold freely?[1]

---

1. Hitler's "Meinkampf" reached a sale of over ten million. Would the Majority say that that book did not have an evil influence and did not contribute to the horrible atrocities perpetrated on the Jewish people?

The Majority Opinion calls the central character in "Candy" the "heroine." This "heroine" is a prostitute, a degenerate, a deviate, and a defiler of the truth. The Majority Opinion appends glowing testimonials of the book from certain periodicals. It quotes from one review:

> "Nowhere has sex been sicker than in the U.S., and sick for so long we have forgotten it is supposed to be healthy."

How healthy a book is "Candy"? What salubriousness does it contribute to the moral health of the nation? The book revoltingly describes in detail a sexual act between a father and his daughter, it portrays the debauching of a niece by her uncle, it relates a disgusting perversion between a girl and a depraved, deformed man, it speaks of unnatural practices which would make the beasts of Sodom and Gomorrah ashamed. And this is what the periodical the Majority cites with approval calls healthy sex!

One book quoted by the Majority declares the book is not pornographic but concedes it is "dirty as hell."

The Majority Opinion states:

> "It is generally conceded, by the book's friends and foes, that it is a satire or at least an attempt at satire upon the cultural ideals of our contemporary society."

This statement is wholly unsupported by the facts. I can be listed as one of the book's foes and I certainly do not regard it as a "satire upon the cultural ideals of our contemporary society." There is nothing in the ideal culture of our contemporary society which remotely resembles the reprehensible conduct, the bestial practices described in "Candy."

Then the Majority quotes from one of the defenders of the book who said that "Candy" is a "spoof on sex." "Candy" is as much a spoof on sex as a garbage dump is a spoof on a garbage dump. "Candy" is the garbage dump. It is rotten-core pornography. It is not a satire on pornography, it is not a spoof on sex, it is plainly an outrageous display of depravity in its most loathsome forms. Those who attempt to defend the book as a work of satire, culture, or literary art would never admit that they would look without favor upon their children reading it.

The Majority is not content to quote from reviews of "Candy." It gratuitously shovels into its Opinion, and thus further burdens, as well as contaminates, the pages of the Pennsylvania Reports, libidinous comments on another book, as they appeared in a Federal court case. The Majority points out that there are other books more obscene than "Candy." In this, the Majority apparently proceeds on the theory that since "Candy" is surpassed in degeneracy by other vile works, "Candy" should not be subject to injunction under Pennsylvania laws. This is like saying that a person in the early stages of a contagious venereal disease may not be excluded from waiting on the dining table because there are syphilitics working in the kitchen.

Thus, the Majority tells of other purveyors of sewage, such as "Memoirs of a Woman of Pleasure," "Naked Lunch," "Tropic of Cancer" and similar pornographic junk, and argues that since they were not banned, "Candy" has at least a minimum or modicum of social value. But the Majority does not give the slightest hint of what that "social value" is. It apparently advances the theme that a community of people should not object to being pushed into a mud pond because there are other communities which permit cesspools where frogs and lizards revel in natatorial slime.

The Majority admits that "Candy" is an obscene book, but then in an astonishing non sequitur declares that it cannot be banned because it does not go "far beyond customary limits of candor." What does the majority regard as the limits of candor? Is it customary candor for decent people to discuss in intimate detail the dung-covered incestuous conduct described in the book? Do people in decent society employ the gutter language spoken by the execrable radish-white humped back creton in the book? The answer is obvious, yet the Majority finds that this maggoty language is customary candor. In what neighborhood does the Majority hear this "customary candor" Billingsgate?

The Majority Opinion is a long one; it is erudite, complicated, and as studded with citations and footnotes as a broken plank with bent nails, but it never comes to grips with the problem the litigation presents. The Act of June 1, 1956, P.L. (1955) 1997, as amended, 18 P.S. s 3832.1, under which the District Attorney proceeded in this case, proclaims against the sale or distribution of a book which "constitutes a danger to the welfare" of the community. Nowhere in the Majority Opinion is there the slightest discussion of the baleful effects on communities of an obscene book. One of the specific findings of fact of the Court below reads:

> "Circulation, distribution and sale of the book 'Candy' constitutes a threat to the morals and welfare of the community."

The Majority Opinion makes no mention of this formidable finding which has the standing of a jury's verdict. It disposes of the case by saying that the decision of the Court below was "subjective." What else could it be? A judge trying a murder case does not go out and commit a murder in order to learn what murder is. He reaches a conclusion after hearing the evidence, and that is what the lower Court did, and that is what the Majority of this Court did not do. If there is an Opinion that is subjective, it is the Majority Opinion. It is not only subjective, it is academic, theoretical and discursive, with considerable hypothesis and it contains even a dash of prediction as to what the Supreme Court of the United States will do, a daring proposition indeed.

Prohibition against obscenity is not only a matter of cleanliness and godliness; the health of the community is involved. It has been established in thousands of cases that there can be a direct connection between abnormal sex books and sex crimes. Those who profess not to see this connection are either abysmally ignorant or refuse to accept the truth. *   *   *

Why have there been laws against obscenity reaching back into the days of antiquity? It is because obscenity, lewdness, lasciviousness strike at the very moral fiber of a people and, when that disintegrates, a nation perishes. Justice Harlan said in the *Roth-Alberts* case (354 U.S. 495, 77 S.Ct. 1318) that "(t)he State can reasonably draw the inference that over a long period of time the indiscriminate dissemination of materials, the essential character of which is to degrade sex, will have an eroding effect on moral standards." We know that Rome was great and went into decline; that Greece was the flower of culture, and that weeds finally grew in the Acropolis; that the Persian, Egyptian, Babylonian and numerous other civilizations were powerful, rich and indomitable but something happened to them and they moldered into decay—not because of armed invasion from without their gates, but from moral deterioration within their walls.

In 1874 Justice Swayne, speaking for an unanimous United States Supreme Court, declared: "The foundation of a republic is the virtue of its citizens. They are at once sovereigns and subjects. As the foundation is undermined, the structure is weakened. When it is destroyed, the fabric must fall. Such is the voice of history * * *"

The contemporary United States Supreme Court has drifted far from the wisdom and fundamental democratic philosophy inherent in the above quotation. The Majority Opinion in the case at bar seeks to justify its conclusions citing from recent decisions of the Court on Capitol Hill in Washington. Those decisions are a lighthouse with broken beams. The majority opinions of the present U.S. Supreme Court, on the subject of obscenity, constitute a never-never land of confusion and self-contradiction. Taken in the aggregate, those opinions suggest a region hazy with drifting fogs, beset with contrary wind currents, criss-crossed with labyrinthian, tortuous foot trails, perforated with pitfalls and tortured with quicksands, which no legal travelers could hope to traverse and emerge therefrom with a precise knowledge as to where he had been, what he had seen, and where he was now going. It is with regret that I say this, but it is with conviction, based on intensive study of late Supreme Court decisions, that I say that Court itself does not seem to know where it is going on this subject which affects the homes, the welfare, and the moral standards of the nation.

I state, again with reluctance, that the Supreme Court of the United States has failed to measure up to its responsibilities in this area of the law. I have respect for the highest Court in the land, I am bound by its decisions, but I wish it would make up its mind as to what is its decision in this realm of jurisprudence. * * * The decisions are a conglomeration of personal views, individual tangents and private predilections, without much thought apparently being given to the effect those decisions will have on the nation as a whole. I state, again with disinclination, that the Supreme Court of the United States has failed to live up to its solemn responsibility of protecting, through a serious interpretation and firm enforcement, of the laws of the land, the ramparts of moral standards, the crumbling of which will bring disaster to our country. The Supreme Court has simply refused to meet its obligations in considering a grave situation which affects American youth, into whose hands the destiny of our nation will one day be committed.

When this case was in the hands of the Court below, decision was delayed awaiting clarification of the whole problem of obscenity by the highest court of the land. On March 21, 1966, the Supreme Court spoke through 14 opinions handed down in three cases. The lower Court called the Supreme Court decisions "a congeries of pronouncements," in which it looked "in vain for the anticipated illumination." Also, "we feel that the mountain has labored and brought forth a litter of mice."

*   *   *

The Supreme Court of the United States has written scores of decisions on obscenity. It has laid down rules, expounded principles, established standards and then later ignored or dismissed them all. It draws fine line distinctions in the areas of community standards, prurient appeal, contemporary society, social value, etc., and then proceeds in effect, to offer in one form or another, a free passport to every book which comes before it, no matter how degraded or vile it may be. It is a significant fact, as admitted by the Majority Opinion in this case, and I quote from the Opinion: "The Court (Supreme Court of the United States) has yet to find a published work obscene per se."!!

I do not believe that the framers of our nation's Constitution ever intended that the judges of the Supreme Court were to perform as super-censors on books. The question of the propriety of the distribution of questioned literature should be left to the States where it was prior to 1787 and which no one at that time ever thought of transferring to the nation. In 1887 the Supreme Court acknowledged that it was the province of the legislative department of government to exercise the necessary police powers to stand guard over public morality:

> "[The] [p]ower to determine such questions, (what is offensive to public morality) so as to bind all, must exist somewhere; else society will be at the mercy of the few, who, regarding only their own

appetites or passions, may be willing to imperil the peace and security of the many, provided only they are permitted to do as they please. Under our system that power is lodged with the legislative branch of the government. It belongs to that department to exert what are known as police powers of the state, and to determine, primarily, what measures are appropriate or needful for the protection of the public morals, the public health, or the public safety." (*Mugler v. State of Kansas*, 123 U.S. 623, 8 S.Ct. 273, 31 L.Ed. 205.)

Nevertheless, the Supreme Court has deliberately assumed jurisdiction over the millions of books, pamphlets, magazines and newspapers in the land, a jurisdiction it cannot possibly cope with. And then, to make matters worse, it attempts to apply a yardstick which can have no application to realities. The standard for determining obscenity, as laid down in the *Roth* case, is "whether to the average person, applying contemporary community standards, the dominant theme of the material taken as a whole appeals to prurient interest."

What is a community? It is a region, a circumscribed area as a town, village, neighborhood. In its broadest concept it could possibly envelop a State, but it is contrary to common usage to apply the word "community" to a nation, and this is what the Supreme Court has done.

But, even after arbitrarily giving to community a national significance, the Supreme Court has ignored the moral standards of the American people as a whole. It has fashioned most of its decisions on obscenity on the views and attitudes of an infinitesimal minority, literary critics and book reviewers, who, with their admitted talents, cannot possibly speak for the masses not so sophisticated as those who made the reviewing of books their profession.

This summary seizure of jurisdiction by the Supreme Court in this field has worked, and continues to work, havoc in the individual states which are frequently compelled to wait for decisions from Washington as to whether a certain book may or may not be sold at a newsstand in a village in North Dakota. And more often than not, the expected decision turns out to be so cloudy in exposition and disposition that the pornographic culprit escapes under cover of the rhetorical smoke.

The decisions of the United States Supreme Court in obscenity cases have raised alarm in the most venerable places of the nation—the home, the church, and the school.

*   *   *

The Pennsylvania Supreme Court missed a coveted opportunity in the case at bar to strike a blow for decency, since the U.S. Supreme Court has not yet passed on the book which is the subject of the current legislation. Of course, one could well imagine that, after the U.S. Supreme Court allowed the British pandering whore Fanny Hill to pass into the temple of purity, it would not bar entrance to the frowzy, streetwalking, subterranean harlot "Candy." Still, this Court could have made the effort to save a few Pennsylvania children from the stench of "Candy" because a little time might elapse between our banning it and the Supreme Court's striking down the ban. And then there could always be the possibility, as remote as it seems today, that the U.S. Supreme Court might respect its historical pronouncements that freedom of the press does not include the publication of obscenity. *   *   *

From all this we conclude that the Majority of this Court, by taking into the chamber of consideration and consultation an arithmetic table, a block, an ax, and circular logic, arrived at the conclusion that there could be no use in waiting to see what the Supreme Court might say in "Candy", and thus, with a circular saw, it sawed away the rights of the people of Pennsylvania to be saved from the inundation of filth gushing from the pages of a book which the Majority finds possesses a minimum of social importance but never explains why.

Because, of course, it cannot!

From Pittsburgh to Philadelphia, from Dan to Beersheba, and from the ramparts of the Bible to Samuel Eliot Morison's Oxford History of the American People, I dissent!

World's shortest opinion . . .?

"It is truly a model of brevity. If more judicial opinions were like this one, lawyers and judges who have to read them would be much happier, and the forests would be much safer."

—Justice, Arizona State Court

DENNY

v.

RADAR INDUSTRIES, INC.

Court of Appeals of Michigan
Dec. 2, 1970
184 N.W.2d 289, 28 Mich.App. 294

J.H. GILLIS, Judge.

The appellant has attempted to distinguish the factual situation in this case from that in *Renfroe v. Higgins Rack Coating and Manufacturing Co., Inc.* (1969), 17 Mich.App. 259, 169 N.W.2d 326. He didn't. We couldn't.

Affirmed. Costs to appellee.

Chapter 7
Love and Marriage

It is perhaps not surprising that a large number of the cases suggested to us deal with love and marriage. We share our meals, our homes, our lives with those who are closest to us. But, unfortunately, we also share our anger, frustration and unhappiness with those same people. Emotions can be volatile at times and, when there are problems, the emotions escalate. And so we sometimes find that we cannot resolve our differences over the dinner table. Instead, we end up discussing them in court.

We begin with the story of a love that should not have been and that ultimately went sour. The facts are by no means unique. But Vice Chancellor Jayne's language is delightful, and the ridicule he heaps upon the defendant was undoubtedly more telling, and longer lasting, than any outraged denunciation of a gigolo-turned-cad could ever have been.

TAMI

v.

PIKOWITZ

Court of Chancery of New Jersey
July 30, 1946
48 A.2d 221, 138 N.J. Eq. 410

JAYNE, Vice Chancellor.

In several of its aspects this cause is an unfashionable one to be introduced to a court of equity for determination. Basically it pertains to the title and possession of a Plymouth automobile which, in the existing industrial conditions, is alleged to be a rare and unique article of personalty. In retaining jurisdiction I have preferred to recognize the suit as one prosecuted to nullify a bill of sale alleged to have been procured fraudulently and without consideration.

The controversy recoils from the indiscretions of the parties. In its broad factual appearance, the indecorous acts of the complainant are manifestly surpassed by the dishonorable perfidy of the defendant. The story can be readily summarized.

The parties were employed at the establishment of a war industry, where their acquaintance and ensuing associations originated. Both were married persons, but in the initial period of their companionship neither thought it prudent or necessary to divulge that incidental fact to the other.

While the defendant is noticeably lacking in the physical comeliness of an Adonis, nevertheless the complainant's interest in him, like Aphrodite's, gradually ascended to an altitude of infatuation. When released from work, they frequently convened at a neighboring tavern, where they enjoyed, and she paid for, the refreshments. She bestowed upon him many gifts, such as a wrist watch, a wallet (he conserved his earnings), gloves, neckties, and sun glasses. Indeed, he smoothly persuaded her to loan him $200. Up to this point he rejoiced in playing the role of a subsidized escort. He subsequently permitted her to contemplate the dissolution of their former marriages and their future alliance in matrimony.

On December 14, 1945, she purchased the automobile at the price of $1,000. She did not have a license to operate a motor vehicle, but the vendor had promised to instruct her. The defendant forthwith expressed to the complainant his ardent desire to visit his relatives in Pennsylvania, and he implored her to permit him to have the use of the car for the accomplishment of that journey but, according to the testimony of the complainant, he shrewdly informed her that if, perchance, the vehicle should be involved in some accident, she, by virtue of her ownership of it, might incur some personal pecuniary liability. He accordingly recommended that it would be entirely feasible and extremely precautious for her to transfer temporarily the apparent ownership of the vehicle to him. She did so on December 20, 1945, whereupon the defendant departed for Pennsylvania.

During his absence, his wife either fortuitously or designedly met the complainant. The interview inspired the complainant to make an unexpected personal visit at the address in Pennsylvania where the defendant had assured her he intended to sojourn. The defendant was not at that address. The complainant was informed that the defendant could be reached at a designated residence in a near-by village in the company of one "Amelia." It may be inferred that Amelia was no more pleased to meet the complainant than the latter was pleased to meet Amelia.

The circumstances of that occasion caused the curtain of implicit faith to drop from the complainant's eyes, and she discovered that the pretended fidelity of the defendant was merely a deceptive shadow. "Now sighs steal out and tears begin to flow," said Pope.

The defendant returned to Middlesex County, New Jersey, early in January 1946. The complainant immediately requested him to surrender the automobile and its title to her. He refused. She intimated her intention to consult an attorney. He threatened that should she do so, he would impart to her husband full knowledge of their associations. He then retired as a gigolo to become a cad. But let me continue.

Upon the institution of the present cause, the defendant filed an answer in which he averred that "the complainant meretriciously had sexual relations with this defendant on many occasions since the month of October 1945," and that the complainant gave him the automobile "in consideration of the meretricious relation existing between the complainant and this defendant."

Furthermore, the defendant at the final hearing, and in the presence of the complainant's husband, related brazenly and without a blush of humility, his sexual performances with the complainant, and he sought to multiply the number of such occurrences as if he were endeavoring to establish an adequate quantum meruit. Thus again the defendant retrogrades; this time to the level of venality.

The words of Justice Kalisch, expressive of the sentiment of the Court of Errors and Appeals in *Letts v. Letts*, 79 N.J.Eq. 630, 635, 82 A. 845, 848, Ann.Cas.1913A, 1236, reverberate: "I doubt if there can be found in the history of the divorce court anywhere such a rara avis, a male co-respondent, who had voluntarily come forward in aid of an injured husband suing for a divorce; who had sunk his manhood his morals, and his honor so low as to go voluntarily upon the witness stand and with brazen impunity proclaimed his triumph over his victim, to irretrievably disgrace and ruin her. The experience of mankind has been to the contrary; and therefore when a case arises which is contrary to this experience, it is such an aberration from the normal trend of human action that it requires convincing proof to confirm it."

The complainant denied that her associations with the defendant had included any sexual indulgences. I can attribute some measure of credibility to her testimony, but I do not hesitate to declare that I cannot repose any credence whatever in that of the defendant. The defendant claims the automobile as a remunerative reward for his "meretricious" servitude. His counsel confronts the complainant with the maxim "He who comes into equity must come with clean hands." It is the defendant himself who has sought to soil and besmear the hands of the complainant. The maxim has its limitations. It does not banish all sinful suitors from a court of equity. The iniquitous conduct must be related proximately to the act of the defendant which is the subject matter of the cause of action; it must be evil practice or wrongful conduct in the particular transaction in respect to which the complainant seeks redress.

It must be realized that the doctrine of unclean hands has its logical justification only in considerations of good conscience and natural justice. There are cases in which a court of equity in fulfillment of the reasons and objects of its creation and existence may in furtherance of natural justice aid the one who comparatively is the more innocent. The complaint's benevolence and the defendant's malevolence do not escape attention. In the posture of the proof in this case I shall not permit the defendant to profit from the feminine weaknesses of the complainant. The defendant acknowledges that he never contributed a penny to the purchase price of the automobile. When first interviewed by an attorney of the complainant, he suggested a compromise by which he might purchase the vehicle by means of instalment payments. He has since chosen to darken some corner in which to hide his loot. Indeed, it required some coercion from the bench to induce the defendant to disclose where he was concealing the automobile.

I am unable to accept the doctrine of unclean hands as a positive defense to the complainant's cause of action. I have, however, paused to consider whether there was an absolute, unconditional, and unqualified gift under the rigid rules of the common law. I think not. Notwithstanding the unwholesome motives of the complainant, I conclude that she intended the transfer to be essentially a bailment. The transfer on her part was undoubtedly conditional and deceitfully procured by means of an imposition upon her enchantment.

Neither my judgment derived from an observation of the witnesses nor my conception of equity and natural justice permits me to absolve the defendant. The decisions of our courts are intended to be expressive or explanatory of the rules that are to govern the relations and conduct of individuals in our social organization. There must be an organic connection between the community sentiment and opinion upon such subjects as manhood, integrity, honor, and fairness, and the laws and decisions of our courts. It would seem to me to be a bar-

barian rule of human conduct that would enable this defendant to succeed in his deliberate brigandage and attempted extortion.

I shall advise a decree for the complainant.

The days and weeks before the wedding are very busy ones for the happy couple. There is so much to do, and it seems that, no matter how many people are available to help, something always gets overlooked. Like the need to divorce the first wife before marrying the second. Or the third. Or . . .

In the Matter of the
ESTATE OF WILLIAMS

Court of Appeals of Michigan
Dec. 7, 1987
417 N.W.2d 556, 164 Mich.App. 601

DANHOF, Chief Judge.

Respondent, Rosebud Williams (Rose), appeals from a November 7, 1985, order of the Wayne County Probate Court, which removed her as personal representative of the estate of decedent Tommie Williams and determined that petitioner, Betty Williams, not Rose, was decedent's lawful spouse.

Decedent died intestate on July 15, 1984. Three days later, on July 18, 1984, Rose petitioned the court for commencement of probate proceedings, asserting that she was decedent's wife. Pursuant to her petition, Rose was appointed personal representative. On July 20, 1984, Betty petitioned the court to remove Rose as personal representative. Betty asserted that she, not Rose, was decedent's wife.

It is undisputed that decedent married four times. The factual dispute of the instant case centers on whether the decedent was equally prolific in obtaining decrees of divorce. The probate court found that decedent was negligent in this area and had divorced no one. However, decedent's third marriage (to Estelle) ended with the death of his third wife.

Decedent and Betty, his fourth wife, entered into a ceremonial marriage on January 7, 1974, at which time a marriage certificate was duly executed. The two lived together as man and wife until decedent's death in 1984. Betty testified when she married decedent it was her understanding that decedent had been married only once previously and that his former wife, Estelle, had died. Betty's marriage certificate supported her claim. It indicated only one previous marriage for decedent. The probate court found that Betty entered into marriage in good faith without knowledge of decedent's first and second marriages and without knowledge that decedent had not divorced his previous wives.

Betty testified further that she later learned that decedent had been married two other times. Decedent told her that Rose had divorced him and married another man. Betty contends that she did not learn of Rose's claim that decedent had not divorced her (Rose) until after decedent's death, when it was too late to remedy the situation.

In 1973, prior to their marriage, Betty and decedent purchased a rental home. However, the home was deeded in decedent's name alone. The rental home is the predominant estate asset. Betty contended, and the probate court so found, that she contributed to the purchase price of the home from her personal funds, that both Betty and decedent were obligated on the mortgage, and that Betty contributed to the monthly mortgage payments. Betty asserts she would be unable to meet her obligations on the mortgage if the spousal intestacy share of the house and rents were awarded to Rose.

Rose testified that she married decedent on July 21, 1951, and presented a copy of the marriage certificate. During their marriage, Rose gave birth to a daughter, Bertina. Bertina's status as heir is not contested.

In a document filed with the probate court on July 18, 1984, when Rose sought appointment as personal representative, Rose acknowledged that she deserted decedent in 1957. Sometime after this separation, Rose learned through "hearsay" that decedent had divorced her. Rose testified that after decedent married Estelle, the third wife, she married John Lewis on December 14, 1968. Lewis died on March 22, 1970. Estelle died on February 12, 1972.

Rose testified that, when she was helping decedent with funeral arrangements for Estelle, she asked to see the divorce papers. Decedent responded that he had never divorced her. Rose testified that she had never divorced decedent. Thus, Rose argued that Betty could not be decedent's lawful spouse.

Rose also testified that after Estelle died she helped decedent care for three nephews and nieces of whom he was guardian. Rose suggested he hire a baby-sitter. Evidently, Betty was the baby-sitter decedent hired.

Decedent's first marriage was to Daisy Mae Jones, whom he married in Pickens County, Alabama, on December 1, 1945. In a brief filed with the probate court, Betty asserted that a diligent search had been made of the divorce records of two counties in Alabama where decedent and Daisy were known to reside and of the Wayne County divorce records and that no record of divorce had been found. Thus, Betty argued that decedent had not divorced Daisy and therefore Rose could not be decedent's lawful spouse. The problem with this argument was that it also impaired Betty's status as lawful spouse.

The probate court attempted to notify decedent's first wife of the probate proceedings. A letter, dated November 19, 1984, from a Detroit attorney appears in the file. It begins: "The 'real' Mrs. Williams is alive and well in St. Louis, Missouri." The attorney explained that an attorney from St. Louis had contacted him to investigate the situation and that he might be employed to assist in presenting Daisy's claim. The letter asserted without explanation that decedent and Daisy never divorced. However, despite the fact she was notified and indicated some initial interest, Daisy never filed an appearance in the probate proceedings.

*   *   *

On appeal, Rose first attempts to avoid the probate court's factual finding that decedent and Daisy never divorced. Rose asserts that Daisy failed to file an appearance or claim of the estate and introduced no evidence to rebut the claims of "any subsequent spouse." However, Daisy is not the only one who was entitled to introduce evidence on the validity of Rose's marriage. Betty, as a potential heir, could, and did introduce proof contesting Rose's claim of heirship. However, we find that the proofs relative to Daisy were insufficient to support the probate court's conclusion that decedent and Daisy never divorced.

In Michigan, where the validity of a marriage is attacked on the ground that one of the parties was married to another, a very strong presumption exists in favor of the validity of the second marriage. The presumption is not rebutted by testimony of the first spouse that, to the best of her knowledge, her husband never attempted to procure a divorce from her and that she had never received or been served with divorce papers, or by testimony that a search was made in the county wherein decedent was known to have resided and no record of divorce was discovered, The possibility exists that an absent spouse could have obtained a divorce elsewhere.

In the instant case, no evidence was introduced indicating where decedent resided after he left Alabama. It is possible that decedent divorced Daisy in a county where the records were not searched. The evidence was insufficient to rebut the presumption of the validity of a subsequent marriage. The probate court erred in finding that decedent and Daisy had never divorced.

However, there was sufficient evidence to support the court's finding that decedent had not divorced Rose. Betty testified that decedent told her Rose had divorced him. Rose testified she had never divorced decedent. It is an important distinction from prior precedents that the person who was to have obtained the divorce testified. Since the probate court gave credence to the testimony that no divorce was obtained, there was clear and convincing evidence to rebut the presumption of the validity of the marriage between decedent and Betty. The probate court erred in concluding, on equitable grounds, that Betty was entitled to the status of lawful spouse. Rose was decedent's lawful spouse.

While the equitable grounds relied upon by the probate court are not relevant to the question of legal status, we conclude that the equitable positions of the parties are important considerations with which the probate court was properly concerned. Over matters of which it has jurisdiction, the probate court has the same powers as the circuit court to make any proper order, including the power to provide equitable relief.

We conclude that Rose is estopped from asserting her legal status. We base our conclusion on several grounds. Rose deserted decedent in 1957. Rose herself remarried without obtaining a divorce and without making reasonable efforts to ascertain whether decedent had divorced her. Equally important is the fact that Rose learned that no divorce existed in 1972 yet remained silent when decedent married Betty in 1974.

It also appears Rose had the opportunity to bring the defect to Betty's attention so that the defect could be cured since Rose acknowledges in her appellate brief that she maintained "consistent social contact throughout the term of the deceased's life." After ten years of purported matrimony ended with decedent's death only then did Rose step forward to announce that she was his lawful spouse. The apparent object of Rose's claim is the bounty produced by decedent's and Betty's ten years of labor.

While we have discovered no case law in which a Michigan appellate court has considered the question of estoppel in the context presented here, courts of other states have reached similar results. The equitable approach which many of our sister states have adopted is summarized in Anno: Estoppel or laches precluding lawful spouse from asserting rights in decedent's estate as against putative spouse. It has long been the majority rule that desertion or abandonment is generally held to be a bar to any right to share in the estate of a deceased spouse. It has also been held that a surviving spouse is estopped from asserting rights under a marriage, even when her husband informed her he had obtained a divorce, when at the time she entered into her second marriage she knew her first husband was still alive and that she had not obtained a divorce from him and that she had not been served with any papers in any divorce proceeding that he may have instituted. Finally, estoppel has been applied in situations where a wife slept on her rights "year in and year out and who, by her silence and acquiescence, allowed the rights of a third party to intervene." Brown v. Brown, 274 Cal.App.2d 178, 190, 79 Cal.Rptr. 257, 82 Cal.Rptr. 238. The instant case presents a situation where all three of the above grounds are present.

Since we conclude that Rose is estopped from asserting her legal status as decedent's lawful spouse, she did not have standing to rebut the presumption of the validity of decedent's subsequent marriage to Betty. Although upon a slightly different rationale, the decision of the probate court is affirmed.

The law applied by the South Dakota Supreme Court, while stated with admirable clarity and conciseness, was not groundbreaking. But the facts of paternity, though not commented on by the court, are surprising.

In the Matter of F.J.F. and F.M.F.

Supreme Court of South Dakota
Nov. 25, 1981
312 N.W.2d 718

FOSHEIM, Justice.

This case began as a dependency and neglect proceeding. Following the adjudication hearing an order was entered declaring F.J.F. and F.M.F., nonidentical twins, dependent and neglected children. Six days later, on February 5, 1980, a dispositional hearing was held. The court ordered termination of the parental rights of the mother and F.R., the alleged father. The order noted that F.R. appeared personally, denied paternity, and consented to the termination of any parental rights in the twins which he may have had. The court thereupon granted the Department of Social Services permanent custody of the twins for purposes of adoption.

On May 29, 1980 Mr. Henkel petitioned the court to reopen the dependency and neglect proceedings for the purpose of determining his claimed paternity of, and custody rights to, the twins. Mr. Henkel alleged he was not given notice of the dependency and neglect proceedings. The trial court granted his petition and on June 25, 1980 heard his testimony and accepted evidence, introduced by the State, of the cost incurred by the State of South Dakota for the care and medical expenses of the twins. The trial court then ordered that the mother, the children and Mr. Henkel submit to blood tests for the purpose of determining paternity. The State and Mr. Henkel stipulated that if such blood tests showed a paternity index of 95 percent or greater, in support of Mr. Henkel's claim, his paternity would be established.

*   *   *

On March 6, 1981, the trial court held the final paternity hearing to determine whether Mr. Henkel was the twins' father. Subsequent to this hearing the trial court entered findings of fact which stated, in part, that the parental rights of the mother were terminated by the court; that the mother named one F.R., her live-in companion, as the twins' father; that F.R. denied paternity, and that any parental rights to the twins which he may have had were terminated; that Mr. Henkel and the mother of the twins had sexual intercourse on December 10 and 11, 1978, and that the twins were born nine months later; that the blood tests showed a 97.27 percent likelihood that Mr. Henkel was the father of the male twin and a 0 percent possibility that he was the father of the female twin; and that although it is rare for twins to have separate fathers, it is possible. The trial court determined that Mr. Henkel is the father of the male twin but not the female twin and ordered the Department of Social Services to retain custody of the twins until the matter was decided on appeal or the time for appeal had elapsed. The State thereupon appealed from the trial court's judgment. We affirm.

We first address the issue of whether the trial court had jurisdiction to reopen the proceedings to determine paternity. The State contends that the jurisdiction of the trial court to hear dependency and neglect actions is governed by SDCL ch. 26–8 and, since these proceedings were instituted pursuant to that chapter, SDCL 26–8–63 expresses the controlling procedure. The State argues that no "new evidence has been discovered which was not known and could not with due diligence have been made available at the original hearing and which might affect the decree," as SDCL 26–8–63 requires.

The State maintains that Mr. Henkel had actual or constructive notice of the adjudication hearing and that his evidence of sexual intercourse with the mother was then known to him and should have been presented at that time. Although the notice testimony is conflicting as to the adjudication hearing, the record clearly indicates that Mr. Henkel had actual knowledge of the disposition hearing and that he believed he was the father. Mr. Henkel's stated reason for not then asserting paternity was that he did not want to disturb the possibility of the mother's family obtaining custody of the twins, if they so desired.

The claim upon which Mr. Henkel petitioned could not be termed "new evidence" until the trial court had an opportunity to judge whether Mr. Henkel's suspicions that he was the father were more than that. When Mr. Henkel appeared on the scene, no one, including Mr. Henkel, knew for certain who was the father of the twins. The mother did not claim he was the father and F.R., the alleged father, denied paternity. When parentage had been scientifically tested, however, new and material evidence clearly was available which might affect the original decree and the trial court could revise its disposition accordingly.

We believe, however, that an additional, fundamental question of law was activated by the facts. It relates to whether Mr. Henkel could be denied the opportunity to be heard on his claim of paternity. We believe the Due Process Clause of the Fourteenth Amendment to the United States Constitution required the trial court to hear Mr. Henkel's paternity claim and transcended any statute that might otherwise preclude such a hearing. Mr. Henkel had a right to an opportunity to establish his liberty interest as a parent. This interest is guaranteed by the Fourteenth Amendment and protected by the Due Process Clause. *   *   *

The State also claims the trial court erred when it refused to allow it to introduce evidence concerning Mr. Henkel's parental fitness. The trial court properly excluded that evidence. The sole issue before the court at this hearing was his paternity.

The State next complains that Mr. Henkel must prove his paternity by clear and convincing evidence and that he failed to do so. The State cites *Smith v. Smith*, 71 S.D. 305, 24 N.W.2d 8 (1946), as authority for the clear and convincing burden. In Smith the appellant attempted to prove he was not the father of a child born of his former wife. The child was born eight months after the appellant and his former wife were divorced. There is a presumption of legitimacy which operates under such circumstances, and the *Smith* court correctly held such presumption could only be overcome by the greater burden of clear and convincing evidence. Here there is no presumption to overcome. In a civil paternity proceeding the quantum of required proof is a preponderance of the evidence. *Vander Werf v. Anderson*, 86 S.D. 321, 195 N.W.2d 145 (1972).

Although *Vander Werf* was an action brought by the mother of the child against the alleged father, we see no reason to impose a different burden of proof upon Mr. Henkel.

Additionally, the State's argument ignores the fact that it proposed to Mr. Henkel the stipulation stating that his paternity would be established if the blood tests indicated a paternity index of 95 percent or greater in his favor. Mr. Henkel agreed to this proffered stipulation and, based thereon, his paternity of the male twin would be established.

*   *   *

We affirm the trial court's order that Mr. Henkel is the father of the male twin. We remand for a determination of reimbursement to the State for the expense incurred for the care and medical expenses of the male twin.

Judge Ruark is justly known for his wit. It is his concluding tribute to hillbillies that makes this case so well known.
But this opinion is also notable for its gentleness and warmth.
It reveals a deep understanding of what it takes to make a
marriage. There is a sense that the court cares about Minnie
and Lowell, and wants their marriage to work.

MOORE

v.

MOORE

Springfield Court of Appeals, Missouri
Aug. 24, 1960
337 S.W.2d 781

RUARK, Judge.

On the evening of November 18, 1958, what had apparently been a successful marriage exploded in the presence of
neighbor friends when the husband, having discovered that
his wife had failed to make a telephone call which he had
requested her to make, announced that "I just want my soul
back. I want my freedom." His explanation to an attempted
peacemaker neighbor who was present at the time was that
he wanted to be his own boss.

Later he sought this recovery of soul and freedom by filing
a petition for divorce based on "general indignities." To his
petition defendant filed answer and cross bill. During trial of
the case, however, the defendant announced and testified that
she did not want a divorce and that she believed a recon-
ciliation could be effected, and in the argument in this court
she renounced any desire for judgment on the cross bill. The
judgment of the court granted a divorce on plaintiff's petition,
and from that judgment the defendant has appealed.

Plaintiff rests his claim of indignities largely on two things,
(a) that his wife was domineering and interfered with his personal and business affairs, and (b) that she indicated a dislike
for his relatives and friends and made them feel unwelcome.

Plaintiff and defendant are middle-aged. Both have been married previously. Both have grown children by their former marriages, none by this marriage. They were married on September 16, 1952, and separated on November 18, 1958. Plaintiff husband was (since 1946) and still is a rural mail carrier. Defendant had been an "Avon" saleslady and after the marriage continued to work at such employment on a part-time basis. Financially the union was moderately successful. Shortly before the marriage plaintiff had bought, on credit, a farm located near Galena either on or near James River. He said that at the time of marriage he had no money, and he appears to have had little else, except the farm he owed for. Defendant had, at the time of the marriage, a Chevrolet automobile and some money (the amount is in dispute) which went into the furnishing and improvement of the home. During the six years of marriage the parties paid about $3,000 in reduction of the mortgage and purchased another forty acres to add to it (cost $1,800). They remodeled and added to the home; added to the furnishings; redrilled the well and brought water into the house; rebuilt or repaired the barn; rebuilt the fencing; and in general made an attractive place known as "Sky Farm," complete with equipment and machinery, some cattle, riding horses, and, essential to the way of life of people living along James River, a boat and motor.

It is not disputed that defendant's efforts contributed to the prosperity of the parties and that she was a good housekeeper and a hard worker. In addition to her household duties and part-time work as Avon saleslady she sometimes did a man's work with the farm tractor and in taking care of the stock. Plaintiff conceded that she was "a good cook," "a pretty good lover and pretty good wife," "at times, when she wanted to be."

But respondent in his brief, in all sincerity, asserts that among the Four Freedoms recognized in Stone County (sometimes referred to as "The Kingdom of the James" because of the James River) are the right of a man to be master in his own house, the right of a man to fish and hunt with his friends at reasonable times without interference from the wife, and the right to deal and trade in livestock without the wife's intervention. The respondent contended, and here contends, that the defendant was domineering and bossy in interfering with these rights. Running through the whole of plaintiff's testimony and the testimony of a number of his friends is the firm idea that, since the marriage, the plaintiff's old hunting, fishing, swapping (and, shall we say, occasionally imbibing) cronies have gradually come to feel that they are *persona non grata* at Sky Farm. In the words of one of them, the reception they got at the Moore house "sometimes * * * was kinda cool," and of another one, " a little on the cool side, like I wasn't more or less wanted to visit with Lowell." And the occasions of plaintiff's joinder and participation in their ventures have probably become fewer as time has passed. Plaintiff and some of his witnesses testify to the effect that defendant was domineering toward the plaintiff. A number of defendants's witnesses, on the other hand, are equally firm in the belief that plaintiff *couldn't* be dominated. The sum total of their beliefs concerning him in this respect could be summed up in a good James River word by the expression "bullheaded." Such general characterizations, however, unless accompanied by specific incidents or occurrences, have very little probative value. So we will attempt to take the evidence of the claimed indignities item by item. For the sake of clarity we will refer to the parties by their first names, as did most of the witnesses.

* * *

Item—The turkey shoot: In the fall of 1954 Guilliams and Lowell were going to a turkey shoot at Crane (on Flat Creek). "Lowell and I stopped at Jake Watts store down here, and his wife drove up, and was opposed to him going to this turkey shoot, and said, 'I married you to be with me, and I intend for you to stay with me. And she told him that he wasn't going to the turkey shoot, and she made a few slaps at him, and embarrassed him very much; me, also—" The witness said, however, that Lowell went on to the turkey shoot. He doesn't think he had been drinking on that occasion but he didn't remember.

We find nothing in Lowell's testimony concerning the turkey shoot. Minnie's version is that it didn't happen. She says that what happened was that, after she and Lowell had been married about three weeks, Guilliams came over to the place with a fifth of whisky and the two of them (Lowell and Guilliams) sat out in the yard and drank awhile and then left; that she was a stranger and scared, and when Lowell failed to return by 9:00 she went hunting for him. She found the two "at this end of the bridge—sitting there drinking." She says she urged Lowell to come home, and that Mr. Guilliams observed, "You know, that is funny about you women. My wife just left here. She has been hunting me too." Lowell came home "when he got ready," but afterwards apologized.

Item—The houseboat incident: The same witness, Guilliams, tells it: "My brother and I dropped by, and Lowell agreed to go down to the houseboat and fish, and just visit. We hadn't been together for some time. * * * Well, she wanted to go along, and she agreed to get out at Branson and stay with her sister. And when we got to Branson, why, she didn't want to get out, she went on down to the houseboat with us." He said this happened in 1954. Minnie said this incident was also shortly after she and her husband were married (in 1952). She admits she did not get out at Branson and did go along on the houseboat but that "it was after dark. They weren't fishing. They didn't go to fish."

Item—Another anti-fishing incident ("a good long time ago"): Doc Young and witness Sheriff Walker came by to get Lowell to go fishing. "And we had the boat loaded up, and ready to go, and directly Lowell went out to the car, and got in and shut the car door, and said, 'Let's go, let's go. And about that time Stevie [Minnie] run up there and grabbed the door, and the handle, and begin to hollering at Lowell. And of course, I couldn't say just what everything was that was said, but there was quite a commotion there, and—* * * I just don't know all the words that was said, but there was quite a loud commotion going on, and finally, she told him that if he went on with us that she wouldn't be there whenever he got back. And of course he kept telling Doctor and I to drive on, and finally, the doctor drove on off and left her." Note Lowell went on fishing.

* * *

Item—Insistence on putting farm in defendant's name: Lowell said that Minnie was insistent on his putting the title to Sky Farm in both their names because she was afraid "my kids would throw her off, if anything happened to me, and she would be set out in the cold," and finally, in 1953, he acceded to her demands because he "had rather do it than listen to it." After that she "started being more domineering."

Item—Refusal to sell or mortgage the home: Lowell was offered the chance to go into a Table Rock lake shore property development. Minnie refused to join in mortgaging the home in order to raise the necessary $10,000. Admittedly this was a speculative proposition, and it is doubtful that Lowell himself would have gone through with it. In a letter written to his stepdaughter he said the offer 'might be a fleece job' and expressed some doubt concerning the proposition. In another letter he said he was "bowing out" because his proposed partner had promised a real estate dealer ten per cent instead of five per cent for sale of lots.

On what may or may not have been another occasion Lowell said that he wanted to sell Sky Farm and move to town, and according to Lowell they had an interested prospective buyer, but Minnie, without his knowledge, removed the property from the real estate listing.

Item—Criticism of trades: Lowell said that his wife refused to sign notes "on some of my stupid trades." He said that she criticized most of his cattle trades, and when he would buy a cow on his mail route he usually "got the devil about it" when he got home. But he bought the cows anyway. One of his witnesses (Gladys Hicks) said Minnie told her Lowell was always making stupid trades. Lowell's stepmother testified Minnie said he "wasn't any business man" that he was a good worker, but "didn't know how to handle his money, or do business, and if it hadn't been for her they wouldn't have had anything." Minnie denies she made any of these statements.

* * *

Item—Lowell says Minnie picked out his clothes, that she chose the pants and shirts he wore. He did not testify that those she chose for him were unsuitable or unsatisfactory to him, or how many times she bought clothes for him, or whether he was prevented from buying what he wanted, or what steps he had taken to prevent her from doing this shopping.

* * *

Item—Lowell says that Minnie made it disagreeable for his children to visit and at one time threatened (to him) not to cook for them anymore. Plaintiff's witness Gladys Hicks, who said that she and her husband had fished and deer hunted with the Moores, testified about an incident when Lowell's daughter Sharon came downstairs in the morning, clad only in what might be called a "negligee," and wanted to go out to the barn to see her father. Minnie forbade her to go out so clothed and made Sharon cry. There is evidence of another occasion when this same daughter was quarreling at Lowell, and Minnie told her in substance either to desist or to take her bag and get out—but note this was in defense of the now complaining plaintiff.

Item—The quail hunting incident: This is the incident which probably triggered the blowup. The parties had an old Chevrolet and a comparatively new Plymouth. On Sunday before the separation Lowell left at 4:30 in the morning to go quail hunting. He asked for the keys to the Plymouth. Minnie refused because "you are not hauling that bird dog in the Plymouth" and because she had Avon products in that car. Lowell said he would unload it. Minnie said she would do it herself "when I get ready." With that, plaintiff "told her what to do with the car" and went in the old one.

Item—The telephone incident: Minnie's daughter and son-in-law were both employed in Detroit. The evidence, including Lowell's testimony, shows that he was fond of them and had written several letters concerning business opportunities in the Galena neighborhood, including boat dock, tourist court, and television business. Finally they decided to move to Galena and go into the television business. The correspondence indicates that Lowell, if not actually urging the move, was favorably disposed toward it, whereas Minnie says she was not so favorable because she felt her daughter and son-in-law were used to making more money than was possible in Galena. They quit their jobs and loaded their equipment in trucks. Lowell had written that he would come to Detroit and drive one of the trucks to Galena. The daughter had sent plane tickets and a neighbor had arranged to drive Lowell and Minnie to the airport at Springfield. On Monday after the quail hunting incident above mentioned, Lowell told Minnie to call the children and tell them that he and Minnie were not coming. She did not make the call because, so she says, the next morning he told her not to call. This precipitated the declaration of Lowell concerning his freedom. He said her failure to make the call indicated that he couldn't place dependence in what she said.

Item—Finally, the witness Gladys Hicks testified that on one occasion Minnie referred to Lowell's folks as "hillbillies."

There are still a number of other incidents which we cannot relate because of the length of this opinion. They are more trivial than those we have heretofore described, but in general they are along the same line. In concluding our statement of the evidence we should say that neither of the parties impugned the morals of the other and both proved to have excellent reputations among their neighbors.

We are cognizant that in passing on cases of this kind it is the practice to give deference to the circuit judge in respect to the credibility of witnesses. Nevertheless, it is our responsibility to review the whole case and reach our own conclusions and render such judgment as should have been given. The question here is, do the acts and transactions which we have described amount to a course of conduct such as to render plaintiff's condition intolerable. Each case of this kind must necessarily be judged on its own facts. No "indignities" case is exact precedent for another, and no hard, fast rule can be followed, because the sensitivities of people differ. "It has long been established as the law that where the action is based on indignities, such indignities, in the statutory sense, must amount to a species of mental or physical cruelty, or of injury accompanied with insult or hatred, and they must be such as cannot be relieved by any exertions of the injured party. Indignities such as to warrant the granting of a divorce, ordinarily must amount to a continuous course of conduct. A single act or word, or occasional acts or words, will not suffice. *The course of conduct must be such as to connote settled hate and a plain manifestation of alienation and estrangement. Indignities are such acts as consist of unmerited contemptuous conduct, or words and acts of one spouse toward the other which manifests contempt, or contumely, incivility or injury accompanied with insult and amounting to a species of cruelty to the mind.*" (Our emphasis.) *Hoffman v. Hoffman*, Mo.App., 224 S.W.2d 554, 561. And the indignities sufficient to sustain a decree of divorce are wrongful acts over a course of time which are of sufficient gravity or magnitude to make plaintiff's life as defendant's spouse intolerable.

Applying the general rule to the present case, we find no settled or continuous course of conduct which indicates hatred, contempt or estrangement, and we find no great injury to have been suffered by the plaintiff. The incidents which he produced are scattered out over more than six years of married life. Some of the instances of insistence upon going fishing with him occurred shortly after the marriage, and we believe that it is not unusual for a bride of short duration to insist upon her husband's presence and company at that time. Plaintiff himself said Minnie was a "pretty good lover." One instance in which she made an unladylike objection to his going fishing with his friends is not dated, except that it was "a good long time ago." We will agree with respondent in his definition of Stone County freedoms that a husband has a *right* to go fishing. And we will go further and say that this *right* extends to fishing without the constant and ever-present impediment of female presence and participation, if such be against the will of the husband. It is a wise wife who accords her husband that freedom—in moderation—and a foolish wife who interferes. The studied, constant, and repeated interference with that right over a long period of time could be, under certain conditions, an indignity, but two or three or four isolated instances of insistence upon going along, or insistence upon his not going (either fishing or turkey shooting), over a period of six years do not, in and of themselves, constitute a constant and studied course of conduct amounting to indignities which render life intolerable. Further, the record convinces us that the plaintiff did, with and without his wife's consent or presence, indulge in a fair amount of fishing, hunting and swapping.

As to plaintiff's charge of domination in financial affairs: We think it was not unusual or unseemly that defendant was insistent upon conveyance of the (then mortgaged) farm into joint title. She was putting her work and money into the venture, and we see no reason why she should not have insisted upon the record title evidencing her interest, especially in view of the plaintiff's trading proclivities. Plaintiff himself agrees that they were partners in the operation of the farm business. Neither can we say that defendant was unjustified in being unwilling to sell or mortgage the farm home to finance his proposed essay into a speculative venture.

Concerning the accusation and criticism in respect to "stupid trades": As to whether Lowell's trades were stupid we cannot say, but the evidence is, by his own statement, that he was not affluent before the marriage, and further, by his admission, he and Minnie were joint owners and "partners over there and in business together. What I owed she owed, didn't she?" Being an equal partner, she was entitled to exercise some rights of a partner in respect to partnership property. It is probable that repeated and constant harping and criticism of every act and endeavor in respect to trading could become extremely wearisome and distasteful and ultimately one form of "indignities." We are inclined to believe that Minnie did, from time to time, assume a critical, or at least an impolitic, attitude in respect to Lowell's trading and swapping activities, but we are likewise inclined to believe that some of her criticism was justified and that Lowell exaggerates when he would have it appear that it was constant. There is an old saying that criticism hurts the most when it is true. And we note he *did* continue to trade.

The accusation that Minnie made it disagreeable for Lowell's children to visit is not borne out by the evidence. The children *did* frequently visit and vacation at Sky Farm, and the evidence indicates that they *did* enjoy themselves and she *did* cook for them, along with her other chores and duties. We can find no place where she communicated any expression of ill will to plaintiff's children, and we note that neither of his children testified against her.

As to the incident concerning her having made his daughter, Sharon, cry because she forbade Sharon to go out in her negligee, we can only say that even in the pleasant and relaxed atmosphere of our clean, forthright Ozarks it is not customary for grown women (Sharon was twenty) to run around outdoors, in the daytime, in their nightgowns. We do not find that the restriction on the daughter was unreasonable.

We are satisfied that the defendant did, with only the best of intentions, attempt to channel her husband's activities into courses which she thought were best for the marriage and best for him, but that in so doing she adopted a course of conduct and attitude which occasionally tended to have a "smothering" effect on plaintiff. It is a close question and one subject to human frailties of judgment as to whether this smothering reached the degree which amounts to the "indignities" as defined by the case law heretofore stated. The defendant probably, but understandably, preferred that the plaintiff spend his time with her, or in useful or profitable occupation, rather than with his fishing-hunting-swapping-horseriding companions, and we deduce that she probably was afraid of his trades. No doubt she desired to direct him toward (what she considered to be) "a better life," and she no doubt found it difficult to compromise her sense of what was best with any great understanding or comprehension of what her husband's views, habits, and masculine desires might demand. To use a Southern Missouri expression, she wanted to tie the stake rope a little too short. But all this was without conscious desire to dominate or oppress and was with the love which promotes the complete desire to do that which was best for her husband. The trouble arose because she perhaps failed to take into account that her husband had, and was entitled to have, ideas of his own on these subjects. We are convinced that he manfully and patiently (or so he thought) submerged his somewhat unconscious desire to pull up the stake until finally the pressure proved overpowering and he "blew up." It was not wholly the fault of either one and neither of them was entirely innocent.

In respect to plaintiff's evidence that Minnie once referred to relatives of the plaintiff as hillbillies: We suggest that to refer to a person as a "hillbilly," or any other name, for that matter, might or might not be an insult, depending upon the meaning intended to be conveyed, the manner of utterance, and the place where the words are spoken. Webster's New International Dictionary says that a hillbilly is "a backwoodsman or mountaineer of the southern United States;—often used contemptuously." But without the added implication or inflection which indicates an intention to belittle, we would say that, here in Southern Missouri, the term is often given and accepted as a complimentary expression. An Ozark hillbilly is an individual who has learned the real luxury of doing without the entangling complications of *things* which the dependent and over-pressured city dweller is required to consider as necessities. The hillbilly foregoes the hard grandeur of high buildings and canyon streets in exchange for wooded hills and verdant valleys. In place of creeping traffic he accepts the rippling flow of the wandering stream. He does not hear the snarl of exhaust, the raucous braying of horns, and the sharp, strident babble of many tense voices. For him instead is the measured beat of the katydid, the lonesome, far-off complaining of the whippoorwill, perhaps even the sound of a falling acorn in the infinite peace of the quiet woods. The hillbilly is often not familiar with new models, soirees, and office politics. But he does have the time and surroundings conducive to sober reflection and honest thought, the opportunity to get closer to his God. No, in Southern Missouri the appellation "hillbilly" is not generally an insult or an indignity; it is an expression of envy.

We are of the opinion that the indignities complained of were too scattered and remote, and, in general, too inconsequential, to be termed a continuous or studied course of conduct amounting to a species of cruelty, injury, insult, contempt, settled hatred or estrangement. Practically all marriages have their moments of discord. Few run their course without some occasional "indignity" offered and suffered. Most marriage ceremonies take that into account when the parties promise to take each other for better or worse. Occasional exhibition of traits which offend the other is a part of the "worse," but it is not the intolerable indignities contemplated by the statute.

Appellant's second contention is that, because of certain acts and conduct on the part of the plaintiff, he was not the innocent and injured party and was therefore not entitled to a decree. Since we have held the plaintiff did not prove sufficient indignities to entitle him to a divorce, and since the cross bill has been abandoned, we see no reason to consider such alleged acts and it would be of no service to the parties to this already crippled marriage to spread them upon the published record. It is our judgment that the divorce should be denied and the whole cause dismissed. It is so ordered.

In contrast to the Moore's marriage in the prior case, it seems obvious that this one can't be, and probably shouldn't be, saved—although it is not hard to understand why the husband thinks everything is just fine. One wonders, was it ever really a marriage?

COWIE

v.

COWIE

Missouri Court of Appeals
Feb. 9, 1982
628 S.W.2d 727

CRIST, Judge.

Marriage dissolution proceeding. Husband denied the marriage was irretrievably broken and the trial court agreed. Wife appeals. We reverse and remand for new trial.

The trial court found "there has not been a meeting of the burden of proof in terms of irretrievability of the marriage." Accordingly, the question is whether or not there was sufficient evidence for the trial court to find that the marriage was irretrievably broken. At the close of wife's case, the trial court indicated husband's behavior, as described by wife, had been reprehensible. At the close of all the evidence, the trial court indicated that husband had been guilty of "gross insensitivity." The trial court stated: "I personally believe that these people should get divorced because I believe she's depressed because she's in an unhappy marriage. . . ."

The pertinent part of § 452.320–2(1)(b), RSMo. 1978 reads:

> That the respondent has behaved in such a way that the petitioner cannot reasonably be expected to live with the respondent.

In *Gummels v. Gummels*, 561 S.W.2d 442, 443 (Mo. App.1978) the court said: "We note that (the) statute refers to a spouse's behavior not-misbehavior." *In re Marriage of Pate*, 591 S.W.2d 384, 388 (Mo.App.1979), the court stated: "The question of fault is not determinative of whether a marriage should be dissolved. . . ."

The parties were married on November 6, 1975. One child was born on July 11, 1979. The trial began on September 9, 1980. Wife testified there was no reasonable likelihood that the marriage can be preserved and therefore the marriage is irretrievably broken. Husband had behaved in such a way that she found it unreasonable to live with him. The wife then testified to specific instances as to why husband had behaved in such a way that she found it unreasonable to live with him.

One of husband's most disturbing propensities was his unwillingness to communicate with wife for long periods of time lasting up to six weeks. This behavior was engendered, for example, by wife's failing to pick husband up from work shortly after they returned from their honeymoon, wife's misloading of a gun at a gun club competition, and his failing to enjoy himself on a trip through Europe.

Wife related numerous instances where husband refused to sleep in the same bed with her, sometimes for periods lasting up to two weeks. One time, husband even called the couple's dog to the bed after he had forced wife to sleep on the couch. Husband was employed by Anheuser-Busch and worked six or seven days a week. He would also go up to eight weeks without bathing and would wear the same clothes for a week at a time.

Husband expected wife to take care of all household details, such as snow shoveling, taking out trash, doing laundry, cooking, handling household expenditures, and grocery shopping. All of the bills were to be paid from wife's salary, plus $30.00 per week from husband's earnings. Husband did not permit wife to watch television after 9:00 p.m. When he would work evenings, husband regularly woke wife when he would arrive home and keep her awake until he was ready to go to sleep.

Husband refused to purchase new furniture for the couple's apartment, nor would he allow wife to replace an old canning machine. Even so, he bought a new electric welder for himself. Husband would continually berate wife, telling her she was disgusting, crazy, that he did not love her and that she lived in "Utopia" if she expected love.

Husband refused to allow wife to use their clothes dryer when she did the laundry because to do so would be too expensive. He would also go through the trash to determine whether wife had thrown away items he believed to be of value, such as Michelob bottles or frozen cake pans. Husband also criticized wife for volunteering to drive for the Meals on Wheels program because the cost of gasoline ($1.00 per week) was too high.

When wife was pregnant with the couple's only child, husband forced wife to walk four blocks, in sub-zero temperature, from a house they were rehabilitating back to their apartment. Husband also began to smoke during her pregnancy and would purposely blow smoke in wife's face. According to wife, husband stated that he believed he was not the father of the child as the couple had only one act of intercourse during the period of conception.

Husband denied most of the allegations testified to by wife. However, the trial judge did not decide the case on credibility. Rather, the case turned upon the fact that there was insufficient proof of unreasonable behavior. Under *Gummels* and *In re Marriage of Pate, supra,* wife's evidence was sufficient for her burden of proof.

Judgment reversed and remanded for a new trial.

The May-December romance is one of the stock themes of literature. This particular instance is presented gently, but nonetheless in the inimitable style of Justice Michael Musmanno.

George J. PAVLICIC

v.

Sara Jane VOGTSBERGER
a/k/a Sara Jane Slesinski,
a/k/a/ Sara Jane Mills

Supreme Court of Pennsylvania
Nov. 18, 1957
136 A.2d 127, 390 Pa. 502

MUSMANNO, Justice.

George J. Pavlicic has sued Sara Jane Mills for the recovery of gifts which he presented to her in anticipation of a marriage which never saw the bridal veil. At the time of the engagement George Pavlicic was thrice the age of Sara Jane. In the controversy which has followed, Pavlicic says that it was Sara Jane who asked him for his hand, whereas Sara Jane maintains that Pavlicic, following immemorial custom, offered marriage to her. We are satisfied from a study of the record that it was Sara Jane who took the initiative in proposing matrimony— and, as it will develop, the proposal was more consonant with an approach to the bargaining counter than to the wedding altar.

George Pavlicic testified that when Sara Jane broached the subject of holy wedlock, he demurred on the ground that he was too old for her. She replied that the difference in their ages was inconsequential so long as he was "good to her." Furthermore, she said that she no longer was interested in "young fellows"—she had already been married to a young man and their matrimonial bark had split on the rocks of divorce. Hence, she preferred an older man. George qualified. He was 75. Sara Jane was 26.

The May-December romance began on a very practical footing in April, 1949, when Sara Jane borrowed from George the sum of $5,000 with which to buy a house, giving him a mortgage on the premises. In three and one-half years she had paid back only $449 on the mortgage. On the night of November 21, 1952, she visited George at his home and advanced the not illogical proposition that since they were to be married, there was no point in their having debts one against the other and that, therefore, he should wipe out the mortgage he held on her home. George said to her: "If you marry me, I will take the mortgage off." She said: "Yes," and so he promised to satisfy the mortgage the next day. To make certain that there would be no slip between the promise and the deed, Sara Jane remained at George's home that night; and on the following morning drove him in her automobile to the office of the attorney who was to make, and did make, arrangements for the satisfaction of the mortgage.

Being enriched to the extent of $4,551 by this transaction, Sara Jane expatiated on another rational thesis, namely, that since they were going to be married and would be riding around together she should have a better car than the dilapidated Kaiser she was driving. She struck home with her argument by pointing out that in a new car he would not fall out, for it appears this was an actual possibility when he rode in her worn-out Kaiser. Thus, without any tarrying, she drove George from the Recorder of Deed's Office, where she and the mortgage had been satisfied, to several automobile marts and finally would up at a Ford agency. Here she selected a 1953 Ford which she said would meet her needs and keep him inside the car. George made a down payment of $70 and on the following day he gave her $800 more, the latter taken from his safety deposit box. Still later he handed her a check for $1,350, obtained from a building and loan association—and Sara Jane had her new car.

Less than a year later, Sara Jane complained that her feet got wet in the Ford and she proposed the purchase of an Oldsmobile. She explained that by trading in the Ford, which she characterized as a "lemon," she would need only $1,700 to acquire the Oldsmobile. George was not averse to transportation which would keep his future wife's feet dry, but he said that since they were to be man and wife, and he apparently was paying for all the bills, it might be more businesslike if title to the car were placed in his name. This suggestion, according to George's testimony at the trial, made Sara Jane "mad" and he practically apologized for being so bold and inconsiderate as to ask title to an automobile which he was buying with his own money. Accordingly he withdrew his suggestion, said: "All right," and made out a check in Sara Jane's name for $1,700. And thus Sara Jane got her new Oldsmobile.

In January, 1953, in the enthusiastic spirit of an anxious swain, George presented Sara Jane with a $140 wrist watch. Sara Jane selected the watch.

In February, 1953, Sara Jane represented to George that they would both make a better appearance if she had an engagement and wedding ring. George took her to a jewelry store and she made a selection consistent with discretion. George paid $800.

Sara Jane then asked George to take care of the repairing of a ring she had received from her mother. It was a mere matter adding a diamond. George paid the bill.

Even before George's bank book became Sara Jane's favorite literature she had prevailed upon him to advance substantial sums to her. In June, 1952, she told George she needed $800 to cover her house with insulbrick. George gave her $800 to cover her house with insulbrick.

It is not to be said, however, that Sara Jane was completely lacking in affectionate ante-nuptial reciprocity. In June, 1953, she bought George a wedding ring for him to wear. She conferred upon him at the same time a couple of woolen shirts. There is no way of learning how much the ring and shirts cost because she did not take George into her confidence or into the store where she purchased the items.

George testified that when he wore the wedding ring people laughed and asked him when he was to be married. He replied: 'Pretty soon.' He tried to live up to the prediction and asked Sara Jane for the wedding date. She said she could not name the month. In view of what was to develop, she could have added with truth that she could not name the year either.

In October, 1953, Sara Jane expounded to George the economic wisdom of purchasing a business which would earn for them a livelihood in his old and her young age. She suggested the saloon business. George agreed it was a good idea. She contacted a saloon-selling agent and George accompanied her to various saloons which the agent wished to sell. George was impressed with one saloon called the "Melody Bar," but the price was above him. Sara Jane then said that if he would give her $5,000 she would buy a cheap saloon outside of Pittsburgh. George gave her $5,000. And Sara Jane disappeared—with the $5,000.

The next time she was heard from, she was in Greensburg operating Ruby's Bar—with George's $5,000. from Ruby's Bar she proceeded to the nuptial bower where she married Edward Dale Mills. Although she had many times assured George she would marry him because she liked the idea of an old man, the man she then actually married was scarcely a contender for Methuselah's record. He was only 26—two years younger than Sara Jane.

When George emerged from the mists and fogs of his disappointment and disillusionment he brought an action in equity praying that the satisfaction of the mortgage on Sara Jane's property be stricken from the record, that she be ordered to return the gifts which had not been consumed, and pay back the moneys which she had gotten from him under a false promise to marry. Sara Jane filed an Answer and the case came on for trial before Judge Marshall of the Allegheny County Court of Common, Pleas. Judge Marshall granted all the plaintiff's prayers and entered a decree from which the defendant has appealed to this Court.

The defendant urges upon us the proposition that the Act of June 22, 1935, P.L. 450, 48 P.S. § 171, popularly known as the "Heart Balm Act," outlaws the plaintiff's action. This is the first time that the Act of 1935 has come before this Court for interpretation and ruling. Although the Act contains several sections, the heart of it lies in the first sentence, namely, "All causes of action for breach of contract to marry are hereby abolished."

There is nothing in that statement or in any of the provisions of the Act which touches contracts subsidiary to the actual marriage compact. The Act in no way discharges obligations based upon a fulfillment of the marriage contract. It in no way alters the law of conditional gifts. A gift given by a man to a woman on condition that she embark on the

sea of matrimony with him is no different from a gift based
on the condition that the donee sail on any other sea. If, after
receiving the provisional gift, the donee refuses to leave the
harbor,—if the anchor of contractual performance sticks in the
sands of irresolution and procrastination—the gift must be re-
stored to the donor. *A fortiori* would this be true when the
donee not only refuses to sail with the donor, but, on the
contrary, walks up the gangplank of another ship arm in arm
with the donor's rival.

The title to the gifts which Sara Jane received, predicated
on the assurance of marriage with George, never left George
and could not leave him until the marital knot was tied. It
would appear from all the evidence that the knot was fully
formed and loosely awaiting the ultimate pull which would
take title in the gifts from George to Sara Jane, but the final
tug never occurred and the knot fell apart, with the gifts legally
falling back into the domain of the brideless George.

The appellant in her argument before this Court would
want to make of the Act of June 22, 1935, a device to per-
petuate one of the very vices the Act was designed to prevent.
The Act was passed to avert the perpetration of fraud by ad-
venturers and adventuresses in the realm of heartland. To allow
Sara Jane to retain the money and property which she got
from George by dangling before him the grapes of matrimony
which she never intended to let him pluck would be to place
a premium on trickery, cunning, and duplicitous dealing. It
would be to make a mockery of the law enacted by the Legislature in that very field of happy and unhappy hunting.

The Act of 1935 aimed at exaggerated and fictional claims
of mortification and anguish purportedly attendant upon a
breach of promise to marry. The legislation was made necessary
because of the widespread abuse of the vehicle of a breach
of promise suit to compel overly-apprehensive and naive defendants into making settlements in order to avoid the embarrassing and lurid notoriety which accompanied litigation
of that character. The legislation was intended to ward off injustices and incongruities which often occurred when, by the
mere filing of breach of promise suits innocent defendants became unregenerate scoundrels and tarnished plaintiffs became
paragons of lofty sensibility and moral impeccability. It was
not unusual in threatened breach of promise suits that the

defendant preferred to buy his peace through a monetary settlement rather than be vindicated by a trial which might leave his good name in shreds.

There is no doubt that in the history of romance a nation could be populated with the lovers and sweethearts (young and old) who have experienced genuine pain and agony because of the defection of their opposites who promised marriage and then absconded. Perhaps there should be a way to compensate these disillusioned souls, but it had been demonstrated that the action of breach of promise had been so misemployed, had given rise to such monumental deceptions, and had encouraged blackmail on such a scale, that the Legislature of Pennsylvania, acting in behalf of all the people, concluded that the evil of abuse exceeded to such an extent the occasional legitimate benefit conferred by a breach of promise suit that good government dictated its abolition.

Thus the law of 1935 prohibited, but prohibited only, the suing for damages based on contused feelings, sentimental bruises, wounded pride, untoward embarrassment, social humiliation, and all types of mental and emotional suffering presumably arising from a broken marital promise. The Act did not in any way ban actions resulting from a tangible loss due to the breach of a legal contract. It could never be supposed that the Act of 1936 intended to throw a cloak of immunity over a 26–year old woman who lays a snare for a 75–year old man and continues to bait him for four or five years so that she can obtain valuable gifts and money from him under a false promise of marriage.

George Pavlicic is not asking for damages because of a broken heart or a mortified spirit. He is asking for the return of things which he bestowed with an attached condition precedent, a condition which was never met. In demanding the return of his gifts, George cannot be charged with Indian giving. Although he has reached the Indian summer of his life and now at 80 years of age might, in the usual course of human affairs, be regarded as beyond the marrying age, everyone has the inalienable right under his own constitution as well as that of the United States to marry when he pleases if and when he finds the woman who will marry him. George Pavlicic believed that he had found that woman in Sara Jane. He testified that he asked her at least 30 times if she would marry him and on each occasion she answered in the affirmative. There is nothing in the law which required him to ask 31 times. But even so, he probably would have continued asking her had she not taken his last $5,000 and decamped to another city. Moreover he had to accept 30 offers of marriage as the limit since she now had married someone else. Of course, mere multiplicity of proposals does not make for certainty of acceptance. The testimony, however, is to the effect that on the occasion of each proposal by George, Sara Jane accepted—accepted not only the proposal but the gift which invariably accompanied it.

* * *

As already stated, the Act of 1935 provides that "All causes of action for breach of contract to marry are hereby abolished." This language is as clear as the noonday sun. The appellant would darken it with the eclipse of artificial reasoning. The appellant would want us to read into the statute the provision that "All causes of action *for the recovery of property* based on breach of contract to marry are abolished." The appellant would want the statute to be read: "All actions *resulting from* a breach of contract are abolished." But we cannot so read or so interpret the statute. The abolition is confined to actions for breach of contract to marry, that is, the actual fracture of the wedding contract.

It thus follows that a breach of any contract which is not the actual contract for marriage itself, no matter how closely associated with the proposed marriage, is actionable.

After a thorough review of the pleadings, the notes of testimony, the briefs and the lower Court's Opinion, we come to the conclusion that the final decree entered by Judge Marshall is eminently just and in accordance with established principles of law and equity. It is accordingly

Decree affirmed at appellant's costs.

The old saying that "All's fair in love" is simply not true, at least as far as the law is concerned. While it is generally accepted that couples do not disclose *everything* about themselves to each other, some misrepresentations are so great as to entitle the unsuspecting spouse to relief.

KEYES
v.
KEYES

Superior Court of New York City
December, 1893
26 N.Y.Supp. 910, 6 Misc. 355

I

McADAM, J. The defendant, by fraudulently misrepresenting himself as an honest, industrious man, induced the plaintiff, a confiding young woman, to become his wife. If the misrepresentation had been as to the defendant's social position, rank, fortune, manners, or the like, they would have furnished no ground for declaring the marriage void. Fabrications and exaggerations of this kind, while not commendable, are so common as to be tolerated by the law on grounds of public policy. Persons intending to act upon such representations must verify them at their peril, for, though they enter into the inducements to marriage, they are not considered as going to the essentials of the relation, on the theory that the parties take each other for better or worse. Indeed, in some cases, marriage likens itself to the veritable mouse trap, which is "easier to get into than out." In this case the defendant represented himself as an honest, industrious man, and appearances favored him, when in truth he was a professional thief, whose picture has a place in the rogues' gallery, and he is now "doing time" in the Clinton prison for crime. It was an unholy alliance, begotten in fraud, and the plaintiff is the victim. What fraud, in kind and amount, should be deemed sufficient to annul a marriage, has led to a fruitful amount of discussion and contrariety of opinion. The statute provides that a marriage may be annulled, where the consent of one of the parties was obtained by force, duress, or fraud, any one being sufficient. This provision was intended to protect the party imposed upon and to punish the one guilty of the wrong. The difficulty in inducing courts to act upon this provision is the stupefying fear that dissolution may lead to carelessness and blind credulity on the part of those contemplating marriage. But "love is blind," always has been, and will be. Nothing born of the law will prevent indiscreet and unsuitable marriages. The average individual judges and acts on appearances, on his own likes and dislikes; and if he or she exercises his or her best judgment, and is deceived by the arts and wiles of an unscrupulous, designing person, there should be no unwillingness, in a proper case, to afford relief to the injured, when it can be done without injury to any one except the guilty. There can be no consent to a contract unless it be voluntary. If it be induced by misrepresentation, duress, or constraint, the guilty party will be allowed to obtain no benefit from it. It has been said in some cases that the misrepresentation must be such as to deceive persons of ordinary prudence. But the better rule is that if the pretense is capable of defrauding it is sufficient. The real question is how far the representation affected the mind of the party defrauded, and this is one of fact. In *People v. Court of Oyer*, 83 N.Y., at page 449, the court held:

> "The law was intended to protect the weak and credulous as well as the careful and intelligent, and the materiality and influence of the pretense is for the jury to determine. * * * It is quite as accurate to say merely that the pretense must be calculated to deceive, leaving that to be determined from the circumstances of each particular case."

In all these matters, much is left to the good sense and judgment of the court or jury, if there be one. Chancellor Kent says, (2 Comm. 77:)

> "It is said that error will in some cases destroy a marriage, and render the contract void, as if one person be substituted for another. This, however, would be a case of palpable fraud, going to the substance of the contract."

In the present instance the plaintiff found, after marriage, that a professional thief had, by fraud, been substituted for the honest, industrious man she was led to believe she had married. While the cases are dissimilar, the result in either is substantially the same. Companionship, with its reciprocal duties, is the basis of marriage, and no respectable young woman should be obliged to divide the life companionship of a husband between herself and the penal institutions of the state. No conception of married life or reciprocal duties would tolerate such a thing. There could be nothing more degrading in its influence. Such a husband is not a fit subject for the household, nor one to be looked up to for advice and guidance. Men may have vices at the time of their marriage, and, if these are dropped at or before the time of their vows, they should not be resurrected, and made the basis of domestic strife, but where they are continued after marriage they may give rise to serious matrimonial difficulties. In *Wier v. Still*, (31 Iowa, 107,) a widow induced to marry a "jail bird" by means of false representations as to his respectability was refused relief on the ground of her folly and credulity. Bigelow, in his work on Fraud, (page 93,) cites the above case "as especially applicable to a widow." And in *Moot v. Moot*, 37 Hun, 288, the court, in granting a decree of nullity, was influenced by the fact that the plaintiff was a "school girl,"—distinctions obviously founded more on the judicial policy or discretion of the courts than upon strict legal principles. They find warrant in the precept which permits the court or jury to determine in their own way the influence and effect of misrepresentations as applied to the case at hand, and the special equity therein calling for relief; and in this manner the age, experience, and gullibility of the victims play their part. As the plaintiff's age is between that of the school girl and the widow, there would seem to be a discretionary choice of alternatives left for the court to determine which rule it will adopt to satisfy the requirements of this controversy. If the defendant had reformed after marriage, and become exemplary in conduct, the court might have required the plaintiff to overlook the past, and screen it from the world with the mantle of charity, but he has not chosen the pathway of the penitent, and is, in consequence, again under state surveillance, in its penitentiary at Clinton. Consortium and conjugal society have scarcely risen to the dignity of memories. The consequence is not a temporary sorrow, which may be buried under the oblivion of recurring time, or forgotten in the solitude of despair, but an ever-present affront and reproach that "will not down." The fraud perpetrated upon the plaintiff goes to the substance and essence of the contract, and while this may be regarded as an exceptional case, resting on its own peculiar merits, yet, if the statute authorizing a decree of nullity for fraud does not reach such a case, it is difficult to imagine one it is capable of comprehending. There are, fortunately, no children to bear the obloquy of the marriage; and unless a premium is to be placed on fraud, and the guilty taken under the protecting aegis of the law, there is no reason founded on principle or policy why the plaintiff should not have that justice which the decree prayed for will afford. The application must be granted.

Chapter 8
Seeking Justice

Originally, courts of law were limited to providing money damages to an injured party, even if that might not be effective relief. In order to promote more perfect justice, courts of equity were developed with the power to issue various writs and orders. At the same time, narrow limits were imposed on the use of those powers to prevent the courts from becoming too powerful. Similarly, strict procedures were adopted to be followed by those who called upon the courts to exercise their powers.

Today, the distinction between courts of law and courts of equity has been all but eliminated. However, courts still attempt to find ways to use their powers, within limits, to achieve justice.

The very concept of justice presupposes that the decision maker, the judge, will be fair. In order to maintain the trust of the community, the judge must not only be fair but, like Caesar's wife, above suspicion. Thus, it is appropriate for judges to disqualify themselves if they might be biased, or if there is reason to think that their fairness might reasonably be questioned by others. The motion to disqualify a black judge in an employment discrimination action raised a number of difficult and troubling questions. Although Judge Higginbotham denied the motion, his decision was written with the utmost respect for the issue before him.

"I endorse the decision because Judge Higginbotham did not apologize for being black. The opinion shows the erudition of a federal district court judge, a person with over 50 honorary degrees, author of many law review pieces, author of the book IN THE MATTER OF COLOR, *a former Chief Judge of the Second Circuit, a person who had achieved senior status when he left the circuit bench in 1993 and a person who, had politics been different, might have been a justice of the United States Supreme Court."*

—Professor, Northwestern University School of Law

COMMONWEALTH OF PENNSYLVANIA, *et al.*
v.
LOCAL UNION 542, INTERNATIONAL UNION OF OPERATING ENGINEERS, *et al.*

United States District Court, E.D. Pennsylvania
Dec. 4, 1974
388 F.Supp. 155

HIGGINBOTHAM, District Judge.

INTRODUCTION

Defendants, Local 542, International Union of Operating Engineers, the Contractors Association of Eastern Pennsylvania and the General Building Contractors Association, Inc., have moved this Court pursuant to 28 U.S.C. § 144 to refrain from further participation in this case. In support of their motions, defendants have filed the affidavits of Robert Walsh, the business manager of Local 542, of Angelo A. Antonucci, the executive secretary of the Contractors Association of Eastern Pennsylvania, and of Charlson I. Mehl, the executive director of the General Building Contractors Association, Inc. Each of these affidavits alleges a personal bias on my part in favor of the plaintiff class in the instant action. For reasons that will hereinafter appear, I have concluded that these affidavits are, as a matter of law, insufficient to justify my disqualification as judge in the instant action. Defendants' motions for disqualification must therefore be denied.

I.

DEFENDANTS' AFFIDAVITS

In support of their motion for recusal, defendants allege in their affidavits:

1. That the instant case is a class action, brought under the Civil Rights Act of 1964 and other civil rights statutes, charging that defendants have discriminated against the twelve black plaintiffs and the class they represent on the basis of race, and seeking extensive equitable and legal remedies for the alleged discrimination;

2. That I will try the instant case without a jury, and that I am black;

3. That on Friday, October 25, 1974, I addressed a luncheon meeting of the Association for the Study of Afro-American Life and History, during the 59th Annual Meeting of that organization, "a group composed of black historians";

4. That in the course of that speech I criticized two recent Supreme Court decisions which involved alleged racial discrimination, and said, inter alia, that:

    (a) "I do not see the [Supreme] Court of the 1970's or envision the Court of the 1980's as the major instrument for significant change and improvement in the quality of race relations in America";

(b) "The message of these recent decisions is that if we are to deal with the concept of integration, we must probably make our major efforts in another forum";

(c) "As I see it, we must make major efforts in other forums without exclusive reliance on the federal legal process."

5. That I used the pronoun "we" several times in the course of the speech, and that my use of this pronoun evidences my "intimate tie with and emotional attachment to the advancement of black civil rights";

6. That by my agreement to deliver the speech I presented myself as "a leader in the future course of the black civil rights movement";

7. That my speech took place in "an extra-judicial and community context," and not in the course of this litigation;

8. That the following day, Saturday, October 26, 1974, *The Philadelphia Inquirer* published "an article appearing under a predominant headline on the first page of the metropolitan news section, . . . describing the October 25th meeting and publishing the aforementioned quotes";

9. That approximately 450,000 copies of *The Philadelphia Inquirer* containing this account were distributed publicly on or about October 26, 1974;

10. That this account made "the community at large" aware of my "significant role as a spokesman, scholar and active supporter of the advancement of the causes of integration";

11. That I believe "that there has been social injustice to blacks in the United States"; "that these injustices must be corrected and remedied"; and "that they must be remedied by extra-judicial efforts by blacks, including [myself];

12. That "the very invitation to speak," "the content of [my] remarks" and my "posing for photographs" after the address identify me as "a leader for and among blacks," and "one of the country's leading civil rights proponents";

13. That I am a "celebrity" within the black community;

14. That "I [have] identified, and [do] identify, [myself] with causes of blacks, including the cause of correction of social injustices which [I believe] have been caused to blacks"; that I have made myself "a participant in those causes, including the cause of correction of social injustices which [I believe] have been caused to blacks";

15. That "in view of the applicable federal law," and by reason of my "personal and emotional commitments to civil rights causes of the black community, the black community expectation as to [my] leadership and spokesmanship therein, and the basic tenet of our legal system requiring both actual and apparent impartiality in the federal courts," my "continuation . . . as trier of fact, molder of remedy and arbiter of all issues constitutes judicial impropriety."

These allegations commingle conclusions with facts to an extraordinary degree. Conclusions, of course, are not relevant to this inquiry. Even if they were, it is difficult to ascertain what defendants mean by certain of the conclusionary allegations they have made. For example, they state that my interest in these matters indicates an "emotional attachment." If, by "emotional attachment," they were implying that I believe that blacks should, in a nonviolent, rational fashion, strive to eliminate racial injustice, I would accept that characterization. If, by the use of the phrase "emotional attachment," they were implying a degree of irrationality, I do not accept that conclusion as a reasonable inference from either my appearance before the Association for the Study of Afro-American Life and History, or the contents of my speech to it, or the newspaper article reporting on the speech.

No matter what defendants assert in their conclusionary allegations, the factual core of their affidavits is the newspaper article in *The Philadelphia Inquirer* of October 26, 1974. The legal sufficiency of the affidavits stands or falls on the basis

of what I said and did on the occasion of my October 25th
speech, as reported in the *Inquirer* article of the following day,
and on any rational inferences that can be drawn from that
article.

II.

THE LAW OF DISQUALIFICATION

* * *

**The court sets forth the basic law of disqualification, which
holds that it is the judge's obligation to determine whether
the affidavits give fair support to a charge of bias. The court
may not question the good faith of those seeking disqualification or the truth of the allegations. And, if the facts do not
warrant disqualification, the court has an affirmative duty not
to withdraw.**

* * *

III.

THE LEGAL SUFFICIENCY OF DEFENDANTS' AFFIDAVITS

The legal issue raised by defendants' motion is easily disposed of. I have examined the factual allegations of defendants'
affidavits in the light of the law, as set forth above, which
governs the recusal of a trial judge for reasons of bias or prejudice. That examination leads me inescapably to the conclusion
that, as a matter of law, defendants' affidavits are insufficient
to justify my disqualification.

Defendants base their motions on my remarks at the 59th
Annual Meeting of the Association for the Study of Afro-American Life and History. Those remarks in no way manifest the
personal prejudice and bias that must be shown in order to
satisfy the requirements of § 144. They contain no reference
to these defendants or to these plaintiffs or to this suit. They
relate to my background and my associations, not to any party
in this action personally, and are therefore insufficient to show

the personal bias required by the statute. In the words of Chief Judge Parker, they show "at most, zeal for upholding the rights of Negroes under the Constitution and indignation that attempt should be made to deny them their rights. A judge cannot be disqualified merely because he believes in upholding the law, even though he says so with vehemence." *Baskin v. Brown*, 174 F.2d at 394. The affidavits which recite these remarks are therefore clearly insufficient, as a matter of law, to justify my disqualification.

IV.

DEFENDANTS' AUTHORITIES

Because these motions for disqualification touch me personally, I resolved, when they were filed, to give defendants' arguments the fullest possible consideration. Accordingly, I carefully reviewed all of the cases cited by Local 542 in its memorandum in support of the § 144 motion. This research has convinced me that defendant's position, though rich in good faith, is devoid of merit. Each of those cases arose out of a factual context radically different from this one. None of them compels the result that defendant urges me to reach here. Only a handful of them, those in which a judge recused himself voluntarily when he had no legal obligation to do so, even suggest that result. And, for reasons that I will presently set out, I emphatically do not believe that these cases of voluntary recusal are apt precedents for my decision on these motions to disqualify.

Defendant Local relies primarily on the sweeping language of Justice McKenna in *Berger v. United States*, [55 U.S. 22, 41 S.Ct. 230, 65 L.Ed. 481]. Its reliance, however, is totally misplaced. In *Berger*, the affidavit filed in support of the motion for disqualification alleged that the presiding judge in an espionage trial, the Honorable Kenesaw Mountain Landis, was prejudiced against the defendants because they were German-Americans. The affidavit further alleged that Judge Landis had said, inter alia, that "if anybody has said anything worse about the Germans than I have I would like to know it so I can use it"; that "one must have a very judicial mind, indeed, not to be prejudiced against the German-Americans in this country. Their hearts are reeking with disloyalty"; and that "you are of the same mind that practically all the German-Americans are in this country, and you call yourselves German-Americans.

Your hearts are reeking with disloyalty." Unquestionably, these remarks, made in the context of an espionage trial with German-American defendants, gave "fair support to the charge of a bent of mind that may prevent or impede impartiality of judgment," and amply justified the broad language of Justice McKenna's opinion. The instant case is altogether different on its facts. My remarks, as recited in defendants' affidavits, were in no way related to this case. They were addressed to a group of scholars, not to union men generally or to operating engineers in particular. They referred neither to the defendants here nor to the plaintiffs, neither to employment discrimination suits generally nor this cause in particular. They did not promise partiality to blacks in civil rights actions. If anything, they encouraged blacks to explore forums other than the federal courts for the redress of their grievances. While it is concededly difficult for a man to act as judge in his own case, I do not find that my remarks gave "fair support to the charge of a bent of mind that may prevent or impede partiality of judgment." Consequently, *Berger v. United States, supra,* is, on its facts, clearly distinguishable from the instant case. According to William Shakespeare, "Macduff was from his mother's womb untimely ripp'd." Macbeth, Act V, Scene VIII. Similarly, in an attempt to buttress defendant's memorandum, Mr. Justice McKenna's language in *Berger* was from its context irrelevantly "ripp'd."

* * *

The court discusses a number of cases in which judges did not recuse themselves despite having a special familiarity with the subject matter, such as having helped to draft the law at issue.

* * *

V.

BEING BLACK, AND THE APPEARANCE OF IMPARTIALITY

When stripped to its essence, the gravamen of defendants' objection seems primarily based on the following express or implicit allegations:

(1) I am black;

(2) Some of the defendant union's members are white;

(3) The instant case involves a claim of racial discrimination;

(4) "By agreeing to appear before such group (The Association for the Study of Afro-American Life and History) Judge Higginbotham presented himself as a leader in the future course of the black civil rights movement," and

(5) By my appearance at the Association's meeting and/or by the substance of the remarks I actually made or as they were quoted in the newspaper, "the continuation of [Judge Higginbotham] as finder of fact, molder of remedy, and arbiter of all issues constitutes judicial impropriety."

A. Being Black

I concede that I am black. I do not apologize for that obvious fact. I take rational pride in my heritage, just as most other ethnics take pride in theirs. However, that one is black does not mean, *ipso facto*, that he is anti-white; no more than being Jewish implies being anti-Catholic, or being Catholic implies being anti-Protestant. As do most blacks, I believe that the corridors of history in this country have been lined with countless instances of racial injustice. This is evident by the plain historical fact that for more than two and a half centuries, millions of blacks were slaves under the rule and sanction of law—a fate which confronted no other major minority in this country. Every presidential commission and almost every Supreme Court opinion dealing with racial matters have noted the fact that in this country, there has often been racial injustice for blacks.

Thus a threshold question which might be inferred from defendants' petition is: Since blacks (like most other thoughtful Americans) are aware of the "sordid chapter in American history" of racial injustice, shouldn't black judges be disqualified *per se* from adjudicating cases involving claims of racial discrimination? Defendants do not go so far as to precisely assert that black judges should *per se* be disqualified from hearing cases which involve racial issues, but, as will be demonstrated hereinafter, the absolute consequence and thrust of their rationale would amount to, in practice, a *double standard* within the federal judiciary. By that standard, white judges will be permitted to keep the latitude they have enjoyed for centuries in discussing matters of intellectual substance, even issues of human rights and, because they are white, still be permitted to later decide specific factual situations involving the principles of human rights which they have discussed previously in a generalized fashion. But for black judges, defendants insist on a far more rigid standard, which would preclude black judges from ever discussing race relations even in the generalized fashion that other justices and judges have discussed issues of human rights. Under defendants' standards, if a black judge discusses race relations, he should thereafter be precluded from adjudicating matters, involving specific claims of racial discrimination.

* * *

Would it have been permissible for a black to have talked to white historians, or is there something particularly opprobrious about speaking to any group of historians which thereafter taints one's ability to participate in the judicial process? Do petitioners suggest that it is more sinister for a black judge to speak to black historians than for the Chief Justice of the United States Supreme Court to speak to the National Conference of Christians and Jews? Should the distinguished Chief Justice be barred in the future from adjudicating cases where claims of religious or racial bigotry are urged, simply because he spoke to a distinguished group which supports the concepts of the brotherhood of man, the golden rule, and fair play?

Many judges of this court have spoken to bar associations, including those specialized sections of the bar such as the plaintiff's personal injury bar, or the defense bar. Should such judges be forever barred from adjudicating personal injury cases involving plaintiffs or defendants? Is there anything more malevolent in speaking to a group of black historians about equal justice under the law than for a Catholic, Jewish, or Protestant judge to speak in his cathedral, synagogue or church on the Sermon on the Mount, or the Torah? If a Catholic judge spoke to a group of Catholic historians, should he be forever barred from adjudicating cases involving the constitutionality of state appropriations disbursed to parochial schools? Was my speech malevolent because its occasion was a national meeting? Does something inherently more pernicious occur when 100 black historians get together at a national conference than when 20 meet in a local setting?

C. Is it Permissible for Black Judges to be Scholars in the Race Relations Field?

* * *

The court answers that question in the affirmative, noting that other judges have been recognized for their expertise in areas that may be relevant to cases that come before them.

* * *

IX.

THE OLD AND NEW ORDER OF THINGS

If, for the reasons previously discussed, defendants' motions are meritless, and since the motions are presumably filed in good faith, what other rationale could explain why defendants so vehemently assert their claim that I be disqualified in the instant case? Perhaps, among some whites, there is an inherent disquietude when they see that occasionally blacks are adjudicating matters pertaining to race relations, and perhaps that anxiety can be eliminated only by having no black judges sit on such matters or, if one cannot escape a black judge, then by having the latter bend over backwards to the detriment of black litigants and black citizens and thus assure that brand of "impartiality" which some whites think they deserve.

* * *

X.

THE ROLE OF JUDGES

Thus, the critical issue is, what conduct by black judges will assure their impartiality? Should they be robots? Should they demean their heritage by asking for less than first class citizenship for other blacks? Should they not tell the truth about past injustices? Of course, there is a dramatic difference between the role which legislator, politicians, and elected officials play in our society, one which is far closer to the cutting edge of policy development, and the role which could be tolerated or expected from a federal judge. I willingly accept those limitations; they are inherent in the judicial process. I am aware that Judge Higginbotham is not Senator Higginbotham, or Mayor Higginbotham, or Governor Higginbotham, but I also know that Judge Higginbotham should not have to disparage blacks in order to placate whites who otherwise would be fearful of his impartiality.

Obviously, black judges should not decide legal issues on the basis of race. During my ten years on this court, I have not done so. I have, depending on the facts, sentenced numerous black and white criminal defendants to substantial terms of imprisonment. I have placed other criminal defendants, both black and white, on probation. Depending on the relevant fact, some civil cases have been decided in favor of and others against black litigants. In this case, plaintiffs similarly will enjoy no advantage because they are black; defendants will not be disadvantaged because some of them are white. The outcome of this case will be directed by what the evidence shows, not by the race of the litigants.

I am pleased to see that my distinguished colleagues on the bench who are Jewish serve on committees of the Jew-Community Relations Council, on the boards of Jewish publications, and are active in other affairs of the Jewish community. I respect them, for they recognize that the American experience has often been marred by pervasive anti-Semitism. I would think less of them if they felt that they had to repudiate their heritage in order to be impartial judges.

Many Catholic judges have been active in their church, as have been Episcopalian and other Protestant judges. It would be a tragic day for the nation and the judiciary if a myopic vision of the judge's role should prevail, a vision that required judges to refrain from participating in their churches, in their nonpolitical community affairs, in their universities. So long as Jewish judges preside over matters where Jewish and Gentile litigants disagree; so long as Protestant judges preside over matters where Protestants and Catholic litigants disagree; so long as white judges preside over matters where white and black litigants disagree, I will preside over matters where black and white litigants disagree. Defendants are patently aware of the variety of extra-judicial activities which has been the accepted standard for judges in this District Court, in this circuit, and in the nation. It is inconceivable, then, that rational lawyers would object to the aforementioned speeches made by Chief Justice Burger and Justice Stewart, or even the speech which Justice Douglas made on December 2, 1974, to the Jewish Community Relations Council of Philadelphia.

I concluded my address to the historians by quoting Langston Hughes' famous poem "Dream of Freedom":

"THERE IS A DREAM IN THE LAND WITH ITS BACK AGAINST THE WALL,
BY MUDDLED NAMES AND STRANGE SOMETIMES THE DREAM IS CALLED.
THERE ARE THOSE WHO CLAIM THIS DREAM FOR THEIRS ALONE—
A SIN FOR WHICH, WE KNOW, THEY MUST ATONE.
UNLESS SHARED IN COMMON LIKE SUNLIGHT AND LIKE AIR,
THE DREAM WILL DIE FOR LACK OF SUBSTANCE ANY WHERE.
THE DREAM KNOWS NO FRONTIER OR TONGUE THE DREAM NO CLASS OR RACE,
THE DREAM CANNOT BE KEPT SECURE IN ANY ONE LOCKED PLACE.
THIS DREAM TODAY EMBATTLED, WITH ITS BACK AGAINST THE WALL—
TO SAVE THE DREAM FOR ONE IT MUST BE SAVED FOR ALL."

In a nation which had a revolution theoretically based on the declaration that "we hold these truths to be self-evident, that all men are created equal," a judge should not be disqualified if two centuries later he believes that the rhetoric must be made real for all citizens, including blacks, and that the dream must be "saved for all."

CONCLUSION

In many ways this opinion may appear to be too long and prolix. But if defendants' arguments are asserted in good faith and sincerity, they nevertheless represent an almost subconscious expression of their expectation of the deportment of blacks and, more specifically, of black judges. If America is going to have a total rendezvous with justice so that there can be full equality for blacks, other minorities, and women, it is essential that the "instinct" for double standards be completely exposed and hopefully, through analysis, those elements of irrationality can be ultimately eradicated. It is regrettable that in this case I must take substantial time and effort to answer defendants' meritless allegations, but in some respects the motions merely highlight the duality of burdens which blacks have in public life. Blacks must meet not only the normal obligations which confront their colleagues, but often they must spend extraordinary amounts of time in answering irrational positions and assertions before they can fulfill their primary public responsibilities.

* * *

Of course, I do have feelings that this nation must fulfill its theoretical commitment to equal justice under the law. I do not apologize for these feelings, nor do I apologize for my remarks. Given the same opportunity, I would make those remarks again today. If I had not in fact made them, I would wish that I had.

Defendants' Motions for Disqualification are denied.

Unlike the issue before Judge Higginbotham, Justice Davis' potential bias would probably not have been recognized by anyone but himself. However, if a judge is biased, or might appear to be so, he or she has an obligation to raise the issue on his or her own.

"I enjoy reading this opinion by [Justice] Matt Davis declining to participate in a case for a lot of reasons I would never have stated. It is an excellent example of one of our illustrious predecessors on this Court who, for many reasons other than those stated in this opinion, was legendary for his colorfulness while on the Court."

—Judge, Texas State Court

CARROLLTON–FARMERS BRANCH INDEPENDENT SCHOOL DISTRICT
v.
KNIGHT

Court of Civil Appeals of Texas
Aug. 1, 1967
418 S.W.2d 535

This case arose when two high school students, ages 17 and 18, were suspended from school after they married each other. The trial court granted a temporary injunction requiring the school district to allow the students to attend school. The appellate court affirmed, ruling that their marriage was in all respects a legal marriage and that marriage alone is not a proper ground for a school district to suspend a student from attending high school for scholastic purposes only.

Justice Fanning wrote the opinion for the court, but Justice Davis wrote separately, disqualifying himself from participating in this decision.

*   *   *

DISQUALIFICATION

DAVIS, Justice.

The writer honestly feels that he should disqualify himself from the decision in the above and foregoing case for the following reasons:

I was one of seven children of tenant farmers. My Mother passed away when I was only nine years of age. It was always her ambition, and it became mine, to get an education and become a lawyer. I finished Glenwood, unaffiliated, High School when I was 18 years old. I tried to enter college, but, met with two most embarrassing situations, and could not do so. I worked as a common laborer. Finally, I decided to get married, accumulate enough wealth to attend college, get a law degree and pursue my profession. I married on October 26, 1929. The Crash of 1929 was really felt in 1930. I was a tenant farmer and, although I was plagued with my difficulties, I managed to hold my own.

When I decided it was impossible for me to attend college, I decided to get my law degree by home study. I traded two "frying size chickens and a mess of turnip greens" for my first lawbook.

The only law that I know is what I have read from the lawbooks at home (many nights I have studied all night without any sleep), and have gained from experience. In 1934, I notified the Board of Legal Examiners that I was ready to take the examination for a license. In return, I was notified that I would have to furnish an "AFFILIATED HIGH SCHOOL DIPLOMA", file an application, and then wait 27 months before I would be permitted to take the Bar Exams. No one can imagine the depressed feeling that was brought upon me. I was married, then the father of two children, and was too poor to think about going to school. After much serious consideration, and a talk with Superintendent Henry McClelland and Principal John W. Avery of the Gilmer Affiliated High School, I decided to make the race for Justice of the Peace. While serving as Justice of the Peace, I would get an affiliated high school diploma. To my surprise, they told me that I could attend the school without any payment of tuition whatever, if I had the ambition and the "Guts" to do it. I made the race and was elected. I entered Gilmer High School in the fall of 1935 and received my AFFILIATED HIGH SCHOOL DIPLOMA on June 1, 1936, at which time I was 27 years old, the father of three children and had another one on the way. I did not receive my license to practice law until April 29, 1940, at which time I was 31 years old.

I have always been taught that the best education that you can get, the better off you will be. To me, there is nothing immoral, wrong, or degrading about a legal and moral marriage. Of course, no one approves of the marriage of teen-agers, unless there is a good reason. My wife and I were teen-agers when we married. The school trustees of the Gilmer Affiliated Independent School District were so proud of the fact that I was attending the school because of my ambition that they did not charge any tuition. I was permitted the same privileges that were permitted all other school children. In the beginning, it was an awful experience. To me, any Board of Trustees who would do anything to punish or delay anyone that does not do anything that is morally wrong is not thinking in the terms of the Gospel.

As a result of my being permitted to attend High School, after I was married, I have served one term in the Texas Legislature, and I am now serving my third term on the Court of Civil Appeals. Although, I am not a perfect man, I am quite proud of the experience that I have had, and am still married to a wonderful woman and we have four children of whom we are justly proud.

Where would I be today if I had not been permitted to attend a high school because of my marriage? For this reason, I disqualify myself.

One newspaper journalist compared the anguish caused by the lottery ticket in this next case to that depicted in John Steinbeck's novel *The Pearl*. In addition to this suit involving the store that issued the ticket and the clerk who "bought" it, the clerk who "sold" the ticket filed suit to get the winnings. Her claim was rejected. Likewise, a group of citizens filed suit contending that there was not a true winner and that the money should go back in the pot. That claim was also rejected. Eventually, the parties to this suit agreed to divide the proceeds, but not before the episode had created a lot of bitterness and division in Gregory, South Dakota.

DACY, *et al.* d/b/a Mr. "G's"
v.
GORS and KLEIN

Supreme Court of South Dakota
June 5, 1991
471 N.W.2d 576

MILLER, Chief Justice.

This is an original mandamus proceeding commenced seeking to require a circuit judge to grant an application for a preliminary injunction and to require that certain disputed lottery proceeds be deposited with his court pending final determination of the litigation below. This court issued an alternative writ of mandamus requiring the circuit judge to enter an order temporarily requiring the deposit of funds into court to be placed in interest-bearing accounts and further directed him to show cause why the writ should not remain in effect until the litigation below is completed on its merits. This court has now received extensive briefs and heard the argument of the litigants at the hearing on the alternative writ. For reasons set forth below, the alternative writ will be quashed and the order maintaining the status quo vacated.

FACTS

"Mr. G's" is a convenience store in Gregory, South Dakota, operated by Dacshutz, Inc., a South Dakota corporation. The owners of Dacshutz, Inc. are Michael and Diane Dacy, and Scott M. and Julie A. Anshutz. Dacshutz, Inc. entered into an extensive agreement with the South Dakota Lottery to sell Lotto America tickets. The specific provisions of the agreement are not particularly relevant in these proceedings.

On Thursday, April 4, 1991, an employee of "Mr. G's" printed a Lotto America ticket for a customer who then refused to pay for it because it was not the specific type of ticket he wanted. (This was a $5.00 ticket eligible for the Lotto America drawings on April 6, 10, 13, 17, and 20, 1991. Apparently the customer wanted five $1.00 tickets for the April 6 drawing.) The employee then placed the ticket on the lottery ticket terminal in hopes of selling it to another customer.

A Lotto America drawing was held on April 6, 1991. The next day at approximately 8:30 a.m., Ionia Klein, an employee of "Mr. G's," noticed the lotto ticket lying on top of the Lotto America ticket terminal. Upon examination of the lotto ticket, she noticed that the numbers corresponded with the winning numbers randomly selected at the Lotto America drawing the previous evening. She also noticed that the lotto ticket had not been signed. Klein then claims to have purchased the lotto ticket by taking $5.00 from her purse and placing it in a separate cash box maintained by Dacshutz, Inc. for money paid for the purchase of Lotto America tickets. Klein then signed the lotto ticket with her name on the line provided on the back of the ticket.

On Monday, April 8, 1991, Klein presented the ticket to the South Dakota Lottery, which then proceeded to determine if the ticket was valid and if Klein was entitled to receive the proceeds. On April 9, 1991, upon completion of the investigation by the South Dakota Lottery, its Executive Director, Susan Walker, officially determined that Klein was entitled to the prize money of $12.4 million to be paid in twenty annual installments.

On Wednesday, April 10, "negotiations" over the proceeds of the lottery ticket began between the owners of "Mr. G's" and Klein. Included in these discussions were accusations of theft of the lottery ticket by Klein. There were also efforts to reach a settlement agreement. Klein ultimately refused the settlement.

On April 11, 1991, Dacys, Anshutz, and Dacshutz, Inc. commenced an action in circuit court against Klein, asserting that they were the owners of the lottery ticket. The complaint sought declaratory relief of their ownership rights and damages for Klein's alleged fraud and conversion. These owners of "Mr. G's" also sought an injunction requiring that the first year's proceeds of nearly $630,000 of the lottery winnings be deposited into court pending a determination of the true ownership of the ticket. After a four-hour evidentiary hearing, Circuit Judge Gors denied the request for a temporary injunction. He later entered extensive written findings of fact and conclusions of law. Among other things, Judge Gors concluded that plaintiffs had not shown irreparable harm or a reasonable probability of success on the merits.

Upon appropriate application, this court entered an order preserving the status quo in the circuit court action and exercised original jurisdiction by issuing the alternative writ of mandamus referred to earlier, and which we now quash.

DECISION

Before proceeding further with this opinion, some preliminary comments are appropriate. This case has fostered much media attention and various correspondence to members of this court from private citizens taking varied positions. It seems clear to us that there is a vast misunderstanding of the precise legal issue presented before this court at this time.

WE ARE NOT DECIDING WHO OWNS THE LOTTERY TICKET OR WHO GETS THE LOTTERY PRIZE!! That will be decided later at the trial court level. THE SOLE ISSUE BEFORE THIS COURT IS WHETHER CIRCUIT JUDGE GORS SHOULD BE MANDATED TO ISSUE A TEMPORARY INJUNCTION TO REQUIRE THE DEPOSIT OF THE FIRST YEAR'S LOTTERY WINNING PROCEEDS DURING THE PENDENCY OF THE LITIGATION. We hold that we cannot and should not order Judge Gors to do so.

Under Article V, § 5 of the South Dakota Constitution, this court has authority to issue, hear and determine any original or remedial writs. By rule of this court, codified at SDCL 15–25–1, the exercise of such original jurisdiction "is reserved for the consideration of matters of prerogative, extraordinary, and general concern."

SDCL 21–29–1 provides:

> The writ of mandamus may be issued by the Supreme and Circuit Courts, to any inferior tribunal, corporation, board, or person, to compel the performance of an act which the law specially enjoins as a duty resulting from an office, trust, or station; or to compel the admission of a party to the use and enjoyment of a right or office to which he is entitled, and from which he is lawfully precluded by such inferior tribunal, corporation, board, or person.

Further, it "must be issued in all cases where there is not a plain, speedy, and adequate remedy, in the ordinary course of law." SDCL 21–29–2.

* * *

As noted previously, petitioners requested Judge Gors to issue a preliminary injunction. Pursuant thereto, a hearing was held on April 19, 1991. At the hearing, there was testimony from five witnesses. The transcript of the hearing contains 119 pages. At the conclusion of the hearing, Judge Gors denied petitioners' request for a preliminary injunction. Certainly, the issuance or denial of an injunction is discretionary with a trial court.

"Whether a preliminary injunction should issue involves consideration of (1) the threat of irreparable harm to the movant; (2) the state of the balance between this harm and the injury that granting the injunction will inflict on other parties litigant; (3) the probability that movant will succeed on the merits; and (4) the public interest."

It is obvious from reading Judge Gors' findings of fact and conclusions of law that he considered each and every one of the foregoing criteria and factors. He made specific findings and conclusions as they relate to the same. Quite appropriately, in that preliminary injunction proceeding, he made no judicial determination of the ownership of the lottery ticket. That must be done at the trial on the merits. Also, we cannot, at this juncture, make a final determination of ownership of the lottery ticket. Typically in mandamus proceedings, courts do not consider questions as to the ownership of property. Any ultimate determination of ownership by this court may only be made on direct appeal following the trial court's final judgment.

The dissents principally assert that Klein will not prevail on the merits. Those assertions are premature at best. The trial court has entered findings of fact which we cannot say are clearly erroneous. The principle assertions of petitioners sound in fraud and deceit, which raise questions of fact to be resolved by a jury. Further, since we believe questions of fact remain: "It [is] necessary, therefore, that the rights of the parties should be determined by a judgment of the court in an ordinary action, and not in the first instance by mandamus." "We are of the opinion that the ends of justice will be better [served] by having this cause . . . first tried in the circuit court[.]" Finally, whether we agree with Judge Gors findings and conclusions is immaterial. The crucial question, as stated earlier, is whether he abused his discretion under the facts of the case.

* * *

We believe that Judge Gors, in light of the evidence before him, did not abuse his discretion. Since the granting or denial of a preliminary injunction rests within the sound discretion of the trial court, and we find no abuse of that discretion, mandamus will not issue. Therefore, the Alternative Writ of Mandamus is hereby quashed.

WUEST, Justice (dissenting).

I agree with the special writing of Justice Sabers and with the law cited in the majority opinion. Where I part company with the majority opinion is the application of the law to the facts of this case. There is no doubt the trial court has discretion to grant or deny injunctive relief, particularly where the facts are in dispute. Here, however, the relevant facts are not in dispute and the claim of Ionia Klein to the prize money is precarious at best. Whether she is entitled to the money is a question of law and not a question of fact.

An essential element of the game of lottery is chance. When the element of chance is absent, "the game's character as a lottery ceases to exist." *Horan v. State of Calif.*, 220 Cal.App.3d 1503, 1508, 270 Cal.Rptr. 194, 196 (1990). The undisputed facts before the trial court show Ms. Klein ventured no chance with respect to the April 6th Lotto America drawing; she acquired the winning ticket after the drawing and with the knowledge that it was the winning ticket. Therefore, as to Ms. Klein, there was no lottery.

The majority opinion correctly states we are not determining ownership of the ticket in this proceeding. But we are considering the probability of Mr. G's success in a trial on the merits. The facts before the trial court tend to show that Mr. G's was the owner of the ticket at the relevant time. Under its agreement with the South Dakota Lottery, Mr. G's was liable for all tickets issued at the store, whether sold or not. And, at the time of the drawing, the winning ticket had not been sold and Mr. G's was liable for it. Thus, there exists a strong probability that Mr. G's will ultimately prevail at trial.

Moreover, given the financial status of Ms. Klein, Mr. G's faces irreparable harm in that she will likely be judgment proof after a trial on the merits, at least to the extent her legal counsel is compensated from the first disbursement of the lottery proceeds. Indeed, it is in the public interest to insure that all who take a chance in the lottery, take an equal chance.

* * *

SABERS, Justice (dissenting).

We should maintain the freeze on these funds to preserve them for the rightful owner, prevent harm and avoid multiple lawsuits.[1]

1. Further harm from additional lawsuits could result from releasing these funds. Robin Parsons, the clerk from whom the ticket was ordered, has already started a lawsuit claiming ownership. The presently unknown person who is said to have "refused" the ticket, among others, could also jump into the fray.

Under the majority opinion in *McFarland v. McFarland*, No. 17043, slip op. (S.D. May 29, 1991) relating to "tracing of funds," the rightful owner of the ticket could bring more lawsuits to trace and recover these presently frozen funds against Klein's lawyers, bankers and any other paid creditors. If we permit the funds to be released to Klein, it could produce a trial lawyers "Valhalla."

In view of the rare opportunity this Court has to prevent this kind of wasteful litigation, a decision to permit the release of the funds to Klein will rank high on the historical list of legal opportunities known and blown. Releasing these funds solves no problems, only creates more problems.

A basic premise of the law is that a person cannot profit from her own wrong. The law also prevents an employee from taking advantage of her employer. Ionia Klein knew she was taking advantage of her position as an employee and she knew she was doing wrong because she lied about the time and circumstances of the claimed purchase. This is not based on employer's version, but hers. She cannot claim a more favorable version of the facts than her own testimony.

Klein neither participated in nor won the lottery drawing because she knew the ticket was a winner before she took possession of it. Since she took no risk in acquiring the ticket, as to her, there was no lottery. Because the ticket was issued but not sold at 8:00 p.m. on April 6, 1991, the employer's account was responsible to pay for it at the time of the drawing and the employer became the winner of the lottery.

Since it is clear that Klein is not the owner, irreparable harm will occur to the owner if the first installment of $500,000 is released to her. Therefore, the owner is entitled to maintain the status quo, and, there being no adequate remedy at law, injunctive relief is appropriate. To hand the check over to Klein under these circumstances, although it may be more popular, would constitute a clear abuse of discretion. One cannot mask this abuse of discretion by failing to make the obvious findings and legal conclusions.

Despite this, to avoid claimed temporary hardship to Ionia Klein and her husband, who terminated their employment upon "winning" the lottery, I would vote to let Klein obtain a monthly amount of $1,000 from these lottery funds during the pendency of the action. Any amounts obtained would be subject to repayment when ownership is conclusively determined.

The idea of holding a computer in contempt of court may strike one as silly. Or as a darned good idea and long overdue. Or both. Whichever, a rogue computer led to a unique sanction, as explained in this opinion, which may or may not have been written with tongue firmly in cheek.

In re VIVIAN

United States Bankruptcy Court, S.D. Florida
Dec. 8, 1992
150 B.R. 832

ORDER ON LETTER FROM JOHN C. VIVIAN DATED DECEMBER 3, 1992 AND MARKED "IMPORTANT" AND DETERMINING ROGUE COMPUTER IN CIVIL CONTEMPT

A. JAY CRISTOL, Bankruptcy Judge.

On December 7, 1992, the court received a letter from John C. Vivian referring to the Bankruptcy Case of John Coffey Vivian and Margaret Vivian, as above numbered. The court will treat the letter as a motion to determine the NationsBank computer in contempt of this court.

Following the entry of discharge in bankruptcy to John Coffey Vivian and Margaret Vivian, NationsBank sent them a dunning letter on a debt which had been discharged. The court set the matter on an order to show cause and the court's order was taken quite seriously by NationsBank. The bank went to the expense of flying a high executive from North Carolina to Miami to appear and testify that the letter was sent in error and the court was satisfied that no intentional violation of the injunction had occurred. The NationsBank computer had generated the notice and NationsBank wrote a letter of apology to the Vivians and proceeded to appropriately chastise their computer and directed it not to send anymore notices to the Vivians.

Only a month went by and the Vivians received a computer generated document from the bank which contained the words, "Please make checks payable to NationsBank and remit with top part of this statement to". Never mind that the document also showed no balance due and no payment due date, the Vivians were annoyed. It appearing to the court that this was not an intentional act of any human at NationsBank but rather the rampage of a rogue computer, the court entered an order on December 3, 1992, docketed December 4, suggesting that counsel for the bank communicate with the bank and the Vivians and try and make clear that this was not an intentional violation and it would not happen again.

Lo and behold, another month rolled around and that rogue computer did it again. The account statement showing no balance due and no date to make payment was mailed on NationsBank's red, white and blue stationery (also containing some shades of gray and black print) to Mr. and Mrs. Vivian.

It is this final document that has truly established, beyond any reasonable doubt, that Mr. and Mrs. Vivian have no sense of humor and no gratitude whatsoever for the court's prior efforts on their behalf. They have, in their letter of December 3, queried "May I ask a question? Why can't you or your Court get these continuing and very annoying letters STOPPED." (The question mark was omitted by the Vivians, not by the court but the court understood what they meant.) The Vivians were so annoyed that they went on to threaten that perhaps they should write to their family friend, a very well known, renowned and respected federal judge, about this serious matter. They then went on to say "May I hear from you or your secretary by return mail?". It is apparent that the Vivians are mad as you know what and they are not going to take it anymore. Likewise, this court is mad as you know what and is not going to take it anymore. Accordingly, and pursuant to Federal Rule of Bankruptcy Procedure 9020, the court determines the NationsBank computer to be in civil contempt of this court. Upon consideration, it is

ORDERED that the NationsBank computer, having been determined in civil contempt, is fined 50 megabytes of hard drive memory and 10 megabytes random access memory. The computer may purge itself of this contempt by ceasing the production and mailing of documents to Mr. and Mrs. Vivian.

It is obvious that a monetary fine against a computer would not be effective. Sometimes, a monetary fine is not the most effective sanction against a person either, especially if the court is more concerned with preventing future transgressions than in punishing a past offense.

CURRAN

v.

PRICE

United States District Court, D. Maryland
Aug. 18, 1993
150 F.R.D. 85

SMALKIN, District Judge.

This case is before the Court on the defendant's attorney's response to the Court's *sua sponte* direction that he show cause why sanctions should not be imposed upon him under Fed.R.Civ.P. 11 for his having filed a notice of removal in a case that was not removable under any conceivable notion of federal removal jurisdiction. No oral hearing is needed, as will be discussed more fully below.

* * *

In its original consideration of this matter, the Court had thought it appropriate to impose a monetary penalty of $2,500.00 on defendant's attorney. Because, however, a primary purpose of Rule 11—making the opponent whole for fees and expenses—can readily be served in this case under the remand statute itself, and because the improper filing here resulted as much or more from ignorance of the law as from anything else, the Court feels that it should, in the exercise of its discretion, impose a non-monetary penalty. Certainly, non-monetary penalties may be imposed under Rule 11. It is evident that, at least where fees and costs can be recovered separately, the "sparing principle" in imposing Rule 11 sanctions weighs against imposing any significant monetary penalty.

The proper purpose of a non-monetary penalty should be to educate, especially in a case like this, where the attorney fails to grasp the issue even after it has been explained to him by the Court. In his submission showing cause, the attorney here, though citing to *Caterpillar*, [482 U.S. 386, 393, 107 S.Ct. 2425, 2430, 96 L.Ed.2d 318], seems to miss its point entirely, confusing a filing under 42 U.S.C.A. § 1983 with the removal of an ongoing state case.[2]

* * *

The Court has considered, but rejects, the notion of forcing attendance at a CLE course, largely because it is questionable whether the specific gap in counsel's knowledge of federal law would be adequately filled by such a course. Instead, the Court, in the exercise of its discretion, has determined that a more laser-like approach is warranted, consisting of remedial education in federal removal law, to be gained and reinforced through the mnemonic device of copying appropriate materials out in longhand. Counsel will, thus, not have to miss office or court time, to attend classes. Instead, he may accomplish his remedial education during what would otherwise be his leisure time.

Specifically, defendant's counsel, Timothy F. Umbreit, Esq., will be, by a separate order, directed to copy out, legibly, in his own handwriting, and within 30 days of the date hereof, the text (*i.e.*, without footnotes) of section 3722 in 14A C. Wright, A. Miller, and E. Cooper, Federal Practice and Procedure: Civil (1985), together with the text of that section's update at page 43 of the 1993 pocket part of volume 14A. Mr. Umbreit will turn in the resulting product to the Clerk of this Court, with a certification that it was made solely by himself and in his own handwriting. This sanction is, to the Court, the least drastic—and likely a very effective—way of impressing the appropriate principles of federal removal jurisdiction upon counsel's long-term memory.

2. Oddly enough, he also takes the opportunity to criticize the Attorney General for "cumulated logic," whatever that might be.

The circumlocution of legal writing is a standard source of humor. In reality, even lawyers require that documents be comprehendible, at least to other lawyers. In the federal courts, Rule 8 of the Federal Rules of Civil Procedure requires that pleadings contain a "short and plain statement." Still, some lawyers seem to be not quite clear on the concept.

❖–❖–❖–❖–❖

GORDON

v.

GREEN, *et al.*

United States Court of Appeals
Fifth Circuit
Sept. 18, 1979
602 F.2d 743

JOHN R. BROWN, Chief Judge:

As we see it, the only issue currently before the Court in these five consolidated cases is whether verbose, confusing, scandalous, and repetitious pleadings totaling into the thousands of pages comply with the requirement of "a short and plain statement" set forth in F.R.Civ.P. 8. We think that the mere description of the issue provides the answer: we direct the District Court to dismiss the complaints—with leave to amend—because of appellant's failure to comply with F.R.Civ.P. 8(a) and (e).

The Pleadings: Gobbledygook

The appellant, Edwin F. Gordon, invested several million dollars in a series of Florida real estate syndications. When the promises of substantial profits failed to materialize, appellant filed suit against the sellers and promoters of the syndications, claiming various violations of the federal securities laws.

Under F.R.Civ.P. 8, a party seeking relief must submit a pleading containing a "short and plain statement of the grounds upon which the court's jurisdiction depends," F.R.Civ.P. 8(a)(1), and "a short and plain statement of the claim showing that the pleader is entitled to relief." F.R.Civ.P. 8(a)(2).

In addition, F.R.Civ.P. 8(e)(1) states that "[e]ach averment of a pleading shall be simple, concise, and direct." As the following factual account demonstrates, nothing was further from the minds of appellant and his lawyer than the clear directions contained in F.R.Civ.P. 8(a) and (e).

These five consolidated cases were originally brought in the Southern District of New York in March and April of 1976. At this initial stage, appellant filed five separate long, verbose, and confusing verified complaints containing a total of 165 typewritten pages and an additional 413 pages of exhibits. In one of the five cases, appellant filed an amendment to the verified complaint (8 pages plus 39 pages of exhibits).

By stipulation, the cases were transferred to the Southern District of Florida. The Florida Court proposed to dismiss appellant's complaints for violation of Rule 8, but did not actually do so when appellant introduced a single complaint and filed a motion to consolidate. The motion to consolidate was eventually denied.

In September 1976, the Trial Court ordered a hearing on various motions, primarily motions to dismiss under Rule 12(b). One week prior to the hearing and without seeking leave to amend appellant filed an "Amendment to Verified Complaint" for each of the actions. Each "Amendment to Verified Complaint" was 19 pages. On September 30, 1976, the Trial Court dismissed the action, but *not* for failure to comply with Rule 8. Rather, after combing through the mountain of pages before him, the Trial Judge concluded that appellant failed to establish federal court jurisdiction. Subsequently, appellant topped his mountain of legal papers with a fourth set of complaints and a motion for leave to amend. The motion was summarily denied.

"Let Thy Speech Be Short,
Comprehending Much In Few Words"[5]

The various complaints, amendments, amended amendments, amendments to amended amendments, and other related papers are anything but short, totaling over 4,000 pages,

5. Ecclesiasticus 32:8.

occupying 18 volumes, and requiring a hand truck or cart to move.[6] They are not plain, either. The Trial Court described the pleadings as being "extremely long and combin(ing) into single counts detailed recitation of evidence and legal arguments complete with extensive citations of authority." The Court also observed that a paragraph from one typical complaint was single spaced, "extend[ed] the full length of a legal page and constitute[d] a single sentence." Much of the pleadings are scandalous as well.[7] Moreover, we cannot tell whether complaints filed earlier in time are to be read in conjunction with those filed later or whether the amended versions supersede previous pleadings.

6. Appellant's filings demonstrate once and for all that history does in fact repeat itself. In discussing Dr. J. H. Baker's second volume of Spelman's Reports, the 1978 Report of the Council and Abstract of the Accounts of the Selden Society reveals (p. 6): "It is in the 16th century that the sheer physical bulk of the (plea) rolls (became) truly daunting, with a mile or two of parchment used in a term." If every party filed the massive pleadings submitted here, we would only hasten the speed at which our country's trees are being transformed into sheets of legal jargon. Moreover, we would need to build another courthouse simply to store legal documents.

7. At the risk of further polluting the legal waters by immortalizing this gibberish in the annals of the Federal Reporter, we quote some typically scandalous language from one of appellant's many filings:

> Green and Broberg worked closely together to keep their grandiose "Money making monster" scheme in operation . . . (3) by forcing the investors in various syndications to continue to make payments through the loyalty and enthusiasm of those investors who had compromised themselves to the scheme by making money by means of the Green-Broberg scheme, . . . Broberg aided and abetted Green in actively working to police compliance with the "pay or you are out of the deal completely" enforcement concept in this scheme that can only be described as diabolical and monstrous, by Broberg's legal advice that the forfeiture clause was legal (thus Broberg bears an awesome burden towards the investors because of his special fiduciary responsibilities as an Attorney at Law), (4) by not only failing to register this securities investment scheme to bring it under the supervision and censure of the S.E.C. but to openly operate in what was, in fact, an outlaw fashion, based on the spurious so-called "legal opinion" of Attorney Broberg, rendered to investors and potential investors, to the effect that this scheme did not constitute securities but that, on the contrary, it was simple country-style real estate with lots of country-style profit in it for all collaborators, but destruction for the defector who will be cannibalized by the rest of the group, again based on the so-called "legal opinion" of Broberg to the effect that failure to make payments for whatever reason constitutes a breach of the so-called "trust agreement" and subjects the defector to losing his entire interest and having it assumed (cannibalized) by the remaining investors. . . .

One option before us is to struggle through the thousands of pages of pleadings in an effort to determine (assuming we possibly could) whether the Trial Court correctly dismissed for lack of jurisdiction. However, such a course of action would be unwise from the standpoint of sound judicial administration. All would know that there is no longer any necessity for paying the least bit of heed to F.R.Civ.P. 8(a) in its demand for "a short and plain statement" reiterated by the 8(e) requirement that each averment "be simple, concise, and direct." Lawyers would see that in the face of even gross violations of Rule 8, we would undertake the burden of trying to parse out 18 volumes of words, disorganized and sometimes conflicting, with a mish-mash of so-called evidentiary materials, citations of authority, and other things that a pleader, aware of and faithful to the command of the Federal Rules of Civil Procedure, knows to be completely extraneous. And the District Courts who come on the firing line are the first victims of this paper mill. We think that the Trial Court should have dismissed the complaints with leave to amend. While a Trial Court is and should be given great leeway in determining whether a party has complied with Rule 8, we think that as a matter of law, verbose and scandalous pleadings of over 4,000 pages violate Rule 8.

In finding a violation of Rule 8, we do not recede even one inch from the position expressed by this Court in *Blue Cat, Plimsoll Club*, and a host of other cases sounding an approach of liberality under F.R.Civ.P. 12 in reading a pleading as an adequate statement or claim. Appellant asks not that we adopt a liberal approach, but that we stand liberality on its head by accepting 4,000 pages of chaotic legal jargon in lieu of a short and plain statement. We would be hindering, not promoting, the underlying purpose of Rule 8, which is "to eliminate prolixity in pleading and to achieve brevity, simplicity, and clarity." *Knox v. First Security Bank of Utah*, 10 Cir., 1952, 196 F.2d 112, 117. We fully agree with the observation of the District Court for the Eastern District of Michigan that "the law does not require, nor does justice demand, that a judge must grope through (thousands of) pages of irrational, prolix and redundant pleadings." *Passic v. State*, E.D.Mich., 1951, 98 F.Supp. 1015, 1016.

*   *   *

The court held that the plaintiff would be granted leave to file a proper, decent, and acceptable amended complaint.

*   *   *

If our holding results in more time and expense to the appellant, that would be fair recompense for these marked, unjustifiable violations of the letter and spirit of the Federal Rules of Civil Procedure and an indifference as though they had never been adopted 41 years ago.[13]

We vacate the judgment of the District Court and remand for dismissal of the complaint without prejudice to the right promptly to file a complaint in compliance with Rule 8.

VACATED and REMANDED.

13. Counsel as scrivener would have been fair game for the discipline meted out by the Chancellor in 1596. As Professor Richard C. Wydick of Davis Law School reports:

> In 1596 an English chancellor decided to make an example of a particularly prolix document filed in his court. The chancellor first ordered a hole cut through the center of the document, all 120 pages of it. Then he ordered that the person who wrote it should have his head stuffed through the hole, and the unfortunate fellow was led around to be exhibited to all those attending court at West Minister Hall.

> Wydick, Plain English For Lawyers, 1978, 66 Calif.L.Rev. 727.

Obviously this applies only to counsel who filed the papers, not to the appellate counsel who briefed and argued the case here.

The interpretation of provisions in the United States Constitution by the United States Supreme Court are binding on state courts. Rights secured by the federal Constitution must be honored by state courts, even if a state court would not interpret similar language in the state constitution as providing that right. But what if the United States Supreme Court says that the federal Constitution does not guarantee a particular right? Can an almost identical provision in a state constitution be interpreted by the state court as securing that right?

"This is a major case in establishing the rights and power of state courts to independently interpret their own state constitutions as an independent basis for their decisions."

—Justice, South Dakota State Court

STATE

v.

OPPERMAN

Supreme Court of South Dakota
Nov. 12, 1976
247 N.W.2d 673.

WINANS, Justice.

On April 15, 1975, this court reversed a judgment against petitioner because we found that the contraband used to convict petitioner had been seized pursuant to an inventory search which was unreasonable under the Fourth Amendment to the United States Constitution. On November 3, 1975, the United States Supreme Court granted certiorari; in a 5–4 decision it reversed the judgment of this court and remanded for further proceedings not inconsistent with its opinion. On August 26, 1976, this court granted a rehearing to ascertain whether the inventory search of petitioner's automobile was in violation of his rights under Article VI, § 11 of the South Dakota Constitution. We find that the inventory procedure followed in this instance constitutes an unreasonable search under our state constitution; accordingly we reverse the decision of the trial court.

We are mindful that the United States Supreme Court found that the inventory procedure followed in this case did not amount to an "unreasonable search" in violation of the Fourth Amendment. That decision is binding on this court as a matter of federal constitutional law. "However, manifestly the question remains for us to decide whether it offends any of the provisions of our own constitution and we are under no compulsion to follow the United States Supreme Court in that regard." *House of Seagram v. Assam Drug Co.*, 1970, 85 S.D. 27, 32, 176 N.W.2d 491, 494.

There can be no doubt that this court has the power to provide an individual with greater protection under the state constitution than does the United States Supreme Court under the federal constitution. This court is the final authority on interpretation and enforcement of the South Dakota Constitution. We have always assumed the independent nature of our state constitution regardless of any similarity between the language of that document and the federal constitution. Admittedly the language of Article VI, § 11 is almost identical to that found in the Fourth Amendment;[4] however, we have the right to construe our state constitutional provision in accordance with what we conceive to be its plain meaning. We find that logic and a sound regard for the purposes of the protection afforded by S.D.Const., Art. VI, § 11 warrant a higher standard of protection for the individual in this instance than the United States Supreme Court found necessary under the Fourth Amendment.

---

4. S.D.Const., Art. VI, § 11 provides:

"The right of the people of be secure in their persons, houses, papers and effects, against unreasonable searches and seizures shall not be violated, and no warrant shall issue but upon probable cause supported by affidavit, particularly describing the place to be searched and the person or thing to be seized."

U.S.Const., Amend. 4 provides:

"The right of the people to be secure in their persons, houses, papers and effects, against unreasonable searches and seizures, shall not be violated, and no Warrants shall issue but upon probable cause, supported by Oath or affirmation, and particularly describing the place to be searched, and the persons or things to be seized."

Article VI, § 11 of our state constitution guarantees our citizens the right to be free from "unreasonable searches and seizures." We have held that a determination of reasonableness requires a balancing of the need for a search in a particular case against the scope of the particular intrusion. *State v. Catlette*, 1974, S.D., 221 N.W.2d 25. In that opinion we relied on *United States v. Lawson*, 8 Cir., 1973, 487 F.2d 468, and held that an inventory was a search, but found that it was not an unreasonable search as long as it was conducted without investigative motive and its scope was limited to things within plain view.

We also find persuasive the reasoning in *Lawson* that for an inventory search to be reasonable, absent a warrant or circumstances constituting an exception to the warrant requirement, there must be a "minimal interference" with an individual's protected rights. We now conclude that as a matter of protection under S.D.Const., Art. VI, § 11, "minimal interference" with a citizen's constitutional rights means that non-investigative police inventory searches of automobiles without a warrant must be restricted to safeguarding those articles which are within plain view of the officer's vision. We therefore affirm the rationale of our original decision as a matter of state constitutional law.

* * *

It is called the Great Writ. It is the writ of habeas corpus (literally "you have the body"), which is the method by which a prisoner can challenge the legality of his or her confinement. It is used to raise constitutional issues and is generally not available to challenge the sufficiency of the evidence to support a conviction or to present new evidence. This is especially true when the prisoner asks a federal court to overturn a state court conviction. Because of concerns for finality, a prisoner is generally precluded from bringing successive petitions.

Although those considerations presented formidable obstacles, they did not prevent the court from remedying an apparent injustice suffered by James Dean Walker some twenty years earlier.

"A sole practitioner . . . undertook the representation of James Dean Walker, an indigent defendant prisoner, and orchestrated a successful effort lasting over several years which freed Walker from an apparently unjust conviction and imprisonment."

—Judge, United States Court of Appeals

WALKER

v.

LOCKHART,

Superintendent of the Arkansas
Department of Corrections

United States Court of Appeals
Eighth Circuit
Decided May 17, 1985
763 F.2d 942

BRIGHT, Circuit Judge.

In January 1984, this court, in a five to four decision, affirmed the district court's denial of James Dean Walker's second petition for a writ of habeas corpus. Thereafter, new evidence surfaced relating to the crime for which Walker had been convicted. We recalled our mandate on June 13, 1984, and remanded the case to the district court with instructions to hold a hearing on the new evidence and to certify its findings to this court. Upon careful review of the new evidence and the district court's findings, we conclude that the ends of justice will be served by now directing the district court to grant the writ unless the State of Arkansas commences proceedings to retry Walker within ninety days from issuance of the mandate of this court.

I. BACKGROUND

The factual background and lengthy procedural history of this case are set forth in some detail by both the majority and the dissent in this court's recent en banc opinion. Briefly, on April 16, 1963, James Dean Walker and a companion, Russell Kumpe, were at a Little Rock nightclub with two women, Linda Ford and Mary Louise Roberts. Following an altercation in which another patron was shot, Walker, Kumpe, and Ford left the Little Rock area in Kumpe's Oldsmobile. Roberts, who was concerned about Ford, followed in a cab driven by Aaron Paul Alderman. Police Officer Gene Barentine pursued and stopped the Oldsmobile and parked his vehicle behind it. Officer Jerrell Vaughan arrived on the scene almost immediately thereafter, as did cabdriver Alderman and another cabdriver, Thomas Short.

Barentine ordered Kumpe out of the driver's side of the car and began to search him. Vaughan approached the Oldsmobile on the passenger's side of the car. At this point, the precise order of events becomes uncertain, but following an exchange of gunfire, Officer Vaughan lay dead or near death with a single bullet wound to his heart. Walker, who sustained five gunshot wounds, lay face down beside the Oldsmobile a few feet from Vaughan. In his right hand, Walker held a fully-loaded, undischarged gun. Kumpe, who tried to escape at some point during the confusion, had been shot twice by Barentine.

It is undisputed that the gun found in Walker's hand was not the murder weapon. Police found a second gun, a fully loaded Colt .38, under the front seat of the Oldsmobile. A third gun, found either underneath or near Walker's body, was later identified as the murder weapon.

The State charged Walker with first degree murder. At trial, the prosecution proceeded on the theory that Walker shot Vaughan with the gun that was found near his body, and that Barentine then shot Walker. Linda Ford and cabdriver Thomas Short offered evidence indicating that Walker shot at Vaughan. Ballistics evidence indicated that the bullet which killed Vaughan was fired from the gun found on the ground near Walker. The jury convicted Walker of first degree murder and sentenced him to death. The Arkansas Supreme Court reversed his conviction and remanded the case for a new trial.

Prior to Walker's second trial, defense counsel moved to disqualify the state trial judge on the ground that he was grossly prejudiced. The defense presented uncontradicted evidence that the judge, after granting Walker's request to go to church to be baptized, had instructed the deputy sheriff that if Walker "made a move to shoot him down, because he didn't want him brought back to him because he intended to burn the S.O.B. anyway." The trial judge declined to recuse himself. During the retrial, he made a number of rulings and comments adverse to Walker.

Before the second trial, defense counsel obtained disclosure of ballistics evidence demonstrating that Vaughan, not Barentine, had shot Walker. Consequently, the State changed its theory at the second trial and contended that Walker fired first, and that Vaughan, although fatally wounded, managed to shoot Walker five times before he died. To support this theory, the State adduced essentially the same evidence as at the first trial. However, Linda Ford was not present at the second trial. The prosecution claimed that she was unavailable, and over defense counsel's objections, read her testimony from the prior trial into the record. The defense was thus unable to cross-examine Ford in light of the State's altered theory. The jury again convicted Walker of first degree murder, but sentenced him to life imprisonment. The Supreme Court of Arkansas affirmed the conviction.

Walker then filed his first petition for habeas corpus relief alleging, inter alia, that the trial judge was biased and that the prosecution had suppressed testimony of cabdriver Aaron Paul Alderman which would have been highly favorable to Walker. At the habeas hearing, Alderman testified that Kumpe had scrambled underneath the Oldsmobile when the shooting started. Alderman claimed that he saw Vaughan fire several shots at Walker, and that Vaughan remained standing after Walker had fallen to the ground. There was a momentary lull in the shooting, and then Alderman heard a final shot which had a hollow, muffled sound—as though it had been fired from a barrel or pipe. Vaughan fell immediately after that shot. The police then told Kumpe to come out from under the car. Alderman testified that he removed the fully-loaded gun from Walker's hand. As he walked away, he saw another gun near the rear end of the Oldsmobile where Kumpe had been during the exchange of gunfire.

* * *

The district court (Judge Henley) denied the writ, concluding, inter alia, that it was not convinced that the State had suppressed Alderman's testimony, and that the prejudice of the trial judge was not sufficient to deny Walker due process. A panel of this court affirmed the judgment of the district court.

The present litigation originated in 1981 when Walker filed a second application for habeas relief. The district court (Judge Woods) ruled that four of the seven claims asserted by Walker in his second petition had previously been determined adversely to him in his original application for habeas relief. The court considered the guidelines for successive habeas petitions and concluded that because the prior determinations were on the merits, no intervening change in the law had occurred, and Walker had presented no new evidence, the "ends of justice" would not be served by reconsideration of the same claims. The trial court permitted Walker to present evidence on his newly asserted claims, but found the additional grounds to be without merit and denied the writ.

On appeal, following arguments before a panel of this court, the case was referred to the court en banc. The court requested additional briefing on several issues, including whether the constitutional violations alleged (prejudice of the trial judge, suppression of evidence, or other violations) had grossly flawed the guilt determination in this case. After an en banc hearing, this court affirmed the judgment of the district court, holding that Walker had failed to show that the ends of justice required reconsideration of issues determined adversely to him in his first habeas application.

The four dissenting judges concluded that a great injustice had been done, and that Walker was entitled to habeas relief. In particular, the dissent emphasized that the admitted prejudice of the trial judge had deprived Walker of a fair trial, that the prosecution had suppressed evidence favorable to Walker, and that "the record as a whole indicates the strong probability that Walker did not shoot Vaughan."[6]

Judge Arnold, although voting with the majority to deny the writ, agreed in a concurring opinion that Walker had been tried before a prejudiced trial judge. He pointed out that "[i]f due process means anything, it means a trial before an unbiased judge and jury." Judge Arnold further indicated that he disagreed with this court's 1969 decision denying Walker's first habeas petition. He noted, however, that mere disagreement is not enough to justify granting relief on a successive habeas application. Something more is required, such as a change in the law or "new evidence unrevealed at the time of the first habeas proceeding." *Id.* at 1250.

In sum, notwithstanding the denial of relief, a majority of the en banc court concluded that this court erred in 1969 when it denied Walker's application for habeas relief because Walker had not received a fair trial before an unbiased judge.

After issuance of our mandate denying the writ of habeas corpus, Walker, on March 15, 1984, filed a petition for recall of mandate on the ground that new evidence about the crime had surfaced. That evidence came in the form of a diary entry written in 1968 by Russell Kumpe, Walker's companion on the night Officer Vaughan was killed. The entry indicated that Kumpe fired a gun at or near the time Vaughan was shot. In addition, Walker's counsel offered to prove that Kumpe admitted to his former wife that he, not Walker, shot the officer. In response, the State indicated that it possessed a tape-recorded statement, which it had never offered into evidence, in which Walker allegedly confessed to the crime.

---

6. Judge Heaney served on the panel of this court which denied Walker relief in 1969. He joined the dissent on Walker's second petition, and joins with the majority in this opinion, underscoring his strong belief that the previous panel erred, and that only by granting Walker habeas relief can we right a grievous miscarriage of justice.

*   *   *

Judge Arnold, in a separate concurrence to the order recalling the mandate, observed that if the new evidence could establish that Kumpe had in fact fired his gun on the night in question, such evidence would give credibility to Alderman's account of the shooting, which exonerates Walker and which has never been heard by a jury. Judge Arnold concluded that the new material "sufficiently adds to the uncertainties of this case to justify additional proceedings."

Pursuant to our instructions, the district court held an evidentiary hearing in October 1984. The court heard testimony from some thirty witnesses, and considered the evidence specifically mentioned in our remand order, as well as additional evidence which surfaced after the recall of mandate. The district court concluded that the record contained no credible evidence which merited a new trial; that only part of the new evidence would be admissible if another jury trial were held; that Walker's right to due process had not been violated by the suppression of exculpatory material; and that the new evidence did not sufficiently tip the balance of the "ends of justice" standard to require that a new trial be held.

This matter is now before us for further review in light of the evidence presented and the district court's findings.

II. DISCUSSION

The question before this court is whether the new evidence sufficiently tips the balance of the ends of justice standard to permit us to reconsider the merits of the claims raised in Walker's first habeas petition. We must assess, among other things, the admissibility and credibility of the evidence presented, but as to credibility, the issue is not whether the district court or this court would find the new evidence credible, but whether the evidence possesses sufficient credibility that it should be heard by the real factfinder: the jury.

*   *   *

The court discusses newly discovered evidence, including the diary kept by Kumpe, Kumpe's testimony at an evidentiary hearing, Kumpe's statements to his former wife, and a record-

ing of a conversation between Kumpe and his sister, Mildred
Eisner. All the evidence strongly indicated that it was Kumpe
who fired the fatal shot.

*   *   *

In sum, the Kumpe-Eisner transcript constitutes powerful
corroboration of newly discovered evidence favorable to Walker
which we asked the district court to consider on remand. Although the transcript may be weighed into the balance under
the ends of justice standard, it also provides an independent
basis for setting aside Walker's conviction. We conclude that
the transcript itself, when considered in the context of the
entire record, is sufficient to create a reasonable doubt about
Walker's guilt. Suppression of the document therefore constituted a violation of Walker's due process rights.

III. CONCLUSION

After careful review of the record, we conclude that the
newly discovered evidence sufficiently tips the balance of the
ends of justice standard to permit this court to reconsider
Walker's habeas petition, specifically his claim concerning the
bias of the state trial judge. Although none of the evidence
presented at the remand hearing relates to the state trial judge's
actions, the evidence casts sufficient doubt on the factual basis
for Walker's conviction to justify reexamination of our prior
legal conclusions. We now hold that the trial judge's bias deprived Walker of a fair trial. Walker is therefore entitled to
habeas corpus relief. The suppressed Kumpe-Eisner transcript,
although relevant to the ends of justice inquiry, provides an
independent basis for granting Walker's petition for relief.

The dissent asserts that the court is granting the writ on
the basis of newly discovered evidence. That is not the case.
We quite agree with the dissent that a claim of newly discovered evidence relevant only to guilt is not a ground for
habeas relief. The federal habeas power goes only to the constitutionality of detention, not to the question of guilt or innocence. In this case, Walker's detention is unconstitutional
not because new questions have been raised about guilt or innocence, but because the judge who tried his case was prejudiced against him. The newly discovered evidence is relevant

only because it casts sufficient doubt on the factual basis for the conviction to justify reexamination of a legal ground (bias of the trial judge) previously rejected by this court.

The dissent further suggests that the court has summarily concluded that bias supports granting the writ without any analysis or review of prior decisions reaching a different conclusion on this issue. Again, that is not the case. In the previous en banc opinion of this court, four dissenting judges and Judge Arnold in his concurring opinion considered the merits of the bias issue and concluded that Walker did not receive a fair trial before an impartial judge. The newly surfaced evidence gives us the power, in order to attain the ends of justice, to reach the bias question. The state trial judge's statements about Walker's forthcoming trial stand undisputed, particularly the judge's statement that he "intended to burn the S.O.B. [Walker] anyway." In no way can that statement be squared with the requirement that a defendant be tried before a fair tribunal. We need not repeat all of this court's prior discussions on this point. Given the undisputed expression of prejudice by the state trial judge (Judge Kirby), the previous legal conclusion, which we readopt, that Walker was tried before a prejudiced judge impels us to grant the writ.

In his concurrence to this court's en banc decision, Judge Arnold emphasized that, although justice to the petitioner is crucial in our system, we must consider as well the State's right to fairness, and the effect on the State of granting this writ. We agree. We note, however, that at the remand hearing, the Attorney General of Arkansas remarked that the State had come before the district court "seeking to do justice," and that if the court recommended a new trial, the State wins because justice has been done. We are convinced on the record before us that Walker's trial and conviction before an admittedly prejudiced trial judge constituted a gross miscarriage of justice. Retrial of Walker after more than two decades might present some difficulties for the State, but none that would seriously prejudice the prosecution. Many of the State's witnesses are still available, notably Barentine and McDonald—and now Kumpe as well. Testimony of witnesses no longer available has been preserved on the record and presumably could be offered in record form as it was for witnesses said to be unavailable at the time of Walker's second trial. Surely here, where justice has been so long delayed, the equities weigh heavily in favor of correcting this stain on our criminal justice system.

Accordingly, we conclude that James Dean Walker is entitled to habeas corpus relief. We direct the district court to grant the writ unless the State of Arkansas commences proceedings to retry Walker within ninety days from May 17, 1985, the date of this opinion.

LET OUR MANDATE ISSUE FORTHWITH.

ARNOLD, Circuit Judge, concurring.

Some of the arguments made in the dissenting opinion deserve, in my view, a brief comment.

1. The statement is made that "[t]he Court today frees James Dean Walker. . . ." Post, at 962. That is not at all what the Court is doing. We are simply holding that fundamental fairness, embodied in the Due Process Clause of the Fourteenth Amendment, requires a new trial. If Walker is ultimately freed, it will only be because he is acquitted by a jury, assuming that the state does not drop the matter on its own motion, which seems most unlikely.

                              *   *   *

4. Our holding today benefits not only James Dean Walker. It benefits also all the people of Arkansas, who have a vital interest in the honor and fairness of their own courts. Walker, like anyone else accused of crime, should have a fair trial before an impartial judge. Unless and until he receives such a trial, he should not be deprived of his liberty.

With these additional comments, I join the Court's opinion in its entirety.

JOHN R. GIBSON, Circuit Judge, dissenting, joined by ROSS, FAGG, and BOWMAN, Circuit Judges.

                              *   *   *

The court's exercise in reviewing the newly discovered evidence issue is merely a springboard to justify a reconsideration of the judicial bias claim. The court concludes that newly discovered evidence justifies reconsideration of the bias issue, then immediately determines that the question has been decided by the dissent in the earlier en banc opinion, which found bias in the trial court's denying Walker a recess to locate witnesses and its rejection of a ballistics report. In reality, the court is reaching this conclusion independent of any findings by a district court.

In the first habeas proceeding Judge Henley rejected Walker's argument of judicial bias and this finding was unanimously affirmed on appeal. In the second habeas proceeding, Judge Woods refused to consider the claim because he found that Sanders had not been satisfied. Following the recall, Judge Woods did not consider the merits of the bias argument because the new evidence did not concern the issue. Thus, the only district court findings relating to bias in this extensive history are adverse to *Walker*. Moreover, in an earlier opinion, Judge Arnold wrote that while he believed there was bias on the part of the trial judge, he was not persuaded that it "did Walker any actual harm that would not have occurred if the case had been tried by another judge." He specifically concluded that the denial of the recess was not crucial and that the ruling on the ballistics report was not to be faulted.

Now the court summarily concludes that bias supports granting the writ. Even without the opinions in the first round of habeas proceedings, the court would be arrogating the role of the district court by making initial factual findings on appeal. But this zealousness is rendered doubly improper because the court contradicts the earlier district court finding and our prior approval of that finding without any effort to analyze or review these decisions. The court thus seriously abuses its authority in deciding the bias issue.

The history of the *Walker* habeas efforts demonstrates the eagerness of the court to find its own facts and to free Walker. The first habeas proceedings, the earlier decision of this court en banc, and the opinion today reflect *Walker's* shifting factual claims. From the speculative reexamination of the facts engaged in by the dissent in this court's earlier en banc consideration, the court today proceeds to discard the district court's carefully reached findings and to take the most appealing path of finding its own facts. It has no power to do so. The application for a writ of habeas corpus should be denied.

Chapter 9
Metered Justice

Every so often, for no apparent reason, a judge is smitten by Calliope and responds to that Muse with an opinion in rhyme. Although seldom, if ever, reminiscent of anything in an anthology, these efforts seem to become favorites of attorneys. Two of the cases in this chapter, *Fisher* and *Mackensworth*, were the two most frequently called to our attention. Some of the cases in rhyme were even called classics. More than one was accompanied by a note in verse explaining the case's appeal. Whether they are, in fact, classics, and what that means, we will leave to the reader.

As our last case in this section points out, not everyone is enamored with judicial poetry. Some object because they believe that it indicates a frivolous lack of concern for the parties before the court. Others object because they think that the poetry is poor and represents an unsuccessful attempt at humor. Nonetheless, it is a good bet that the Muse will continue to capture judges from time to time.

"The case is a shiny little light in the perpetual gloom of a profession which all too often appears both smug and humorless to those outside it."

—Professor, University of Oklahoma School of Law

FISHER

v.

LOWE, *et al.*

Court of Appeals of Michigan
Jan. 10, 1983
333 N.W.2d 67, 122 Mich.App. 418

J.H. GILLIS, Judge.

> We thought that we would never see
>   A suit to compensate a tree.
> A suit whose claim in tort is prest
>   Upon a mangled tree's behest;
> A tree whose battered trunk was prest
>   Against a Chevy's crumpled crest;
> A tree that faces each new day
>   With bark and limb in disarray;
> A tree that may forever bear
>   A lasting need for tender care.
> Flora lovers though we three,
>   We must uphold the court's decree.

Affirmed.[1]

     1. Plaintiff commenced this action in tort against defendants Lowe and Moffet for damage to his "beautiful oak tree" caused when defendant Lowe struck it while operating defendant Moffet's automobile. The trial court granted summary judgment in favor of defendants pursuant to GCR 1963, 117.2(1). In addition, the trial court denied plaintiff's request to enter a default judgment against the insurer of the automobile, defendant State Farm Mutual Automobile Insurance Company. Plaintiff appeals as of right.

     The trial court did not err in granting summary judgment in favor of defendants Lowe and Moffet. Defendants were immune from tort liability for damage to the tree pursuant to § 3135 of the no-fault insurance act.

     The trial court did not err in refusing to enter a default judgment against State Farm. Since it is undisputed that plaintiff did not serve process upon State Farm in accordance with the court rules, the court did not obtain personal jurisdiction over the insurer.

In this next case, defense counsel's motion to dismiss included a limerick. Plaintiff's reply likewise contained some verse, and Judge Becker followed suit in his written opinion and order. Here is the result. (Afterwards, the Chief Judge of the district circulated a memo cautioning against such frivolity. It was, of course, in verse.)

MACKENSWORTH

v.

AMERICAN TRADING TRANSPORTATION CO.

United States District Court, E.D. Pennsylvania
Nov. 19, 1973
367 F.Supp. 373

EDWARD R. BECKER, District Judge.

The motion now before us
has stirred up a terrible fuss.
And what is considerably worse,
it has spawned some preposterous doggerel verse.
The plaintiff, a man of the sea,
after paying his lawyer a fee,
filed a complaint of several pages
to recover statutory wages.[1]

The pleaded facts remind us of a tale that is endless.
A seaman whom for centuries the law has called "friendless"
is discharged from the ship before voyage's end
and sues for lost wages, his finances to mend.
The defendant shipping company's office is based in New York City,
and to get right down to the nitty gritty,
it has been brought to this Court by long arm service,[2]
which has made it extremely nervous.

---

1. In nautical terms, the wage statute is stowed
   at § 594 of 46 U.S.Code.

2. Long arm service is effected, not by stealth,
   but through the Secretary of the Commonwealth.

Long arm service is a procedural tool
founded upon a "doing business" rule.
But defendant has no office here, and says it has no mania
to do any business in Pennsylvania.

Plaintiff found defendant had a ship here in June '72,
but defendant says that ship's business is through.
Asserting that process is amiss,
it has filed a motion to dismiss.

Plaintiff's counsel, whose name is Harry Lore,
read defendant's brief and found it a bore.
Instead of a reply brief, he acted pretty quick
and responded with a clever limerick:

> "Admiralty process is hoary
> With pleadings that tell a sad story
> Of Libels in Rem-
> The bane of sea-faring men
> The moral:
> Better personally served than be sorry."

Not to be outdone, the defense took the time
to reply with their own clever rhyme.
The defense counsel team of Mahoney, Roberts, & Smith
drafted a poem cutting right to the pith:

> "Admiralty lawyers like Harry
> Both current and those known from lore
> Be they straight types, mixed or fairy
> Must learn how to sidestep our bore.
>
> For Smith, not known for his mirth
> With his knife out for Mackensworth
> With Writs, papers or Motions to Quash
> Knows that dear Harry's position don't wash."

Overwhelmed by this outburst of pure creativity,
we determined to show an equal proclivity.
Hence this opinion in the form of verse,
even if not of the calibre of Saint-John Perse.

The first question is whether, under the facts,
defendant has done business here to come under Pennsylvania's long
    arm acts.[3]
If we find that it has, we must reach question two,
whether that act so applied is constitutional under
    Washington v. International Shoe.[4]

Defendant runs a ship known as the SS Washington Trader,
whose travels plaintiff tracked as GM is said to have followed Nader.
He found that in June '72 that ship rested its keel
and took on a load of cargo here which was quite a big
    business deal.

In order for extraterritorial jurisdiction to obtain,
it is enough that defendant do a single act in Pa. for
    pecuniary gain.
And we hold that the recent visit of defendant's ship to
    Philadelphia's port
is doing business enough to bring it before this Court.

We note, however, that the amended act's grammar[5]
is enough to make any thoughtful lawyer stammer.
The particular problem which deserves mention
is whether a single act done for pecuniary gain also requires
    a future intention.

3. Designed to relieve the plaintiff's service burdens,
   Pennsylvania's latest long arm law may be found
   at § 8309 of 42 Purdon's.

4. That decision of the Supreme Court of Courts
   may be found at page 310 of 326 U.S. Reports.

5. The words of the statute are overly terse,
   still we will quote them, though not in verse:

   (a) General rule.—Any of the following shall constitute "doing business"
   for the purposes of this chapter:

   . . . . .

   (2) The doing of a single act in this Commonwealth for the purpose of
   thereby realizing pecuniary benefit or otherwise accomplishing an object
   with the intention of initiating a series of such acts.

   (3) The shipping of merchandise directly or indirectly into or through this
   Commonwealth.

42 Pa. S. § 8309.

As our holding suggests, we believe the answer is no,
and feel that is how the Pa. appellate cases will go.
Further, concerning § (a)(3)'s "shipping of merchandise"
the future intention doctrine has already had its demise.[6]

We do not yet rest our inquiry, for as is a judge's bent,
we must look to see if there is precedent.[7]
And we found one written in '68 by three big wheels
on the Third Circuit Court of Appeals.

The case, a longshoreman's personal injury suit,
      is *Kane v. USSR*,
and it controls the case at bar.
It's a case with which defendants had not reckoned,
and may be found at page 131 of 394 F.2d.

In *Kane*, a ship came but once to pick up stores
and hired as agents to do its chores a firm of local stevedores.
Since the Court upheld service on the agents,
      the case is nearly on all fours,
and to defendant's statutory argument *Kane* closes the doors.

Despite defendant's claim that plaintiff's process is silly,
there have been three other seamen's actions against defendant, with
      service in Philly.
And although they might have tried to get the service corrected,
the fact of the matter is they've never objected.[8]

---

6. See *Aquarium Pharmaceuticals Inc. v. Industrial Pressing and Packaging*
(E.D.Pa.1973).

> Prospects for suit on a single goods shipment are decidedly greener
> because of the *Aquarium* decision of Judge Charles R. Weiner,
> holding that, in a goods shipment case no future intention is needed;
> the message of *Aquarium* we surely have heeded.
> Anyone who wishes to look *Aquarium* up
> can find it at p. 441 of 358 F.Supp.

7. We thus reject the contention that one of the judicial vices
      is too much reliance on stare decisis.

8. *Berrios v. American Trading & Production Co.* (AT&P) (defendant's
predecessor), C.A. 68–47; *Gibson v. AT&P*, C.A. 68–1466.

> And in *Battles v. AT&P.*, C.A. 73–102, in this very annum,
> service on the Secretary of the Commonwealth was authorized
>   by Judge John B. Hannum.

We turn then to the constitutional point,
and lest the issue come out of joint,
it is important that one thought be first appended:
the reason the long arm statute was amended.

The amendment's purpose was to eliminate guess
and to extend long arm service to the full reach of due process.
And so we now must look to the facts
to see if due process is met by sufficient "minimum contacts."

The visit of defendant's ship is not yet very old,
and so we feel constrained to hold
that under traditional notions of substantial justice and fair play,
defendant's constitutional argument does not carry the day.

This Opinion has now reached its final border,
and the time has come to enter an Order,
which, in a sense, is its ultimate crux,
but alas, plaintiff claims under a thousand bucks.

So, while trial counsel are doubtless in fine fettle,
with many fine fish in their trial kettle,
we urge them not to test their mettle,
because, for the small sum involved, it makes more sense to settle.
In view of the foregoing Opinion, at this time
we enter the following Order, also in rhyme.

ORDER

Finding that service of process is bona fide,
the motion to dismiss is hereby denied.
So that this case can now get about its ways,
defendant shall file an answer within 21 days.

"Although certainly the rights of persons before the Court are to be treated with the utmost gravity, I believe that if judges and counsel alike would 'lighten up' a bit from time to time, it would be greatly conducive to restoring an atmosphere of professionalism that seems to have vanished from the practice of law over the past generation."

—Professor, Mercer Law School

BROWN

v.

STATE

Court of Appeals of Georgia
May 9, 1975
216 S.E.2d 356, 134 Ga.App. 771

EVANS, Judge.

The D. A. was ready
His case was red-hot.
Defendant was present,
His witness was not.

He prayed one day's delay
From His honor the judge.
But his plea was not granted
The Court would not budge.

So the jury was empaneled
All twelve good and true
But without his main witness
What could the twelve do?[3]

---

3. This opinion is placed in rhyme because approximately one year ago, in Savannah at a very convivial celebration, the distinguished Judge Dunbar Harrison, Senior Judge of Chatham Superior Courts, arose and addressed those assembled, and demanded that if Judge Randall Evans, Jr. ever again was so presumptuous as to reverse one of his decisions, that the opinion be written in poetry. I readily admit I am unable to comply, because I am not a poet, and the language used, at best, is mere doggerel. I have done my best but my limited ability just did not permit the writing of a great poem. It was no easy task to write the opinion in rhyme.

The jury went out
To consider his case
And then they returned
The defendant to face.

"What verdict, Mr. Foreman?"
The learned judge inquired.
"Guilty, your honor."
On Brown's face—no smile.

"Stand up" said the judge,
Then quickly announced
"Seven years at hard labor"
Thus his sentence pronounced.

"This trial was not fair,"
The defendant then sobbed.
With my main witness absent
I've simply been robbed."

"I want a new trial—
State has not fairly won."
"New trial denied,"
Said Judge Dunbar Harrison.

"If you still say I'm wrong,"
The able judge did then say
"Why not appeal to Atlanta?
Let those Appeals Judges earn part of their pay."

"I will appeal, sir"—
Which he proceeded to do—
"They can't treat me worse
Than I've been treated by you."

So the case has reached us—
And now we must decide
Was the guilty verdict legal—
Or should we set it aside?

Justice and fairness
Must prevail at all times;
This is ably discussed
In a case without rhyme.

The law of this State
Does guard every right
Of those charged with crime
Fairness always in sight.

To continue civil cases
The judge holds all aces.
But it's a different ball-game
In criminal cases.

Was one day's delay
Too much to expect?
Could the State refuse it
With all due respect?

Did Justice applaud
Or shed bitter tears
When this news from Savannah
First fell on her ears?

We've considered this case
Through the night—through the day.
As Judge Harrison said,
"We must earn our poor pay."

This case was once tried—
But should now be rehearsed
And tried one more time.
This case is reversed!

Judgment reversed.

This case was called to our attention by one who appreciates not only the judge's poetry, but also the defense lawyer's claim of error.

WHEAT
v.
FRAKER

Court of Appeals of Georgia
Feb. 7, 1963
130 S.E.2d 251

EBERHARDT, Judge.

"Foul, foul play," the defendant cried.
"That I by kinsman be not trammeled
Let the issue again be tried
Before another jury impanelled.

Remember how from John at Runnymede
The Charta was forced and wrested
That no matter what the issue or the deed
By my peers it must be tried and tested.

With juror mine adversary durst
Try the cause, whose wife is second cousin to my wife
And to plaintiff's wife a first.
A new trial, sire, I demand to settle strife."

"No foul play do I find or see,"
The judge replied. "Foreman's wife to thine
And to plaintiff's wife may kinsman be,
But to Doug and thee no kinship do I find.[1]

---

1. "The groom and bride each comes within
      The circle of the other's kin;
   But kin and kin are still no more
      Related than they were before."

Thus, it doth not appear
For any cause or reason told
That the juror was not thy peer
The case to try and verdict mold

Moreover, when kinships we sought to learn
It doth not appear that as best befits
One who would a kinsman spurn
Thou revealed that cousin did on the panel sit.

Thy day in court thou hast had,"
The judge asserted, "and law commands
That, no error made, whether good or bad,
The issue tried and settled stands."

Judgment affirmed.

The next two cases were authored by two judges from the
Fifth Circuit Court of Appeals who were well-known for their
display of wit in their opinions. Wisely, neither attempted to
write the entire opinion in verse, as both opinions are over
seven pages long in print.

UNITED STATES
v.
VEN–FUEL, INC.

United States Court of Appeals
Fifth Circuit
Sept. 18, 1979
602 F.2d 747

JOHN R. BROWN, Chief Judge:

This case presents a vicious duel,
Between the U.S. of A. and defendant Ven-Fuel.
Seeking a license for oil importation,
Ven-Fuel submitted its application.
It failed to attach a relevant letter,
And none can deny, it should have known better.
Yet the only issue this case is about,
Is whether a crime was committed beyond reasonable doubt.
Ven-Fuel was convicted of fraudulent acts,
By the Trial Court's finding of adequate facts.
We think it likely that fraud took place,
But <u>materiality</u> was not shown in this case.
So while the Government will no doubt be annoyed,
We declare the conviction null and void.

*   *   *

The court determined that certain representations made in
connection with an application for a license to import oil were
immaterial to the granting of the license. Thus, the defendants
could not be convicted of fraud, even if the representations
were false.

UNITED STATES
v.
BATSON, *et al.*

United States Court of Appeals
Fifth Circuit
Feb. 18, 1986
782 F.2d 1307

GOLDBERG, Circuit Judge:

> Some farmers from Gaines had a plan.
> It amounted to quite a big scam.
> But the payments for cotton
> began to smell rotten.
> 'Twas a mugging of poor Uncle Sam.
> The ASCS and its crew
> uncovered this fraudulent stew.
> After quite a few hearings,
> the end is now nearing—
> It awaits our judicial review.

The United States initiated these seven suits in 1979 to enforce administrative determinations of the Agricultural Stabilization and Conservation Service (ASCS), which ordered appellants to refund overpayments of cotton subsidies obtained in 1972 and 1973 through a scheme or device to defeat the purpose of the Upland Cotton Price Support Program, 7 U.S.C. s 1444(e), or to evade the program payment limitation. The scheme first came to the attention of the ASCS when audit reports revealed that program payments to recipients in Gaines County, Texas, were five times that of comparable cotton producing regions.

* * *

The defendants appeal the district court's grant of summary judgment, and the government seeks an award of interest in accord with its reading of the regulation. We affirm the judgment of the district court, but we reverse as to its award of interest.

*   *   *

With thought and comment most candid,
affirmance shall now be commanded.
But the court below missed
the prejudgment interest:
The cases are therefore remanded.

Not to be lost in the poetry is the unusual posture of this case. The judge had moved on his own to dismiss this case. After considering the merits, he decided to deny his own motion.

In re LOVE

United States Bankruptcy Court
S.D. Florida
June 9, 1986
61 B.R. 558

A. JAY CRISTOL, Bankruptcy Judge.

This cause came on to be heard sua sponte upon the court's own motion to dismiss this chapter 7 petition pursuant to 11 U.S.C. § 707(b) and the court having received the inspiration for the motion from a little old ebony bird and not from any party in interest or any other person and having considered the presumption in favor of debtor provided in 11 U.S.C. § 707(b) and not deeming it appropriate to take evidence, the court finds:

Once upon a midnight dreary,
while I pondered weak and weary
Over many quaint and curious files of chapter seven lore
While I nodded nearly napping, suddenly there came a tapping
As of some one gently rapping, rapping at my chamber door,
"Tis some debtor" I muttered, "tapping at my chamber door—
Only this and nothing more."

Ah distinctly I recall, it was in the early fall
And the file still was small
The Code provided I could use it
If someone tried to substantially abuse it
No party asked that it be heard.
"Sua sponte" whispered a small black bird.
The bird himself, my only maven, strongly looked to be a raven.

Upon the words the bird had uttered
I gazed at all the files cluttered
"Sua sponte," I recall, had no meaning; none at all.
And the cluttered files sprawl, drove a thought into my brain.
Eagerly I wished the morrow—vainly I had sought to borrow
From BAFJA, surcease of sorrow—and an order quick and plain
That this case would not remain as a source of further pain.

The procedure, it seemed plain.
As the case grew older, I perceived I must be bolder.
And must sua sponte act, to determine every fact,
If primarily consumer debts, are faced,
Perhaps this case is wrongly placed.
This is a thought that I must face, perhaps I should dismiss
    this case.
I moved sua sponte to dismiss it for I knew I would not miss it.

The Code said I could, I knew it.
But not exactly how to do it, or perhaps some day I'd rue it.
I leaped up and struck my gavel.
For the mystery to unravel
Could I? Should I? Sua sponte, grant my motion to dismiss?
While it seemed the thing to do, suddenly I thought of this.
Looking, looking towards the future and to what there was to see.

If my motion, it was granted and an appeal came to be,
Who would be the appellee?
Surely, it would not be me.
Who would file, but pray tell me, a learned brief for the appellee
The District Judge would not do so
At least this much I do know.
Tell me raven, how to go.

As I with the ruling wrestled
In the statute I saw nestled
A presumption with a flavor clearly in the debtor's favor.
No evidence had I taken
Sua sponte appeared foresaken.
Now my motion caused me terror
A dismissal would be error.

Upon consideration of § 707(b), in anguish, loud I cried
The court's sua sponte motion to dismiss under § 707(b) is denied.

The final case in this chapter is not in verse. Rather, it involves a judge whose efforts at poetry and humor went awry, at least in the eyes of the Kansas Supreme Court. While one can certainly question the wisdom of writing the verse, the poem itself may be, from a purely technical standpoint, one of the better efforts called to our attention.

In re ROME

Supreme Court of Kansas
Nov. 8, 1975
542 P.2d 676, 218 Kan. 198

PER CURIAM:

This is an original proceeding in discipline against the Honorable Richard J. Rome, Judge of the Magistrate Court of Reno County. The Commission on Judicial Qualifications found that respondent Judge Rome, in issuing a written memorandum decision in a criminal case before him, had violated Canon 3A.(3) of the Code of Judicial Conduct, for which it recommended that he be publicly censured. Judge Rome rejected the commission's finding and recommendation and the matter is here for determination.

The rule which respondent is charged with violating is a part of the code of judicial conduct adopted by this court effective January 1, 1974. It provides:

"CANON 3

"A Judge Should Perform the Duties of His Office Impartially and Diligently

". . . His judicial duties include all the duties of his office prescribed by law. In the performance of these duties, the following standards apply:

"A. Adjudicative Responsibilities.

"(3) A judge should be patient, dignified, and courteous to litigants, jurors, witnesses, lawyers, and others with whom he deals in his official capacity. . . ." (Rule No. 601, 214 Kan. xciv–xcv.)

The evidence before the commission on judicial qualifications consisted of exhibits stipulated to by its examiner and respondent, plus the testimony of respondent.

On January 30, 1974, a woman was arrested in the south part of Hutchinson and charged with agreeing to perform an act of sexual intercourse for hire. Her arrest derived from her unwitting solicitation of a Hutchinson police officer to engage her services. Thereafter the defendant made bond for her court appearance. Trial to the court was had on February 26, 1974, in the tribunbal presided over by respondent. Defendant was represented by a Hutchinson attorney, Kerry Granger. She was found guilty and given the maximum sentence—six months' confinement in the Kansas correctional institution for women and a fine of $1,000. The defendant then filed a notice of appeal to the district court. The appeal was subsequently dismissed with her consent and the case was remanded to the magistrate court. There, on May 20, 1974, defendant appeared with her attorney and applied for probation. Respondent took the matter under advisement and on May 23, 1974, he placed the defendant on probation for a period of two years. In addition to filing an order of probation and making routine notations in his docket respondent also filed in the case a written instrument entitled "Memorandum Decision." The writing, which constitutes the subject matter of this proceeding, states (name of defendant deleted):

This is the saga of ____ ____
Whose ancient profession brings her before us.
On January 30th, 1974,
This lass agreed to work as a whore.

Her great mistake, as was to unfold,
Was the enticing of a cop named Harold.
Unknown to ____ ____, this officer, surnamed Harris,
Was duty-bent on ____ ____'s lot to embarrass.

At the Brass Rail they met,
And for twenty dollars the trick was all set.
In separate cars they did pursue,
To the sensuous apartment of ____ ____.

Bound for her bed she spared not a minute,
Followed by Harris with his heart not in it.
As she prepared to repose there in her bay,
She was arrested by Harris, to her great dismay!

Off to the jailhouse poor ____ ____ was taken,
Printed and mugged, her confidence shaken.
Formally charged by this great State,
With offering to Harris to fornicate.

Her arraignment was formal, then back to jail,
And quick as a flash she was admitted to bail.
On February 26, 1974,
The State of Kansas tried this young whore.

A prosecutor named Brown,
Represented the Crown.
___ ____, her freedom in danger,
Was being defended by a chap named Granger.

Testimony was presented and arguments heard,
Poor ____ ____ waited for the Judge's last word.
The finding was guilty, with no great alarm,
And ____ ____ was sentenced to the Women's State Farm.

An appeal was taken, to a higher court ____ ____ went,
The thousand dollar fine was added to imprisonment.
Trial was set in this higher court,
But the route of appeal ____ ____ chose to abort.

And back to Judge Rome, came this lady of the night,
To plead for her freedom and end this great fight.
So under advisement ____ ____'s freedom was taken,
And in the bastille this lady did waken.

The judge showed mercy and ____ ____ was free,
But back to the street she could not flee.
The fine she'd pay while out on parole,
But not from men she used to cajole.

From her ancient profession she'd been busted,
And to society's rules she must be adjusted.
If from all of this a moral doth unfurl,
It is that Pimps do not protect the working girl!

Subsequent to its filing the memorandum decision was widely published by quotation in the local news media, as well as over the state. This publicity evoked complaint against Judge Rome from a feminist group in Hutchinson in the form of a letter to the editor of the Hutchinson newspaper, with copies to bar association and judicial authorities. The burden of the complaint was that the defendant in the case had been held up to public ridicule by Judge Rome. Publication of the protest letter evoked a citation by respondent of its three signers to appear in magistrate court and show cause why they should not be held in indirect contempt of court. The three engaged legal counsel and appeared as directed. There, in an overcrowded courtroom, after voicing his views on the prostitution problem in the city of Hutchinson, respondent dismissed the contempt charges. The whole matter eventually reached the commission on judicial qualifications and this proceeding ensued.

In defending himself before the commission respondent raised jurisdictional as well as other issues, which were decided adversely to his position, and he renews all of them here.

* * *

Judge Rome claimed that the commission did not have jurisdiction over the matter, that he was entitled to have a jury decide whether he was guilty of malfeasance, that his actions were within the discretion accorded to judges, and that his actions were protected by the First Amendment. These arguments were rejected.

* * *

Is the evidence here of such character as to sustain the conclusion reached by the commission? As already indicated the evidence in the record consisted of exhibits stipulated to by the examiner and respondent, plus respondent's testimony and in a sense the facts may be said to be undisputed so there is little reason for deference to the commission's superior opportunity to resolve sharply conflicting factual disputes. Respondent, who has served as city attorney, as deputy county attorney and county attorney in his home county, and is a respected member of the Kansas bar practicing law in Hutchinson, testified as to his concern about the problem of prostitution in a particular area of Hutchinson: Prostitutes or their pimps were openly accosting people on the streets or waiting for stoplights; some prostitution cases had been tried in police court; he gave the maximum sentence in the defendant's case; his concern was "to jolt the south end and, more particularly, the pimps" and the memorandum decision was used "to get that point across"; he had no intent to degrade or ridicule the defendant; neither she nor her parents made complaint to him about the memorandum; her case had been previously publicized by the news media; he believed that women have been treated unfairly under our sex laws; he did not believe a judge should be denied the privilege of writing an opinion in poetic form.

Respondent cites several cases in which the decision was written in poetic form and argues he should not be chastised for doing that. He has not been proceeded against, nor found derelict, for use of the poetic form. The complaint is that in his decision he held the defendant up to public ridicule or scorn.

Judges have long been enjoined from the use of humor at the expense of the litigants before them for reasons which should be apparent. Under the heading of 'Ancient Precedents in the canons of judicial ethics adopted in 1924 by the American Bar Association this appears:

> "Judges ought to be more learned than witty; more reverend than plausible; and more advised than confident. Above all things, integrity is their portion and proper virtue. . . .
>
> "'Patience and gravity of hearing is an essential part of justice; and an over speaking judge is no well-tuned cymbal. . . .
>
> —Bacon's Essay 'of Judicature.' " (198 Kan. xi.)

In 1967 a long time member of the supreme court of Arkansas in advising new judges on opinion writing had more to say on the subject. We quote:

"Judicial Humor

> " . . Judicial humor is neither judicial nor humorous. A lawsuit is a serious matter to those concerned in it. For a judge to take advantage of his criticism-

insulated, retaliation-proof position to display his
wit is contemptible, like hitting a man when he's
down."

(Smith, *A Primer of Opinion Writing, For Four New Judges,*
21 Ark.L.Rev. 197, 210.)

Judges simply should not "wisecrack" at the expense of anyone connected with a judicial proceeding who is not in a position to reply. When judges do this the stage is set for an
imbroglio like that which apparently occurred after respondent
here cited the three objectors for contempt of court, and respect
for the administration of justice suffers. Nor should a judge
do anything to exalt himself above anyone appearing as a litigant before him. Because of his unusual role a judge should
be objective in his task and mindful that the damaging effect
of his improprieties may be out of proportion to their actual
seriousness. He is expected to act in a manner inspiring confidence that even-handed treatment is afforded to everyone
coming into contact with the judicial system.

Our reading of this memorandum decision leads to the conclusion the defendant in the prostitution case was portrayed
in a ludicrous or comical situation—someone to be laughed
at and her plight found amusing. She was referred to throughout in terms designed to evoke chuckles over her activities.
Her own integrity as an individual, convicted of crime though
she was, was disregarded. The fact that neither she nor her
parents made complaint is scarcely persuasive that she was not
held out as a subject for public amusement. Respondent may
not have intended to ridicule her or hold her out to public
scorn yet that appears to be the effect of that which was done.
Publicity about the memorandum was obviously expected.

Our code of judicial conduct and its implementing rules
deal with a wide range of problems of varying degrees of seriousness. This particular proceeding does not present one of
the greatest magnitude. Neither venality nor criminality is present nor can it be said the memorandum decision was written
with deliberate intent to harm anyone. Yet, everything considered, we believe a violation of the canon in question has
been shown. A litigant was not afforded the kind of treatment
mandated.

It is therefore ordered that respondent Richard J. Rome be and he is hereby censured by this court. He is further ordered to pay the costs of this proceeding.

Chapter 10
The Fickle Finger of Fate

Although some misfortune underlies most lawsuits, this chapter features people who were truly the victims of bad luck and who are seeking redress from those they hold responsible. Some of the fact situations involve scenarios worthy of Rube Goldberg. Others, seemingly, could happen to any of us. Whichever, the very term "luck" indicates the involvement of the fickle finger of fate beyond the control of any human. This may explain the overall lack of success enjoyed by the plaintiffs in these types of lawsuits. We begin with the case that the courts often use as the cornerstone of law when called upon to resolve these disputes.

The unlikely chain of events that resulted in injury to Helen Palsgraf as she waited for a commuter train ultimately led to one of the most important cases in American jurisprudence. Mrs. Palsgraf, a janitress who received $10 per month for services in a $24-per-month apartment and also earned about $8 per week doing housework, had the grave misfortune of being in the wrong place at the wrong time. The railroad offered to settle for $250, but her attorney held out for $1,000. Initially, that proved to be a wise decision because the lower courts entered judgment in favor of Mrs. Palsgraf. But on appeal to the Court of Appeals. . . .

"Palsgraf shall always be my favorite case, for it changed my life. I first heard about it from my father, since it was a litigation which took place during his first years at the Bar and was the subject matter of discussions between young lawyers in 1927. It was my father's recital of the case and its theoretical implications which he used as bait to convince me to go to law school. It worked."

—Professor, Rutgers University

PALSGRAF

v.

LONG ISLAND R. CO.

Court of Appeals of New York
May 29, 1928
248 N.Y. 339, 162 N.E. 99

CARDOZO, C. J.

Plaintiff was standing on a platform of defendant's railroad after buying a ticket to go to Rockaway Beach. A train stopped at the station, bound for another place. Two men ran forward to catch it. One of the men reached the platform of the car without mishap, though the train was already moving. The other man, carrying a package, jumped aboard the car, but seemed unsteady as if about to fall. A guard on the car, who had held the door open, reached forward to help him in, and another guard on the platform pushed him from behind. In this act, the package was dislodged, and fell upon the rails. It was a package of small size, about fifteen inches long, and was covered by a newspaper. In fact it contained fireworks, but there was nothing in its appearance to give notice of its contents. The fireworks when they fell exploded. The shock of the explosion threw down some scales at the other end of the platform many feet away. The scales struck the plaintiff, causing injuries for which she sues.

The conduct of the defendant's guard, if a wrong in its relation to the holder of the package, was not a wrong in its relation to the plaintiff, standing far away. Relatively to her it was not negligence at all. Nothing in the situation gave notice that the falling package had in it the potency of peril to persons thus removed. Negligence is not actionable unless it involves the invasion of a legally protected interest, the violation of a right. "Proof of negligence in the air, so to speak, will not do." Pollock, Torts (11th Ed.) p. 455; "Negligence is the absence of care, according to the circumstances." Willes, J., in *Vaughan v. Taff Vale Ry. Co.*, 5 H. & N. 679, 688. The plaintiff, as she stood upon the platform of the station, might claim to be protected against intentional invasion of her bodily security. Such invasion is not charged. She might claim to be protected against unintentional invasion by conduct involving in the thought of reasonable men an unreasonable hazard that such invasion would ensue. These, from the point of view of the law, were the bounds of her immunity, with perhaps some rare exceptions, survivals for the most part of ancient forms of liability, where conduct is held to be at the peril of the actor. If no hazard was apparent to the eye of ordinary vigilance, an act innocent and harmless, at least to outward seeming, with reference to her, did not take to itself the quality of a tort because it happened to be a wrong, though apparently not one involving the risk of bodily insecurity, with reference to some one else. "In every instance, before negligence can be predicated of a given act, back of the act must be sought and found a duty to the individual complaining, the observance of which would have averted or avoided the injury." McSherry, C. J., in *West Virginia Central & P. R. Co. v. State*, 96 Md. 652, 666, 54 A. 669, 671 (61 L. R. A. 574). "The ideas of negligence and duty are strictly correlative." Bowen, L. J., in *Thomas v. Quartermaine*, 18 Q. B. D. 685, 694. The plaintiff sues in her own right for a wrong personal to her, and not as the vicarious beneficiary of a breach of duty to another.

A different conclusion will involve us, and swiftly too, in a maze of contradictions. A guard stumbles over a package which has been left upon a platform. It seems to be a bundle of newspapers. It turns out to be a can of dynamite. To the eye of ordinary vigilance, the bundle is abandoned waste, which may be kicked or trod on with impunity. Is a passenger at the other end of the platform protected by the law against the unsuspected hazard concealed beneath the waste? If not, is the result to be any different, so far as the distant passenger is concerned, when the guard stumbles over a valise which a truckman or a porter has left upon the walk? The passenger far away, if the victim of a wrong at all, has a cause of action, not derivative, but original and primary. His claim to be protected against invasion of his bodily security is neither greater nor less because the act resulting in the invasion is a wrong to another far removed. In this case, the rights that are said to have been violated, the interests said to have been violated, are not even of the same order. The man was not injured in his person nor even put in danger. The purpose of the act, as well as its effect, was to make his person safe. If there was a wrong to him at all, which may very well be doubted it was a wrong to a property interest only, the safety of his package. Out of this wrong to property, which threatened injury to nothing else, there has passed, we are told, to the plaintiff by derivation or succession a right of action for the invasion of an interest of another order, the right to bodily security. The diversity of interests emphasizes the futility of the effort to build the plaintiff's right upon the basis of a wrong to some one else. The gain is one of emphasis, for a like result would follow if the interests were the same. Even then, the orbit of the danger as disclosed to the eye of reasonable vigilance would be the orbit of the duty. One who jostles one's neighbor in a crowd does not invade the rights of others standing at the outer fringe when the unintended contact casts a bomb upon the ground. The wrongdoer as to them is the man who carries the bomb, not the one who explodes it without suspicion of the danger. Life will have to be made over, and human nature transformed, before prevision so extravagant can be accepted as the norm of conduct, the customary standard to which behavior must conform.

The argument for the plaintiff is built upon the shifting meanings of such words as "wrong" and "wrongful," and shares their instability. What the plaintiff must show is "a wrong" to herself; *i.e.*, a violation of her own right, and not merely a wrong to some one else, nor conduct "wrongful" because unsocial, but not "wrong" to any one. We are told that one who drives at reckless speed through a crowded city street is guilty of a negligent act and therefore of a wrongful one, irrespective of the consequences. Negligent the act is, and wrongful in the sense that it is unsocial, but wrongful and unsocial in relation to other travelers, only because the eye of vigilance perceives the risk of damage. If the same act were to be committed on a speedway or a race course, it would lose its wrongful quality. The risk reasonably to be perceived defines the duty to be obeyed, and risk imports relation; it is risk to another or to others within the range of apprehension. * * * The range of reasonable apprehension is at times a question for the court, and at times, if varying inferences are possible, a question for the jury. Here, by concession, there was nothing in the situation to suggest to the most cautious mind that the parcel wrapped in newspaper would spread wreckage through the station. If the guard had thrown it down knowingly and willfully, he would not have threatened the plaintiff's safety, so far as appearances could warn him. His conduct would not have involved, even then, an unreasonable probability of invasion of her bodily security. Liability can be no greater where the act is inadvertent.

Negligence, like risk, is thus a term of relation. Negligence in the abstract, apart from things related, is surely not a tort, if indeed it is understandable at all. Bowen, L. J., in *Thomas v. Quartermaine*, 18 Q. B. D. 685, 694. Negligence is not a tort unless it results in the commission of a wrong, and the commission of a wrong imports the violation of a right, in this case, we are told, the right to be protected against interference with one's bodily security. But bodily security is protected, not against all forms of interference or aggression, but only against some. One who seeks redress at law does not make out a cause of action by showing without more that there has been damage to his person. If the harm was not willful, he must show that the act as to him had possibilities of danger so many and apparent as to entitle him to be protected against the doing of it though the harm was unintended. Affront to personality is still the keynote of the wrong.

* * *

The judgment of the Appellate Division and that of the Trial Term should be reversed, and the complaint dismissed, with costs in all courts.

ANDREWS, J. (dissenting).

Assisting a passenger to board a train, the defendant's servant negligently knocked a package from his arms. It fell between the platform and the cars. Of its contents the servant knew and could know nothing. A violent explosion followed. The concussion broke some scales standing a considerable distance away. In falling, they injured the plaintiff, an intending passenger.

Upon these facts, may she recover the damages she has suffered in an action brought against the master? The result we shall reach depends upon our theory as to the nature of negligence. Is it a relative concept—the breach of some duty owing to a particular person or to particular persons? Or, where there is an act which unreasonably threatens the safety of others, is the doer liable for all its proximate consequences, even where they result in injury to one who would generally be thought to be outside the radius of danger? This is not a mere dispute as to words. We might not believe that to the average mind the dropping of the bundle would seem to involve the probability of harm to the plaintiff standing many feet away whatever might be the case as to the owner or to one so near as to be likely to be struck by its fall. If, however, we adopt the second hypothesis, we have to inquire only as to the relation between cause and effect. We deal in terms of proximate cause, not of negligence.

* * *

Due care is a duty imposed on each one of us to protect society from unnecessary danger, not to protect A, B, or C alone.

It may well be that there is no such thing as negligence in the abstract. "Proof of negligence in the air, so to speak, will not do." In an empty world negligence would not exist. It does involve a relationship between man and his fellows, but not merely a relationship between man and those whom he might reasonably expect his act would injure; rather, a relationship between him and those whom he does in fact injure. If his act has a tendency to harm some one, it harms him a mile away as surely as it does those on the scene.

*   *   *

The proposition is this: Every one owes to the world at large the duty of refraining from those acts that may unreasonably threaten the safety of others. Such an act occurs. Not only is he wronged to whom harm might reasonably be expected to result, but he also who is in fact injured, even if he be outside what would generally be thought the danger zone. There needs be duty due the one complaining, but this is not a duty to a particular individual because as to him harm might be expected. Harm to some one being the natural result of the act, not only that one alone, but all those in fact injured may complain. We have never, I think, held otherwise. Indeed in the *Di Caprio Case* [131 N. E. 746,] we said that a breach of a general ordinance defining the degree of care to be exercised in one's calling is evidence of negligence as to every one. We did not limit this statement to those who might be expected to be exposed to danger. Unreasonable risk being taken, its consequences are not confined to those who might probably be hurt.

*   *   *

The Keystone Cops. The Marx Brothers. Larry, Moe and Curly. One can imagine any of them in the scene described in our next offering. The case is a standard, and a favorite, in law school casebooks. The language of Justice Carlin is delightful. But do not overlook his sound legal analysis, which relies on *Palsgraf*, among other cases.

"I like it because of its Elizabethan description of the facts of a rather bizarre negligence case. The contrast created between the down-to-earth facts of the case and the deliberately florid language of the court causes me to chuckle every time I read it."

—Professor, Drake University

CORDAS, *et al.*

v.

PEERLESS TRANSP. CO., *et al.*

City Court of New York, New York County
April 3, 1941
27 N.Y.S.2d 198

CARLIN, Justice.

This case presents the ordinary man—that problem child of the law—in a most bizarre setting. As a lowly chauffeur in defendant's employ he became in a trice the protagonist in a breach-bating drama with a denouement almost tragic. It appears that a man, whose identity it would be indelicate to divulge was feloniously relieved of his portable goods by two nondescript highwaymen in an alley near 26th Street and Third Avenue, Manhattan; they induced him to relinquish his possessions by a strong argument ad hominem couched in the convincing cant of the criminal and pressed at the point of a most persuasive pistol. Laden with their loot, but not thereby impeded, they took an abrupt departure and he, shuffling off the coil of that discretion which enmeshed him in the alley, quickly gave chase through 26th Street toward 2d Avenue, whither they were resorting "with expedition swift as thought" for most obvious reasons. Somewhere on that thoroughfare of

escape they indulged the stratagem of separation ostensibly to
disconcert their pursuer and allay the ardor of his pursuit. He
then centered on for capture the man with the pistol whom
he saw board defendant's taxicab, which quickly veered south
toward 25th Street on 2d Avenue where he saw the chauffeur
jump out while the cab, still in motion, continued toward 24th
Street; after the chauffeur relieved himself of the cumbersome
burden of his fare the latter also is said to have similarly departed from the cab before it reached 24th Street. The chauffeur's story is substantially the same except that he states that
his uninvited guest boarded the cab at 25th Street while it
was at a standstill waiting for a less colorful fare; that his "passenger" immediately advised him "to stand not upon the order
of his going but to go at once" and added finality to his command by an appropriate gesture with a pistol addressed to his
sacro iliac. The chauffeur in reluctant acquiescence proceeded
about fifteen feet, when his hair, like unto the quills of the
fretful porcupine, was made to stand on end by the hue and
cry of the man despoiled accompanied by a clamorous con-
course of the law-abiding which paced him as he ran; the con-
catenation of "stop thief", to which the patter of persistent
feet did maddingly beat time, rang in his ears as the pursuing
posse all the while gained on the receding cab with its quarry
therein contained. The hold-up man sensing his insecurity suggested to the chauffeur that in the event there was the slightest
lapse in obedience to his curt command that he, the chauffeur,
would suffer the loss of his brains, a prospect as horrible to
an humble chauffeur as it undoubtedly would be to one of
the intelligentsia. The chauffeur apprehensive of certain dissolution from either Scylla, the pursuers, or Charybdis, the pursued, quickly threw his car out of first speed in which he was
proceeding, pulled on the emergency, jammed on his brakes
and, although he thinks the motor was still running, swung
open the door to his left and jumped out of his car. He con-
fesses that the only act that smacked of intelligence was that
by which he jammed the brakes in order to throw off balance
the hold-up man who was half-standing and half-sitting with
his pistol menacingly poised. Thus abandoning his car and passenger the chauffeur sped toward 26th Street and then turned
to look; he saw the cab proceeding south toward 24th Street
where it mounted the sidewalk. The plaintiff-mother and her
two infant children were there injured by the cab which, at
the time, appeared to be also minus its passenger who, it appears, was apprehended in the cellar of a local hospital where
he was pointed out to a police officer by a remnant of the

posse, hereinbefore mentioned. He did not appear at the trial. The three aforesaid plaintiffs and the husband-father sue the defendant for damages predicating their respective causes of action upon the contention that the chauffeur was negligent in abandoning the cab under the aforesaid circumstances. Fortunately the injuries sustained were comparatively slight. Negligence has been variously defined but the common legal acceptation is the failure to exercise that care and caution which a reasonable and prudent person ordinarily would exercise under like conditions or circumstances. It has been most authoritatively held that "negligence in the abstract, apart from things related, is surely not a tort, if indeed it is understandable at all." Cardozo, C. J., in *Palsgraf v. Long Island Railroad Co.*, 248 N.Y. 339, 345, 162 N.E. 99, 101, 59 A.L.R. 1253.

* * *

Negligence is "not absolute or intrinsic," but "is always relevant to some circumstances of time, place or person." In slight paraphrase of the world's first bard it may be truly observed that the expedition of the chauffeur's violent love of his own security outran the pauser, reason, when he was suddenly confronted with unusual emergency which "took his reason prisoner". The learned attorney for the plaintiffs concedes that the chauffeur acted in an emergency but claims a right to recovery upon the following proposition taken verbatim from his brief: "It is respectfully submitted that the value of the interests of the public at large to be immune from being injured by a dangerous instrumentality such as a car unattended while in motion is very superior to the right of a driver of a motor vehicle to abandon same while it is in motion even when acting under the belief that his life is in danger and by abandoning same he will save his life". To hold thus under the facts adduced herein would be tantamount to a repeal by implication of the primal law of nature written in indelible characters upon the fleshy tablets of sentient creation by the Almighty Law-giver, "the supernal Judge who sits on high". There are those who stem the turbulent current for bubble fame, or who bridge the yawning chasm with a leap for the leap's sake or who "outstare the sternest eyes that look outbrave the heart most daring on the earth, pluck the young sucking cubs from the she-bear, yea, mock the lion when he roars for prey" to win a fair lady and these are the admiration of the generality of men; but they are made of sterner stuff than the ordinary man upon whom the law places no duty of emulation. The law would

indeed be fond if it imposed upon the ordinary man the obligation to so demean himself when suddenly confronted with
a danger, not of his creation, disregarding the likelihood that
such a contingency may darken the intellect and palsy the
will of the common legion of the earth, the fraternity of ordinary men,—whose acts or omissions under certain conditions
or circumstances make the yardstick by which the law measures
culpability or innocence, negligence or care. If a person is
placed in a sudden peril from which death might ensue, the
law does not impel another to the rescue of the person en-
dangered nor does it condemn him for his unmoral failure
to rescue when he can; this is in recognition of the immutable
law written in frail flesh. Returning to our chauffeur. If the
philosophic Horatio and the martial companions of his watch
were "distilled almost to jelly with the act of fear" when they
beheld "in the dead vast and middle of the night" the dis-
embodied spirit of Hamlet's father stalk majestically by "with
a countenance more in sorrow than in anger" was not the
chauffeur, though unacquainted with the example of these
eminent men-at-arms, more amply justified in his fearsome reactions when he was more palpably confronted by a thing of
flesh and blood bearing in its hand an engine of destruction
which depended for its lethal purpose upon the quiver of a
hair? When Macbeth was cross-examined by Macduff as to any
reason he could advance for his sudden despatch of Duncan's
grooms he said in plausible answer "Who can be wise, amazed,
temperate and furious, loyal and neutral, in a moment? No
man". Macbeth did not by a "tricksy word" thereby stand justified as he criminally created the emergency from which he
sought escape by indulgence in added felonies to divert suspicion to the innocent. However, his words may be wrested
to the advantage of the defendant's chauffeur whose acts cannot be legally construed as the proximate cause of plaintiff's
injuries, however regrettable, unless nature's first law is arbitrarily disregarded.

* * *

In the classic case of *Laidlaw v. Sage*, 158 N.Y. 73, 89, 90,
52 N.E. 679, 685, 44 L.R.A. 216, is found a statement of the
law peculiarly apropos: "That the duties and responsibilities
of a person confronted with such a danger are different and
unlike those which follow his actions in performing the ordinary duties of life under other conditions is a well-established
principle of law. * * * 'The law presumes that *an act or omission*

done or neglected under the influence of pressing danger was done or neglected involuntarily. It is there said that this rule seems to be founded upon the maxim that self-preservation is the first law of nature, and that, where it is a question whether one of two men shall suffer, each is justified in doing the best he can for himself". (Italics ours.) *Kolanka v. Erie Railroad Co.,* 215 App.Div. 82, 86, 212 N.Y.S. 714, 717, says: "The law in this state does not hold one in an emergency to the exercise of that mature judgment required of him under circumstances where he has an opportunity for deliberate action. He is not required to exercise unerring judgment, which would be expected of him, were he not confronted with an emergency requiring prompt action". The circumstances provide the foil by which the act is brought into relief to determine whether it is or is not negligent. If under normal circumstances an act is done which might be considered negligent it does not follow as a corollary that a similar act is negligent if performed by a person acting under an emergency, not of his own making, in which he suddenly is faced with a patent danger with a moment left to adopt a means of extrication. The chauffeur— the ordinary man in this case—acted in a split second in a most harrowing experience. To call him negligent would be to brand him coward; the court does not do so in spite of what those swaggering heroes, "whose valor plucks dead lions by the beard", may bluster to the contrary. The court is loathe to see the plaintiffs go without recovery even though their damages were slight, but cannot hold the defendant liable upon the facts adduced at the trial. Motions, upon which decision was reserved, to dismiss the complaint are granted with exceptions to plaintiffs. Judgment for defendant against plaintiffs dismissing their complaint upon the merits. Ten days' stay and thirty days to make a case.

At first glance, Mr. Huber might seem more foolish than unlucky. But anyone who has been fortunate enough to visit the Apostle Islands in Lake Superior will understand the desire to have a home on Madeline Island. The problem for Mr. Huber was the home he desired on Madeline Island was located in Bayfield, Wisconsin.

PROVOST, d/b/a Vet's Salvage Diving
v.
HUBER

United States Court of Appeals
Eighth Circuit
March 23, 1979
594 F.2d 717

VAN SICKLE, District Judge.

The Appellant Provost brings this timely appeal from an order of the district court which dismissed his complaint and first amended complaint for lack of subject matter jurisdiction. The action was brought under the admiralty or maritime jurisdiction of the federal courts, and sought a salvage award. The district court, in ruling upon Appellee Huber's Rule 12(b)(1) motion, found lacking a nexus with traditional maritime activity and dismissed the action upon that ground.

The basic facts of this novel case are undisputed. From the allegations of the complaints (original and amended) and the affidavits submitted by the parties in connection with the motion to dismiss, it appears that Huber purchased a two-story frame house in Bayfield County, Wisconsin, with the purpose in mind of moving the structure from the mainland to a lot on Madeline Island situated in Lake Superior. Huber hired a housemover to transport the building and contents by truck-trailer over the frozen surface of Lake Superior. The move was attempted in March of 1977 and, at a point approximately three-fourths of the way to the island, the truck, trailer, house and contents broke through the ice.

While the house was partially submerged in the waters of Lake Superior, Huber was approached by an individual who represented himself to be an underwater contractor and who suggested that the structure be sunk to the bottom of the lake to preserve and protect it from ice damage until such time that it could be raised when weather permitted. Huber and his insurer agreed to the plan and the house was thereupon lowered to the lake bottom by placing sandbags on the floor.

In May of 1977 the Plaintiff and a second diver (not a party to this litigation) were approached by Mr. Edward Erickson (the underwater contractor who had lowered the structure to the lake bed). After the situation concerning the submerged house was discussed, the Plaintiff and his fellow diver agreed to assist in retrieving the building, although no specific terms of compensation were reached. Plaintiff spent about sixty hours of underwater work removing sandbags from the floor of the house. While Plaintiff was recharging his air tanks and absent from the jobsite, Erickson commenced to raise the structure. That attempt resulted in the house breaking up to the point of total destruction. Erickson retrieved substantially all of the pieces and disposed of them in a landfill at a cost of $500.00 to the Defendant and his insurer.

Prior to the move in March of 1977, the Defendant secured insurance on the structure (but not the contents) in the sum of $20,000.00. It is unclear from the record, but we may safely assume for purposes of this decision, that the insurer paid the full amount of the policy limits.

Some time after the unsuccessful attempt to retrieve the house intact from the bottom of Lake Superior, the Plaintiff billed the Defendant for $500.00 for his services rendered. The bill remains unpaid, and this suit claiming a maritime salvage of $10,000.00 followed.

As stated above, the district court dismissed Plaintiff's action for lack of a nexus with traditional maritime activity. This Court recently, in *Shows v. Harber*, 575 F.2d 1253 (1978) determined the necessity of such nexus in maritime cases. The Supreme Court has established that proposition in tort actions brought under the admiralty jurisdiction, and the same has been fixed for salvage cases, *Cope v. Vallette Dry Dock Co.*, 119 U.S. 625, 7 S.Ct. 336, 30 L.Ed. 501 (1887).

In *Cope* the Supreme Court, 7 S.Ct. at page 337, rejected a salvage claim in connection with a floating drydock on the basis that "no structure that is not a ship or vessel is a subject of salvage." "Vessel" is defined at 1 U.S.C., Section 3, as "every description of water craft or other artificial contrivance used, or capable of being used, as a means of transportation on water." The short answer to Appellant's assertion that the tractor-trailer being used to carry the house was a vessel within the meaning of maritime law because it was transporting the structure over water is that such transportation was on ice, not water, and that immediately upon the transporter breaking through the ice, it sank to the bottom of the lake. By no stretch of the imagination can we equate a multi-wheeled device, designed and built for the purpose of transportation over a hard, defined surface such as roads, highways, and even ice with a vessel or ship as those terms are used in maritime law.

The Appellant argues that even if the transporter cannot be considered a vessel, the house is still the proper subject of salvage, thereby bringing this action with the admiralty jurisdiction of the federal courts.

* * *

In the instant case we do not and cannot find that, prior to breaking through the ice and submerging, the house had embarked upon a "maritime" adventure. In other words, circumstances attending the placement of property in or upon navigable waters must be considered and are decisive when dealing with the question of admiralty jurisdiction and salvage. The fact that certain property may be the proper subject of salvage, standing alone, does not confer admiralty jurisdiction upon the federal courts. A nexus with traditional maritime activities must still be shown.

We recognize that cases decided since *Cope, supra,* have broadened the somewhat restrictive view therein enunciated by the Supreme Court as to what may properly be the subject of maritime salvage. For example, the Second Circuit concluded in *Lambros Seaplane Base v. The Batory,* 215 F.2d 228 (1954), that a seaplane down at sea is subject to the maritime law of salvage. *Lambros* is distinguishable on the ground that a seaplane—as opposed to a wheeled land vehicle—is designed and used for taking off of, flying over, and landing upon a water surface. Also, the district court in *Colby v. Todd Packing*

Co., 77 F.Supp. 956, 12 Alaska 1 (D.Alaska, 1948), allowed a salvage claim involving floating fish trap frames found adrift. The distinguishing feature in *Colby* is obvious: Fish trap frames are designed to float upon and be transported across a water surface.

We conclude, upon the facts present in this case, that the district court was correct in dismissing the action for lack of a nexus with traditional maritime activities.

Affirmed.

In this case, we encounter a danger of tobacco use that even the Surgeon General has probably not considered.

"This is my current favorite case because the fact pattern is even more improbable than in the Palsgraf *case. Furthermore, it has the added feature of an absolutely disgusting injuring agent."*

—Professor, SUNY Buffalo

PEEVEY, *et al.*

v.

BURGESS

Supreme Court, Appellate Division
April 14, 1993
596 N.Y.S.2d 250, 192 A.D.2d 1115

MEMORANDUM:

On the morning of November 12, 1987, defendant drove his pickup truck to Sharrow Ford, Inc. (Sharrow) for service. Defendant, a tobacco chewer, had attached a homemade spittoon to the emergency brake release handle under the dashboard of the truck. That morning the spittoon contained about six ounces of spit. After Sharrow mechanic Robert Shaff completed his work on the truck's alignment, he opened the driver's door to get a better view as he backed the truck off the service ramp. Shaff shifted the truck into reverse and bent to find the emergency brake release. When he pulled the handle and released the brake, the brake pedal popped up and struck the spittoon, spraying its contents into Shaff's face. As a result, Shaff's eyes burned and he became disoriented, lost control of the truck and fell out. Defendant's truck continued down the ramp and struck a vehicle being repaired by plaintiff Johnnie W. Peevey, a Sharrow employee, causing serious injury. Defendant acknowledged that, when the emergency brake was released, the brake pedal would spring up and strike the spittoon, ejecting its contents. Defendant stated that, because that occurred, he "paid attention" when he released the emergency brake.

Supreme Court erred in granting defendant's motion for summary judgment dismissing the complaint. To establish a prima facie case, plaintiff must show that defendant's conduct was a substantial cause of the event that resulted in the injury and that the conduct created a danger of foreseeable harm. "Whether a breach of duty has occurred * * * depends upon whether the resulting injury was a reasonably foreseeable consequence of the defendant's conduct" (*Danielenko v. Kinney Rent A Car*, 57 N.Y.2d 198, 204, 455 N.Y.S.2d 555, 441 N.E.2d 1073). It is not necessary, however, for plaintiff to establish that the precise manner in which the accident occurred was foreseeable. Questions concerning foreseeability and proximate cause are generally questions for the jury. Here, we cannot say, as a matter of law, that it was not reasonably foreseeable that defendant's conduct in placing a spittoon above the emergency brake pedal, with the knowledge that its contents would be ejected on the driver when the brake was released, could cause a driver to lose control of the vehicle and be a proximate cause of injury to a third party.

Order unanimously reversed on the law with costs, motion denied and complaint reinstated.

Courts will take "judicial notice" or "judicial knowledge" of well-known facts, thus eliminating the need to present evidence in order to prove them. Scientific, historical and geographical facts are commonly noted, as are the basic uses and qualities of common items and, occasionally, aspects of human nature. But the design, construction and manner of approaching a commode were, in this case, beyond the limits of the courts judicial knowledge.

ELLIOTT

v.

DOLLAR GENERAL CORPORATION, *et al.*

Supreme Court of Tennessee
Feb. 1, 1971
On Rehearing April 5, 1971
475 S.W.2d 651, 225 Tenn. 658

JENKINS, Special Justice.

The plaintiff below, Dorothy W. Elliott, hereinafter referred to as the plaintiff, sued the defendants, Dollar General Corporation, the lessee of the premises, Joe V. Williams, Jr., individually and as Trustee, and Robert Scholze Williams, individually and as Trustee, the owners and lessors of the premises, claiming damages for personal injuries in the amount of $50,000.00. The defendants demurred to the declaration, and said demurrers were sustained by the trial judge and the plaintiff has appealed.

The declaration in short says that plaintiff entered the defendant's mercantile establishment which was old and run down and that in the course of her shopping, she was confronted with an emergency and had to go to the rest room. Plaintiff says that she was directed to the rest room, also old and run down and unlighted; that in order to see she lowered the commode seat, climbed thereupon, and was reaching for a pull cord to illuminate the place when she, due to a defective commode seat and lid, fell one foot in the commode and one out as a result of which she was severely injured and damaged.

The defendants demurred to plaintiff's declaration on several grounds, the main one, that the plaintiff was guilty of contributory negligence in climbing on the commode and reaching for the light cord; that the commode was to sit on for the purpose for which it was made, installed and maintained.

The trial court sustained the demurrer and the plaintiff has appealed.

The issue is simple. Was the plaintiff guilty of such contributory negligence as a matter of law which would bar a recovery herein? To decide this question, we, of necessity, must consider the facts as alleged and the surrounding circumstances and the law applicable thereto.

When plaintiff entered this private of all private places, referred to in the pleadings as a rest room, a water closet, bathroom—and by the country term privy—she looked about and saw the commode or toilet (she apparently could see the seat and seat cover thereon) and desiring more illumination in said rest room, she saw an electric light cord hanging from the ceiling, and she lowered the seat and lid, and then proceeded to mount the same on foot. This, she either accomplished or was in the act of accomplishing, when she slipped or was caused to fall therefrom, landing with one foot in the commode or water closet, the other foot and rest of her body falling backward onto the floor, said fall from her perch on the closet lid causing her serious injuries.

The record does not reveal whether the plaintiff was accustomed to running water and lights in the house and the convenience of an inside toilet, and while the defendants' toilet, bathroom or rest room did not measure up to the standards of luxury as described in The Ladies Home Journal or Good Housekeeping with brilliant lighting, bath towels, soap and other accessories pastel colored and delicately scented, we cannot say that it was dangerous or unsafe to the public if it had been used for the purpose for which it was designed. It is true that according to the pleadings it was nearer in construction to the old outside privy referred to in the defendants' brief. This, we vividly remember, for "how dear to our hearts are the scenes of our childhood,"—except "in the good ole winter time."

The defendants go into great detail about what a commode is for, quoting Funk & Wagnall to support their contention. This makes us wonder if the defendants think this Court has reached the point in life where we need a re-education along this line. We know that counsel cannot be too presumptuous but it must be presumed that the Court knows at least the elementary principles of our way of life, and we do not need to be told what a toilet, rest room or privy is used for. It is a matter of common knowledge that the older one gets the more accustomed one becomes to that fact. Judicial notice in this instance is indeed not necessary.

The defendants, in their brief, ask the Court to use our imagination and take judicial knowledge of "the general construction of a water closet seat, usually being oval or rounded and sloping toward the inside. Usually the seat is designed to conform generally to the contours of the human posterior. Sometimes the seat is a complete oval and sometimes it is so designed as to leave an opening at one end." This, we can and will do—not that it helps either side or the Court in the decision of this case.

The defendants, in their brief, also ask this Court to be violently presumptuous and to take judicial knowledge of the following, and we quote: "that when the commode seat is in use by a member of the feminine gender that the standard or usual method of approach to it is to draw near, to then turn to face away from it, and to assume a sitting position with a portion of the user's weight on the user's feet." This, we cannot do, for never having witnessed such a described approach, whether proper or improper, and having no desire to do so, we would have to use our jaded imagination in this respect. We have no desire to do that. So, the matter of the proper way for a person of the female gender to approach a toilet or commode is left to the conclusion of the pleader.

We cannot, as suggested, take judicial knowledge of any mathematical formula whereby so much percentage of the user's weight shall rest on the posterior and so much on the feet. We are not aware that toilet makers (the modern-day Chick Sales) have progressed to such a scientific point.

The defendants say that the plaintiff should have called for help when she saw or failed to see the commode so as to use it in the proper manner. But we are not advised by the pleadings whether she was shy, or in a hurry; and we admire her tenacity, whether born of desperation or modesty, and are not in a position to criticize her action in this moment of crisis. But, are we to say that the defendants are to be charged with negligence as a result of her predicament?

The defendants move to strike a portion of the plaintiff's brief, reading as follows:

> "Doubtless, the members of this Court know from experience that an ordinary commode seat and lid is strong and safe.
>
> "In my own bathroom the medicine cabinet with fluorescent lights is turned on and off by a small switch at the side of the cabinet; but the overhead light is controlled by a light switch at the entrance of the bathroom, and it has overhead a large light bulb, and this is shaded by a glass light shade in the form of a bowl upside down, screwed into the ceiling. This light bulb is almost directly over the commode; and it burns out about every twelve or eighteen months and it is necessary to unscrew the screws holding up the light shade so as to get in and remove the light bulb and place a new one in its place. I weigh 185 pounds and instead of going to the basement to get a step ladder, I let down the commode seat and the commode lid and step upon it and unscrew the light shade with a screw driver. I know of my own knowledge that it has never broken or even cracked . . ."

The Court views this as a conclusion of the pleader, interesting reading, and harmless. The Court envies plaintiff's attorney's agility and ability to perform such acrobatic feats from a toilet seat, but questions his judgment and feel we must warn said attorney to cease and desist such conduct lest he befall the same fate as did his client in the instant case.

While the toilet seat or commode may have been unsafe to stand on, there is nothing in the record to show that it was unsafe to sit on or use in the conventional manner, so we must conclude that the plaintiff was putting the toilet seat and lid to a use that the defendants could not foresee, when she heisted herself thereon and was standing or attempting to turn on a light when she fell.

It is a fact recognized down through the ages, or since the toilet seat has been in general use, that it was designed for one part of the body, the human posterior. It was not designed to fit the pedal extremity or to be used as a step stool or a ladder.

Even though plaintiff's declaration alleges that the defendants' acts constituted "negligence that was almost gross negligence," (a new degree), such allegations are nothing more than conclusions of the plaintiff which are not admitted by the defendants' demurrers. A demurrer does not admit inferences from facts or conclusions of law.

But even if it can be assumed that the defendant, Dollar General Corporation, was negligent, the plaintiff is nevertheless barred from any recovery. The declaration states conduct on behalf of the plaintiff which, absent any explanation, compels reasonable minds to conclude that she was guilty of contributory negligence which proximately caused her injuries. In *Stewart v. City of Nashville* (1896), 96 Tenn. 50, at page 57, 33 S.W. 613, at page 615, it was said:

> "Whenever plaintiff's own case . . . raises a presumption of negligence on his part, the burden of repelling it is at once placed upon him. (A)nd where the circumstances attending the injury were such as to raise a presumption against him in respect to the exercise of due care, the law requires him to establish affirmatively his freedom from contributory negligence."

This rule has been applied to pleadings.

Therefore, where the plaintiff, as an invitee on the premises, alleges that she stood upon a commode lid in order to reach a light cord, knowing full well that the lid was not intended for such a purpose, we must hold as a matter of law that she did not exercise ordinary care for her own safety; and any resulting injury was necessarily attributable to her own negligence.

Since the declaration discloses on its face facts from which proximate contributory negligence can be inferred and does not manifest other facts to rebut the inference, we are of the opinion that the trial judge was correct in sustaining the demurrers.

Neither may plaintiff's unwise actions be excused simply because she was confronted with an emergency, *i.e.*, she found it necessary to use the rest room. The declaration alleges that the rest room was dark if the door was closed, but that the plaintiff could see the light cord hanging down. If there was sufficient light for the plaintiff to see the light cord, then there was sufficient light for the plaintiff to use the commode for its intended purpose.

For the foregoing reasons the order of the trial judge sustaining the demurrers is affirmed.

"[Gray] remains one of my favorite opinions, because it indicates how a stubborn plaintiff can bring even a tough litigant to heel. The plaintiff, a law professor, was embarrassed and infuriated when American Express mistakenly had his credit card destroyed in a public restaurant because the Company thought he was delinquent. Even after the Company discovered its mistake and tried to make amends, the plaintiff persisted in pursuing his legal claim. As a result, the case resulted in a substantial change in the way credit card companies do business. Law professors can teach more than their students, as long as persistence is one of their qualities."

—Judge, U.S. Court of Appeals

GRAY

v.

AMERICAN EXPRESS COMPANY

United States Court of Appeals
District of Columbia Circuit
Aug. 31, 1984
743 F.2d 10, 240 U.S.App.D.C. 10

MIKVA, Circuit Judge.

We are called upon to determine what rights, if any, appellant Oscar Gray has against American Express arising from the circumstances under which it cancelled his American Express credit card. The District Court granted summary judgment to American Express; we vacate that judgment and remand for further proceedings.

I. BACKGROUND

Gray had been a cardholder since 1964. In 1981, following some complicated billings arising out of deferred travel charges incurred by Gray, disputes arose about the amount due American Express. After considerable correspondence, the pertinence and timeliness of which we will detail below, American Express decided to cancel Gray's card. No notification of this cancellation was communicated to Gray until the night of April 8, 1982, when he offered his American Express card to pay for a wedding anniversary dinner he and his wife already had consumed in a Washington restaurant. The restaurant informed Gray that American Express had refused to accept the charges for the meal and had instructed the restaurant to confiscate and destroy his card. Gray spoke to the American Express employee on the telephone at the restaurant who informed him, "Your account is cancelled as of now."

The cancellation prompted Gray to file a lengthy complaint in District Court, stating claims under both diversity and federal question jurisdiction. See 28 U.S.C. § §1331, 1332; see also 15 U.S.C. § 1640. He alleged that the actions of American Express violated the contract between them, known as the "Cardmember Agreement," as well as the Fair Credit Billing Act (the "Act"), 15 U.S.C. §§1666–1666j. The District Court granted summary judgment for American Express and dismissed the complaint.

The surge in the use of credit cards, the "plastic money" of our society, has been so quick that the law has had difficulty keeping pace. It was not until 1974 that Congress passed the Act, first making a serious effort to regulate the relationship between a credit cardholder and the issuing company. We hold that the District Court was too swift to conclude that the Act offers no protection to Gray and further hold that longstanding principles of contract law afford Gray substantial rights. We thus vacate the District Court's judgment and remand.

II. DISCUSSION

A. The Statutory Claim

* * *

1. The Billing Error

The billing dispute in issue arose after Gray used his credit card to purchase airline tickets costing $9312. American Express agreed that Gray could pay for the tickets in 12 equal installments over 12 months. In January and February of 1981, Gray made substantial prepayments of $3500 and $1156 respectively. He so advised American Express by letter of February 8, 1981. There is no dispute about these payments, nor about Gray's handling of them. At this point the numbers become confusing because American Express, apparently in error, converted the deferred payment plan to a current charge on the March bill. American Express thereafter began to show Gray as delinquent, due at least in part to the dispute as to how and why the deferred billing had been converted to a current charge.

The District Court held that Gray failed to trigger the protection of the Act because he neglected to notify American Express in writing within 60 days after he first received an erroneous billing. Gray insists that his first letter to American Express on April 22, 1981, well within the 60 day period set forth in the statute, identified the dispute as it first appeared in the March, 1981 billing. According to Gray's complaint, the dispute continued to simmer for over a year because American Express never fulfilled its investigative and other obligations under the Act.

The District Court made no mention of the April 22, 1981 letter, deeming instead a September, 1981 letter as the first notification from Gray as to the existence of a dispute. We conclude that the District Court erred in overlooking the April letter.

* * *

3. The Act and the Cardmember Agreement

As we have indicated above, the District Court summarily resolved Gray's statutory claims by wrongly concluding that the Act did not apply. On appeal, American Express also urges that, even if the Act is otherwise pertinent, Gray was bound by the terms of the Cardmember Agreement which empowered American Express to cancel the credit card without notice and without cause. The contract between Gray and American Express provides:

> [W]e can revoke your right to use [the card] at any time. We can do this with or without cause and without giving you notice.

American Express concludes from this language that the cancellation was not of the kind prohibited by the Act, even though the Act regulates other aspects of the relationship between the cardholder and the card issuer.

Section 1666(d) of the Act states that, during the pendency of a disputed billing, the card issuer, until it fulfills its other obligations under § 1666(a)(B)(ii), shall not cause the cardholder's account to be restricted or closed because of the failure of the obligor to pay the amount in dispute. American Express seems to argue that, despite that provision, it can exercise its right to cancellation for cause unrelated to the disputed amount, or for no cause, thus bringing itself out from under the statute. At the very least, the argument is audacious. American Express would restrict the efficacy of the statute to those situations where the parties had not agreed to a "without cause, without notice" cancellation clause, or to those cases where the cardholder can prove that the sole reason for cancellation was the amount in dispute. We doubt that Congress painted with such a faint brush.

The effect of American Express's argument is to allow the equivalent of a "waiver" of coverage of the Act simply by allowing the parties to contract it away. Congress usually is not so tepid in its approach to consumer problems. * * *

Moreover, the consumer-oriented statutes that Congress has enacted in recent years belie the unrestrained reading that American Express gives to the Act in light of its contract. Waiver of statutory rights, particularly by a contract of adhesion, is hardly consistent with the legislature's purpose. The rationale of consumer protection legislation is to even out the inequalities that consumers normally bring to the bargain. To allow such protection to be waived by boiler plate language of the contract puts the legislative process to a foolish and unproductive task. A court ought not impute such nonsense to a Congress intent on correcting abuses in the market place.

Finally, American Express also contends that, even if the Act is not waived totally, its cancellation was proper because it was for reasons other than those prohibited by the statute. A showing of whatever limited grounds for cancellation remain available under § 1666(d) while a dispute is pending calls for substantial evidentiary proceedings, however. If American Express seeks to avail itself of these grounds, a more substantial factual predicate than that established through summary judgment is necessary.

Thus we hold that the Act's notice provision was met by Gray's April 22, 1981 letter and remand the case to the District Court for trial of Gray's statutory cause of action. American Express will be obliged to justify its conduct in this case as fully satisfying its obligations under the Act.

B. The Contract Claim

* * *

2. Notice

We are asked to interpret the "without notice" provision in the Cardmember Agreement. Gray challenges the card issuer's extreme and, in our view, unreasonable interpretation of this language. The District Court concluded that the notice provision was enforceable. We disagree.

It is certainly true that, from the common law immemorial, parties have been free to include whatever conditions and limitations that they may desire in a contract. Absent a statutory prohibition or some public policy impediment, the very essence of freedom of contract is the right of the parties to strike good bargains and bad bargains. However traditional "cancellation for cause" and "with notice" provisions are to a contract, parties sometimes agree to give them up. Appellant thus would not be the first nor the last cardholder to have surrendered substantial rights. Nor does the fact that Gray paid $35.00 per year for his cardholding privileges automatically entitle him to receive notice or to insist on some showing of cause before his card is cancelled. Indeed, American Express generously provides for a pro-rata refund of the annual charge in the event of cancellation.

The problem, then, is not, as Gray would suggest, the unconscionable nature per se of this clause. Nor is it that this clause contradicts in any actionable way the advertising and puffing that he claims American Express used to entice him into the relationship. (*E.g.*, "When you're out of cash, you're not out of luck."; " . . . flexibility to travel and entertain when and where you want, virtually without interruption.") The problem stems from the card issuer's attempt to interpret the "without notice" provision so as to give the creditor's internal cancellation decision effect as against irreversible transactions that already have been completed.

Commonly understood, the function of notice is to provide forewarning of an event. Similarly, in the context of contractual relations, notice allows the party notified to contemplate, and to prepare for, an action that will occur. By contrast, and reasonably interpreted, a contract that is cancelable without notice implies that it can be terminated without forewarning. Such a contract provision ordinarily does not suggest, however, that the cancellation is effective retrospectively to events that transpired prior to notification of the decision to cancel. Indeed, counsel for American Express made this point for us indirectly at oral argument. When he was asked whether, based on his client's interpretation of the "without notice" clause, American Express was empowered to cancel the agreement "retroactively," he answered "yes," but was quick to add that his client would never take such action against a cardholder. We see little, if any, principled distinction, however, between admittedly "retroactive" cancellation and cancellation effective against irreversible obligations incurred after cancellation but before the cardholder learns his card has been cancelled.

* * *

American Express suggests that if the clauses are not upheld in the manner it urges, there will be a great risk thrown on the credit card business. We think they protest too much. Within the limits of state and federal statutes, credit cards can still be cancelled without cause and without notice. But the cancellation can affect only transactions which have not occurred before the cancellation is communicated to the cardholder. In practical terms American Express will have to make an effort to communicate its cancellation decision to the cardholder. The effort may be as informal as a phone call or a telegram. We leave to future cases the question of what constitutes a good faith effort to communicate the cancellation decision to the cardholder.

Nor need we decide what fact situations would allow the communication of the cancellation to take place through the merchant involved in the transaction. If a cardholder seeks to use his American Express card to buy a car, for example, we think that a communication, through the car dealer, that the card has been cancelled prior to title passing to the cardholder may effect notice in reasonable fashion. But where the meal has been consumed, or the hotel room has been slept in, or the service rendered, the communication through the merchant comes too late to void the credit for that transaction.

*   *   *

III. CONCLUSION

The District Court's order of summary judgment and dismissal is hereby vacated. The case is remanded for further proceedings consistent with this opinion.

Although most people would agree that it would be incredibly unfortunate to buy a home that was supposedly haunted, it would be even more unfortunate to have to go before a court of law and admit that one had unwittingly done so. However, one New York home buyer not only made such a claim in his attempt to rescind the contract of sale, he convinced the court that the house was haunted—at least as a matter of law.

"With tongue in cheek but clarity in its head, the court took an intrinsically absurd situation, treated it with precisely the dignity it deserved, and issued a just ruling that establishes good law for cases of much broader applicability."

—Professor, Columbia University

STAMBOVSKY
v.
ACKLEY, *et al.*

Supreme Court, Appellate Division
July 18, 1991
572 N.Y.S.2d 672, 169 A.D.2d 254

RUBIN, Justice.

Plaintiff, to his horror, discovered that the house he had recently contracted to purchase was widely reputed to be possessed by poltergeists, reportedly seen by defendant seller and members of her family on numerous occasions over the last nine years. Plaintiff promptly commenced this action seeking rescission of the contract of sale. Supreme Court reluctantly dismissed the complaint, holding that plaintiff has no remedy at law in this jurisdiction.

The unusual facts of this case, as disclosed by the record, clearly warrant a grant of equitable relief to the buyer who, as a resident of New York City, cannot be expected to have any familiarity with the folklore of the Village of Nyack. Not being a "local," plaintiff could not readily learn that the home he had contracted to purchase is haunted. Whether the source of the spectral apparitions seen by defendant seller are parapsychic or psychogenic, having reported their presence in both a national publication ("Readers' Digest") and the local press (in 1977 and 1982, respectively), defendant is estopped to deny their existence and, as a matter of law, the house is haunted. More to the point, however, no divination is required to conclude that it is defendant's promotional efforts in publicizing her close encounters with these spirits which fostered the home's reputation in the community. In 1989, the house was included in a five-home walking tour of Nyack and described in a November 27th newspaper article as "a riverfront Victorian (with ghost)." The impact of the reputation thus created goes to the very essence of the bargain between the parties, greatly impairing both the value of the property and its potential for resale. The extent of this impairment may be presumed for the purpose of reviewing the disposition of this motion to dismiss the cause of action for rescission and represents merely an issue of fact for resolution at trial.

While I agree with Supreme Court that the real estate broker, as agent for the seller, is under no duty to disclose to a potential buyer the phantasmal reputation of the premises and that, in his pursuit of a legal remedy for fraudulent misrepresentation against the seller, plaintiff hasn't a ghost of a chance, I am nevertheless moved by the spirit of equity to allow the buyer to seek rescission of the contract of sale and recovery of his downpayment. New York law fails to recognize any remedy for damages incurred as a result of the seller's mere silence, applying instead the strict rule of caveat emptor. Therefore, the theoretical basis for granting relief, even under the extraordinary facts of this case, is elusive if not ephemeral.

"Pity me not but lend thy serious hearing to what
I shall unfold"

(William Shakespeare,
Hamlet, Act I, Scene V [Ghost])

From the perspective of a person in the position of plaintiff herein, a very practical problem arises with respect to the discovery of a paranormal phenomenon: "Who you gonna' call?" as the title song to the movie "Ghostbusters" asks. Applying the strict rule of caveat emptor to a contract involving a house possessed by poltergeists conjures up visions of a psychic or medium routinely accompanying the structural engineer and

Terminix man on an inspection of every home subject to a contract of sale. It portends that the prudent attorney will establish an escrow account lest the subject of the transaction come back to haunt him and his client—or pray that his malpractice insurance coverage extends to supernatural disasters. In the interest of avoiding such untenable consequences, the notion that a haunting is a condition which can and should be ascertained upon reasonable inspection of the premises is a hobgoblin which should be exorcised from the body of legal precedent and laid quietly to rest.

It has been suggested by a leading authority that the ancient rule which holds that mere non-disclosure does not constitute actionable misrepresentation "finds proper application in cases where the fact undisclosed is patent, or the plaintiff has equal opportunities for obtaining information which he may be expected to utilize, or the defendant has no reason to think that he is acting under any misapprehension" (Prosser, Law of Torts § 106, at 696 [4th ed., 1971]). However, with respect to transactions in real estate, New York adheres to the doctrine of caveat emptor and imposes no duty upon the vendor to disclose any information concerning the premises unless there is a confidential or fiduciary relationship between the parties or some conduct on the part of the seller which constitutes "active concealment". Normally, some affirmative misrepresentation or partial disclosure is required to impose upon the seller a duty to communicate undisclosed conditions affecting the premises.

* * *

The doctrine of caveat emptor requires that a buyer act prudently to assess the fitness and value of his purchase and operates to bar the purchaser who fails to exercise due care from seeking the equitable remedy of rescission For the purposes of the instant motion to dismiss the action pursuant to CPLR 3211(a)(7), plaintiff is entitled to every favorable inference which may reasonably be drawn from the pleadings, specifically, in this instance, that he met his obligation to conduct an inspection of the premises and a search of available public records with respect to title. It should be apparent, however, that the most meticulous inspection and the search would not reveal the presence of poltergeists at the premises or unearth the property's ghoulish reputation in the community.

Therefore, there is no sound policy reason to deny plaintiff relief for failing to discover a state of affairs which the most prudent purchaser would not be expected to even contemplate.

* * *

Where a condition which has been created by the seller materially impairs the value of the contract and is peculiarly within the knowledge of the seller or unlikely to be discovered by a prudent purchaser exercising due care with respect to the subject transaction, nondisclosure constitutes a basis for rescission as a matter of equity. Any other outcome places upon the buyer not merely the obligation to exercise care in his purchase but rather to be omniscient with respect to any fact which may affect the bargain. No practical purpose is served by imposing such a burden upon a purchaser. To the contrary, it encourages predatory business practice and offends the principle that equity will suffer no wrong to be without a remedy.

Defendant's contention that the contract of sale, particularly the merger or "as is" clause, bars recovery of the buyer's deposit is unavailing. Even an express disclaimer will not be given effect where the facts are peculiarly within the knowledge of the party invoking it. Moreover, a fair reading of the merger clause reveals that it expressly disclaims only representations made with respect to the physical condition of the premises and merely makes general reference to representations concerning "any other matter or things affecting or relating to the aforesaid premises". As broad as this language may be, a reasonable interpretation is that its effect is limited to tangible or physical matters and does not extend to paranormal phenomena. Finally, if the language of the contract is to be construed as broadly as defendant urges to encompass the presence of poltergeists in the house, it cannot be said that she has delivered the premises "vacant" in accordance with her obligation under the provisions of the contract rider.

* * *

In the case at bar, defendant seller deliberately fostered the public belief that her home was possessed. Having undertaken to inform the public at large, to whom she has no legal relationship, about the supernatural occurrences on her property, she may be said to owe no less a duty to her contract vendee. It has been remarked that the occasional modern cases which permit a seller to take unfair advantage of a buyer's ignorance so long as he is not actively misled are "singularly unappetizing" (Prosser, Law of Torts § 106, at 696 [4th ed. 1971]). Where, as here, the seller not only takes unfair advantage of the buyer's ignorance but has created and perpetuated a condition about which he is unlikely to even inquire, enforcement of the contract (in whole or in part) is offensive to the court's sense of equity. Application of the remedy of rescission, within the bounds of the narrow exception to the doctrine of caveat emptor set forth herein, is entirely appropriate to relieve the unwitting purchaser from the consequences of a most unnatural bargain.

Accordingly, the judgment of the Supreme Court, New York County (Edward H. Lehner, J.), entered April 9, 1990, which dismissed the complaint pursuant to CPLR 3211(a)(7), should be modified, on the law and the facts and in the exercise of discretion, and the first cause of action seeking rescission of the contract reinstated, without costs.

SMITH, Justice (dissenting).

I would affirm the dismissal of the complaint by the motion court.

* * *

The parties herein were represented by counsel and dealt at arm's length. This is evidenced by the contract of sale which, inter alia, contained various riders and a specific provision that all prior understandings and agreements between the parties were merged into the contract, that the contract completely expressed their full agreement and that neither had relied upon any statement by anyone else not set forth in the contract. There is no allegation that defendants, by some specific act, other than the failure to speak, deceived the plaintiff. Nevertheless, a cause of action may be sufficiently stated where there is a confidential or fiduciary relationship creating a duty to disclose and there was a failure to disclose a material fact, calculated to induce a false belief. However, plaintiff herein has not alleged and there is no basis for concluding that a confidential or fiduciary relationship existed between these parties to an arm's length transaction such as to give rise to a duty to disclose. In addition, there is no allegation that defendants thwarted plaintiff's efforts to fulfill his responsibilities fixed by the doctrine of caveat emptor.

Finally, if the doctrine of caveat emptor is to be discarded, it should be for a reason more substantive than a poltergeist. The existence of a poltergeist is no more binding upon the defendants than it is upon this court.

Chapter 11
The Good Old Days

As the old saying goes, "The only thing constant is change"—and the older we get, the more apparent that statement becomes. For the most part, change is good. But sometimes it can be somewhat discouraging, and changes in our judicial system are no exception. State and federal courts, which have expanded considerably over the years, are inundated with an unprecedented number of lawsuits, some of which involve millions of dollars and will take years to resolve. In addition, the already flooded criminal dockets seem to grow with each passing day. It can all be quite overwhelming. That may be why it is not surprising to hear yesterday's generation reminisce about "the good old days," when life was simpler and the pace was a little slower.

Although we cannot turn back the clock, the following selection of cases provides us with a glimpse of the past with respect to law in America. These cases offer a colorful illustration of some of the modest legal disputes that arose during the life and times of the good old days.

Justice Graves authored the majority opinion in the following "celebrated mule case"; however, it was Justice Lamm's concurring opinion that induced one judge to submit it to us.

"Judge Lamm's opinion is humorous, it is eloquent and it applies Missouri tort law in an unusual setting. It is interesting in that the case reached the Missouri Supreme Court even though it involved only [$5.00]. Judge Lamm's opinion indicates that appellate judges had more time to reflect on their opinions than the judges have today."

—Judge, United States District Court

LYMAN

v.

DALE

Supreme Court of Missouri
Dec. 2, 1914
171 S.W. 352, 262 Mo. 353

LAMM, J. (concurring)

It was Dr. Johnson (was it not?) who observed that Oliver Goldsmith had "contributed to the innocent gayety of mankind." (Note bene: If, as a pundit tells me, it was Garrick, and not Goldsmith, Johnson spoke of, and if, in quoting, I misquote, then memory has played a trick upon me, and a learned bar will correct me. Time and weightier matters press me to go on and leave the "quotation"? stand.) The function of this suit is somewhat the same. Beginning with the "J.P.'s" it has reached the "P.J.'s" and in its journey has run the gamut of three courts, one above the other. Now, *secundum regulam,* it, a fuss over $5, has reached the highest court in the state for final disposition—all this because (1) of divergence of opinion among our learned brethren of the Springfield Court of Appeals, and (2) the provisions of the Constitution in that behalf made and provided. However, if the amount at stake is small, the value of the case for doctrine's sake is great.

As I see it, the case is this: Dale, a man of substance, a farmer, owned a brown and a gray mule, both young and of fine growth; one saddlewise, the other otherwise. Both, used to the plow and wagon, were entitled to the designation "well broke and gentle." One Parker was Dale's manservant, and in the usual course of his employment had charge of these mules. On a day certain he had driven them to a water wagon in the humble office of supplying water to a clover huller in the Ozark region hard by its metropolis, to wit, Springfield. Eventide had fallen; *i.e.*, the poetical time of day had come when the beetle wheels his droning flight, drowsy tinkling lulls the distant folds, and all the air a solemn stillness holds. In other words, dropping into the vernacular, it was time to "take out." Accordingly, Parker took out with his mind fixed on the watchdog's honest bark baying deep-mouthed welcome as he drew near home; he mounted the ridable mule. He says he tied the other to the hames of the harness on the ridden one by a four or five foot halter rope, and was plodding his weary way homeward a la the plowman in the Elegy. The vicissitudes of the journey in due course brought him to Walnut street in said city of Springfield. At a certain place in that street the city fathers had broken the pavement and made a "rick of brick" aside a long hole or ditch. Hard by this rick of brick was a ridge of fresh earth capped by a display of red lantern danger signals. It seems the unridden mule crowded against the ridden one and harassed Parker by coming in scraping contact with his circumjacent leg. Any boy who ever rode the lead horse in harrowing his father's field will get the idea. In this pickle he took hold of the halter rope, still fastened to the hames, to keep the unridden mule from rasping his said leg. It might as well be said at this point that witnesses for plaintiff did not observe that the end of the rope was attached to the hames of the ridden mule. As they saw it, Parker was leading the mule. As will be seen a bit further on, at this point a grave question arises, to wit: Is it negligence to lead a mule by hand, or should he be fastened "neck and neck" to his fellow? But we anticipate.

Going back a little, it seems as follows: At about the time Parker had reached said part of Walnut street, plaintiff and two others were in a buggy pulled by a single horse and on their own way home to the country. So equipped, these several parties met face to face. At this point it will do to say that, while the mules were used to being on the water wagon, it is not so clear that these travelers three were. There are signs of that artificial elation in the vehicle party that in the evening springs from drinking ("breathing freely"), but on the morning after produces the condition of involuntary expiation Dr. Von Ihring calls "katzenjammer." They disavow being half seas over or drunk. Their chief spokesman, as descriptive of the situation, in part told his story mathematically in this fashion:

> "I had not drank so much but what I kept count. I can keep count until I take three, and hadn't quit counting yet. * * *"

In the course of their journey they, too, came to the brick rick, the ditch, the ridge of dirt, and the red lights on Walnut street. There they met, as said, the gray and brown mule and Parker face to face. When mules and rider approached and passed the three travelers, all on the same side of the ditch, the led mule (whether scared by the hole in the ground, the rick of brick, or the ridge is dark) shied from his fellow ("spread" himself), and presently his hind leg was mixed up with the shafts and wheel of the buggy. When the status quo ante was re-established, both leg and wheel were found damaged. Subsequently a blacksmith offered to repair the damages to the wheel for, say, a dollar and a half. This sum defendant, though denying liability, was willing and offered to pay; but plaintiff's dander was up, and he, as buggy owner, demanded a new wheel worth $5 and sued. In the justice court defendant lost outright and appealed. In the circuit court the same. The learned judges of the Court of Appeals could not agree (the furor scribendi being much in evidence, and three learned opinions falling from their several pens) and sent the case here—and here it is.

My Brother GRAVES has well disposed of it on certain grounds, [reversing the lower court] but the theme being the Missouri mule, and state pride calling for further exposition, the said furor scribendi has seized me—witness:

(a) It is argued that it was negligence to ride one mule and lead its fellow by hand. That they should be halter-yoked "neck and neck." Parker says he necked them in a way, but plaintiff takes issue on the fact. Allowing credit to plaintiff's evidence, two questions spring, viz.: *First.* Is the neck-and-neck theory "mule law" in this jurisdiction? *Second.* If so, then was the absence of the neck-and-neck adjustment the proximate cause of the injury? We may let the first question be settled in some other mule case and pass to the second as more important. It will be observed that the neck and forequarters of the mule did not do the damage. *Contra*, the hindquarters or "business end" of the mule were in fault. We take judicial notice of facts of nature. Hence we know that haltering a mule neck and neck to another will not prevent his hind parts spreading. His neck might be on one line, but his hind legs and heels might be on another—a divergent one. True, the mental concept relating to shying or spreading would naturally originate in the mule's head. But it must be allowed as a sound psychological proposition that haltering his head or neck can in no wise control the mule's thoughts or control the hinder parts affected by those thoughts. So much, I think, is clear and is due to be said of the Missouri mule whose bones, in attestation of his activity and worth, lie bleaching from Shiloh to Spion Kop, from San Juan to Przemysl (pronounced, I am told by a scholar, as it is spelled). It results that the causal connection between the negligence in hand and the injury is broken, and recovery cannot go on the neck-and-neck theory. This because it is plain, under the distances disclosed by the evidence, that the mule's hind legs could reach the buggy wheel in spite of a neck-and-neck attachment.

(b) The next question is a bit elusive, but seems lodged in the case. It runs thus: There being no evidence tending to show the mule was "wild and unruly" as charged, is such a mule per se a nuisance, a vicious animal, has he a heart devoid of social duty and fatally bent on mischief when led by a halter on the street of a town, and must his owner answer for his acts on that theory? Attend to that view of it:

(1) There are sporadic instances of mules behaving badly. That one that Absalom rode and "went from under" him at a crisis in his fate, for instance. So it has been intimated in fireside precepts that the mule is unexpected in his heel action, and has other faults. In Spanish folk lore it is said: He who wants a mule without fault must walk. So, at the French chimney corner the adage runs: The mule long keeps a kick in reserve for his master. "The mule don't kick according to no rule," saith the American Negro. His voice has been a matter of derision, and there be those who put their tongue in their cheek when speaking of it. Witness the German proverb: Mules make a great fuss about their ancestors having been asses. And so on, and so on. But none of these things are factors in the instant case, for here there was no kicking and no braying standing in the relation of causa causans to the injury to the wheel. Moreover the rule of logic is that induction which pro-

ceeds by merely citing instances is a childish affair, and, being without any certain principle of inference, it may be overthrown by contrary instances. Accordingly the faithfulness, the dependableness, the surefootedness, the endurance, the strength, and the good sense of the mule (all matters of common knowledge) may be allowed to stand over against his faults and create either an equilibrium or a preponderance in the scales in his favor. He then, as a domestic animal, is entitled to the doctrine that, if he become vicious, guilty knowledge (the scienter) must be brought home to his master, precisely as it must be on the dog or ox. The rule of the master's liability for acts of the ox is old. Ex. 21:29. That for the acts of the dog is put this way: The law allows the dog his first bite. Lord Cockburn's dictum covers the master's liability on a kindred phase of liability for sheep killing, to wit: Every dog is entitled to at least one worry. So with this mule. Absent proof of the bad habit of "spreading" when led and the scienter, liability did not spring from the mere fact his hind leg (he being scared) got over the wheel while he was led by a five-foot halter rope, for it must be held that a led mule is not a nuisance per se, unless he is to be condemned on that score out and out because of his ancestry and some law of heredity, some asinine rule, so to speak—a question we take next.

(2) Some care should be taken not to allow such scornful remarks as that "the mule has no pride of ancestry or hope of posterity" to press upon our judgment He inherits his father's ears; but what of that? The asses' ears, presented by an angry Apollo, were an affliction to King Midas, but not to the mule. He is a hybrid, but that was man's invention centuries gone in some province of Asia Minor, and the fact is not chargeable to the mule. So the slowness of the domestic ass does not descend as a trait to the Missouri mule. It is said that a thistle is a fat salad for an ass' mouth. Maybe it is also in a mule's, but, be it so, surely his penchant for homely fare cannot so far condemn him that he does not stand rectus in curia. Moreover, if his sire stands in satire as an emblem of sleepy stupidity, yet that avails nought, for the authorities (on which I cannot put my finger at this moment) agree that the Missouri mule takes after his dam and not his sire in that regard. All asses are not fourfooted, the adage saith, and yet to call a man an "ass" is quite a different thing than to call him "mulish." Vide the lexicographers.

Furthermore, the very word "jackass" is a term of reproach everywhere, as in the literature of the law. Do we not all know that a certain phase of the law of negligence, the humanitarian rule, first announced, it has been said, in a donkey case (*Davis v. Mann*, 10 Mees. & W. 545) has been called, by those who deride it, the "jackass doctrine?" This on the doctrine of the adage: Call a dog a bad name and then hang him. But, on the other hand, to sum up fairly, it was an ass that saw the heavenly vision even Balaam, the seer, could not see and first raised a voice against cruelty to animals. Num. 22:23 *et seq.* So, did not Sancho Panza by meditation gather the sparks of wisdom while ambling along on the back of one, that radiated in his wonderful judgments pronounced in his decision by the common-sense rule of knotty cases in the Island of Barataria? Did not Samson use the jawbone of one effectually on a thousand Philistines? Is not his name imperishably preserved in that of the fifth proposition of the first book of Euclid—the *pons asinorum?* But we shall pursue the subject no farther. Enough has been said to show that the ass is not without some rights in the courts even on sentimental grounds; ergo if his hybrid son, tracing his lineage as he does to the Jacks of Kentucky and Andalusia, inherits some of his traits, he cannot be held bad per se. Q.E.D.

It is meet that a $5 case, having its tap root in anger (and possibly in liquor), should not drag its slow lengths through the courts for more than five years, even if it has earned the soubriquet of "the celebrated mule case."

The premises herein and in the opinion of Brother GRAVES all in mind, I concur.

"[I]t is amusing to watch a dignified court grapple with the vagaries of human conduct and have to explain in legalese what could be said so much easier by any layman on the street."

—Professor, Ohio State University

NORTON and others
v.
KNAPP

Iowa Supreme Court
June 10, 1884
19 N.W. 867, 64 Iowa 112

SEEVERS, J.

Because of the statements contained in an amended abstract we are required to set out the petition as follows:

> "That the plaintiffs sold and delivered to the defendant, about February 17, 1882, a certain flaxseed-cleaner mill, at the agreed price of eighty dollars, no part of which had been paid, and that the same was then due.

> "That on or about April, 1882, plaintiffs drew a sight draft on defendant for the agreed price of said mill, which was in words and figures as follows:

> "$80.   LA CROSSE, WIS., April 18, 1882.

> "At sight pay to the order of Exchange Bank of Nora Springs, Iowa, eighty dollars, value received, and charge the same to the account of
> > "NORTON & KEELER

> *"To Miles Knapp, Nora Springs, Ia."*

—Which was accepted by said Miles Knapp in written words and figures, on the back thereof, as follows: "Kiss my foot. MILES KNAPP." Also alleging "that said draft was still the property of plaintiff, due and unpaid, and claiming judgment for eighty dollars, interest, and costs."

To the foregoing petition the defendant demurred, on the ground "that the draft set out in the petition does not show a legal acceptance." The demurrer was overruled, and the defendant answered, denying the allegations of the petition, and pleaded a special defense as to the flaxseed cleaner. The plaintiffs withdrew or dismissed "so much of their cause of action as was based on the sale of the flaxseed-cleaning machine, leaving the draft as their sole cause of action." A jury was impaneled to try the issue joined, and the plaintiff offered in evidence the draft, as above set out; to which the defendant objected, on the ground that it had not been accepted by him. This objection was sustained, and the jury, under the direction of the court, found for the defendant, and judgment was rendered on the verdict. The amount in controversy being less than $100, the court has certified certain questions upon which the opinion of this court is desired. In substance, two of them are whether the words "kiss my foot," on the back of the draft, signed by the drawee, is a legal and valid acceptance; and whether such acceptance can be introduced in evidence without showing it was the intention to accept the draft. The rule upon this subject is thus stated in 1 Pars. Bills & Notes, 282: "If a bill is presented to a drawee for the purpose of obtaining his acceptance, and he does anything to or with it which does not distinctly indicate that he will not accept it, he is held to be an acceptor, for he has the power, and it is his duty, to put this question beyond all possibility of doubt."

Counsel for the defendant [sic] insist that it was held in *Spear v. Pratt*, 2 Hill, 582, that the words "I will not accept this bill" signed by the defendant, constituted a valid acceptance. As we understand the case, the defendant's name was written "across the face of the bill," and this was held to be a sufficient acceptance, on the ground that the request to accept had not been negatived.

The rule we understand to be, if the drawee does anything with or to the bill, or writes thereon anything, which does not clearly negative an intention to accept, then he can or will be charged as an acceptor. The question, then, is, what construction should be placed on the words "kiss my foot," written on the bill and signed by him? They cannot be rejected as surplusage. Such language is not ordinarily used in business circles or polite society. But by their use the defendant meant either to accept or refuse to accept the bill. It cannot be he meant the former; therefore, it must be the latter. It seems quite clear to us that the defendant intended, by the use of the contemptuous and vulgar words above stated, to give emphasis to his intention not to accept or have anything to do with the bill or with the plaintiff. We understand the words, in common parlance, to mean and express contempt for the person to whom the words are addressed, and when used as a reply to a request, they imply, and are understood to mean, a decided, unqualified, and contemptuous refusal to comply with such request. In such sense they were undoubtedly used when the defendant was requested to accept the bill. The question asked upon this point must be answered in the negative. Whether parol evidence is admissible to show the intent of the defendant, we have no occasion to determine, because no such evidence was offered, and our rule is not to determine mere abstract propositions.

* * *

Affirmed.

"The rule of law regarding the death of a draft horse (vs. its mere injury) is still good law in Texas."

—Professor, Southern Methodist University

CITY OF CANADIAN

v.

GUTHRIE

Court of Civil Appeals of Texas
June 8, 1932
87 S.W.2d 316

HALL, Chief Justice.

Guthrie was engaged in hauling in the city of Canadian, in which occupation he used a wagon and team. One of the animals so used is described as a "by mare, one-eyed, about 12 or 14 years old. That this mare, by reason of the loss of her said eye, which plaintiff alleges to be the left eye, was specially adapted to the work of teaming in connection with the other horse." It appears that on account of the dearth of vitamins from A to Z in her home cuisine, this particular mare was prone to spend her off nights prowling through the city, feasting upon the lawns, shrubbery, and gardens of her neighbors. Some days before the fatal day she had been placed in the city pound, plaintiff was duly notified and failed to pay her board bill, whereupon the city marshal employed one Jess, whose surname was Lemley, more familiarly known as "Panhandle Pete," who, at the direction of the mayor, ruthlessly took said mare's life by shooting her between the bad eye and the one not so bad. In other words, in the vernacular of gangland, when Panhandle Pete's pistol popped, she petered, for which the poundkeeper paid Pete a pair of pesos. The mayor testified that just before her execution he visited the city pound twice to see her and found her in bad shape, that she was sick and prostrate, and had hay and other provender in her nose. That he cleaned out her flues so she could breathe, but, nevertheless, he called out the militia and ordered Pete to put her out of her misery for humanitarian reasons. This established the corpus delicti. His honor testified that he knew nothing about mares, and the jury believed him.

There is testimony that she was thin in flesh, indicating that she had some fine points upon which her harness could be hung. From the record, we conclude that although she may not have had a skin you would particularly love to touch (though she had seen only fourteen joyous summers), yet she had a skin which clung like ivy to her rafters with a beautiful corrugated effect upon the sides of her lithe and spirituelle form.

Plaintiff immediately brought suit, fixing his actual damages at $50, alleging that his mare had no market value, and proudly averring that she was the only mare of her kind in Hemphill county, but that $50 was her actual and intrinsic value, and $100 was her sentimental value. He further sued for $350 for the loss of the services of said mare while pursuing his occupation of hauling, and claimed the further sum of $500 as exemplary damages on account of the malicious act of the city in having her killed. He averred that because of her loss his occupation, like Othello's, was gone and he "had been set out an empty." However, he concluded before the trial that a genial, brotherly-love city like Canadian, which had been converted into a one-horse town by Pete and the mayor, was incapable of harboring malice, and the claim for exemplary damages was abandoned at the trial.

Plaintiff testified that usually he kept her confined in a four-wire corral. The chain of title discloses that Mike Nolan at one time was her proud possessor, and sold her to Mr. Flowers for twelve pieces of silver, payable in installments of two pieces per month. The abstract of title further shows that Flowers sold her to Guthrie, the plaintiff herein, but, according to Flowers' testimony, he had never received even a thin dime of the purchase money since he transferred possession. The testimony of Flowers and the plaintiff conflict upon this issue, but since the title is not involved in this action, that matter is "dismissed for want of jurisdiction," because we do not know what else to do with it.

The record shows that upon at least two occasions

"When night drew her sable curtain down
And pinned it with a star,"

and

"Silence like a gentle spirit
Brooded o'er a still and pulseless world,"

the time lock on her corral mysteriously went off and so did she, in search of tulips, dahlias, and gladioli in the neighboring lawns and flower beds. It is clear from the record that she had at least one eye for the beautiful, and was excessively fond of flowers, but that the tender passion was not reciprocated, for, as stated, he parted with her without consideration. While her origin is shrouded in mystery, her appetite for flora of the rarest and costliest varieties indicates that somewhere back in the line of her ancestry there had been injected a stream of royal blood. Although she had only one eye, appellant contends she could find more edible shrubbery in a single night than an experienced landscape gardener could replant in thirty days. We may assume that in her midnight excursions she had been thrown with porch climbers, joy riders, orchard raiders, and other nocturnal prowlers, which may account for her waywardness and utter disregard for the property rights of others. But after her midnight banquet upon orchids, delphiniums, and hyacinths, the poundkeeper would take her in charge, and set before her a bundle or two of mildewed sorghum of the vintage of 1927 in order to take the taste out of her mouth, but when he sent the meal ticket to the plaintiff, the latter steadfastly refused to pay. It was not denied that she had "went hence" and was cut down in the heyday of her young and fitful life because the mayor found some of the hay in her nose, and he admitted that he was accessory before the fact and had personally ordered her gentle soul sent to the great beyond and the remainder to the municipal dump ground.

While, as bearing upon her sentimental value, it is saddening to know that the beautiful flower beds and onion patches of Canadians, over which she was wont to gambol in the moonlight between the hour when

"Curfew tolled the knell of parting day,"

and some hours later,

> "when greyeyed morn,
> Stood tiptoe upon the misty mountain height
> And flecked the eastern hills with rays of
>   golden light,"

would know her no more forever nevertheless, in the cold unsympathetic eye of the law, sentimental value is not recognized as a basis for damages. 13 Tex.Jur. 155.

A jury was impaneled, who found: (1) That the mare had an intrinsic value; (2) of $25; (3) that plaintiff suffered special damages; (4) which were the proximate result of the city's unlawful act; (5) in the sum of $35. The court defined "proximate cause" in the stereotyped form, and charged the jury that special damages "are such consequences of an injury as are peculiar to the circumstances and conditions of the injured party." Judgment was rendered in favor of Guthrie for $60, with interest from the date of the judgment at 6 per cent.

The city demurred to the petition generally and specially to the item of special damages based upon the loss of the use of the mare by plaintiff in his business as a drayman. This demurrer should have been sustained, and the court's action in overruling it presents fundamental error. Damages occasioned by the loss of the use and hire of an animal are recoverable where the animal is injured so that it cannot be used for a time, or where the possession is illegally detained; but no such damages are recoverable for the total loss or death of an animal. The measure of damages in the case of a wrongful killing of an animal is its market value, if it has one, and if not, then its actual or intrinsic value, with interest.

Appellee's counsel suggested that this being the rule, it is cheaper to kill a mare in Texas than it is to cripple her. The same seems to be true with reference to men, but this court must declare the law as it exists. An eminent Ex Chief Justice of this state doubtless had this in mind when his eloquent pen wrote:

"For nothing so bespeaks a people as their notions of justice. There jurisprudence, comprising those ideas, is the supreme expression of their moral convictions. In it their very character is indelibly written, and hence by it they are to be truly judged.

"That is why I have said that the jurisprudence of Texas embodies the spirit of the Commonwealth. And because it does, is the source of a just pride. It has ever been a spirit valiant, bold and free. As it flamed with an imperishable glory at the Alamo, at Goliad and at San Jacinto, so it has lived and has imparted its virtue to the jurisprudence of the State." 1 Tex.Jur. xxvii.

After the item of $500 claimed as exemplary damages (which, of course, was not recoverable) had been abandoned by plaintiff, the trial court should have sustained the general demurrer to the item of $350 special damages, as the real amount in controversy is only $50, alleged to be the actual value of the mare.

In our original opinion, we held that because the actual damages fixed at $50 was an amount below the jurisdiction of the county court, that that court had no jurisdiction, and therefore this court acquired none by the appeal, and we dismissed the cause. We suggested that as the plaintiff's mare was wont to stray into the wrong curtilage for nourishment, likewise his attorneys had wandered into the wrong court in search of damages. In the light of the motion for rehearing, it appears that that was an unjust criticism of learned counsel, but it is far worse as a legal proposition, because, as counsel say in their motion for rehearing:

I.

"Comes now the plaintiff, appellee,
And moves this Honorable Court to see,
That House Bill Number 304
Threw open wide the Court House door,
Of County Court in Hemphill County
Where Guthrie sought relief and bounty,
And recompense and generous meed,

> For his departed wayward steed,
> Cut down in all her youthful pride,
> When she was taken for a ride."

II.

> "The court did hold, that as this mare,
> To wrong curtilage did repair,
> Likewise, these lawyers who here do pray,
> Into the wrong court below did stray;
> But this Honorable Court overlooked the fact,
> That the Legislature passed an Act,
> In Nineteen Hundred and Fifteen,
> And Jurisdiction since has been,
> In that Court whence this case came,
> As in the Justice Court the same."

Reference to H.B. No. 304 (Laws 1915, c. 125) shows that the Legislature did extend the jurisdiction of the county court of Hemphill county, making it concurrent with the jurisdiction of justices' courts, a law which even this court did not know; but appellee's counsel have found too much law for his good, because section 3 of the act provides that no appeal shall be taken to the Court of Civil Appeals from any final judgment of said county court in civil cases of which said court has concurrent jurisdiction with the justices' court where the judgment or amount in controversy does not exceed $100, exclusive of interest and costs. The judgment as stated is $60. According to the allegations, the real amount in controversy is $50.

* * *

It follows from [earlier] decisions that the county court had jurisdiction, but no appeal could be prosecuted to this court. It therefore becomes our duty to dismiss the appeal.

Appellee generously offers to enter a remittitur of the item of $35 awarded him in the trial court. Since we have no jurisdiction of the appeal, we cannot enter the remittitur here nor pass upon any of the interesting questions presented in the able and exhaustive briefs of counsel. The original opinion is withdrawn, and the appeal is dismissed.

"I nominate [McGinley] v. Cleary, with full confidence that its salt and spice endureth well into today's overly complex and sometimes mundane world of legal opinions. . . . [McGinley] reminds me of the oft told tale of the man who arrived in Las Vegas in a sixty thousand dollar Cadillac and departed in a five hundred thousand dollar Greyhound bus."

—Judge, United States District Court

McGINLEY

v.

CLEARY

Third Division, Fairbanks, Alaska
August 8, 1904
2 A.K. Reports 269

WICKERSHAM, District Judge.

On the 29th of last November the plaintiff was, and for some time previous thereto had been, one of the proprietors of that certain two-story log cabin described in the pleadings as the "Fairbanks Hotel," situate upon lot 1, Front street, in the town of Fairbanks, Alaska. The opening scene discovers him drunk, but engaged on his regular night shift as barkeeper in dispensing whisky by leave of this court on a territorial license to those of his customers who had not been able, through undesire or the benumbing influence of the liquor, to retire to their cabins. The defendant was his present customer. After a social evening session, the evidence is that at about 3 o'clock in the morning of the 30th they were mutually enjoying the hardships of Alaska by pouring into their respective interiors unnumbered four-bit drinks, recklessly expending undug pokes, and blowing in the next spring cleanup. While thus employed, between sticking tabs on the nail and catching their breath for the next glass, they began to tempt the fickle goddess of fortune by shaking plaintiff's dicebox. The defendant testifies that he had a $5 bill, that he laid it on the bar, and that it constituted the visible means of support to the game and transfer of property which followed. That defendant had a $5 bill so late in the evening may excite remark among his acquaintances.

Whether plaintiff and defendant then formed a mental design to gamble around the storm center of this bill is one of the matters in dispute in this case about which they do not agree. The proprietor is plaintively positive on his part that at that moment his brains were so benumbed by the fumes or the force of his own whisky that he was actually non compos mentis; that his mental faculties were so far paralyzed thereby that they utterly failed to register or record impressions. His customer, on the other hand, stoutly swears that the vigor and strength of his constitution enabled him to retain his memory, and he informed the court from the witness stand that while both were gazing at the bill, the proprietor produced his near-by dicebox, and they began to shake for its temporary ownership. Neither the memory which failed nor that which labored in spite of its load enabled either the proprietor or the customer to recall that any other money or its equivalent came upon the board. The usual custom of $500 millionaires grown from wild cat bonanzas was followed, and as aces and sixes alternated or blurringly trooped athwart their vision, the silent upthrust of the index finger served to mark the balance of trade.

They were not alone. Tupper Thompson slept bibulously behind the oil tank stove. Whether his mental receiver was likewise so hardened by inebriation as to be incapable of catching impressions will never be certainly known to the court. He testified to a lingering remembrance of drinks which he enjoyed at this time upon the invitation of some one, and is authority for the statement that when he came to the proprietor was so drunk that he hung limply and vine-like to the bar, though he played dice with the defendant, and later signed a bill of sale of the premises in dispute, which Tupper witnessed. Tupper also testified that the defendant was drunk, but according to his standard of intoxication he was not so entirely paralyzed as the proprietor, since he could stand without holding to the bar. Not to be outdone either in memory or expert testimony, the defendant admitted that Tupper was present, that his resting place was behind the oil tank stove, where, defendant testifies, he remained on the puncheon floor in slumberous repose during the gaming festivities with the dicebox, and until called to drink and sign a bill of sale, both of which he did according to his own testimony. One O'Neil also saw the parties plaintiff and defendant about this hour in the saloon, with defendant's arm around plaintiff's neck in maudlin embrace.

After the dice-shaking had ceased, and the finger-tip book-keeping had been reduced to round numbers, the defendant testifies that the plaintiff was found to be indebted to him in the sum of $1,800. Whether these dice, which belonged to the bar and seem to have been in frequent use by the proprietor, were in the habit of playing such pranks on the house may well be doubted; nor is it shown that they, too, were loaded. It is just possible that mistakes may have occurred pending lapses of memory by which, in the absence of a look-out, the usual numbers thrown for the house were counted for the defendant, and this without any fault of the dice. However this may be, the defendant swears that he won the, score, and passed up the tabs for payment.

According to the defendant's testimony, the proprietor was also playing a confidence game, whereupon, in the absence of money, the defendant suggested that he make him a bill of sale of the premises. Two were written out by defendant. The second was signed by plaintiff and witnessed by Tupper, and for a short time the defendant became a tenant in common with an unnamed person and an equitable owner of an interest in the saloon. The plaintiff testifies that during all this time, and until the final act of signing the deed in controversy, he was drunk, and suffering from a total loss of memory and intelligence. The evidence in support of intelligence is vague and unsatisfactory, and the court is unable to base any satisfactory conclusion upon it.

Above the mists of inebriety which befogged the mental landscape of the principals in this case at that time rise a few jagged peaks of fact which must guide the court notwithstanding their temporary intellectual eclipse. After the dice-throwing had ceased, the score calculated, and the bills of sale written, and the last one conveying a half interest in the premises signed by the plaintiff, he accompanied the defendant to the cabin of Commissioner Cowles, about a block away, on the banks of the frozen Chena, and requested that official to affix his official acknowledgment to the document. Owing to their hilarious condition and the early hour at which they so rudely broke the judicial slumbers, the commissioner refused to do business with them, and thrust them from his chamber. He does not testify as to the status of their respective memories at that time, but he does say that their bodies were excessively drunk; that of the defendant being, according to the judicial eye, the most wobbly. He testifies that the plaintiff was able

435

to and did assist the defendant away from his office without any official acknowledgment being made to the bill of sale. The evidence then discloses that, in the light of the early morning, both principals retired to their bunks to rest; witness Sullivan going so far as to swear that the plaintiff's boots were removed before he got in bed.

The question of consideration is deemed to be an important one in this case. Defendant asserts that it consisted of the $1,800 won at the proprietor's own game of dice, but Tupper Thompson relapses into sobriety long enough to declare that the real consideration promised on the part of the defendant was to give a half interest in his Cleary creek placer mines for the half interest in the saloon; that defendant said the plaintiff could go out and run the mines while he remained in the saloon and sold hootch to the sour-doughs, or words to that effect. Tupper's evidence lacks some of the earmarks; it is quite evident that he had a rock in his sluice box. The plaintiff, on the other hand, would not deny the gambling consideration; he forgot; it is much safer to forget, and it stands a better cross-examination.

The evidence discloses that about 3 or 4 o'clock p.m. on the evening of the 30th the defendant went to the apartment of the proprietor, and renewed his demand for payment or a transfer of the property in consideration of the gambling debt. After a meal and a shave they again appeared, about 5 o'clock, before the commissioner; this time at his public office in the justice's court. Here there was much halting and whispering. The bill of sale written by Cleary was presented to the proprietor, who refused to acknowledge it before the commissioner. The commissioner was then requested by Cleary to draw another document to carry out the purpose of their visit there. The reason given for refusing to acknowledge the document then before the commissioner was that it conveyed a half interest, whereas the plaintiff refused then to convey more than a quarter interest. The commissioner wrote the document now contained in the record, the plaintiff signed it; it was witnessed, acknowledged, filed for record, and recorded in the book of deeds, according to law.

The deed signed by McGinley purports to convey "an undivided one-fourth (¼) interest in the Fairbanks Hotel, situate on lot No. one (1) Front street, in the town of Fairbanks." The consideration mentioned is one dollar, but, in accordance with the finger-tip custom, it was not paid; the real consideration was the $1,800 so miraculously won by the defendant the previous night by shaking the box. Plaintiff soon after brought this suit to set aside the conveyance upon the ground of fraud (1) because he was so drunk at the time he signed the deed as to be unable to comprehend the nature of the contract, and (2) for want of consideration.

It is currently believed that the Lord cares for and protects idiots and drunken men. A court of equity is supposed to have equal and concurrent jurisdiction, and this case seems to be brought under both branches. Before touching upon the law of the case, however, it is proper to decide the questions of fact upon which these principles must rest, and they will be considered in the order in which counsel for plaintiff has presented them.

Was McGinley so drunk when he signed the deed in controversy that he was not in his right mind, or capable of transacting any business, or entering into any contract? He was engaged, under the ægis of the law and the seal of this court, in selling whisky to the miners of the Tanana for four bits a drink, and more regularly in taking his own medicine and playing dice with customers for a consideration. Who shall guide the court in determining how drunk he was at 3 o'clock in the morning, when the transaction opened? Tupper or the defendant? How much credence must the court give to the testimony of one drunken man who testifies that another was also drunk? Is the court bound by the admission of the plaintiff that he was so paralized by his own whisky that he cannot remember the events of nearly 24 hours in which he seems to have generally followed his usual calling? Upon what fact in this evidence can the court plant the scales of justice that they may not stagger?

Probably the most satisfactory determination of the matter may be made by coming at once to that point of time where the deed in question was prepared, signed, and acknowledged. Did the plaintiff exhibit intelligence at that time? He refused to acknowledge a deed which conveyed a half interest, and caused his creditor to procure one to be made by the officer which conveyed only a quarter interest; he protected his property to that extent. Upon a presentation of the deed prepared by the officer, he refused to sign it until the words "and other valuable consideration" were stricken out; thus leaving the deed to rest on a stated consideration of "one dollar." Upon procuring the paper to read as he desired, he signed it in a public office, before several persons, and acknowledged it to be his act and deed.

Defendant says that the deed was given to pay a gambling debt lost by the plaintiff at his own game, and his counsel argues that for this reason equity will not examine into the consideration and grant relief, but will leave both parties to the rules of their game, and not intermingle these with the rules of law. He argues that they stand in pari delicto, and that, being engaged in a violation of the law, equity ought not to assist the proprietor of the game to recover his bank roll. It may be incidently mentioned here, as it has been suggested to the court, that the phrase pari delicto does not mean a "delectable pair," and its use is not intended to reflect upon or characterize plaintiff and defendant.

*   *   *

There are cases where courts will assist in the recovery of money or property lost at gambling, but this is not one of them. The plaintiff was the proprietor of the saloon and the operator of the dice game in which he lost his property. He now asks a court of equity to assist him in recovering it, and this raises the question, may a gambler who runs a game and loses the bank roll come into a court of equity and recover it? He conducted the game in violation of law, conveyed his premises to pay the winner's score, and now demands that the court assist him to regain it. Equity will not become a gambler's insurance company, to stand by while the gamester secures the winnings of the drunken, unsuspecting, or weak-minded in violation of the law, ready to stretch forth its arm to recapture his losses when another as unscrupulous or more lucky than he wins his money or property. Nor will the court in this case aid the defendant.

The cause will be dismissed; each party to pay the costs incurred by him, and judgment accordingly.

We have all heard of someone who experienced a broken wedding engagement. Although it is a difficult decision to make, it is usually the result of one or both of the parties realizing that they are incompatible. But whatever the reason may be, the basis for breaking an engagement in the following case from 1890 would be not only unfathomable, but quite ridiculous in the 1990s. It is yet another example of how times have changed.

HARDIN

v.

HARSHFIELD

Court of Appeals of Kentucky
Jan. 23, 1890
12 S.W. 779, 11 Ky.L.Rptr. 638

BENNETT, J.

The appellant, an unmarried young lady, about 20 years of age, who sues by her father, as her next friend, alleges that the appellee falsely, maliciously, and with a design to injure her standing in society, and to bring her into public ridicule, shame, and disgrace, and to break off a marriage agreement existing between her and Charles Bean, a person altogether eligible, spoke of her, in the presence and hearing of quite a number of persons, in substance, these slanderous words: "Boys, I have a damned hard tale on Cordie Hardin. I will tell you after dinner." After dinner he said: "Cordie Hardin went to the store of Chris Pauley to buy some groceries, and while Chris Pauley was waiting on her she let a big fart that was heard all over the house. Two or three young men being present, Chris Pauley looked at them and laughed, and they walked out of doors. Chris Pauley having fixed up the groceries, she took them, left the house and got on her horse, and forgot her gloves. She got down, and came back into the store. He supposed she was demoralized by what she had done, the fact being impressed on her mind so strongly. She said when she came back into the store: 'Mr. Pauley, did you see anything of that fart I let in here a while ago?' His reply was 'No, but

I smelt it damned strong.' Boys, ain't that a damned hard one on her?" That the utterance of the foregoing words injured her standing in society, and brought her into public ridicule, shame, disgrace, etc., and caused said Bean, he having heard and believing said report, to break off said engagement.

In an action to recover special damages for the utterance of words not actionable in themselves it is not necessary that the words of themselves should convey the meaning of an injurious imputation. It is sufficient if the words used were intended to convey such imputation, and did in fact convey it to the minds of the persons who heard them, and had the effect intended. All that is required is that the words used, coupled with the manner, tone, look, or wink of the person using them, are capable of conveying the meaning intended. For instance, to say of a woman that she was fond of showing her petticoat to men, coupled with such manner, tone, gesture, or wink as to convey to the minds of the speaker's listeners that the woman was lewd or lascivious, and such meaning was so intended, and the listeners did in fact so understand it, such language, if uttered falsely and maliciously, and did degrade the woman in public estimation, would be actionable. To falsely and maliciously say of a physician, lawyer, or shoemaker that he is a quack, jackleg, or cobbler, entitles the person thus spoken of to damages commensurate with the injury that such language has done his profession or trade. The reason is much stronger for protecting defenseless and helpless woman against false and malicious imputations, that tend to humiliate and degrade them in society. Kentucky manhood demands that they should be protected, and the guilty party mulcted in damages commensurate with the humiliation and degradation thus inflicted. The language, taken all together, attributed to the appellee, was capable of making the impression upon the hearers that the appellant was an immodest, indiscreet, coarse, vulgar young woman, which, if so understood and believed, would lower and degrade her in the estimation of good and refined society. If any man had engaged to marry her because of her supposed modesty, discretion, and exemplary conduct, such a report, if believed by him, would doubtless, and should, cause him to break the engagement. It is alleged that the appellee falsely and maliciously used said language for the purpose of humiliating and degrading the appellant, etc., and of breaking off said engagement, and it did have the desired effect; and, as said, the language, taking it all together, was capable of producing such an effect. The person speaking the words and intending them to have an injurious effect, it is enough that such words, taken all together, have, in common sense and reason, some connection with the damage said to have ensued from them; but it is not enough that the unwarrantable caprice of some person has caused a damage to result from them which the speaker did not intend, and had no reason to apprehend. It is said that, the accusation being false, Bean, though believing it, and acting on that belief, wrongfully broke the engagement. If the words had been true, as just intimated, Bean would have been perfectly justified in breaking off the engagement, provided he had made it in consideration of the belief that the appellant was a modest, discreet, and innocent young lady. It turns out, however, that the words, the truth of which he believed and acted on as true, were false and slanderous, and Bean made a mistake in believing them to be true; but appellee spoke them, as is alleged, for the purpose that they should be believed, and produce a damaging effect upon the standing and marital prospects of the appellant; and it does not lie in his mouth to say that Bean should not have believed his slanderous language to be true. He caused the wrongful impression to be made that brought such serious consequences upon the appellant, and is responsible to her for it.

It is also said that there is no allegation that the appellee uttered this language in the presence of Bean, and, if other persons repeated the appellee's language to Bean, which caused him to break off the engagement, the appellee is not responsible, unless he authorized such person to repeat the language. There are two objections to this proposition: *First*. It would allow the appellee to invent and utter a slander in the hearing of persons, and if they spread it far and wide, believing it to be true, the appellee would not be responsible for their utterances thus made. It cannot be true that a person may invent and utter language damaging to another, and say to the other that "the person who acted on these utterances did not get them from me, but from the persons that heard me speak them; therefore I am not liable to you for the injury." It seems to us that the reply that "you were the author of this language, and the persons repeating simply acted as your mouth-piece, and the foundation of the person's action is traceable to you, and you are responsible for it. Besides, *second*, you did not utter this language to these persons in confidence, rather with an injunction not to repeat it, but you uttered it as though they were at perfect liberty to repeat it; and you, by thus uttering it, authorized them to repeat it, and you doubtless intended them to repeat it, so you are responsible for any damage that has ensued from uttering said language." The judgment is reversed, with directions for further proceedings consistent with this opinion.

When greeting someone in public, it is customary to say "Hello," nod your head and smile or shake hands. However, some people prefer to break from tradition and develop their own style. . . . In this next instance, the defendant greeted an acquaintance in such a fashion that it resulted in his conviction for disorderly conduct.

PEOPLE ex rel. SHANNON

v.

GARSTENFELD

Kings County Court
November, 1915
156 N.Y.S. 991, 92 Misc. 388

ROY, J.

Is it disorderly conduct for one individual to publicly greet another by placing the end of his thumb against the tip of his nose, at the same time extending and wiggling the fingers of his hand? That momentous question is involved in this appeal. What meaning is intended to be conveyed by the above-described pantomime? Is it a friendly or an unfriendly action; a compliment or an insult? Is it a direct invitation to fight, or is it likely to provoke a fight?

Dr. Holmes, that delightful wit and philosopher of a former generation, remarked in his 'Autocrat of the Breakfast Table' that 'there are a good many symbols even that are more expressive than words.' In the Knickerbocker History of New York we read that, when William the Testy sent an expedition to treat with the belligerent powers of Rensselaerstein, the ambassador who accompanied the expedition demanded the surrender of the fortress. 'In reply the wachtmeester applied the thumb of his right hand to the end of his nose, and the thumb of his left hand to the little finger of the right, and, spreading each hand like a fan, made an aerial flourish with his fingers.' No breach of the peace ensued, but this was apparently owing to the fact that the ambassador was ignorant of the significance of the wachtmeester's salutation. It is, however, recorded that the practice became widespread, and that up to the author's day the thumb to the nose and the fingers in the air is apt to be a reply made by tenants to their landlord when called upon for any long arrears of rent.

The practice still persists, and is not limited to tenants who are indisposed to pay their rent. Among boys it serves as a harmless vent for injured feelings, which lack the proper vocabulary to relieve themselves through audible speech. But when boys become men they should 'put away childish things.' In the case at bar the circumstances attending the enactment of the nasal and digit drama aforesaid tend to show a design to engender strife. Moreover, the defendant had committed the same offense toward the complaining witness on previous occasions, thus indicating a determination to annoy him to the limit of patient endurance. My answer to the question stated at the beginning of this opinion is: It depends on circumstances. And under the circumstances disclosed I am satisfied the magistrate was fully warranted in reaching the conclusion he arrived at, and I therefore affirm the conviction.

Judgment affirmed.

Contributors List

We would like to thank the following judges and law professors who submitted their favorite opinion for our consideration:

Prof. Kenneth J. Abdo
Prof. Charles R. Adams III
Hon. David H. Adams
Hon. Charles M. Allen
Prof. Albert W. Alschuler
Prof. Lynn L. Alstadt
Hon. Armand Arabian
Prof. John D. Ayer
Hon. Charles F. Baird
Prof. Gordon B. Baldwin
Prof. Roger M. Baron
Hon. James E. Barrett
Hon. Betty Barteau
Prof. Joseph P. Bauer
Hon. Thomas E. Baynes, Jr.
Prof. Martin D. Begleiter
Prof. Fred Warren Bennett
Prof. Robert W. Bennett
Prof. Dawn D. Bennett-Alexander
Prof. Carole C. Berry
Prof. Gerry W. Beyer
Prof. G. Robert Blakey
Prof. Albert P. Blaustein
Hon. Charles Bleil
Prof. Joan Bohl
Prof. Mark Healy Bonner
Prof. James B. Boskey
Prof. Craig M. Bradley
Prof. Richard E. Brennan
Hon. Hugh W. Brenneman, Jr.
Hon. Peg Breslin
Hon. Myron H. Bright
Prof. Joseph F. Brodley
Hon. John G. Brosky
Prof. Pamela H. Bucy

Hon. Juan G. Burciaga
Prof. John M. Burkoff
Prof. Robert K. Calhoun, Jr.
Ms. Cathryn Campbell
Prof. John J. Cannon
Prof. Edward V. Cattell, Jr.
Prof. James H. Cawley
Prof. William M. Champion
Hon. Herbert Y. C. Choy
Hon. James P. Churchill
Hon. Vincent A. Cirillo
Hon. Russell G. Clark
Hon. Sam Houston Clinton
Prof. Rebecca Cochran
Prof. Henry S. Cohn
Mr. Robert W. Cole
Hon. Sara Walter Combs
Hon. Julian Abele Cook, Jr.
Prof. Corinne Cooper
Prof. Steven M. Cooper
Mr. John J. Copelan, Jr.
Hon. William J. Cornelius
Hon. Robert E. Cowen
Prof. Randall Coyne
Hon. Gary L. Crippen
Hon. Thomas F. Crosby, Jr.
Prof. John T. Cross
Prof. Lawrence A. Cunningham
Prof. Anthony D'Amato
Prof. Michael J. Dale
Hon. Stewart Dalzell
Hon. James C. Dauksch, Jr.
Prof. Frederick Davis
Hon. Bob Dickenson
Prof. Joel C. Dobris

Prof. Frank W. Donaldson
Hon. Allen L. Donielson
Prof. Charles H. Dougherty
Prof. David R. Dow
Prof. Marjorie Downing
Prof. James J. Duane
Hon. Conrad B. Duberstein
Prof. Anne Proffitt Dupre
Hon. Charles P. Dykman
Prof. Herbert A. Eastman
Mr. Emmanuel E. Edem
Mr. Ed Edmonds
Prof. Frank W. Elliott
Hon. Albert J. Engel
Prof. David Ensign
Prof. Marie A. Failinger
Prof. Mary R. Falk
Prof. Daniel A. Farber
Hon. Michael W. Farrell
Hon. Peter T. Fay
Hon. Ralph Adam Fine
Prof. Jill E. Fisch
Prof. Thomas C. Fischer
Hon. Clarkson S. Fisher
Prof. Bruce E. Friedman
Hon. William D. Friedmann
Hon. Gary Gaertner
Hon. Robert S. Gawthrop, III
Prof. Michael B. Gerrard
Ms. Sharon Stern Gerstman
Mr. Elmer Gertz
Hon. Janine P. Geske
Hon. Floyd R. Gibson
Prof. Ronald Lee Gilman
Prof. Martin D. Ginsburg
Hon. Richard M. Givan
Ms. Susan Goering
Hon. Myron L. Gordon
Prof. Mark F. Grady
Prof. Lino A. Graglia
Hon. Ben Z. Grant
Prof. David M. Grant

Ms. Laura Graser
Mr. Erwin N. Griswold
Prof. Ronald X. Groeber
Hon. Richard P. Guy
Ms. Emily E. Haddad
Hon. Martin L. Haines
Mr. Halbritter
Prof. Marilyn Hanzal
Prof. Lee Hargrave
Prof. Jerome R. Hellerstein
Prof. Richard H. Hiers
Prof. David R. Hodas
Hon. Thomas E. Hollenhorst
Prof. Edwin P. Horner
Hon. J. Gorman Houston, Jr.
Hon. Alex T. Howard, Jr.
Hon. Procter Hug, Jr.
Prof. Joyce A. Hughes
Prof. John Huston
Prof. Roger J. Illsley
Prof. Herbert P. Jacoby
Prof. Robert M. Jarvis
Prof. Vincent R. Johnson
Prof. F. K. Juenger
Prof. Michael D. Kaminski
Prof. Thomas M. Kerr
Hon. Howard H. Kestin
Hon. Mary Louise Klas
Prof. Charles L. Knapp
Hon. Gerald Kogan
Prof. Michael I. Krauss
Hon. Robert J. Kressel
Mr. Kenneth R. Kupchak
Prof. Peter B. Kutner
Hon. Ronald R. Lagueux
Prof. Kimberly J. Laliberte
Prof. Donald E. Lampert
Prof. Richard S. Lane
Hon. Earl R. Larson
Hon. Jerry L. Larson
Prof. J. Al Latham, Jr.
Prof. Robert P. Lawry

Prof. Joseph H. Lawson
Hon. Donald P. Lay
Hon. Alfred J. Lechner, Jr.
Prof. Randy H. Lee
Hon. William C. Lee
Prof. Arthur S. Leonard
Prof. Howard Lesnick
Prof. A. Leo Levin
Prof. David I. Levine
Hon. John B. Lewis, Jr.
Hon. Paul J. Liacos
Hon. Mildred L. Lillie
Ms. Annette Lombardi
Hon. Harold L. Lowenstein
Prof. Richardson R. Lynn
Dean Frank J. Macchiarola
Hon. George E. MacKinnon
Prof. John A. Maher
Mr. Gerald A. Malia
Hon. Paul Mannes
Prof. Calvin K. Manshio
Prof. Thomas C. Marks, Jr.
Hon. Prentice H. Marshall
Hon. Charles A. Marvin
Prof. Marvin W. Maydew
Prof. Stephen R. McAllister
Ms. Nancy M. McCoy
Hon. Charles W. McGarry
Prof. Michael McGonnigal
Prof. Paul L. McKaskle
Hon. Robert M. McRae
Prof. Daniel J. Meador
Prof. Alfred W. Meyer
Hon. James H. Michael, Jr.
Hon. Abner J. Mikva
Hon. Richard Mills
Hon. Burley B. Mitchell, Jr.
Prof. Paula A. Monopoli
Hon. John H. Moore, II
Prof. C. Robert Morris
Hon. Stanley Mosk
Prof. Frederick C. Moss

Hon. Florence K. Murray
Hon. James C. Murray
Prof. Gary Myers
Hon. Bernard Newman
Hon. Jerome J. Niedermeier
Prof. David R. Normann
Prof. Curtis W. Nyquist
Prof. Kevin M. O'Connell
Prof. Kevin O'Regan
Hon. Louis F. Oberdorfer
Prof. A. Samuel Oddi
Hon. Marian P. Opala
Dean Lewis H. Orland
Mr. J. Warren Ott
Hon. Mark P. Painter
Hon. Mary Little Parell
Hon. Alexander L. Paskay
Prof. J. Randall Patterson
Prof. Patricia L. Patterson
Prof. George T. Patton, Jr.
Hon. John H. Peay
Prof. Joseph M. Perillo
Mr. Stephen L. Pevar
Hon. Charles W. Pickering, Sr.
Hon. G. Joseph Pierron
Prof. Marc R. Poirier
Prof. Robert Popper
Hon. Richard A. Powers, III
Hon. James K. Prewitt
Hon. James A. Pudlowski
Dean Albert T. Quick
Prof. Robert E. Rains
Hon. R. A. (Jim) Randall
Hon. W. Keith Rapp
Prof. Charles A. Rees
Prof. W. Patrick Resen
Prof. C. Nicholas Revelos
Prof. Carol M. Rice
Prof. J. P. Rooney
Prof. Gilbert S. Rothenberg
Prof. Laura F. Rothstein
Prof. Ronald D. Rotunda

Prof. Thomas D. Rowe, Jr.
Hon. Carl B. Rubin
Hon. Richard W. Sabers
Prof. Arthur J. Sabin
Prof. Michael J. Saks
Prof. Alan Saltzman
Dean Robert M. Saltzman
Prof. Pamela Samuelson
Prof. Verna C. Sanchez
Mr. Michael S. Sands
Mr. Kurt M. Saunders
Hon. William J. Schafer, III
Prof. Michael P. Scharf
Hon. John M. Scheb
Hon. Robert H. Schumacher
Prof. Marin R. Scordato
Hon. Jerry Scott
Hon. Bruce M. Selya
Hon. Ila Jeanne Sensenich
Hon. Curtis G. Shaw
Mr. Arden E. Shenker
Hon. Kenneth W. Shrum
Prof. Joseph J. Simeone
Hon. Paul J. Simon
Prof. William R. Slomanson
Mr. Charles M. Smith
Hon. D. Brooks Smith
Hon. Gerald M. Smith
Prof. Robert B. Smith
Hon. Thomas P. Smith
Prof. Ellen K. Solender
Prof. Edmund B. Spaeth, Jr.
Prof. John M. Speca
Prof. Clyde Spillenger
Prof. Mark Squillace
Prof. Susan J. Stabile
Hon. Thomas L. Steffen
Prof. Laura W. Stein
Prof. N. O. Stockmeyer, Jr.
Prof. William B. Stoebuck

Prof. Donald H. Stone
Mr. Lowell V. Stortz
Prof. Peter L. Strauss
Mr. Stanley S. Stroup
Prof. Edward J. Sullivan
Hon. Robert D. Sundby
Mr. Arthur J. Tarnow
Hon. Daniel H. Thomas
Hon. James D. Todd
Dean Joseph P. Tomain
Hon. Esther M. Tomljanovich
Prof. T. Gerald Treece
Hon. Steven M. Vartabedian
Hon. Robert Vogel
Hon. James A. von der Heydt
Prof. Harvey F. Wachsman
Hon. J. Clifford Wallace
Prof. Sally G. Waters
Prof. Tony Waters
Prof. Ursula Weigold
Prof. Louise Weinberg
Prof. Alan J. Weisbard
Hon. Joseph R. Weisberger
Prof. John Wendt
Prof. Douglas J. Whaley
Prof. John W. Whelan
Hon. Willis P. Whichard
Prof. Barbara Ann White
Prof. Leon Wildes
Hon. Glen M. Williams
Prof. Evelyn L. Wilson
Prof. Edward M. Wise
Hon. Charles R. Wolle
Prof. Thomas A. Woxland
Prof. Charles Alan Wright
Prof. Danaya C. Wright
Hon. Eugene A. Wright
Hon. Thomas A. Zlaket
Prof. Harvey L. Zuckman

✝